THE PREHISTORIC SOCIETY

Fragments of the Bronze Age

THE PREHISTORIC SOCIETY

Fragments of the Bronze Age

The destruction and deposition of metalwork in south-west Britain and its wider context

by
Matthew G. Knight

Prehistoric Society Research Paper No. 13
2022

THE PREHISTORIC SOCIETY
Series Editor: Michael J. Allen
Managing Editor: Julie Gardiner

OXBOW | books
Oxford & Philadelphia

Published in the United Kingdom in 2022 by
The Prehistoric Society

and

OXBOW BOOKS
The Old Music Hall, 106–108 Cowley Road, Oxford, OX4 1JE

and in the United States by
OXBOW BOOKS
1950 Lawrence Road, Havertown, PA 19083

Hardcover Edition: ISBN 978-1-78925-697-0
Digital Edition: ISBN 978-1-78925-698-7 (epub)

A CIP record for this book is available from the British Library

Library of Congress Control Number: 2021950230

Printed in Malta by Melita Press

For a complete list of Oxbow titles, please contact:

UNITED KINGDOM
Oxbow Books
Telephone (01865) 241249
Email: oxbow@oxbowbooks.com
www.oxbowbooks.com

UNITED STATES OF AMERICA
Oxbow Books
Telephone (610) 853-9131, Fax (610) 853-9146
Email: queries@casemateacademic.com
www.casemateacademic.com/oxbow

Oxbow Books is part of the Casemate Group

Front cover
Complete and fragmented replica Bronze Age implements. Photo: M.G. Knight

Rear cover
Top: Gold lunula from Auchentaggart, Dumfries and Galloway © National Museums Scotland
Middle: South Cadbury shield, Somerset © Somerset County Council & South West Heritage Trust
Bottom: Colaton Raleigh hoard, Devon © Royal Albert Memorial Museum & Art Gallery, Exeter

MARC FITCH FUND
DAMUS UT DETUR

THE PREHISTORIC SOCIETY RESEARCH PAPERS

The Prehistoric Society Research Papers publish collections of edited papers covering aspects of Prehistory. These may be derived from conferences, or research projects; they specifically *exclude* the publication of single excavation reports. The Research Papers present the fruits of the best of prehistoric research, complementing the Society's respected *Proceedings* by allowing broader treatment of key research areas.

The Research Papers is a peer-reviewed series whose production is managed by the Society.

Further information can be found on the Society's website (www.prehistoricsociety.org)

THE PREHISTORIC SOCIETY

The Prehistoric Society's interests are world wide and extend from the earliest human origins to the emergence of written records. Membership is open to all, and includes professional, amateur, student and retired members.

An active programme of events – lectures, study tours, day- and weekend conferences, and research weekends – allows members to participate fully in the Society and to meet other members and interested parties. The study excursions cater for all preferences from the relatively luxurious to the more economical, including highly popular student study tours. Day visits to sites are arranged whenever possible.

The Society produces two publications that are included with most categories of membership: the annual journal, *Proceedings of the Prehistoric Society* and the topical newsletter, *PAST*, which is published in April, July and November. In addition the *Prehistoric Society Research Papers* are published occasionally on which members may have discount.

Further information can be found on the Society's website (www.prehistoricsociety.org), or via the Prehistoric Society's registered address: ℅ Institute of Archaeology, University College London, 31–34 Gordon Square, London, WC1H 0PY.

The Society is a registered charity (no. 1000567)

THE PREHISTORIC SOCIETY RESEARCH PAPERS

Other volumes in this series, available from Oxbow Books

No. 1. *From Bann Flakes to Bushmills – papers in honour of Professor Peter Woodman*
eds N. Finlay, S. McCartan, N. Milner & C. Wickham-Jones (2009)

No. 2. *Land and People – papers in memory of John G. Evans*
eds M.J. Allen, N. Sharples & T. O'Connor (2009)

No. 3. *Materialitas: working stone, carving identity*
eds B. O'Connor, G. Cooney & J. Chapman (2010)

No. 4. *Is there a British Chalcolithic? People, place and polity in the later 3rd millennium*
eds M.J. Allen, J. Gardiner, A. Sheridan & D. McOmish (2012)

No. 5. *Image, Memory and Monumentality: archaeological engagements with the material world*
eds A.M. Jones, J. Pollard, M.J. Allen and J. Gardiner (2012)

No. 6. *Settlement in the Irish Neolithic: new discoveries at the edge of Europe*
by Jessica Smyth (2014)

No. 7. *The Beaker People: isotopes, mobility and diet in prehistoric Britain*
eds M. Parker Pearson, A. Sheridan, M. Jay, A. Chamberlain, M. Richards & J. Evans (2019)

No. 8. *First Farmers of the Carpathian Basin: changing patterns in subsistence, ritual and monumental figurines*
by Eszter Bánffy (2019)

No. 9. *Bell Beaker Settlement of Europe: the Bell Beaker phenomenon from a domestic perspective*
ed. Alex M. Gibson (2019)

No. 11. *The Social Context of Technology: non-ferrous metalworking in later prehistory*
by Leo Webley, Sophia Adams & Joanna Brück (2020)

No. 12. *Neolithic stone extraction in Britain and Ireland: an ethnoarchaeological perspective*
by Peter Topping (2021)

Volumes in production

No. 10. *Re-peopling La Manche: new perspectives on Neanderthals lifeways at La Cotte de St Brelade*
eds Matt Pope, Beccy Scott & Andrew Shaw

CONTENTS

LIST OF FIGURES AND TABLES

List of Figures

List of Tables

AUTHOR

MATTHEW G. KNIGHT
National Museum of Scotland
Chambers Street,
Edinburgh EH1 1JF

M.Knight@nms.ac.uk

Matthew Knight is a Senior Curator of Prehistory at National Museums Scotland, responsible for the Scottish Chalcolithic and Bronze Age collections. He specialises in the production, use and deposition of Bronze Age material culture in Britain, particularly metalwork, and his research interests also include the treatment of older material in later contexts.

ABSTRACT

The deliberate destruction and deposition of metalwork is a widely recognised phenomenon across Bronze Age Europe but rarely forms the focus of study. Weapons, tools and ornaments were manipulated, damaged and broken before being deposited in a variety of contexts, including hoards, burials and settlements, as well as singly in natural places. Most research focuses on understanding *why* metalwork was deliberately destroyed and deposited, but understanding *how* is equally important.

This book draws on material science, wear analysis and experimental archaeology to develop a framework for recognising and interpreting deliberate damage on Bronze Age metalwork. The framework, termed the Damage Ranking System, is applied to the case study region of south-west Britain (ie, Cornwall, Devon, Dorset and Somerset) and over 1700 metal objects were studied as part of the research. The results highlight that deliberate destruction of metalwork increased over the course of the Bronze Age.

The assessment of the objects is combined with contextual analyses to present detailed discussions of the practices observed at different stages of the Bronze Age in south-west Britain and how this enabled people to express social beliefs through depositional practices. Destruction in the earlier Bronze Age was less frequent but often associated with funerary contexts; metalwork destruction reached a peak between 1000–800 BC by which time it was commonly associated with hoarding. This book emphasises how a regional case study can be used to understand aspects of prehistoric agency, technology and performance, as well as the people behind these actions, and allows us to recognise how the social role of destruction and deposition transformed over time and space. Looking beyond the study region, it is possible to observe how actions undertaken in south-west Britain relate to the wider context of Bronze Age Britain and Europe.

Résumé

La destruction délibérée et le dépôt d'objets métalliques est un phénomène largement reconnu dans l'Europe de l'âge du Bronze mais qui a rarement fait l'objet d'études. Des armes, des outils et des parures ont été manipulés, endommagés et brisés avant d'être déposés dans divers contextes, comprenant des dépôts non funéraires, des sépultures et des habitats, ainsi que dans des lieux naturels. La plupart des recherches visent à comprendre pourquoi les objets en métal ont été délibérément détruits et déposés mais il est tout aussi important de comprendre comment.

Ce livre s'appuie sur les sciences des matériaux, la tracéologie et l'archéologie expérimentale pour développer un cadre permettant de reconnaître et d'interpréter les dommages délibérés sur les objets métalliques de l'âge du Bronze. Ce cadre, appelé *Damage Ranking System*, est appliqué à la région du Sud-Ouest de la Grande-Bretagne (Cornouailles, Devon, Dorset et Somerset) et plus de 1 700 objets métalliques ont été étudiés dans le cadre de cette recherche. Les résultats soulignent que la destruction délibérée des objets métalliques a augmenté au cours de l'âge du Bronze.

L'étude des objets est combinée avec des analyses contextuelles pour discuter en détail les pratiques observées à différents périodes de l'âge du Bronze dans le Sud-Ouest de la Grande-Bretagne et comment elles ont permis aux gens d'exprimer des croyances sociales à travers des pratiques de dépôt. Au début de l'âge du Bronze, la destruction était moins fréquente mais souvent associée à des contextes funéraires. La destruction des objets métalliques a atteint un pic entre 1000 et 800 avant J.-C., date à laquelle elle était généralement associée aux dépôts non funéraires. Cet ouvrage souligne comment une étude de cas régionale peut être utilisée pour comprendre les aspects de l'agentivité, de la technologie et de la performance préhistoriques, ainsi que les personnes à l'origine de ces actions, et nous permet de reconnaître comment le rôle social de la destruction et du dépôt s'est transformé dans le temps et l'espace. En regardant au-delà de la région étudiée, il est possible d'observer comment les actions entreprises dans le Sud-Ouest de la Grande-Bretagne se rapportent au contexte plus large de la Grande-Bretagne et de l'Europe à l'âge du Bronze.

Zusammenfassung

Die absichtliche Zerstörung und Niederlegung von Metallgegenständen ist ein allgemein bekanntes Phänomen im bronzezeitlichen Europa, das jedoch nur selten im Mittelpunkt von Untersuchungen steht. Waffen, Werkzeuge und Schmuck wurden manipuliert, beschädigt und zerbrochen, bevor sie in ganz unterschiedlichen Kontexten deponiert wurden, darunter Horte, Gräber und Siedlungen, aber auch einzeln an Naturorten. Die meisten Untersuchungen konzentrieren sich auf die Frage, *warum* Metallobjekte absichtlich zerstört und deponiert wurden, aber ebenso wichtig ist zu verstehen, *wie* dies geschah.

Dieses Buch stützt sich auf Materialwissenschaft, Gebrauchsspurenanalyse und experimentelle Archäologie, um einen Rahmen für das Erkennen und Interpretieren von absichtlichen Beschädigungen an bronzezeitlichen Metallgegenständen zu entwickeln. Dieser Rahmen, das so genannte Damage Ranking System, wird auf den Südwesten Großbritanniens (d. h. Cornwall, Devon, Dorset und Somerset) als Fallstudie angewandt, für die über 1700 Metallobjekte untersucht wurden. Die Ergebnisse zeigen, dass die absichtliche Zerstörung von Metallobjekten im Laufe der Bronzezeit zunahm.

Die Analyse der Objekte wird mit kontextuellen Untersuchungen kombiniert, um die in verschiedenen Stadien der Bronzezeit im Südwesten Großbritannien beobachteten Praktiken und die Art und Weise, wie diese es den Menschen ermöglichten, soziale Vorstellungen durch Deponierungspraktiken auszudrücken, detailliert zu erörtern. Die Zerstörung von Metallgegenständen war in der Frühbronzezeit weniger häufig, aber oft mit Bestattungskontexten verknüpft; ihren Höhepunkt erreichten die Zerstörungen zwischen 1000 und 800 v. Chr. und sie waren zu diesem Zeitpunkt häufig mit dem Niederlegen von Horten verbunden. Dieses Buch unterstreicht, wie eine regionale Fallstudie genutzt werden kann, um Aspekte prähistorischer Handlungsweisen, Technologie und Performanz sowie die Menschen, die hinter diesen Handlungen stehen, zu verstehen, und ermöglicht es uns zu erkennen, wie sich die soziale Bedeutung von Zerstörung und Niederlegung in Zeit und Raums verändert hat. Wenn man über die Untersuchungsregion hinausblickt, kann man feststellen, wie die im Südwesten Großbritanniens durchgeführten Handlungen mit dem weiteren Kontext des bronzezeitlichen Großbritanniens und Europas zusammenhängen.

Resumen

La destrucción y el depósito deliberado de objetos metálicos durante la Edad del Bronce es un fenómeno ampliamente reconocido en Europa, pero raramente constituye un foco de estudio. Armas, herramientas y ornamentos fueron manipulados, dañados y rotos antes de ser depositados en una gran variedad de contextos, incluyendo acumulaciones, enterramientos y asentamientos, al igual que en depósitos individuales situados en emplazamientos naturales. La mayor parte de las investigaciones se centran en comprender *por qué* estos objetos metálicos fueron deliberadamente destruidos y depositados, pero comprender *cómo* es igualmente importante.

Este libro recurre a la ciencia de los materiales, el análisis de huellas de uso y la arqueología experimental para desarrollar un marco de identificación e interpretación de los daños deliberados producidos en los objetos metálicos durante la Edad del Bronce. Este marco, denominado "sistema de clasificación del daño" se aplica, como caso de estudio, a la región del suroeste de Gran Bretaña (Cornualles, Devon, Dorset y Somerset) donde se han estudiado, como parte de esta investigación, cerca de 1700 objetos metálicos. Los resultados señalan que la destrucción deliberada de los objetos metálicos se incrementó a lo largo de la Edad del Bronce.

La valoración de los objetos se combina con los análisis contextuales con el objetivo de presentar una discusión detallada de las prácticas observadas en diferentes momentos de la Edad del Bronce en el suroeste de Gran Bretaña y cómo esto posibilitó a los grupos humanos expresar sus creencias sociales a través de las prácticas deposicionales. Estos procesos de destrucción eran menos frecuentes durante el Bronce inicial, pero a menudo se asocian a contextos funerarios; la destrucción de los objetos metálicos alcanza un apogeo entre el 1000–800 BC, momento en el que estuvo comúnmente asociado a los depósitos. Este libro enfatiza cómo un caso de estudio regional se puede emplear para entender aspectos sobre la intencionalidad, la tecnología y las actuaciones prehistóricas, al igual que para comprender a las personas detrás de estas acciones, permitiendo reconocer cómo el papel de los procesos de destrucción y deposición se han transformado a lo largo del tiempo y el espacio. Más allá de nuestra región de estudio, es posible observar cómo las acciones documentadas en el suroeste de Gran Bretaña se relacionan con el contexto más amplio de la Edad del Bronce en Gran Bretaña y Europa.

ACKNOWLEDGEMENTS

The research on which this book is based was conducted between 2015 and 2018 as part of my PhD thesis undertaken at the University of Exeter and University of Bristol. I was fortunate to have been funded by the Arts and Humanities Research Council through the South West and Wales Doctoral Partnership (Grant No. AH/L503939/1). I am also thankful to Santander and Cornwall Archaeological Society who similarly provided funds in support of my thesis. In bringing this book to publication I am grateful for financial support from Cornwall Archaeological Society, Dorset Natural History and Archaeological Society, the Historical Metallurgy Society and the Maltwood Fund of the Somerset Archaeology and Natural History Society.

In terms of academic support, I consider myself lucky to have been supported and encouraged by many people who have generously given their time and expertise over several years. Professor Anthony Harding saw me through my undergraduate and masters degrees at Exeter and encouraged me to go for the PhD that resulted in this book. Even in his well-deserved retirement he continues to steer me in the right direction. As well as Anthony, I was supervised by Professor Joanna Brück (then University of Bristol, now University College Dublin) and Professor Linda Hurcombe (University of Exeter). Both Jo and Linda were endlessly engaged with my research and helped hone my thoughts and writing. I am also grateful to Dr Gill Juleff (University of Exeter) and Professor David Fontijn (Leiden University) for examining my PhD and making the viva a surprisingly pleasant experience! Special thanks also go to David for contributing a foreword to the present volume.

Several people have read (endured!) earlier drafts of chapters of this book, including Jo Brück, Ella Paul (Treasure Trove Unit), Fraser Hunter and Sarah Laurenson (both National Museums Scotland). I am especially grateful to Dr Andy Jones (Cornwall Archaeological Unit) and Anthony Harding who read the full text ahead of submission and to my reviewers for their constructive and productive comments. Finally, thanks to Mike Allen and Julie Gardiner for their firm editing and guidance through the publication process. The combined comments, suggestions and insights received were invaluable, though those listed are in no way to blame for any resulting discrepancies!

For their general help answering queries, providing unpublished data, supplying images and generally offering support while writing this book, my thanks go to Adam Gwilt, Amal Khreisheh, Ann Woodward, Anna Tyacke, Ben Roberts, Bill Britnell, Brendan O'Connor, Ciorstaidh Trevarthen, Clare Randall, Danielle Wootton, Dot Boughton, Emily Freeman, Gail Boyle, Henrietta Quinnell, Ian Richardson, Jim Parry, Laura Burnett, Lucy Shipley, Marion Uckelmann, Martin Green, Mary Cahill, Neil Wilkin, Peter Northover, Peter Reavill, Richard Tabor, Rob Webley, Stuart Needham, Tess Machling, Tobias Mörtz, Tom Cadbury, Trevor Cowie and Valerio Gentile. Special thanks go to Neil Burridge for his support with my experiments and for answering many bronze-related queries!

My data collection involved me visiting 22 museums and institutions across southern England, as well as one private collection, and I want to highlight here the phenomenal contribution of museum staff to enabling this research. I cannot stress enough that there would be no book without them. I am thus indebted to members of staff at Ashmolean Museum, Bristol City Museum and Art Gallery, the British Museum, Blandford Town Museum, Dorset Museum, the Museum of Barnstaple and North Devon, the Museum of Somerset, Penlee House Galley and Museum (Penzance), The Box, Plymouth, Priest's House Museum and Garden (Wimborne), Poole Museum, Russell-Cotes Art Gallery and Museum (Bournemouth), Red House Museum and Gallery (Christchurch), Royal Albert Memorial Museum and Art Galley, Royal Cornwall Museum, Salisbury Museum, Torquay Museum, Totnes Elizabethan House and Museum, Wells and Mendip Museum and Wareham Town Museum. I was also fortunate to study Martin Green's private collection in Cranborne Chase, which contributed a wealth of fascinating data to this book.

Finally, I must thank my friends and family. They tirelessly humour my Bronze Age obsession and often allow me to continue talking even when they have ceased listening or caring! I am lucky to work with some brilliant people at National Museums Scotland who are always on hand to discuss metalwork, hoards and depositions, usually over coffee and scones. Likewise, my mum, dad and brother are endlessly supportive with wit and wisdom, and I cannot thank them enough.

However, my greatest thanks are to my wife and daughter, Robyn and Naomi. Robyn has listened to my musings, supported me with chocolate and cups of tea, read over random bits of text, and generally been the best person imaginable. She is the reason I knew I could finish this book. Naomi, meanwhile, is the reason I knew I *had* to finish this book. She was a reason to take breaks when writing was tough and has kept us smiling and laughing throughout difficult times. Completing this book means I get to spend more time with her, which was all the motivation I needed. It is to these two wonderful people that I dedicate this book.

Matthew G. Knight

The Prehistoric Society would like to add thanks to Marc Fitch Fund. We also thank our referees and members of our Editorial Advisory Committee, and our reviewers for their expert advice and opinions. In particular, I would like to offer my thanks to Oxbow Books and Julie Gardiner (Prehistoric Society Managing Editor), for their advice and assistance, and also to Julie Blackmore of Frabjous Books for typesetting yet another of our volumes with skill, proficiency, design and dexterity.

Michael J. Allen

PREFACE

Bronze Age metalwork deposition fascinates me. It is a collective practice that spanned Europe whereby people gathered large quantities of material, often in good condition, and placed it in the ground in all manner of situations, seemingly for many different reasons. Typically, it is the complete objects that have seen most research but, for me, it is the metalwork in 'bad' condition that captures my imagination. I can recall two deposits that especially stimulated this interest, both of which are discussed within this book.

The first is a hoard of crushed gold bracelets from Priddy, Somerset. At some point, about 3500 years ago, an individual or group gathered these perfectly usable, wearable bracelets and mangled them into a ball and placed them in the ground. To our modern mindsets, gathering gold ornaments and treating them in this way defies rational explanation, not least because they could have been recycled and were never recovered. Traditionally, the destruction of objects is seen as a mundane reduction of material, but this reaches a tension when seemingly valuable materials and objects are decommissioned and buried. It struck me there were some complexities here that had not been fully explored.

The second deposit is a fragment of an axehead from a wooden platform site at Greylake, also Somerset. This axehead was burnt, crushed and broken – a 'triple death' as Linda Hurcombe described it when I told her about it. About ten years ago, I was studying this piece at the Somerset Heritage Centre, and I was asked a very pertinent question: how was it broken? Or in other words, what did people need to do in order to break their objects in the Bronze Age? I was stumped. I realised I did not have a clear answer to give. Like many people, I was very interested in *why* objects were buried, but I had never fully considered *how*. That single, off-hand question, and the consideration that metalwork destruction may have been a more coordinated practice than previously discussed, set me on a rather different path than the one originally intended when I started my study of Bronze Age metalwork deposition.

Flicking through the literature on Bronze Age metalwork, it is common to find many notes about objects that are broken or bent or burnt or damaged in some way. There are, of course, some notable exceptions, but assumptions are typically made about how the objects broke, which will depend on what approach a particular author is taking – that is, whether they see the damage as significant or not. Damage on swords is generally considered deliberate and significant because swords are considered powerful objects; damage on axes is often interpreted as more mundane because axes are viewed as everyday tools. There are descriptions that blades were snapped over knees, axes broke through use, and ornaments were bent by hand, but there is actually very little consideration of, and investigation into, what is actually possible and how it may be enacted.

This information is out there, however, in the hands and minds of those who understand bronze as a material and it is gradually being acknowledged. It is through conversations with metalworkers and experimental archaeologists, as well as my own experiments into the topic, that I have tried to approach metalwork destruction and deposition, as well as drawing on several authorities on depositional practices who have inspired this work.

This book began its life as a PhD thesis

looking at these practices in south-west Britain and that research forms the foundation for what I present here. However, I have tried to expand beyond the initial research aims of the thesis and set my regional study in a wider contextual framework with the hope that it will have applications in other areas and other fields. Of course, I do not profess to have solved the mysteries of metalwork deposition in Bronze Age Europe. Instead, I have simply tried to develop another tool for our interpretive arsenal in the hope we can get a step closer to understanding why they were performed. Fragments of materials and objects seem to crop up everywhere once you start looking for them, and these bits and pieces left behind are endlessly intriguing. Through them, we can reveal complex stories about people and objects in the past, which I hope I have achieved with this book.

Matthew G. Knight
25 July 2021

A note on the text

The data discussed here were collected between February 2015 and March 2017 and they are presented in full in online supplementary material available via the Archaeology Data Service: https://doi.org/10.5284/1090300. Throughout the book, sites and objects studied are followed by catalogue numbers, which correspond with these data.

FOREWORD

One of the challenges of the European Bronze Age is to make sense of the practice of metalwork deposition: the permanent burial of artefacts that could have be re-used or otherwise recycled. All over Europe, in the course of almost 2000 years, massive amounts of recyclable metal were left in the ground only to be uncovered again thousands of years later. From a rationalist, economic perspective, this may seem to us an unnecessary wasting, even 'destruction' of valuable resources. As if this permanent hiding of valuable things and materials were not bizarre enough, a part of that material also appears to have been physically transformed. Things like swords, daggers, axes and ornaments were sometimes bent, broken, smashed to pieces or twisted. It makes one wonder what could have been the Bronze Age rationality behind this 'double destruction'?

This book, aptly titled *Fragments of the Bronze Age*, aims to shed some light onto this remarkable 'double destruction'. Of course, the breaking of bronze would make perfect sense from a purely technological craft perspective: a smith needs metal in manageable chunks that can be put into crucibles for re-melting. There is no doubt that much of metal breaking and bending relates to such practicalities. But as the present book convincingly shows, in some cases there must have been other reasons why Bronze Age people physically transformed tools, ornaments and weapons.

In what is probably the first systematic study of this practice of double destruction for one region, Matthew Knight presents a fascinating analysis, based on a thorough and representative overview of empirical evidence from south-west Britain over the entire Bronze Age. In its systematic rigor, going beyond the anecdotal and fuelled by valuable insights from experimental archaeology, the author gives an impressive insight not only into the practices of destruction itself, but also into its long-term development and social background and motivations. It is a study the significance of which goes beyond the regional. I see it as a source of ideas and inspiration for new studies to be carried out on Bronze Age evidence from other parts of Europe, notably Central and Eastern Europe. Also, Knight's use of insights gained from experimental archaeology are valuable to this field of research and open a new, promising avenue of research.

With this book, Knight opens a window into the past where metal was more than just a material, and where breaking and bending is more than an act of destruction.

Prof. David Fontijn
Leiden University

Author of
Sacrificial Landscapes and *Economies of Destruction*

1

Piece offerings: approaches to the destruction and deposition of Bronze Age metalwork

A peace offering and a piece offering

In March 1993, a peace ceremony was held in southern Ethiopia (Pankhurst 2006; Girke & Pankhurst 2011). It took place at a site of past conflict and several tribes were involved to ensure there was a collective approach to peacekeeping. The event took place over three days and involved three main stages, each accompanied by a series of processes, prayers and rituals embedded with meaning. The first involved anointing leaders and their ritual staffs; this was followed by the destruction and burial of three spears and then the exchange of gifts. It is the destruction of the spears on which I want to focus. These spears were brought by leaders from several groups and the tips and edges were blunted with rocks by the various leaders, within a shelter. The tips were arranged facing west towards the setting sun to symbolise evil being warded off and during the process these weapons were personified and treated as perpetrators of past conflict, banished through a series of chants (Pankhurst 2006, 254). Finally, the spears were taken 500 metres from the site to a termite mound where the wooden shafts were snapped in half and placed on the mound for the insects to devour. Sanctions were set in place against anyone digging up the spears. The final stage of the ceremony, the giving of gifts, involved the exchange of hide bracelets and fatty necklaces as well as agricultural implements to symbolise commensality and the replacement of weapons with productive tools (Pankhurst 2006; Girke & Pankhurst 2011). This represented a one-off event, designed to ensure a commitment to peace was established and maintained, entangling communities in a performative act.

About 3000 years ago, at a freshwater pool on Dartmoor in south-west Britain spearheads were also destroyed and deposited. The Late Bronze Age copper-alloy hoard from the evocatively named Bloody Pool comprised four incomplete spearheads and four fragments of socketed spear ferrules that would have fitted to the end of a wooden spear shaft (Fig. 1.1; Tucker 1855, 84–5). Three of these spearheads were large, possibly ceremonial objects, and each was deliberately broken straight across the widest part of the blade, removing the upper blade and tip. This involved heating the spearheads on a fire and striking with a hard, probably blunt, object to create a sharp, straight fracture (Knight 2019a, 261–5). The sockets and blade edges were also possibly intentionally damaged; the ferrules are similarly fragmentary. The three largest spearheads had rivets in place indicating they may have been attached to the shaft when deposited; the ferrules also indicate the spears may have been deposited complete, or perhaps with broken shafts. We can only speculate whether the spears were heated and broken at the site of deposition or whether the pieces were brought to the site from elsewhere before they were sunk into the pool. This process of destruction and deposition conveys a symbolic nature that might be interpreted as a sacrifice of weapons following a conflict (cf. Coombs

Figure 1.1: The hoard of broken spearheads from Bloody Pool, Devon (RAMM-F005) (photo: author, courtesy of Royal Albert Memorial Museum and Art Gallery, Exeter)

1975; Mörtz 2010; 2013; 2018), a votive offering to the place or to deities (Fox 1973, 120), or, considering the Ethiopian ceremony, a peacekeeping act.

The Ethiopian ceremony is not intended as an analogy for understanding the Bloody Pool hoard; instead the comparison between two superficially similar destructive acts that are so temporally, geographically, and culturally different serves to emphasise two important points. The first is that the destruction and deposition of objects are culturally embedded, performative processes. They are undertaken in particular ways in accordance with specific beliefs for specific purposes and connect those involved through social action. These may be related actions or undertaken at different times. In turn, the destruction event and eventual deposition allow the reproduction of social values that establish, reify and transform beliefs and relations between people (cf. Bourdieu 1977).

The second point is a crucial reminder that what we find archaeologically is very much only a partial record of the event of destruction and deposition and we cannot hope to understand the full event from the surviving material evidence. The Ethiopian peacekeeping ceremony is interesting because archaeologically all we might uncover is three blunted spearheads, perhaps with remnants of shafts if we are lucky, seemingly isolated from an ephemeral structure 500m away. We would have no indication of why the place was chosen nor the purpose of the event or the array of rituals, gift-giving and social interactions that underpinned and contributed to the overall ceremony. Although this allows us to conceptualise the Bloody Pool hoard as a similarly complex social event that linked people, place and objects, it will always remain conceptual. However, the surviving broken spearheads do allow us to reconstruct the processes and physical acts of destruction and deposition that can imply the significance of such an event. It is a focus from this perspective that I feel is important in understanding such actions.

Destruction and deposition of Bronze Age metalwork

> '...it is no longer possible to maintain any clear distinction between the ritual and functional aspects of metal deposits, for both made considerable use of broken objects' (Bradley 2005, 164)

Of course, the destruction and deposition of objects is conducted in innumerable ways and for diverse reasons at different times, serving economic, religious, social and/or political purposes. Bronze Age metalwork was no exception. These practices are widely recognised across Europe and have been the focus of much interest. This book furthers study of this phenomenon, but with a focus on *how* metal objects were destroyed and deposited, as much as *why*.

Throughout I draw on studies from across Europe, but my main area of focus is Britain. Here metalworking began around 2450 BC, with artefacts produced in copper and gold and, from about 2200 BC onwards, copper alloys. These artefacts have been found in a range of conditions and contexts. Daggers were burnt and buried with bodies. Swords and spears were decommissioned and thrown into rivers. Pins and bracelets were crushed, twisted and contorted and placed in certain landscapes, and axes were smashed to pieces and deposited in hoards of hundreds of objects. From individual complete objects to hoards of fragments, from pieces in settlement pits and ditches to curated burial associations, there was clearly no one way to treat and deposit metal objects. These were processes that were linked to and perhaps governed by their eventual context and associations, be that with people, objects, monuments, settled places or natural landscapes. With increased metal-detecting activity in Britain, finds reported through the Portable Antiquities Scheme (PAS) in England and Wales and the Treasure Trove Unit in Scotland are offering an unprecedented resource of material to be understood. Couple this with increased developer-funded activity and improved excavation techniques and scientific analyses, and we are able to disentangle and illuminate some of the previously hidden complexities of prehistoric depositional actions. Similar situations can be observed across Europe.

How, then, should we interpret destruction and deposition? Firstly, we must recognise we are studying two separate practices, even if they are sometimes closely linked (cf. Brandherm 2018, 48). An object does not have to be destroyed to enter the ground. If it is damaged, the destruction of an object may occur shortly before the event of deposition, as might be the case for an object burned on a pyre with a body before burial, or objects may be manipulated at one site and transported to their final depositional location. The meanings behind the treatment of an object and its eventual deposition could therefore be quite different. Secondly, if we accept that these practices were diverse and contextual, then we must also accept that we will be left with a range of acceptable interpretations depending on the situation under study. These need not be mutually exclusive, and they certainly should not be treated as a 'one-size-fits-all'. Whilst traditional analysis, beginning in the 19th century, often viewed broken, bent and burnt Bronze Age metalwork as abandoned scrap (eg, Evans 1881), a greater appreciation of object biographies, depositional contexts and broader practices increasingly demonstrates that the destruction and subsequent deposition of metalwork served a wider range of functions (eg, Hansen 1994; 2016; Turk 1997; 2001; Bradley 1998; 2005 145–64; 2017, 124–41; Chapman 2000; Fontijn 2002; 2020; Chapman & Gaydarska 2007; Becker 2013; Woodward & Hunter 2015; Brandherm 2018). Depositions have commonly been seen through the lens of an opposing ritual-profane dichotomy, but this is too simplistic, especially when it comes to broken objects. Broad concepts of what was considered appropriate for selectively depositing objects applied (cf. Needham 1988; Fontijn 2002), but these were individual actions that show a surprising amount of diversity, which remains underexplored. Within the Bronze Age, there were shifts in the types of objects and materials that were destroyed and different ways of doing this at different times and in different places. Whilst much material culture was deposited (and occasionally destroyed) in prehistory, in this book I focus specifically on metal objects because a range of observable damage was inflicted upon some of them in almost every context in which they are encountered throughout the Bronze Age. This allows for a cross-contextual analysis; however, with the exception of large fragmented hoards, there are relatively few dedicated studies of damaged metalwork, and none to my knowledge that examine it across different contexts.

Moreover, there has been limited attention to examining the destruction and deposition of metalwork as fluid and changing practices that are culturally specific. A rare example is Christopher Hoffman's (1999) study of deliberately broken metal objects in Chalcolithic, Late Bronze Age and Iron Age Spain. Hoffman highlights three instances of destruction and deposition within a relatively close geographical area in Majorca, which indicates changing reactions to how and why metalwork should be destroyed and deposited over time. In the Chalcolithic, he pinpoints a copper ingot that had been deliberately chiselled in half with each piece deposited in a different village; Hoffman (1999, 114–5) suggests the breakage required specialised tools, energy and metallurgical knowledge whilst separation and deposition served as a method for linking different individuals or communities, what we might now refer to as 'enchainment' (following Chapman 2000 *inter alia*; see below). In the Late Bronze Age, a sword piece with its corners hammered up and a deliberately blunted socketed axehead plugged with the blade of another axehead were deposited in association under the entranceway of a Majorcan talayot (a stone built tower); although typically considered a 'scrap' deposit, Hoffman (1999, 116–7) suggests the carefully executed process of damaging these objects indicates the process was undertaken by a skilled metalworker and the deposit may have been an act of safe-keeping or concealment or served a symbolic purpose as part of social reproduction. He contrasts this with the ecstatic, less sophisticated actions undertaken on metal artefacts deposited in a funerary context at Son Matge during the Iron Age: 'ornamental bronze *tintinabula* were hit with heavy objects and crushed, lead plaquettes were bent in half, iron spears were twisted in half and bent into coils' (*ibid.*, 118). These actions are considered a fundamental part of the associated burials. Thus, Hoffman emphasises the potential of combining an analysis of destructive and depositional practices with the spatial and temporal context to enable insights into the changing expression of prehistoric social and technological agency. Furthermore, it illustrates that over a long period of time, multiple reasons may emerge for the destruction of metalwork within a given region, something that I will expand upon in the present study.

Hoffman's study hints at the range of interpretations one might apply to the metalwork destruction and deposition, though it is by no means exhaustive. The key explanations that recur through studies of deliberately damaged metalwork in the Bronze Age include:

- Destruction for recycling, recasting and scrapping
- Fragments possessing a pre-monetary function
- Enchainment and social exchange
- The death of people and objects
- Ritual damage, sacrificial offerings and 'killing' objects

This range of interpretations are briefly considered here largely in relation to Bronze Age Britain. These are not presented as mutually exclusive – indeed breaking or damaging an object may serve multiple purposes – but capture the diversity of approaches towards explaining the destruction of metalwork.

Destruction for recasting, recycling and scrapping

The deliberate fragmentation and reduction of objects for recasting or recycling is one of the most prolific explanations for the large fragmentary hoards of metalwork deposited across Europe (eg, Evans 1881; Briard 1965; Burgess 1968; Eogan 1983, 3–4; Brandherm 2018; Wiseman 2018). Ethnographic studies in Africa, Indonesia and India, for instance, have all identified situations where worn and broken objects form part of exchange systems (Rowlands 1971, 211–2; Lahiri 1995, 125–6); old and damaged objects were traded with a metalsmith either as raw material or in exchange for new objects. Rowlands (1971) highlighted the seasonality associated with these actions; worn-out objects were often brought back towards the end of a season and Rowlands used this as a possible explanation for the accumulation of used and broken objects in Late Bronze Age hoards (*ibid.*, 212). Many hoards during this period consist of fragmentary objects, casting waste (eg, casting jets and slag) and ingots and metallurgical analyses have indicated high rates of recycling were ongoing by the final stages of the Bronze Age (Northover 1982a). Physical evidence for this comes with the occasional identification of objects melted into ingots. Consequently, hoards of predominantly fragmented objects, so-called 'scrap hoards', have been seen as the result of reduction for the casting process with these hoards representing the stock of metalsmiths or the abandonment of worn-out material. This theory has recently garnered strength for Late Bronze Age fragmented hoards in England and Wales through Rob Wiseman's (2018) modelling of the available PAS data which indicates that hoards of fragmented objects were randomly broken and accumulated; by the Ewart Park metalworking assemblage (*c.* 920–800 BC), Wiseman suggests 85–95% of all bronze in circulation was ending up in hoards. This means that the deliberate destruction of metalwork prior to deposition was a regular occurrence by the end of the Bronze Age.

Problems have been raised with these ideas though. Fundamentally, the question remains why was so much material abandoned and never recovered? Moreover, the recasting explanation does not account for the agency behind hoarding practices, nor explain the disproportionate character of hoards, including some types of objects more than others, which infers an element of selectivity (Turk 1997; 2001; Maraszek 2000; 2006; Fontijn 2002; Bradley 2005, 155ff.; Becker 2013; Hansen 2016). Many 'scrap' hoards comprise complete as well as incomplete objects, which likewise warrants explanation: can we consider a complete object 'scrap'? This is not to deny that the destruction of objects is not linked to the recasting and recycling process – clearly objects had to be broken for recasting and in many cases a metalworker was probably needed for destroying objects (Turk 1997, 51; Turner 2010a; Knight 2019a). However, this explanation in isolation remains too functionalist, not taking into appreciation the technological processes and skills that allowed fragmentation, nor the selection processes that resulted in certain objects ending up in hoards in certain locales.

Fragments possessing a pre-monetary function

An alternative argument for the increase in objects broken and deposited across Europe suggests that bronze fragments, occasionally termed 'hack-bronze', served as pre-monetary currency (eg, Sommerfeld 1994; Pare 1999; 2013; Brandherm 2018; Ialongo & Lago 2021). Much of this evidence derives from studies of weights and weighing systems in Central and Eastern Europe, and some analyses suggest that fragmented bronze in Europe may have operated similarly to contemporary systems relating to silver in Mesopotamia (Ialongo & Lago 2021). Although this was perhaps the case for some parts of Europe, such evidence remains limited in north-western Europe. In part, this results from a lack of attention to weights of bronze fragments and fragmentation patterns, though there is also limited proxy evidence, eg, balance weights (Ialongo 2019). Similarly, Wiseman's (2018) study highlighting randomised weights indicates that if this was 'currency', it was not monitored according to specific weighing systems. Of course, this projects a modern ideal of currency and commodification onto the past that is probably not appropriate, and it is clear that sometimes bronze did circulate in fragmented forms. Possible Bronze Age shipwreck assemblages from Langdon Bay, Kent, and Salcombe Bay, Devon comprised complete and fragmentary bronze and gold objects and copper and tin ingots (Needham *et al.* 2013), which highlights how raw metals and other objects were transported. This also illustrates the important observation that fragmentation of objects may take place away from their eventual depositional spot. If bronze fragments were part of an appropriate way to exchange metal, and this metal was considered to have some pre-monetary value, we may thus interpret hoards of fragments as safe-keeping exercises (cf. Brandherm 2018, 50) – though we again must question why so much was never retrieved – or else represented gifts of wealth to the supernatural.

In contrast to the treatment of bronze, there was perhaps greater control over the weights of gold objects (Hawkes 1932; Northover 1989; Needham 1990a; Rahmstorf 2019). In their study of gold fragments in the Late Bronze Age hoard from Rossett in north Wales, Gwilt *et al.* (2005, 45–52) highlight that the fragmentation of some bracelets across Britain and Ireland conform to ratios of separation, whereby they might be cut into eighths, quarters and/or halves. Combinations of the weights of fragments conformed to the production of some complete bracelets of different styles. Rahmstorf (2019) has similarly suggested that Middle and Late Bronze Age gold objects in Britain and Atlantic France may have been deliberately cut for purposes of exchange and production. However, it is clear that a pre-monetary function cannot account for all damaged objects.

Enchainment theory and social exchanges

Enchainment theory, derived from John Chapman's (2000) seminal *Fragmentation in Archaeology*, has held great currency in studies of fragmented objects (also Chapman & Gaydarska 2007). It refers to a chain of personal relationships made through the exchange of inalienable objects with distinctive biographies; this exchange involves two people establishing a transaction or social relationship represented by a specific artefact that is broken into two or more pieces, with the parts kept as tokens by participants until reconstitution of the relationship is necessary (*ibid.*, 6). This might be finalised by the structured deposit of the respective objects, either together or separately, perhaps in similar contexts; in turn this served to create, sustain and manage social identities and relational concepts of personhood. The structured deposition is crucial to our interpretations as the process of prehistoric enchainment is otherwise archaeologically invisible except by inference. Chapman presented instances of clay, stone and metal artefacts, as well as human remains, that suggested people in the past utilised fragmented artefacts and skeletons to preserve connections; of particular note is the refitting of fragments identified across different contexts within Neolithic settlements in Hungary, Bulgaria and Greece, which Chapman (*ibid.* 61–4) uses as evidence of enchainment processes in action. This concept has since been pervasive through studies of fragmentation and prehistoric personhood (eg, Fowler 2004; Brück 2006b). In many respects it stands in tension with the theories presented so far as it emphasises the role of damaged objects, specifically fragments, as socially charged agents in constructing aspects of personhood and identity, rather than holding a pragmatic value.

However, although Chapman was able to demonstrate numerous instances of such events in prehistoric south-eastern Europe, elsewhere various isolated instances remain the only hint that social relationships might be constructed in this way. The split copper ingot deposited in two villages in prehistoric Majorca is one. Another potential comes from Britain, where two refitting Late Bronze Age sword fragments were found in separate, but intervisible hilltop locations in Staffordshire, England (Bradley & Ford 2004); one sword fragment appears to have been in circulation for longer than the other, suggesting diverging histories but linked by the fragmentation event and knowledge that the two pieces were once part of the same object. On their own, these cases hardly speak to a widespread prehistoric notion of utilising fragmented objects to enchain aspects of social relationships (though studies of a similar nature and scale to that by Chapman have, to my knowledge, never been undertaken elsewhere). More broadly we might posit that where fragments and pieces are missing from deposited objects, the removal of pieces served to maintain relationships, perhaps to be kept in circulation, a concept that extends to human remains as well as objects (Brück 2004; 2006a; 2019). Fragmentary 'heirloom' objects, for instance, are commonly identified in the archaeological record and the deposition of one piece while retaining the other may have created links between the living and the dead, such as with jet and amber necklaces (Woodward 2002; Brück 2004; Frieman 2012). Assessing enchainment is most robust when grounded in clear contextual analysis and it is potentially problematic to apply the theory too broadly (Brittain & Harris 2010). That fragmentation and observable enchainment are contextual is unsurprising when one considers that relational personhood is similarly multi-facetted and contextually situated (Fowler 2004; 2016; Brück & Fontijn 2013). Where examples can be identified, this interpretation should be applied with caution.

The death of people and objects

Deliberately broken, burned and manipulated objects were commonly buried with the Bronze Age dead (eg, Ashbee 1960, 96; Brück 1995; 2006a; 2019, 73–6; Needham & Woodward 2008). These cases present some of the clearest links for connections between people and objects and why objects may have been destroyed. In 1961, Leslie Grinsell examined ethnographic and historical evidence for this phenomenon highlighting the range of reasons why objects might be deliberately damaged or 'killed' prior to deposition with the dead (Table 1.1), as well as summarising some of the prolific archaeological evidence for these practices across Europe and north Africa, from the Neolithic onwards (Grinsell 1961; 1973). Grinsell's list highlights practical reasons for deliberate damage (eg, to fit in the grave) as well as culturally specific rationales (eg, superstitions). These reasons are not exhaustive, however. As enchainment theory highlighted above, objects may be broken with some pieces deposited and others retained to preserve links between the living and the dead: this is the case among the Nuer in South Sudan, where a man's metal armrings might be broken and distributed among the men and boys of the family upon his death (Evans Pritchard 1956, 152). Communities may also destroy possessions such as pots, personal ornaments and weapons, to sever links with the dead, eliminate painful reminders or memorialise deaths through the physical transformation of objects (eg, Stayt 1931, 162; Colson 1953, 274–5; Ray 1963, 116–20; Marshall 1965, 260; Maybury-Lewis 1974, 280). The treatment of objects is influenced heavily by their associations with people and communities or the histories and connections they embody, that is, their inalienable nature (Weiner 1992).

Reason
Releasing an object's spirit
Reducing the risk of grave-robbing
Prevention of quarrels amongst the living
'Repugnance' of using them again
Fear of pollution (eg, if the person died of a contagious disease)
To frighten away Charon (Aegean superstition)
Close association between the objects and the dead (eg, swords)
Objects associated with the mortuary ceremony
Symbolising the destruction of enemies of the deceased
Objects too large for the grave
To preserve links between the living and the dead (eg, enchainment)
To sever links between living and dead
As part of 'memory work' to remember or forget people and their possessions

Table 1.1: Summary of Grinsell's (1961; 1973) reasons for the ceremonial 'killing' of objects at funerals with additional reasons in bold

The same seems to have been true of many artefacts deposited with Early Bronze Age burials. Interpretation of these objects has benefited greatly from biographical approaches towards how objects were produced and used (cf. Kopytoff 1986; Gosden & Marshall 1999). Worn, fragmentary and dissembled objects, including ceramics and amber, jet and composite necklaces may have been heirlooms gifted by mourners and establishing genealogical links (Woodward 2002; Frieman 2012; Woodward & Hunter 2015). Here, again, we encounter some overlap with Chapman's 'enchainment theory' and the emphasis on social exchanges, highlighting the destruction, deposition and circulation of objects as part of a multi-faceted social expression. In death, partial and incomplete objects may also represent elements that were deliberately broken as part of the funeral so that some could be retained as tokens of the dead by the living (Brück 2004; 2006a; Fowler 2004; Brück & Fontijn 2013). In this way objects come to embody people. Sasja van der Vaart-Verschoof (2017a) has made similar suggestions for Hallstatt C burials in the Low Countries, emphasising the selectivity of including, manipulating, fragmenting and removing objects at the point of burying the dead; considering grave goods as *pars pro toto* – that is, including a portion of an object as a representative of the whole – it is possible to identify these as objects with ascribed meanings. A common suggestion is that objects may be so intrinsically linked with a person that when an individual died, their object had to be killed as well (Grinsell 1961, 477).

Direct associations between objects and people allow us to compare and contrast their treatment as a way of gaining insights into how they related; such links are less clear for objects destroyed and deposited away from places of human burial or even human activity.

Ritual damage, sacrificial offerings and 'killing' objects

Perhaps the most common interpretation when deliberately damaged metalwork is encountered is that it served a symbolic or 'ritual' aspect in the Bronze Age. It is widely applied to account for intentional destruction in the Bronze Age and here I summarise some of the approaches in relation to single and hoarded finds. Frequently, an object's biography is considered as part of the interpretation, with the deliberate destruction a necessary part of making the object acceptable for deposition, perhaps linked with an associated person or community (York 2002; Brück 2004; 2006a; Fowler 2004, 72–6; Fontijn *et al.* 2012). Hansen (1994; 2016) has suggested a *pars pro toto* theory for fragmented objects in hoards, paralleled with deliberately broken offerings at Classical Greek sanctuaries; this theory is increasingly suggested for some Middle and Late Bronze Age hoards (eg, Fontijn 2002; Webley *et al.* 2020, 118–20). Further, it might explain some single finds deposited in similar locales to hoards (eg, Becker 2013). However, it does not necessarily account for the variety of object types and object conditions found in accumulated deposits, which can include complete and broken objects, as well as metallurgical waste (cf. Bradley 2017, 134–5). More generally, some caution is needed in projecting historical comparisons onto Bronze Age depositions.

Ritually damaged objects are also commonly linked to violent acts (eg, Nebelsick 1997; 2000; Perea 2008; Rezi 2011; Fontijn *et al.* 2012; Mörtz 2018). Deformed and broken objects thus represent emotionally charged ecstatic actions, resulting from a reaction to the contemporary socio-political situations (Nebelsick 2000). Louis Nebelsick, in particular, has advocated this for extreme forms of damage observed on metalwork in Central Europe:

> 'We are dealing with traces of violent behaviour which show no signs of formative or structural intentions. The coarse nature of this destructive process, its unsystematic, fleeting character, and its sometimes terrible intensity can hardly be connected with a well-considered, carefully undertaken, competently performed, reductive or scrapping process. Even given the possibility that the perpetrators were technically incompetent, this would still not explain the signs of explosively exaggerated feats of strength, the evidence for interrupted and ill-considered sequences of action and the signs of hurried, blind violence. This evidence for egregious demolition all points to a context of uncontrolled rage, euphoric frenzy and ecstatic violence' (Nebelsick 2000, 163).

This interpretation is based on modern perceptions of what was or was not 'functional' in the past, but it is difficult to ignore the exaggerated actions taken on some objects. Objects in the Pila del Brancon hoard in Italy, for instance, were bent, broken and burnt before being deposited in a river bank (Bietti Sestieri *et al.* 2013); similar actions were undertaken on weapons in the Duddingston Loch assemblage (Callander 1922) and Peelhill Farm hoard (Mörtz *et al.* forthcoming), both Scotland (Fig. 1.2).

Tobias Mörtz (2013; 2018; Mörtz *et al.* forthcoming) has argued such weapon hoards might constitute sacrificial offerings resulting from bouts of conflict, with the violent acts of deliberate destruction mimicking the violent conflicts in which the weapons were involved. To take other examples, socketed axeheads in Britain and south-eastern Europe were deliberately plugged with fragments of other objects and hammered (Hansen 1998; Dietrich 2014; Dietrich & Mörtz 2019), and metalwork in numerous hoards across Europe were seemingly fragmented beyond a purely practical agenda (Nebelsick 2000; Maraszek 2006; Hansen 2016). However, it is important to recognise that violent damage is not the same as ritual damage. Discussions surrounding extreme forms of damage tend to enter a circular argument where an object was violently damaged as part of a ritual and because it was a ritual the object had to be violently damaged. Furthermore, little consideration is given in these interpretations to *how* exactly one might damage or destroy a bronze object and the material properties that condition the method used; a better understanding of these processes offers the opportunity to reassess what we might actually interpret as 'violent' behaviour and whether this may have been legitimately linked to symbolic actions.

Finally, the 'ritual' aspect of deliberately damaged objects is also inferred from the place in which they were deposited. Typically, complete and damaged objects recovered from watery locations are attributed a votive significance from their depositional location and their perceived irretrievability (Levy 1982; Bradley 1998). Deliberate damage observed on artefacts from these findspots is often considered part of a process for 'killing' the object and ending its life (York 2002). To take swords as an example, these may have been considered animate or personified items as a result of their involvement in past interactions (Pearce 2013; Chapman 2018, 70–2); deliberate bending, burning or breaking prior to their placement in rivers and wetlands was considered essential to ending the perceived life of the object and Henry Chapman has argued this may be a form of prehistoric iconoclasm, transforming the object and removing its potential as a sign (Chapman & Gearey 2013; Chapman 2018, 66–73). By extension, the presence of deliberately destroyed metalwork in certain places has been used to infer significance about that place and the potential reason for the deposit. Hoards of complete and fragmentary material deposited in significant landscape locations, such as hilltops and river valleys, may have been part of a system to manage the socio-political landscape by depositing offerings in significant places to claim the land and assert authority (Fontijn 2002; Needham 2007a). By contrast, deliberately destroyed objects in watery places tend to be interpreted as gifts to deities or the supernatural (Brandherm 2018; Fontijn 2020).

Such is the prevalence of the idea of 'ritually damaged' objects, that one must be wary of equating 'intentional destruction' with 'ritual destruction', which is clearly inaccurate. There has been little discussion about the exact nature of these rituals and a balance is needed between what might be considered 'symbolic' action and what might be related to other interpretations. Indeed, we might question why such a division is needed at all (cf. Brück 1999a; Fontijn 2020).

An important point to derive from these various interpretations is that, to date, almost all studies on intentionally damaged metalwork focus on understanding *why* this material was treated this way with rarely any focus on *how* this was undertaken, and the processes involved. Experimental investigations into how Bronze Age metal artefacts were produced and used demonstrate that there is much we can add to our understanding of the histories of objects that may contribute to their deposition; however, the pre-depositional treatment of objects, especially destructive actions, and the associated depositional actions, have seen comparatively limited exploration. This oversight means we are missing key information that can infer aspects of prehistoric agency. Shifting the focus to thinking about destruction and deposition as technical and performative actions that can be reconstructed can assist our understanding of why such activities were done and the underlying social ontologies. A similar approach focusing on specific practices in Early Iron Age burials in the Low Countries and Central Europe has highlighted how we may use similarities in practices to recognise connections and networks between different areas (Fontijn & van der Vaart-Verschoof 2016, van der Vaart-Verschoof 2017, 158–61; van der Vaart-Verschoof & Schumann 2020). By investigating how similar and different practices were undertaken in time and space, finer details of Bronze Age processes and the relationships held between people and their objects can be gleaned, as well as broader connections. Although much has been done already to highlight the complexities of these practices, I believe we can still go further in adding greater nuance to our interpretations, steering away from catch-all interpretations and focusing on relationships between people, places and objects.

Research aims

It is the aim of striving for more nuanced interpretations that drives this book. There are many ways this might be achieved, but here I focus on the *process of destruction* associated with eventual deposition, something that has rarely been given dedicated study. This must begin with recognising and understanding what does and does not constitute deliberate destruction of metalwork (Chapter 2). Often this relies on the 'obvious' nature of destruction (eg, a sword bent in half), but we can also draw on material science approaches, metalwork wear analysis and experimental archaeology; these are avenues that have yet to be fully applied to the study of damaged Bronze Age metalwork but help us better understand the material. Amongst others, key questions that will be addressed in this volume include:

- Can we identify skills, technology and knowledge involved in processes of metalwork destruction and deposition?
- If we understand how destruction was undertaken, what might we say about the performance of these processes? And who might have been involved?
- Are there patterns in the deposition of deliberately damaged metalwork that might infer broader social understandings? Were certain objects selected over others?
- What links can be identified between complete and incomplete objects? What is the relationship between metal and non-metal objects?
- How is this linked to depositional contexts, including hoards, settlements, burials, and geographical and topographical locations?
- How can we then interpret the meaning behind destruction and deposition events?

These questions offer a series of avenues for us then to explore the social role of the destruction and deposition of metalwork and examine what it can tell us about Bronze Age individuals and communities.

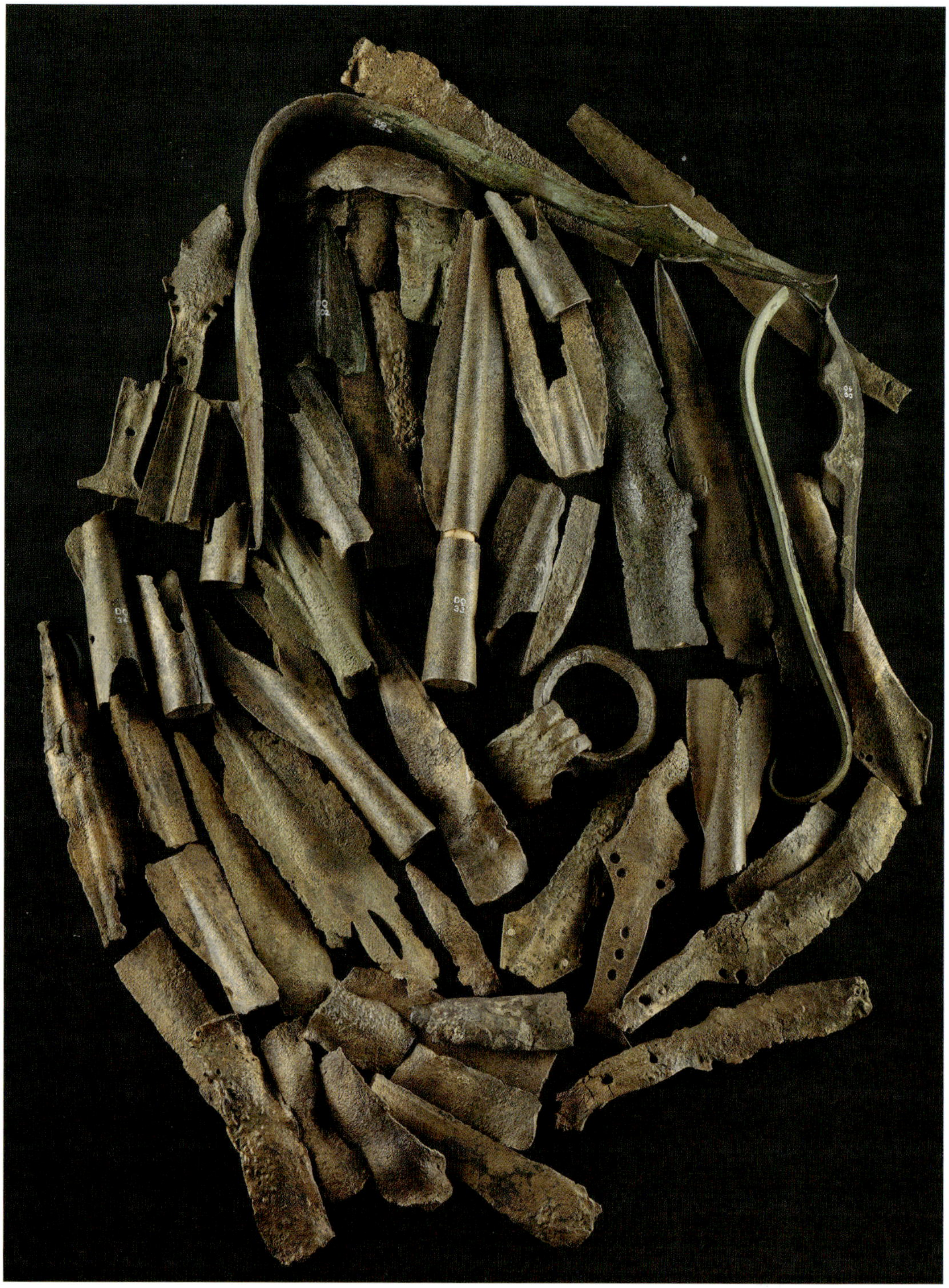

Figure 1.2: The Late Bronze Age assemblage of deliberately destroyed weapons from Duddingston Loch, Edinburgh © National Museums Scotland

South-west Britain as a regional case study for the destruction and deposition of metalwork

The research aims are relevant across Bronze Age Europe, but to achieve a detailed understanding of destructive processes, the phenomenon needs to be approached using a case study region and to involve careful analysis of individual artefacts. Such a region needs a suitably high volume of metal artefacts recovered from a range of contexts and in a

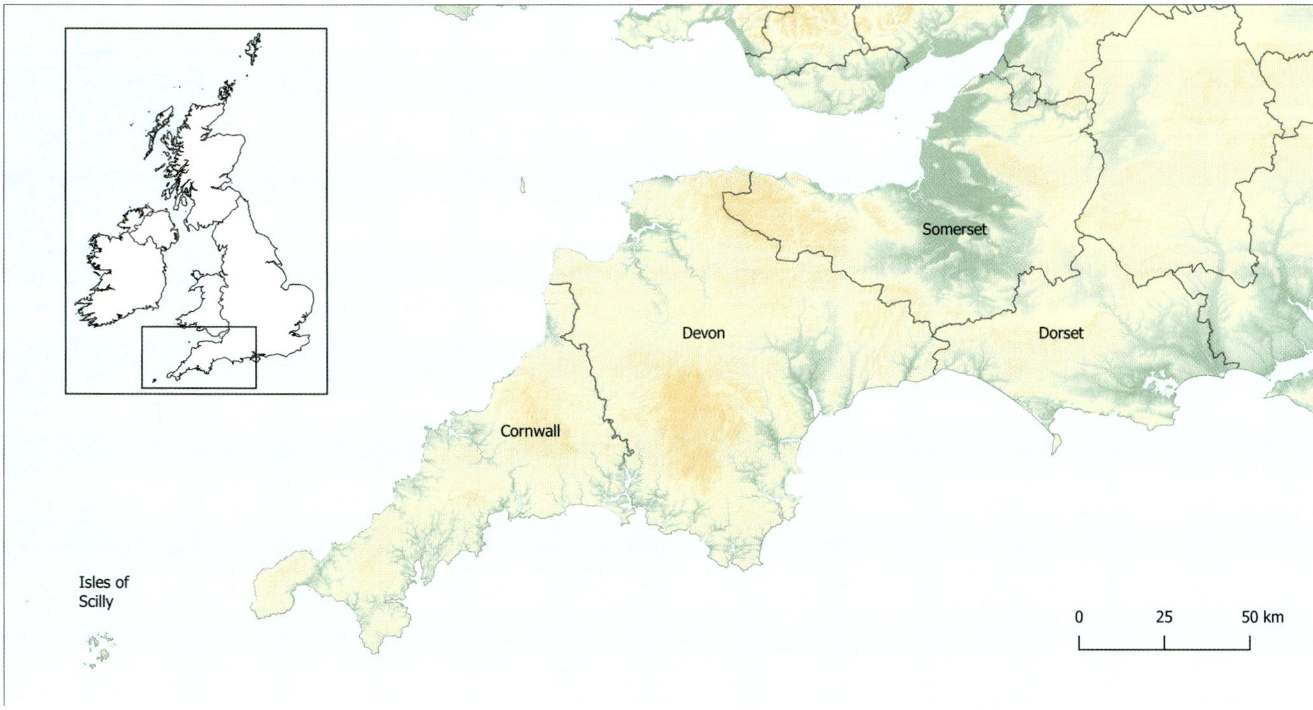

Figure 1.3: The study region: south-west Britain. Contains OS data © Crown copyright and database right 2021

range of conditions to allow us to explore how the treatment of metalwork was related to people and place. South-west Britain provides an ideal case study (Fig 1.3). It comprises a diverse topographic area as well as being one of the most metalliferous regions in Europe, containing deposits of tin, gold, copper and lead, and was exploited for its resources from early in the Bronze Age. Moreover, it occupies an interesting geographical location in Europe, situated on the Atlantic façade between central southern England, Wales, Ireland and north-western France, with far-reaching connections. Finally, there is a readily available dataset for analysis, representing a spatially and temporally broad range of objects and practices (Pearce 1983; Knight *et al.* 2015). This combination of factors means south-west Britain provides a fascinating backdrop for studying destruction and deposition across time, which, as I will show, was variably linked with its geography, local and international connections, and the trade in resources. Over 1700 objects were studied from across the region with the damage carefully assessed for signs of intentional damage (Chapter 2). These were recorded in a database (available via: https://doi.org/10.5284/1090300) and references to database numbers linked with sites are made throughout. This analysis forms the basis for discussing destruction and deposition in this region and more broadly in Bronze Age Britain (Chapter 6).

Terms of destruction

When approaching this topic, it is essential that appropriate terminology is carefully considered. A term like 'destruction' is inherently interpretive and often used wholesale or uncritically. Similarly, damaged objects are frequently described using a variety of terms (eg, broken, notched, burnt) with limited clarification of what this actually means. Clearly defined terms surrounding the theme of destruction are essential if we are to approach this topic adequately.

Damage on objects may, of course, occur in a number of ways, such as through use or accident in the past or post-depositional and recovery processes. Intrinsic to this is the identification of whether damage is ancient or not, a point we will address in Chapter 2. Moreover, damage, as a term, encompasses the full variety of effects on an object, including material displacement, deformation and/or loss. 'Damage' can apply to something as simple as nicks suffered through use, or as complex as a burnt, bent and broken sword, as well as referring to post-depositional corrosion or post-recovery processes. Damage is therefore quite a generalised term and in the subsequent chapters, I have tried to qualify the causes and types of damage observed.

In particular, I have used specific terms when referring to broken objects (ie, objects in two or more pieces), which are commonly encountered in the archaeological record and are most commonly encountered in this study. Like other forms of damage, breakage may be deliberate or accidental and throughout I choose to use the term *break* synonymously with the more mechanical term *fracture*. However, I refer to the resulting portions of objects differently, depending on their level of completeness:

- A *piece* of an object represents more than 25% of the original object;
- A *fragment* of an object represents 25% or less of the original object.

Of course, this relies on the original object form being recognisable from the surviving piece or fragment. Where a broken object is unrecognisable, I refer to these as fragments as well, since an unrecognisable portion of an object is likely to represent less than 25% of the original form. Under these definitions, fragmentation, then, refers specifically to the process of breakage that results in fragments. This distinction has been made to assist with recognising the nature of broken objects from a simple descriptor and allow more meaningful comparisons across a range of objects.

Turning to the central topic, I apply the term *destruction* to refer to damage intentionally inflicted on an object to remove its presumed function. One can think here of the crushing of the socket of a socketed axehead meaning it can no longer be hafted, or the chiselling and breaking of a sword blade meaning it can no longer function as a weapon. Under this definition, destruction is thus always the result of human agency. However, whilst destruction is linked closely with rendering an object unusable in a purely functional sense, destruction does not necessarily mean the end of an object's usefulness or meaning. The fragmentation of a sword serves to destroy the functionality of the weapon, but if the fragments then circulate as part of exchange networks, destruction serves a transformative process. We will see examples of this throughout the present investigation of south-west Britain.

Signs of destruction are not always clear or easy to interpret. Destruction Indicators, as I will refer to them, are important for understanding whether an object has been deliberately damaged but require qualification for us to assess the intentionality of the damage correctly (cf. Knight 2021). This includes varieties of plastic deformation (eg, crushing, bending, twisting), as well as burning and breakage; I will define and develop eight different Destruction Indicators in the next chapter (see Tables 2.4 and 2.5).

Outline of the volume

Chronology

This book covers the period from 2450 BC through to 600 BC (Table 1.2) presenting a long-term view of how the treatment of metalwork transformed across time, from the earliest introduction of copper and copper alloys to the conventional transition towards ironworking. Thus under the term 'Bronze Age', I also include the Chalcolithic and Earliest Iron Age in Britain. By covering the whole of this period, we can encompass and observe the complete range of depositional and destructive actions undertaken in relation to metalwork and how approaches to the treatment of objects changed over time.

Structure

In this introduction I have established the background for the present research, defining key terms and research aims. In Chapter 2, I present a framework for approaching and identifying damaged objects that draws on past analyses, as well as material science approaches and experimental archaeology. This is summarised in a Damage Ranking System (DRS) that applies to copper-alloy objects, as well as gold objects, and can be utilised to structure the data and assess whether damage may be accidental or deliberate. The DRS is used to organise data collected from Bronze Age south-west Britain and to illustrate broad trends in the data in terms of object condition and the depositional contexts. Chapters 3, 4 and 5 present detailed discussions of case studies from south-west Britain, divided according to broad chronological periods (Chalcolithic/Early Bronze Age; Middle Bronze Age; Late Bronze Age/Earliest Iron Age). Chapter 6 brings the discussions

Table 1.2: Southern British Bronze Age metalworking chronology used within this volume

Bronze Age period	*Date (cal BC)*	*Metalworking assemblage (MA)/Phase*	*Periodisation*
Chalcolithic	2450–2200/2150	MA I/II	Period 1/2
EBA	2200/2150–1950	MA III Brithdir/Migdale	Period 2/3
EBA	1950–1875	MA IV Mile Cross/Aylesford	Period 3
EBA	1875–1725	MA V Willerby	Period 3
EBA	1725–1500	MA VI Arreton	Period 4
MBA	1500–1400	Acton Park (Acton 2)	Period 5
MBA	1400–1275	Taunton	Period 5
MBA	1275–1150	Penard	Period 5
LBA	1150–1020	Wilburton	Period 6
LBA	1020–920	Blackmoor/early Ewart Park	Period 6/7
LBA	920–800	Ewart Park	Period 7/8
EstIA	800–600	Llyn Fawr	Period 8

Drawn from Needham 1996; Needham *et al.* 1997; 2010)
E/M/LBA = Early/Middle/Late Bronze Age; EstIA = Earliest Iron Age

together to set the practices observed in the region in the broader context of Bronze Age Britain and north-western Europe. Destruction and deposition are emphasised as important social actions that help us understand how people used these as modes for social reproduction at different times and in different areas. I outline how we can use different features of the material record to interpret deposits of meaning across time and space. In my concluding chapter I return to my research aims, summarising the results of the case study from south-west Britain and emphasising the importance of considering the technical and performative aspects of destruction and deposition.

2

Making sense of the pieces

> It is, of course, fundamental to fragmentation research that all alternatives to deliberate fragmentation and deposition of fragments are explored before a conclusion in favour of that interpretation is reached (Chapman 2012, 132)

What is intentional damage?

We need to address this fundamental question if subsequent interpretations are to hold validity. The identification of deliberate damage is often noted in reports on prehistoric metalwork, but rarely expanded upon. Usually it is approached cautiously, generally due to uncertainty around how the damage may have occurred. When identified it often relies on obvious features and/or patterns of damage, particularly within hoards of material.

A hoard of 40 spearheads and seven axeheads from Bondesgårde, near Torsted, Denmark, exemplifies this (Melheim & Horn 2014, 8–12). Of the spearheads, 14 are fractured at approximately the same point below the tip and 18 have a blow mark in a similar position. Many of the spearheads show signs of intensive use and the hafts may have been deliberately removed prior to deposition. All of these factors in a closed group lead to the conclusion that many of the spears were deliberately destroyed (Melheim & Horn 2014). Similar damage might be regarded as natural or accidental on single finds, but alongside multiple damaged finds, such damage is taken as intentional action. This means that assessing damage on single finds should not be undertaken without considering wider patterns of damage. Commonly, deliberate damage on individual objects, be they single finds or components of hoards, requires more 'obvious' indicators to be considered absolute. A sword from Werkhoven, the Netherlands, for instance, was bent prior to deposition and suffered damage by a blow from a metal object (Fontijn *et al.* 2012); individual objects in the Cassiobridge Farm hoard, England, had crushed sockets or bent blades (Coombs 1979). In both cases, signs of extreme damage were used to conclude intent. Yet an absolute methodology for assessing and identifying deliberate damage is still largely forthcoming.

This is likely to remain the case – any identification of deliberate destruction is still largely a matter of interpretation after all – but the processes for identifying intentional destruction and the significance of physically destroying Bronze Age objects has attracted growing attention in the last two decades (eg, Chapman 2000; York 2002; Becker 2006; Chapman & Gaydarksa 2007; Gabillot & Lagarde 2008; Quilliec 2008; Horn 2011; Rezi 2011; Fontijn *et al.* 2012; Tarbay 2017). Analyses of destruction are hindered, however, by the general lack of knowledge of *how* objects were damaged. For this reason, it is important that some form of methodology is developed.

In this chapter I will consider the various factors that contribute to how we recognise ancient damage, as well as approaches for better understanding it. A first step towards assessing intentional damage is by utilising what I have termed a Damage Ranking System (Knight 2021), which builds on this past research. This system assesses damage observed on individual objects and ranks it on a probability index, 0–3, with 0 being definitely unintentional and 3 being definitely intentional. I conclude this chapter by applying this methodology to a sampled dataset from south-west Britain, which highlights the benefits of this system

Mechanical property	*Description*
Plasticity	The ability to relieve stress on the microstructure by plastically deforming before breakage
Ductility	Plastic deformation under tensile stress causing bending
Malleability	Plastic deformation under compressive stress, leading to a smaller volume
Brittleness	The likelihood an object will break under stress rather than plastically deform
Hardness	The mechanical resistance to compressive force, eg, how easily the surface of an object might be damaged
Fracture	Breakage of an object into two or more pieces, further divided into ductile fractures and brittle fractures (those with or without associated plastic deformation)
Tensile/ultimate strength	The maximum stress a material can withstand before fracturing
Toughness/impact	The ability to absorb energy and plastically deform without fracturing
Yield point/proportional limit	The point at which a material can no longer recover from plastic deformation

Table 2.1: Summary of the mechanical properties of bronze (following Horn & von Holstein 2017, 91)

for understanding deliberate damage across a region and throughout the Bronze Age. This forms the basis for more detailed assessments in subsequent chapters.

Material matters

In Britain, the earliest bronze artefacts were produced from copper alloyed with tin, with low percentages of lead added by the later Bronze Age (Brown & Blin-Stoyle 1959; Northover 1980; 1982a). The respective contents of tin and lead, as well as various post-casting processes, impact the mechanical properties of the resulting bronze artefact (Table 2.1), which means these are important considerations for understanding how an object may be damaged.

A bronze with a higher tin content will be more brittle and less plastic than one with a lower tin content; it may thus be more likely to break than bend (Scott 2012). Similarly, work-hardening a sword edge will improve the toughness and tensile strength of the metal, while decreasing the plasticity and increasing the likelihood that it may fracture under duress. The inclusion of lead is particularly important. Alloying low percentages of lead with tin-bronze assists the casting process, indicating perhaps a practical use for its inclusion (Tylecote 1986, 30; Scott 2012, 242ff.), though more than 5% can lower the tensile strength of the bronze, as lead is immiscible in copper, which would make the material more liable to break along the microstructural bronze-lead boundaries (Tylecote in Allen *et al.* 1970, 22–3; Staniaszek & Northover 1983; Craddock 1991, 55). These planes of weakness mean that when heated the copper-alloy object may fracture, or 'hot short', under stress resulting in a sharp break with limited other evidence of deformation (Kuijpers 2018, 100, 148, 181, 220; Knight 2019a, 252f.). In real terms, this means that if incomplete Bronze Age artefacts are known to be composed of leaded bronze and present a sharp break, it can be suggested they are the result of hot-shorting, whether through accident (eg, through hot-working; Kuijpers 2018, 148, 181, 220–1), or deliberately fragmenting the object by heating and striking it (Knight 2017; 2019a). Therefore, we can see that these factors are important for understanding how and why bronze objects broke in the past. Where compositional data are available these need to be considered. Furthermore, an awareness of the mechanical properties of bronze means that certain damage can be explained based on the material science, as well as the presumed way in which damage was sustained.

Although these features are inherent to understanding *why* bronze performs the way it does, this consideration has only recently come to the fore in studies exploring wear analysis (eg, Gutiérrez Sáez & Martín Lerma 2015; Horn & von Holstein 2017; Andrews *et al.* 2021), though it has been well-established for many years. An appreciation of the mechanical attributes of bronze needs to be integrated into our perspectives of ancient damage.

Figure 2.1: Opposite ends of a piece of spearhead from Dorset with an ancient break at one end (top) and a modern break at the other (bottom) (photo: author, courtesy of Poole Museum Service)

Ancient or not? The role of corrosion and patina

A first step towards damage identification and accurate interpretation of the material is determining that the damage observed on an object is truly ancient. However, complex or unknown object histories post-recovery often render this difficult. Typically, reports on metalwork have not discussed this in any detail, with authors simply stating if the objects were broken in antiquity or not, but it is a process that must be undertaken and thus warrants discussion. A simple method for identifying ancient damage is an assessment of the consistency between the corrosion of the damage and the rest of the object (Needham 1990b, 20; York 2002, 79; Roberts & Ottaway 2003; Becker 2006, 49; Horn & von Holstein 2017; Bell 2019).

The nature and formation of corrosion is reliant on a range of factors, including the surrounding temperature and deposition environment (Robbiola *et al.* 1998; Piccardo *et al.* 2007; Horn & von Holstein 2017). In the right conditions, protective mineralised layers might form preserving the original surface, commonly known as a patina (Robbiola *et al.* 1998). As this type of corrosion is stable and preserves the underlying surface, a fracture in the patina, sometimes revealing the original bronze colour, probably represents more recent damage, perhaps through rediscovery processes (eg, ploughing or dredging). By extension, damage with a consistent patina suggests that it could have occurred in antiquity (Fig. 2.1; Kienlin & Ottaway 1998; Bridgford 2000, 166).

Alternatively, corrosion can be destructive, causing pitting, corrosion deposits, and delamination (Robbiola *et al.* 1998, 2097–8), damaging the original surface and hindering interpretations of manufacture, use-wear and damage (Fig. 2.2; Kienlin & Ottaway 1998, 271; Bell 2019). In extreme cases, the overall object can decay over time, so no original metal remains, sometimes resulting in breakage. Furthermore, because corrosion

Figure 2.2: Extensive corrosion damage on a palstave from Norton Fitzwarren, Somerset, obscuring signs of manufacture and use (photo: author, courtesy of Somerset County Council and South West Heritage Trust, acc. no. 68.A.8/1)

might cause objects to fracture, it can create a false impression of ancient damage or obscure the difference between modern and ancient breaks.

In some cases, if an object is poorly conserved or mistreated after recovery, corrosion can form quickly, sometimes obscuring fresh breaks over the course of a hundred years (Kienlin & Ottaway 1998; Bridgford 2000, 166; Becker 2006, 44–5). Likewise, where corrosion has been cleaned from objects, this method of identification becomes problematic. This largely occurs on finds excavated during the 19th and early 20th centuries, which have been kept out of the ground for a long period of time; knowing when and how objects were discovered is therefore important (cf. Kristiansen 1987).

Despite these issues, assessment of corrosion remains one of the best ways of interpreting the antiquity of damage observed on metalwork, in conjunction with knowledge about the security of the context and the known object history.

After deposition

The context in which an object was deposited or recovered can influence the decay of the object over time and/or the likelihood that it will become damaged through post-depositional or recovery processes. Fontijn (2002, 43–7) discussed natural and anthropogenic processes that would impact the recovery and distribution of objects; many of these would also affect the condition in which an object was found and the likelihood that it would sustain damage (eg, an object recovered from a cultivated field may have been struck by a plough). These offer useful starting points to which other considerations can be added (Table 2.2).

Table 2.2: Post-depositional processes affecting the final condition of the objects (adapted from Fontijn 2002, 43–7)

Natural processes	*Anthropogenic processes*
Corrosion Sedimentation Water movement	Dredging Extractive industries eg, mining, quarrying Agricultural processes eg, ploughing, fertilisation Re-appropriation in later periods

Natural processes

In addition to corrosion, two other natural processes can affect the condition of an object: sedimentation, and water movement. In his study of findspots in the Netherlands, Fontijn (2002, 43) argued sedimentation affected the likelihood of finding metal objects (ie, the greater the sedimentation the deeper they would now be buried) and thus impacted the overall distribution maps. Although one might consider it unlikely to damage the deposited objects, Horn (2013a, 13) suggested that transverse bending might occur through soil pressure post-deposition. This seems unlikely and has yet to be noted for Bronze Age metalwork in Britain, but it remains possible under the right circumstances.

Similarly, the movement of objects through or by water might potentially cause some surface damage to the material and in extreme cases breakage or bending perhaps through collision with rocks in the riverbed or in coastal locations.

Anthropogenic processes

Post-depositional anthropogenic processes are some of the most common causes of damage on prehistoric objects. There are four key examples we can consider here relevant to our case study region of south-west Britain: dredging, extractive industries, agriculture and reappropriation in later periods.

Firstly, the dredging of rivers and the reshaping of waterways and coastlines all involve intrusive equipment that can damage any objects uncovered in the process. Such damage might affect the object surface, or cause deformation and fracturing of the objects. The obvious problem is how to differentiate ancient damage from processes such as dredging (Needham & Burgess 1980, 447). If the object has been recovered relatively recently, modern damage could be indicated by a break in the patina, but this is not guaranteed as objects deposited in wet areas do not necessarily develop an extensive patina (Fontijn 2002, 40; Becker 2006, 41–2). Nonetheless, York (2002, 79) used patina to differentiate 'recent recovery (dredger) damage and ancient damage' on objects recovered from the River Thames, many of which were found while dredging. By comparison, few objects in south-west Britain possess a context associated with dredging, though two swords dredged at Weymouth,

Dorset, present damage that is difficult to ascribe to prehistoric actions (Pearce 1983, 487, 489, nos 476, 491; DCM-F040), whilst one rapier from the River Fowey, Cornwall, was certainly broken upon or after recovery (Pearce 1983, 552, no.866).

Extractive industries on land, such as mining and quarrying, similarly involve processes that can damage metalwork. The exploitation of material resources in south-west Britain over the last 3000 years, and particularly the impact of mechanical diggers and explosives in the modern period, means that many objects have probably been reclaimed and/or destroyed or broken. Unlike wetland deposits, dryland metalwork finds develop more distinct corrosive products and any surface damage should be clearly visible.

Thirdly, the impact of agricultural processes, particularly those involving machinery (eg, ploughing), on the context of finds across the country is commonly noted, but the damaging consequences are only briefly mentioned. Objects deposited at shallow depths may be damaged and/or fragmented in the process of recovery. Furthermore, the increased use of fertilisers and other pollutants over the last 50–100 years has accelerated the rate at which corrosion products form and bronze deteriorates in the ground (Tronner *et al.* 1995; Nord *et al.* 2005). What this means is that many bronze objects recovered in recent decades may be in a worse state that those recovered in the 18th and 19th centuries, and illustrates that one needs to be conscious of *when* artefacts were recovered in the assessment of damage.

Finally, Bronze Age metalwork is occasionally recovered from a context not coherent with the expected typo-chronology, even within prehistoric sites (Hingley 2009; Knight 2019b; forthcoming a). Consequently, some objects were rediscovered and reappropriated at different times and might have been reused, altered, or treated differently from how they were originally discovered (cf. Knight *et al.* 2019). For example, a broken Middle Bronze Age palstave was found in the Iron Age Lexden tumulus near Colchester, Essex, and seems to have been adapted with silver adhesions in the Iron Age (Foster 1986, 78–80). Similarly, in his study of Middle Bronze Age Irish rapiers and swords, Bell (2019) identified damage linked to post-recovery manipulation, rehafting and reuse in the 18th and 19th centuries AD, including a Bronze Age blade rehafted with an iron hilt from Shapwick, Somerset. A broken sword from Rodney Stoke, Somerset, had two rivet holes drilled into the surviving blade (Fig. 2.3), though it is unclear whether this is a prehistoric adaptation or occurred more recently. Although infrequent, occurrences such as these highlight the need for fully understanding any damage linked with reappropriation.

Post-recovery processes

Reappropriation events, which may happen at any time, highlight the need to be aware of various post-recovery actions. The most common for discoveries made in the recent past is cleaning the object, which removes the object's patina and can damage the surface of the object and hinder wear analysis. In their study of wear on socketed axeheads, Roberts and Ottaway noted that 'cleaning' of the objects rendered microscopic wear analysis 'impossible' (2003, 123). Some post-recovery acts can be more extreme, such as the rehafting and reuse of Middle Bronze Age blades noted above. An Early Bronze Age flat axehead from Kentisbeare, Devon, was struck with a chisel-like implement by the finder approximately 33 times across both faces, causing dents, notches and material displacement, before it was donated to the museum in Exeter in 1884 (Fig. 2.4; RAMM-F026). Breaks in the patina indicate the damage is modern. This object also highlights the unusual extent to which objects may become deformed following recovery. Other situations include the almost total obliteration of metal artefacts, such as at Lovehayne Farm, Colyton, Devon, where a hoard of metalwork said to include 'over 100' objects was discovered between 1760 and 1768. It was subsequently sold as scrap metal and melted down (Pearce 1983, 438–9, no.217). The range of ways objects may become damaged that is not linked to intentional prehistoric action is remarkable.

Metalwork wear analysis

The most general assessment for identifying destruction is whether the damage could have occurred through use. If the damage is ancient but could not have occurred through assumed utilitarian functionality, it is often considered

Figure 2.3: An incomplete sword from Rodney Stoke, Somerset, with a reshaped end and two holes drilled into the blade (photo: author, courtesy of Wells & Mendip Museum)

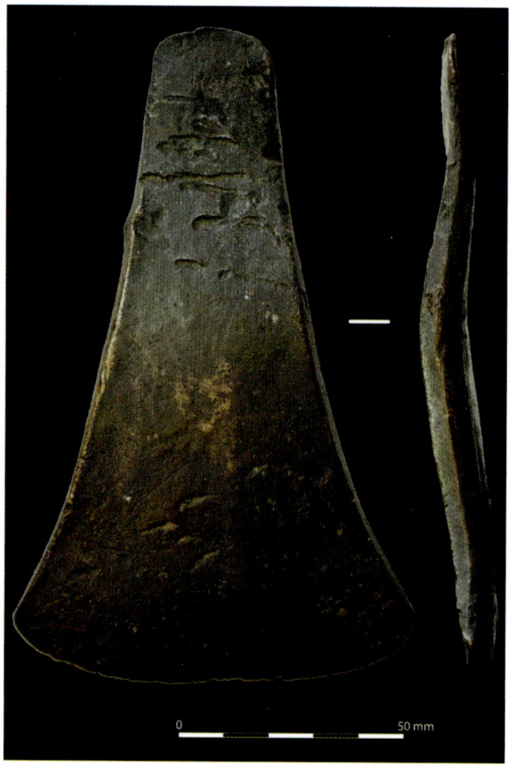

Figure 2.4: Chisel marks and plastic deformation damage caused by a 19th century finder on an Early Bronze Age flat axe from Kentisbeare, Devon (photo: author, courtesy of the Royal Albert Memorial Museum and Art Gallery, Exeter.

intentional (eg, York 2002, 80; Becker 2006, 55–6; Perea 2008; Quilliec 2008, 70–1; Turner 2010a, 60ff.; 2010b; Horn 2011; 2017; Melheim & Horn 2014). However, the rapid increase in metalwork wear analyses in the last two decades, involving both experimentation and microscopic investigations of Bronze Age metal artefacts, offers the opportunity to more accurately assess whether observed damage may be use-related (eg, Soriano Llopis & Gutierrez Sáez 2009; Horn 2013a; 2013b; 2017; Dolfini & Crellin 2016; Horn & von Holstein 2017; Horn & Karck 2019; Hermann *et al.* 2020a, 7–13; Andrews *et al.* 2021).

Damage to objects is frequently assumed to result from material failure following extensive use making it important to consider experimental projects in which bronze implements were used over a long period of time. Unfortunately, few details have been published of bronze implements utilised in such experiments. One example is a reference to a broken bronze axehead used during the construction of the replica Bronze Age Ferriby boat (van de Noort *et al.* 2014, 302–3). This axehead apparently broke during use across the narrowest part, though no further details are given. This axehead was one of 25 tools used during the project from April 2012 to March 2013, including axes, adzes and chisels, all of which suffered varying degrees of use necessitating resharpening and reworking and, in some cases, rehafting (van der Noort *et al.* 2014, 302–3; Hurcombe 2020). All tools were handled by volunteers during the project and used for a variety of purposes; it is possible the single broken axehead may have broken through misuse, or possibly as a result of poor casting. Similarly, in their experiments producing replicas of prehistoric wooden trackways, Coles and Coles (1986, 110–1) noted damage to bronze blades and wooden hafts through improper use.

One innovative study, led by Miriam Andrews, has attempted to study how extended use may affect an object conducted controlled mechanical experiments involving replica cutting edges of palstaves rigged on a drop tower (Andrews *et al.* 2021). Replica edges of different compositions were variably worked post-casting and then repeatedly dropped and struck against an oak block in a series of impact tests, some up to 3000 times. Differential wear was produced, which aligned with differences in metallurgy and microstructure, as well as casting flaws. As-cast cutting edges were prone to fail more quickly, such as deformation of the edge, and those with a higher tin content became more brittle and were prone to fracturing (Andrews *et al.* 2021, 13–4). Although this test focused on cutting edges only, tests such as these provide some clues as to the resilience of bronze objects through use over long periods of time and highlight the potential for similar mechanical studies involving whole objects to simulate extended use.

Damage can and does occur through shorter periods of use, however. During manufacture of a wooden shield as part of the *Bronze Age Combat* project, a bronze chisel snapped across the blade and the butt of a flat axehead became flattened and the body bent under hammering (Marion Uckelmann pers. comm.); again, such damage may result from misuse or poor casting. A rapier, used in repeated strikes in the Bronze Age Combat project, eventually bent and cracked at the edge when struck against a wooden shield, rendering the object unusable (Hermann *et al.* 2020a, 56). Rachel Faulkner-Jones' (2016) experiments involved striking a replica Middle Bronze Age dirk against synthetic skeletal material: this caused the tip to bend and the repercussive force chipped the wooden hilt and broke the metal rivet hole. Broken rivet holes on dirks, daggers and rapiers are frequently encountered in the archaeological record; these experiments all contribute to how we can understand and interpret prehistoric damage.

Notching

Much wear analysis has investigated edge damage on metal artefacts, including swords, axeheads, spearheads, halberds, knives and daggers (Molloy 2006; 2007; 2011; Gutiérrez Sáez & Martín Lerma 2015; Horn & von Holstein 2017; Gentile & van Gijn 2019; Hermann *et al.* 2020a; 2020b). A common form of damage – 'notching' – warrants specific focus for its destructive potential, particularly in relation to swords and spearheads. Notching refers to plastic deformation of an edge when the damage is deeper than it is wide and occurs when a blade edge is struck against another blade edge (eg, sword on sword) (Bridgford 2000; Gentile & van Gijn 2019, 136; Hermann *et al.* 2020b). This can occur in two main forms on weapon edges: v-shaped or u-shaped,[1] depending on the nature of the strike (O'Flaherty *et al.* 2011; Gentile & van Gijn 2019; Hermann *et al.* 2020a).

Extreme notching may render metal artefacts unusable, either through regular occurrence along the blade edge creating a serrated effect, deep marks in the edge weakening the blade (referred to as 'hacking' by Bridgford 2000), or on a blade face, which would weaken the blade on a transverse plane (Mörtz 2010). One may thus avoid edge-on-edge sword-fighting in a genuine combat scenario to reduce the risk of damaging the blade (Harding 2007, 111–2; Molloy 2017, 288). Following this rationale, repeated edge-notching of any form could reflect intent to damage the blade; it is, however, more likely that edge-notching either reflects the inadequacy of the sword-wielder incurring accidental damage, or implies that prehistoric fighters were willing to incur some edge damage as part of the fighting style (Hermann *et al.* 2020a, 119–20; 2020b, 1066–7).

Horn (2013a) noted notching as a destructive feature on weapons (halberds, swords and spearheads); similarly unusual notching around the hilt on a sword from Werkhoven, the Netherlands, was taken as potentially deliberate (Fontijn *et al.* 2012, 207). Although notching on the blade edge through use is different from more regular notching or notching in unlikely locations on the object, the term is still used generically for this type of damage; therefore, caution must be taken in how it has been used in the past and how it is applied here. Bridgford (1997, 106–7), for instance, presented notching on swords as indicating use, but also highlighted that her tabularised results hid a few swords that were deliberately 'hacked'. The point at which notching might be considered intentional was not discussed by Bridgford, though O'Flaherty *et al.* (2011) suggested that the shape of a notch may relate to whether an object was static or yielding when struck and this in turn may indicate deliberate 'hacking' of a blade held in place versus a blade swung in combat. Subsequent actualistic experiments have found that both u-shaped and v-shaped notches may be produced through combat engagements (Gentile & van Gijn 2019; Hermann *et al.* 2020b). In attempting to determine intentional from unintentional notching, we can begin to suggest pertinent parameters, including the depth, position and distribution of notches (Knight 2021; see below).

Other use-related damage

Other use-related damage that may be construed as intentional includes the blunting or flattening of edges and tips and bending, both of which are frequently noted on artefacts (eg, Horn 2015; Molloy 2018; Horn & Karck 2019). Blunting of blade edges and tips of spearheads and swords may occur through use, as indicated through combat experiments (Anderson 2011, 604; Hermann *et al.* 2020a; 2020b), though it has been highlighted as a possible destructive feature as well, designed to remove the functionality of the object (Hermann *et al.* 2020a, 93). Similarly, bent sword blades resulting from experimental combat scenarios are increasingly noted, including striking an animal carcass (Anderson 2012, 89), parrying blows from opponents (Gentile & van Gijn 2019; Hermann *et al.* 2020a, 28–9; 2020b, 1058–9, 1068–70), and striking a shield rim (Hermann *et al.* 2020a, 56); it becomes clear that the plastic nature of bronze can result in deformation of objects through use. In my own experiments, *mis*-using replica swords in ways that might simulate accidental damage, such as deflecting blows with the flat of the sword blade, or striking the flat of the sword against the edge of a shield, likewise produced distinctive bending damage (Knight 2019a, 258–9; Fig. 2.5). These experiments suggest that when observed on prehistoric artefacts, such damage must be more carefully considered. This is especially true as bent swords may be repaired by bending back into shape (Knight 2019a, 259), though this will structurally weaken the metal and can alter the subsequent performance of the object (Molloy 2011, 75; 2018, 295; Hermann *et al.* 2020a, 29).

Repairs

Repaired damage on metal implements is occasionally noted but rarely synthesised; moreover, a skilled repair may almost completely conceal any pre-existing damage. However, a study of copper-alloy spearheads, swords, knives and daggers from northern Germany utilising high-powered microscopy indicates that signs of repair may be relatively common (Horn & Karck 2019; see also Horn 2017; Molloy 2018). Notably, simple repairs, such as damage to sword edges, were not always conducted before deposition (Kristiansen 1999; 2002), and occasionally, used objects have suffered additional deliberate damage (Mörtz 2010, 156). This provides insights into the non-functional purpose of deposition and the decisions made by those utilising metal objects. Results from metalwork wear analysis are an essential tool for analysing deliberate damage.

Experimental destruction

In stark contrast to the numerous experiments exploring the use of metal objects, of which I have presented only a small glimpse, to my knowledge there are only four documented experiments that explore the effects of intentionally damaging replica Bronze Age objects and two of these lie in unpublished theses. These offer crucial insights into the process of destruction that have implications for studying the archaeological record.

During his wear analysis of Scottish Early Bronze Age axeheads, Shaun Moyler (2007) identified several examples that had been broken in half to which he assigned the category 'deliberate breakage'; Moyler attempted to break one of his replica flat axeheads to investigate this practice (*ibid.*, 134–9). The replica axehead was clamped vertically between two stones and the projecting butt was struck repeatedly with a stone hammer; when this failed, a modern steel hammer was employed, which also failed to break the axehead cleanly. Hammer marks were visible on the replica, as well as transverse bending and some fracturing, though the clean fragmentation seen on the prehistoric examples was not reproduced, leading Moyler to suggest that no deliberate breakage had occurred on the axeheads he studied. This conclusion is, however, problematic as Moyler did not explore the effect of heating the axehead before striking it. Moreover, the replica was produced using modern techniques to improve the overall performance of the axehead during use (*ibid.*, 50–4), which was the desired outcome of this project. However, the broken prehistoric examples all possessed 'casting flaws, such as cracks, hollows and air bubbles' (*ibid.*, 147); these inherent prehistoric flaws would have affected an object's predisposition to breakage, and Moyler (*ibid.*, 140) even suggests that those axeheads with obvious flaws might have been chosen for destruction. Despite these limitations, this experiment emphasises the tensile strength of bronze as a material.

Another destruction experiment was conducted by Claudio Giardino and Georges

Verly (2013) who tested whether the 'reverse quenching' of a sword following annealing would improve its malleability to transversely bend into a 'U-shape'. The quenched sword (S1) was bent over the conical section of a steel anvil to approximately 90 degrees before breaking at the bending point. The unquenched sword (S2) was bent manually over the metallurgist's thigh in short stages to distribute the pressure more evenly; this enabled the sword to bend to a u-shape without fracturing. Giardino and Verly were able to build upon their technique for achieving the desired outcome and suggested that the bending of a sword required at least some specialist knowledge of the composition and capabilities of the material (*ibid.*).

Thirdly, John Hardman (2016) investigated the temperatures required to break tin-bronzes to determine differences in deformation patterns. He hypothesised that these differences might then be utilised to determine at what temperature archaeological bronzes were fragmented. Hardman's experiments involved heating bars of 12% tin-bronze to different temperatures and striking them with a steel hammer and anvil to bend and break them (*ibid.*, 13ff.). The extent of transverse bending was measured and the correlation between increasing temperature and reducing angle of deformation was found to be statistically significant. Through his experiments and subsequent comparison with two Late Bronze Age hoards from Wales, Hardman suggested various temperature ranges at which different bronzes were broken. His experiments demonstrate a clear correlation between the increase in temperature and the reduction in tensile strength of bronze, demonstrating that associated damage (such as bending) might indicate the mode of breakage (Hardman 2016).

Figure 2.5: A replica sword bent in two directions after parrying a blow from another sword.

These three experiments represented the starting points for my own series of experiments, investigating the skill and process involved in damaging Late Bronze Age objects (Knight 2017; 2019a), which will be summarised here. Drawing on case studies from south-west Britain, replica socketed axeheads, swords and spearheads were produced by Neil Burridge, an experienced bronzecaster (Figs 2.6–2.8; Table 2.3). Consultation with metalworkers and exploratory experiments indicated that heating the bronze artefacts until they were red-hot, *c.* 500–600°C, would be optimum for achieving the most effective fragmentation. At these temperatures the copper alloys became brittle and fragmenting swords, spearheads and axeheads could be achieved with relative ease.

A bronze hammer and chisel were used to fracture a heated sword into 12 fragments, leaving chisel marks on some fragments; crucially, no associated marks could be observed on the fragments where the chisel broke straight through the sword blade (Fig. 2.9; Knight 2019a, 260). Similarly, heating and

Figure 2.6: Two replica Ewart Park swords produced for experiments

striking one of the spearheads (3.1) and two axeheads (1.3 and 1.6) with a bronze hammer was enough to break the objects, leaving limited associated marks (Knight 2017; 2019a). Spearhead 3.1 broke into three pieces and Axeheads 1.3 and 1.6 fractured into multiple small fragments, leaving the cutting-edge fragment as the largest surviving fragment with a slightly crushed socket aperture (Figs 2.10–2.11). Initial exploratory experiments with metalworkers found that the important part of this process was striking the heated objects with a blunt tool, rather than the material of the tool having an impact. Stone, antler, bone and wooden hammers all achieved effective fragmentation (Knight 2019a, 254).

By comparison, leaving the objects unheated prior to fragmentation was much less effective. In all cases, many more strikes were needed, causing extensive deformation of the surface and profile of the objects. An unheated sword (2.3) bent repeatedly under strikes until fragmentation was eventually achieved (Figs 2.12–2.13). Similarly, it was possible to bend and crush a replica spearhead before breaking (Fig. 2.14; Knight 2019a). In one experiment involving Axehead 1.5 blows with a stone hammer failed to produce any significant damage, such as crushing or fragmentation, whilst in another experiment blows with a bronze hammer caused some crushing of the socket of Axehead 1.8, as well as minor cracking and extensive surface deformation (Fig. 2.15). However, in this latter experiment it took 105 blows to achieve crushing and no fragmentation, compared to three hammer blows to fragment a heated socketed axe (Table 2.3; Knight 2017, 207ff.).

Figure 2.7: One of the replica barbed spearheads produced for the destruction experiments

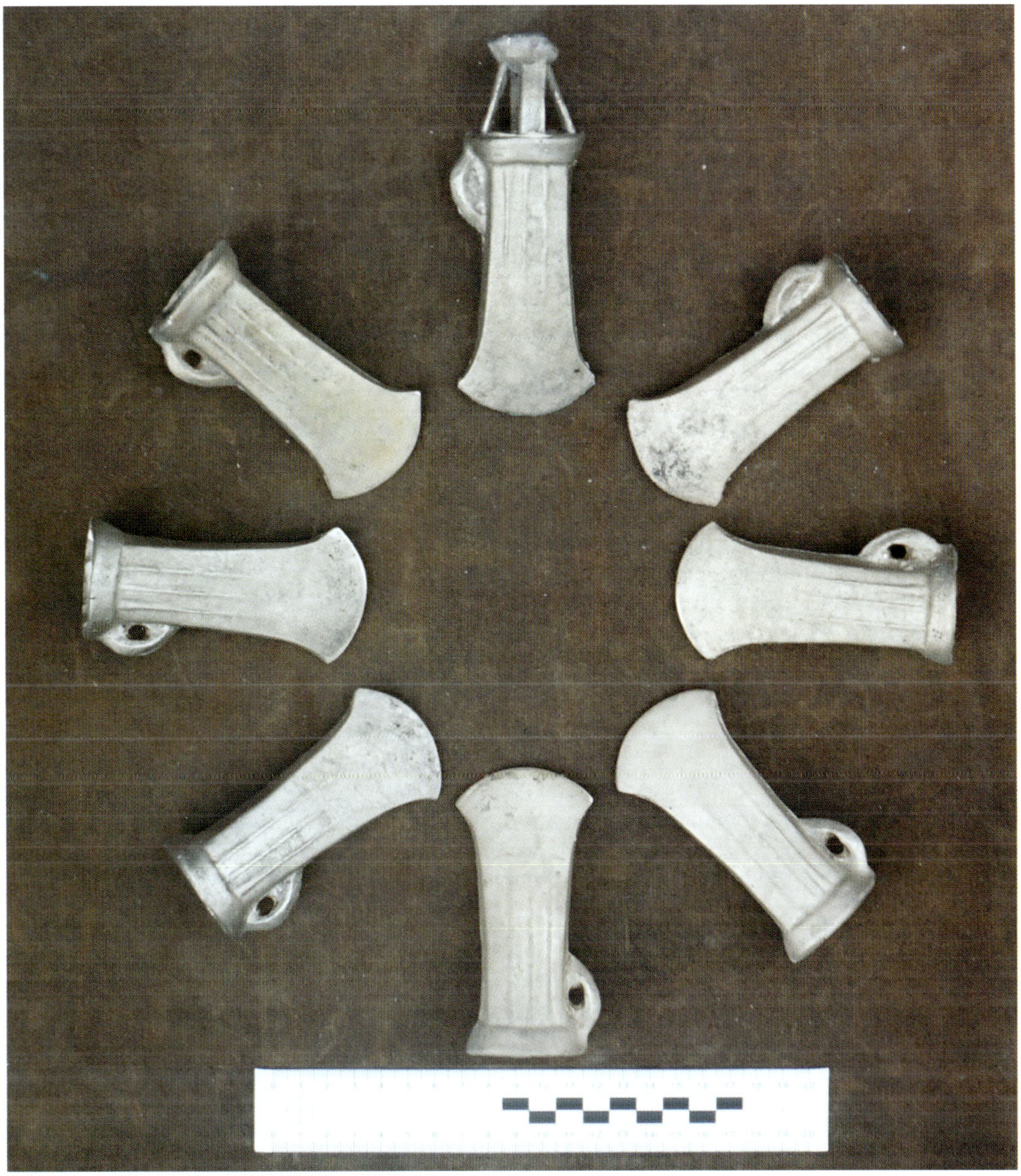

Figure 2.8: Eight replica socketed axeheads produced for the experiments of which four were subjected to destruction

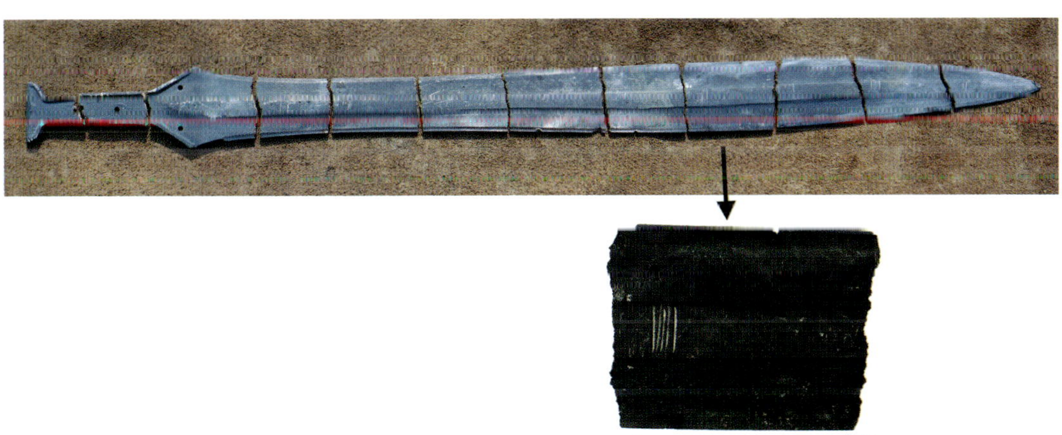

Figure 2.9: Sword 2.2 after destruction experiment. Chisel marks were visible on some pieces (inset image)

Figure 2.10: Spearhead 3.1 after destruction experiment

Additionally, Neil Burridge offered an unworked, mis-cast replica sword to explore how easily it might be bent without the use of tools. It was possible to bend this sword over my thigh into a u-shape, demonstrating the plasticity and tensile strength of tin-bronze in its unworked form (Fig. 2.16; Knight 2019a, 260).

Initial conclusions indicated that whilst damaging and fragmenting objects could have been a relatively unskilled activity, it did require knowledge of how the material will behave as well as the ability to construct a suitable fire, and the possession of adequate tools (Knight 2017; 2019a). The replicas that were heated and broken provided the closest parallels with archaeological examples (Knight 2017, 218–22; 2019a, 264–5). Moreover, discussions with metalworkers indicated they could control the desired fragmentation and predict how the bronze might behave in advance of striking it. This ability to anticipate how a material will behave ahead of manipulating it is characteristic of skilled metalworkers (Kuijpers 2018). Therefore, although metalworking knowledge may not have been essential, it would clearly have been advantageous, and it seems likely that metalworkers were part of the process of deliberately damaging objects in the Bronze Age.

This series of experiments provides the beginnings of a reference collection for assessing archaeological damage in relation to that produced through experimentation, an important step forward in accurately identifying deliberate damage.

Categorising damage: Destruction Indicators and a Damage Ranking System

The complexities of identifying damage mean a clear approach to organising and interpreting damage is required. Past attempts to categorising intentional damage have done so through assessments of object completeness and condition (eg, Bridgford 2000; York 2002; Tarbay 2017) or analysis of patterns of fragmentation in groups of metalwork (Čivilytė 2009, 47–66; Rezi 2011). One of the first and most thorough approaches was presented by Stuart Needham in his analysis of the Late Bronze Age assemblage from Petters Sports Field, Surrey (Needham 1990b). Needham utilised a coded system to classify different features of the metalwork and succinctly present information about each individual object. This incorporated the completeness, use, condition, metallurgical flaws, and non-edge damage, allowing one to cross-reference the treatment of different objects.

However, these approaches do not specifically address what constitutes deliberate damage and a general methodology applicable to all metal objects has never been developed. How does one tell when a bent sword was *deliberately* bent? How can we tell if a fragmented axehead is the result of accident or intent? Having the ability to answer such questions and recognise intentionality allows us insights into the history of an object, its treatment in prehistory, and by extension its role and relationship with an individual or community.

In seeking to address such questions, I have categorised damage observed on Bronze Age copper-alloy objects under eight key 'Destruction Indicators' (Table 2.4), which will be used here to manage evidence of damage across the Bronze Age metalwork of south-west Britain. The Destruction Indicators (DIs) encompass a range of damage most observed on bronze objects (see below for a discussion of gold objects) that may be interpreted as the intentional destruction of an artefact. Previously, I have listed seven (Knight 2021), but here I add an eighth category: 'Stabbed/penetrated', as it is occasionally observed on objects such as shields. An inherent and important first step is the determination that the damage being categorised is indeed ancient, following some of the considerations outlined above; only then can an assessment of the nature of the damage be undertaken. Although they vary depending on object form, DIs can

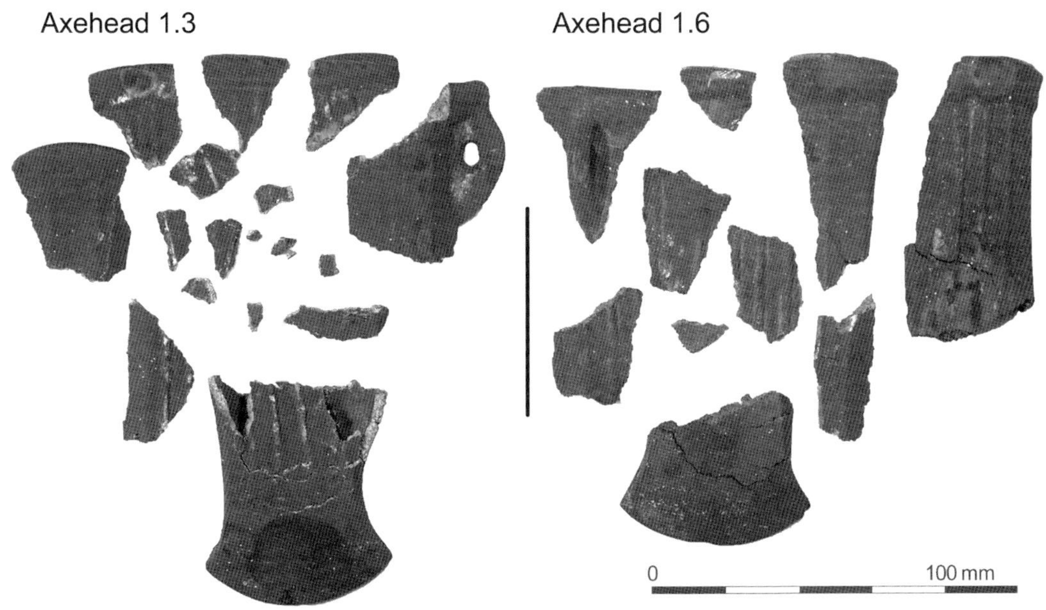

Figure 2.11: Axeheads 1.3 and 1.6 after destruction experiment

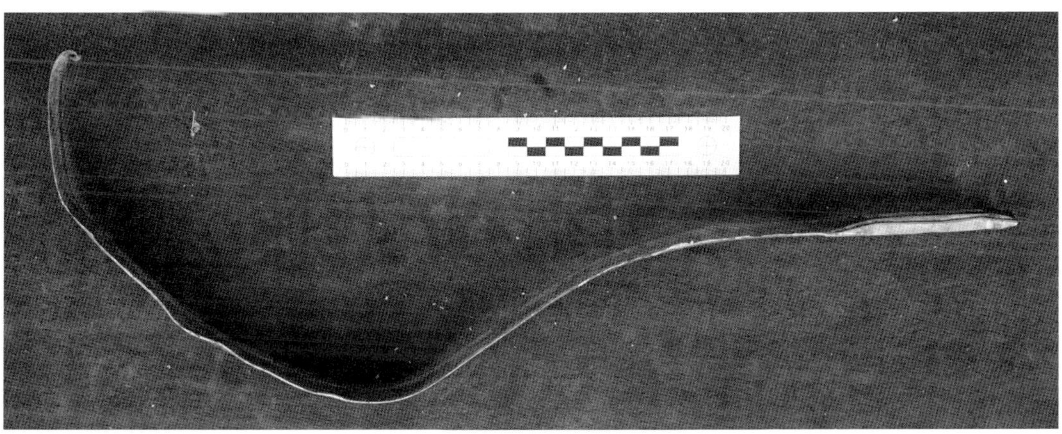

Figure 2.12: Side profile of Sword 2.3 bent during destruction experiment

Figure 2.13: Sword 2.3 after destruction experiment

be assessed according to qualifying criteria, drawing on a background of wear analysis, experimental data, patterns of damage from previous studies, contextual analysis and material science (Knight 2021). Table 2.5 outlines how the Destruction Indicators relate to different copper-alloy object types and indicates where considerations are required.

Assessing whether the bend of a sword is intentional, for instance, should consider the context from which it was recovered and the likelihood of damage post-deposition, as well as its compositional properties, the thickness of the blade, and the position and angle of the bend when possible (Knight 2021, 50–3). Combat experiments have indicated that bronze swords might bend or bow up to *c.* 20 degrees through use (Fig. 2.5; Gentile & van Gijn 2019; Knight 2019a, 258; Hermann *et al.* 2020b), suggesting the extent of use-related bending is unlikely to be particularly extreme, that is, a sword will probably not bend to a right angle through use. A parameter of 30 degrees was proposed as a qualifier for when bent

Figure 2.14: Spearhead 3.3 after destruction experiment

swords might be more confidently considered intentional (Knight 2021, 52). Comparison with the archaeological record assists with this assessment. Hermann *et al.* (2020b, figs 17 and 18) compare a replica sword displaying a bend up to 10 degrees from straight with an almost identical bend on an archaeological example. Moreover, the complete but bent Bronze Age swords from south-west Britain only display up to 15 degrees of deformation. Therefore, it follows that these swords probably bent through use-related activity. However, swords bent to a greater extent are more likely to be the result of intent. As bending associated with use in combat experiments has only been infrequently documented, the parameter of 30 degrees allows for more extreme bending through use not yet recorded. This does not mean that swords bent to less than this might not also be considered intentional, but additional damage or indicators, such as tool marks, breakage or burning, are required to make a confident assessment. Moreover, the parameter is liable to adjustment as more data are recorded. By contrast, slighter objects and objects with a range of potential functions, such as awls, razors and knives, require more careful consideration as they may become bent and damaged through use under exerted pressure, and as they are thinner may be more easily bent accidentally. Furthermore, these are objects for which there has been far fewer experiments exploring use and damage (though see Gutiérrez Sáez & Soriano Llopis 2008; Soriano Llopis & Gutiérrez Sáez 2009; Gutiérrez Sáez & Martín Lerma 2015), making it difficult to conclusively distinguish deliberate from use-related damage unless it is particularly extreme.

These examples outline the principles behind applying all of the DIs. They are not suggested to be absolute parameters, but rather offer a measured approach to assessing damage, subject to change as more factors are understood. Some indicators, such as crushing or folding, can usually be confidently assessed as deliberate, whereas others, such as bending or notching, have the potential to be use-related and require greater consideration, especially where further research is required. Assessment of the damage must be approached in the most comprehensive way to enable the most accurate interpretation. In simplifying this further, and to account for this variability, these

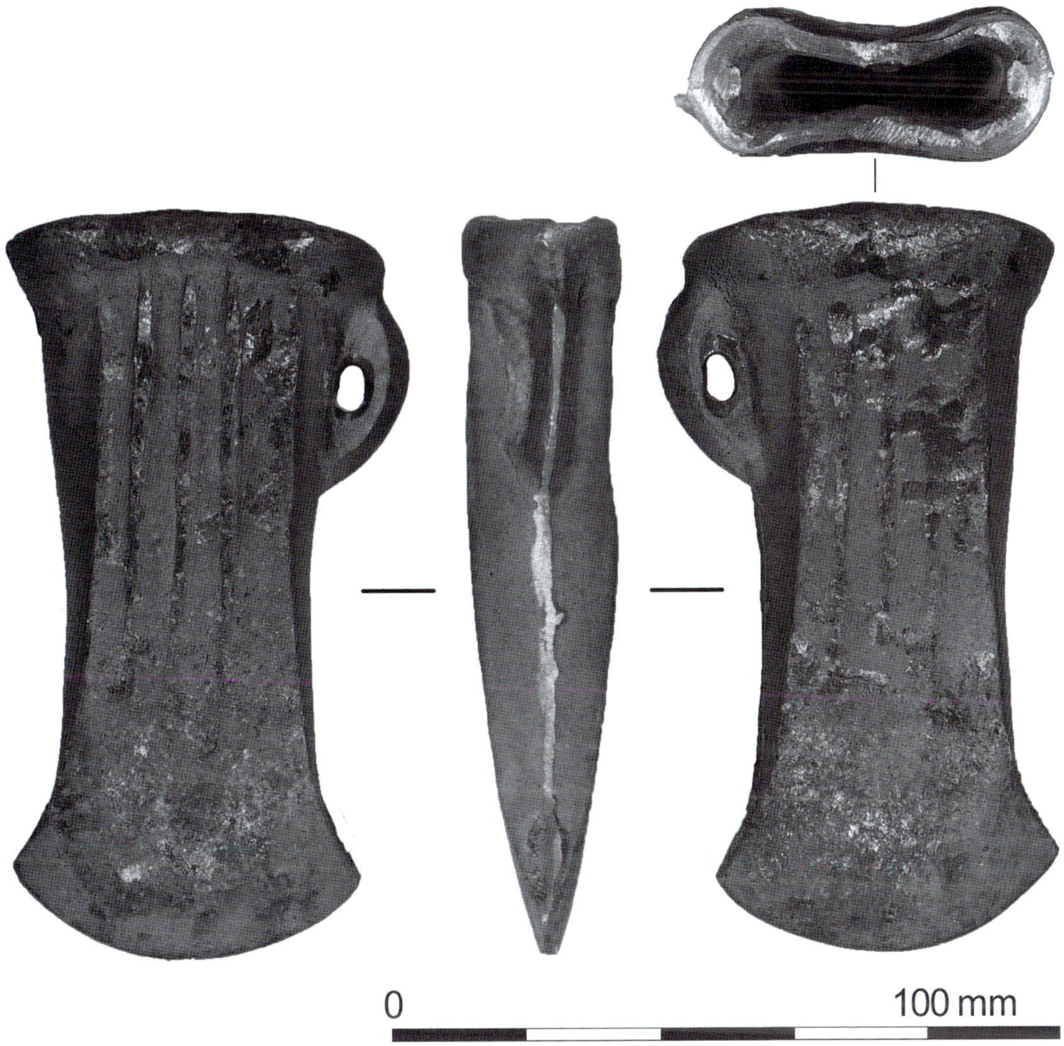

Figure 2.15: Axehead 1.8 after 105 blows with a bronze hammer

Destruction Indicators may be set within a simple six-coded index: the Damage Ranking System (DRS) (Table 2.6; Knight 2021).

The DRS assesses damage on a scale of likelihood. Some damage is object-specific, though the criteria have been presented as a set of considerations applicable to most Bronze Age metalwork (Table 2.7). The DRS is designed to rank individual damage, not an overall object. This is because many objects display multiple forms of unassociated damage and thus an object may be attributed multiple rankings. This in turn enhances how we might construct and understand the biography of an object or the role of certain objects in a broader sphere (Knight 2021).

Damage on gold objects

In this chapter, gold objects have so far received limited attention, though represent an important part of the Bronze Age metalwork repertoire. As a material, gold is softer and more plastic than copper alloys. Many gold objects, particularly the earliest objects, were produced from gold sheet making them thinner and more fragile than bronze objects; these gold artefacts were thus more prone to accidental deformation and breakage and require a more cautious approach when assessing Destruction Indicators. Additionally, because gold does not corrode, determining ancient from modern damage cannot rely on differences in surface condition. Understanding the circumstances of deposition and the associated context, as well as the history of an object, is therefore vital for accurately interpreting the age and nature of the damage. The key Destruction Indicators for gold objects are: *plastic deformation* (divided

Table 2.3: A summary of the replicas produced and the results of the destruction experiments (results from Knight 2017; 2019a)

ID	*Object*	*Composition* Cu	Sn	Pb	*Post-casting processes*	*Heated?*	*Tools used*	*Damage*	*Associated marks?*	*Notes*
1.3	Socketed axehead	84%	15%	1%	Unquenched Casting jets/flash removed Edge left unworked	Y >600°C	Bronze hammer	Broke into 16 frags	Plastic deformation around cutting edge	Initially heated and struck *c.* 490°C but this was ineffective
1.5	Socketed axehead	90%	8%	2%		N	Granite hammer stone	Slight plastic deformation; some crushing to body	Surface deformation	
1.6	Socketed axehead	90%	8%	2%		Y >600°C	Bronze hammer	Broke into 9 frags	Plastic deformation around cutting edge	As Axehead 1.3
1.8	Socketed axehead	88%	8%	4%		N	Bronze hammer	Crushed socket	Surface deformation; cracking	Required 105 blows
2.2	Sword	90%	9%	1%	Unquenched Casting jet removed Edge ground, cold-hammered & sharpened Ash hilt riveted on	Y 575°C	Bronze hammer & chisel	Broke into 12 frags	Some chisel marks on frags	
2.3	Sword	90%	8%	2%	Unquenched Casting jet removed Left as cast	N	Bronze hammer	Bending; broke into 7 frags	Bending; surface damage	Required bending back and forth prior to breakage
–	Sword	88%	12%	-	As cast; mis-cast	N	n/a	Bent into u-shape	None	Manually bent over thigh
3.1	Barbed spearhead	88%	10%	2%	Unquenched Casting jet removed Clay core inserted 2 m ash shaft inserted & riveted	Y *c.* 500°C	Bronze hammer	Broke into 3 frags	None	
3.2	Barbed spearhead	88%	10%	2%	Unquenched Casting jet removed Core removed	N	Bronze hammer & chisel	Crushed; plastic deformation; fragmentation	Hammer marks; cracking	Chisel proved ineffective so changed to hammering only during experiment

Destruction Indicator	*Description*
Bending/folding	Plastic deformation from the expected trajectory of an object Transverse and longitudinal bending possible
Twisting/torsion	Lateral plastic deformation along the longitudinal axis
Crushing	Compression of an object removing its functionality
Notching	Plastic deformation of an edge or surface resulting in an indentation
Breakage	Separation of two or more pieces of an object
Burning	Exposure of an object to high temperatures causing damage to the surface and/or microstructure
Plugged sockets	Filling or blocking of a socket with objects other than hafting material
Stabbed/penetrated	Perforated with another object

Table 2.4: Destruction Indicators observed on copper-alloy objects (adapted from Knight 2021)

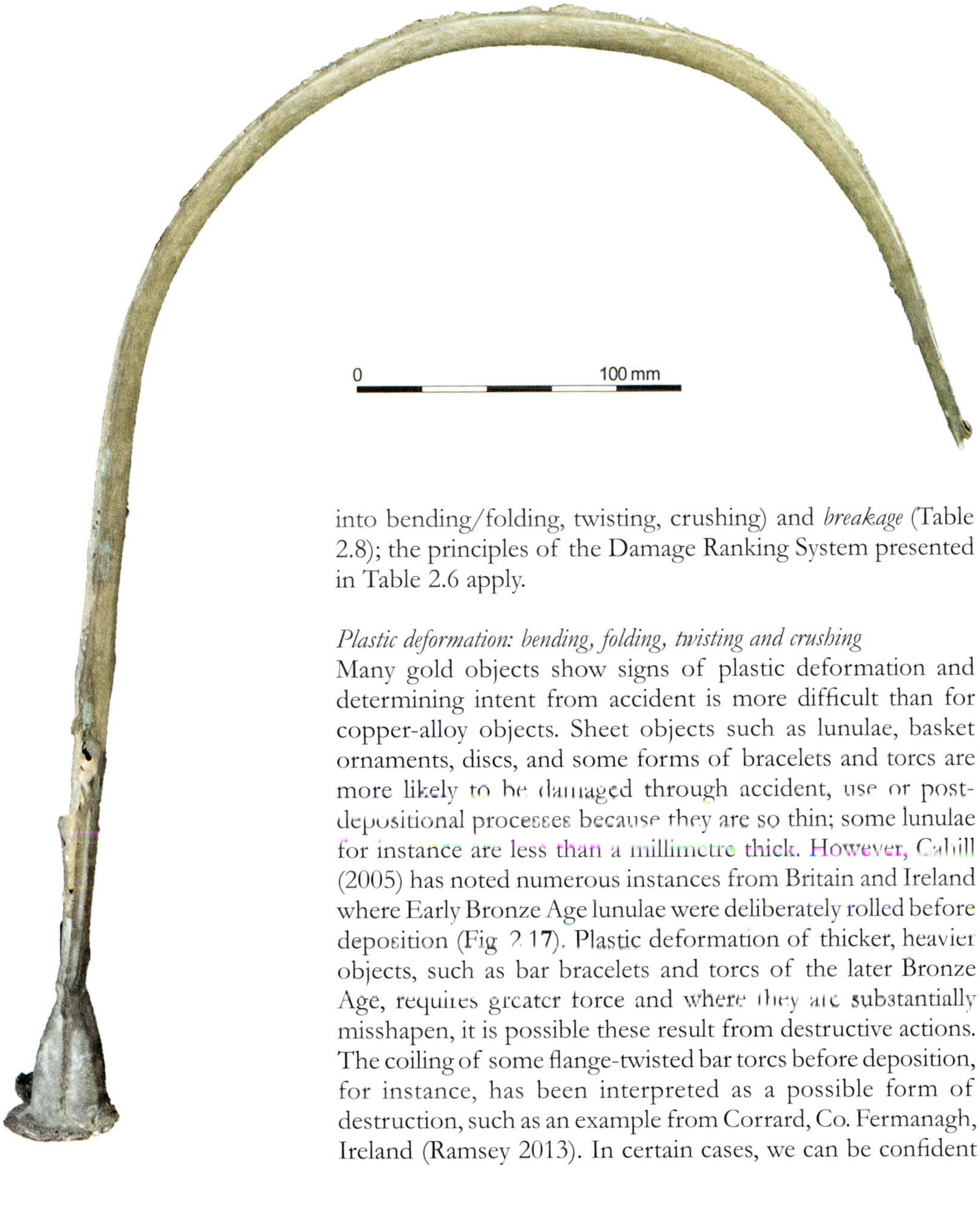

Figure 2.16: An as-cast replica sword bent into a U-shape

into bending/folding, twisting, crushing) and *breakage* (Table 2.8); the principles of the Damage Ranking System presented in Table 2.6 apply.

Plastic deformation: bending, folding, twisting and crushing

Many gold objects show signs of plastic deformation and determining intent from accident is more difficult than for copper-alloy objects. Sheet objects such as lunulae, basket ornaments, discs, and some forms of bracelets and torcs are more likely to be damaged through accident, use or post-depositional processes because they are so thin; some lunulae for instance are less than a millimetre thick. However, Cahill (2005) has noted numerous instances from Britain and Ireland where Early Bronze Age lunulae were deliberately rolled before deposition (Fig 2.17). Plastic deformation of thicker, heavier objects, such as bar bracelets and torcs of the later Bronze Age, requires greater force and where they are substantially misshapen, it is possible these result from destructive actions. The coiling of some flange-twisted bar torcs before deposition, for instance, has been interpreted as a possible form of destruction, such as an example from Corrard, Co. Fermanagh, Ireland (Ramsey 2013). In certain cases, we can be confident

Object(s)	*Destruction Indicators*										
	Transverse bending	*Longitudinal bending*	*Folding*	*Breakage*	*Individual fragments*	*Crushing*	*Twisting*	*Burning*	*Notching*	*Plugged sockets*	*Stabbed*
Swords, rapiers, dirks, daggers and halberds	Y (30°)	Y	Y	P	P Y*	–	Y (45°)	ad	P	–	–
Knives	P (45°)	Y	Y	P	P Y*	–	Y (45°)	ad	P	–	–
Tanged spearheads	Y (45°)	Y	Y	P	P Y*	–	Y (45°)	ad	P	–	–
Socketed spearheads	Y (30°) (tip 45°; nd)	Y	Y	P	P Y*	Y	Y	ad	P	Y	Y
Flat and flanged axeheads	Y	Y	Y	P	P Y*	–	Y	ad	P	–	–
Palstaves	Y	Y	Y	P	P Y*	–	Y	ad	P	–	–
Socketed axeheads	Y	Y	Y	P	P Y*	Y	Y	ad	P	Y	Y
Chisels and gouges	Y	Y	Y	P	P Y*	Y	Y	ad	P	Y	–
Copper-alloy ornaments	P	P	Y	P	P Y*	Y	P	ad	P	–	Y
Miscellaneous copper-alloy objects (eg, awls, razors, saws, sickles, tweezers)	P	P	Y	P	P Y*	–	Y	ad	P	–	–
Copper-alloy sheet objects (eg, shields, decorative plaques)	Y	P	Y	P	P	Y	P	ad	P	–	P

Key: Y = Indicator of deliberate damage; Y* = Refers specifically to fragments that are mid-sections of objects; N = Not an indicator of deliberate damage;
P = possible indicator - determined by a set of factors and/or other destruction indicators;
nd = no additional damage; ad = additional damage or contextual information necessary to determine intent. Some indicators are qualified by statements in brackets

Table 2.5: A summary of Destruction Indicators and criteria for identifying intentional damage

in determining deliberate damage, for example with folded and crushed ornaments.

Breakage

The varied ways that metal objects may break often makes it difficult to interpret what is or is not deliberate. Like copper-alloy objects, one must consider a range of factors for incomplete gold objects, including manufacturing and casting flaws, associated marks (eg, tool marks), patterns of damage, and whether the artefact represents an individual fragment or a multi-piece break (cf. Knight 2021, 54–8). Gold often preserves tool marks, though one needs to be careful to distinguish between hammer marks for working the gold and those intended to cause material failure. Cut or chisel marks near breakage points are clearer indicators (Fig. 2.18); Perea (2008), for instance, notes that the 28 bracelets in the Villena hoard, Portugal, were cut through by a careful process of abrasion.

This also illustrates the importance of recognising patterns of damage. For copper-alloy objects I linked similar patterns of breakage either to points of weakness, or to places repeatedly chosen for intentional breakage (Knight 2021, 55–6). Some areas of gold objects are liable to break under stress, such as the hooked terminals of some torcs or the apex of a penannular bracelet as it is repeatedly opened and closed; alternatively, patterns of breakage not linked to points of weakness is better interpreted as the result of deliberate action. As noted at the start of this chapter, and illustrated by the Villena hoard, this is easier to recognise in a closed group of objects where multiple objects have been treated similarly, but harder to interpret with a single find. However, similar breakage patterns

Presence of damage	Damage Ranking	Description	Criteria
Definitely present	0	Not deliberate	Evidence of corrosion and post-depositional processes or casting flaws that would have caused damage
	1	Probably not deliberate	Damage combined with wear analysis or consistent with unintentional damage
	2	Probably deliberate	No associated marks but consistent with damage one would expect from intentional practices informed by experiments
	3	Definitely deliberate	Damage that could only have been inflicted intentionally, typically with associated marks
Present or presence uncertain	Uncertain	Uncertain	Objects displaying several features that cannot be conclusively determined
Definitely not present	n/a	Not applicable	Complete, undamaged objects

Table 2.6: A summary of the Damage Ranking System and key simplified criteria for Bronze Age metalwork

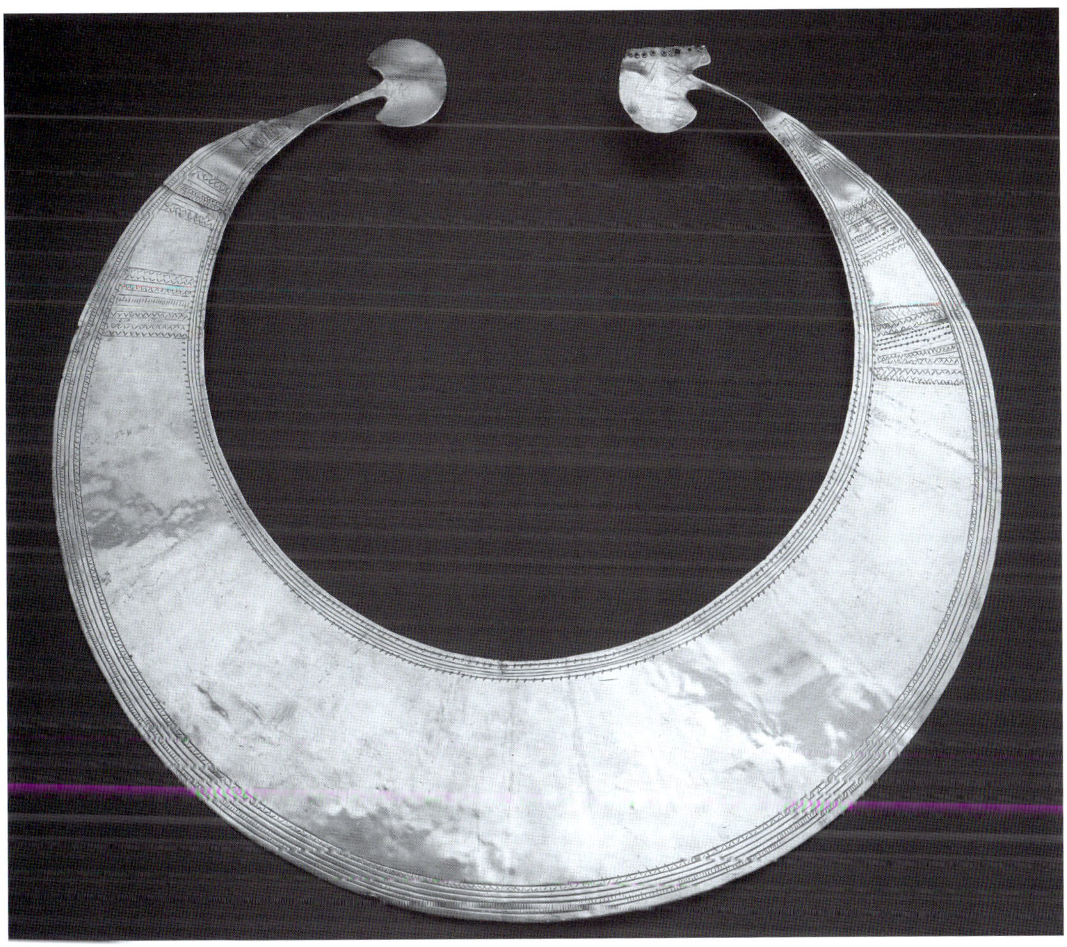

Figure 2.17: The gold lunula from Auchentaggart, Dumfries and Galloway, was discovered rolled up © National Museums Scotland

of fragments of British and Irish Late Bronze Age bar bracelets, both as single finds and in hoards, some with associated cut marks, strengthens the idea that when encountered, this damage should be considered intentional (Gwilt *et al.* 2005, 45–52). Moreover, there is evidence that these fragments may, in some cases, conform to a weight system (Gwilt *et al.*

Table 2.7: Summary of criteria and considerations for applying the Destruction Indicators and Damage Ranking System to copper-alloy objects (adapted from Knight 2021, table 3)

Damage Ranking	*Destruction Indicator(s)*	*Criteria/considerations*	*Object type(s)*
0 Definitely not deliberate	All	Post-depositional/post-recovery processes causing damage (eg, corrosion, ploughing, dredging, cleaning), informed by knowledge of the context/post-recovery history	All
1 Probably not deliberate	Bending	Associated with other use-wear eg, striations, scratches, notches, etc Objects thinner than 7.5 mm suffering bowing	All
		Up to 30° with no associated marks or breakage	Thin-bladed implements, spearheads
		Present on tools put under pressure causing material stress	eg, awls, chisels, gouges, pins, possibly knives
	Twisting	Up to 45° with no associated damage	All
	Notching	Supported by research indicating use eg, use experiments or metalwork wear analysis Irregular edge damage Various depths (<7 mm) and/or single notches	All
	Breakage	Patterns of breakage linked to use or structural weakness (eg, side-loops, blade tips, rivet holes) Casting flaws & evidence of manufacture flaws	All
	Stabbed/ penetrated	Infrequent & present on objects that may incur such damage through use	Shields
2 Probably deliberate	Bending	Up to 30° with associated damage marks	All
	Twisting	Up to 45° with associated damage	Thin-bladed implements, tanged spearheads
	Notching	Deep notches (>7 mm) Regular, repeated notching creating a serrated effect Notches in unusual positions eg, hilts or hafting plates	All
	Breakage	Straight, sharp breaks with no associated plastic deformation Associated transverse bending <45° Patterns of breakage unlikely to be linked to use or structural weakness (eg, bracelet terminals, socketed axehead cutting edges) Fragments & pieces associated with deliberately damaged material eg, frags in a plugged socket Multiple broken pieces of different objects conforming to a similar size &/or weight within single accumulation Associated marks possibly related to breakage but not obviously linked eg, hammer or chisel marks elsewhere on the object	All
3 Definitely deliberate	Bending	Transverse bending >30° Objects thicker than 7.5 mm	All
	Folding		All
	Crushing	Often with associated damage eg, tool marks, cracking, breakage	Socketed objects
	Twisting	Present	Socketed spear-heads, all axe-heads, various tools (eg, chisels)
		Over 45°	Thin-bladed implements, tanged spearheads

Damage Ranking	*Destruction Indicator(s)*	*Criteria/considerations*	*Object type(s)*
3 Definitely deliberate	Breakage	Associated plastic deformation &/or bending >30° Associated tool marks closely related to break eg, tool marks around a fracture Multi-piece breaks (3+ pieces) except where post-depositional processes can be identified Mid-section frag. indicating an object was once in 3+ pieces	All
	Burning	Associated with other burnt material &/or associated DIs	All
	Plugged sockets		Socketed objects
	Stabbed/penetrated	Repeated penetrations across the object or in unexpected places	Thin/sheet objects, eg, shields, decorative objects
Uncertain	–	Applied when damage to objects cannot be classed within the ranking system and it would be misleading to do so. This includes: – Burning evidence with no associated context or damage – Damage to objects for which there are no indicators of how it may have broken (eg, unused broken objects with no Destruction Indicators) – Damage to objects for which there is limited understanding of how such objects were used – Objects for which breakage & damage not clear, such as those obscured by corrosion	All

Figure 2.18: A chiselled gold bar from Cadbury Castle, Somerset (photo: author, courtesy of Somerset County Council and South West Heritage Trust, acc. no. TTNCM 76.AA.165/28)

2005; Warner & Cahill 2012, 100; Rahmstorf 2019).

Finally, as with pieces and fragments of copper-alloy objects, it is worth emphasising that while gold objects may break into two pieces through accident, it is less likely that a gold object will break into three or more pieces unintentionally; a mid-section fragment of a gold artefact may indicate that the object was deliberately broken (cf. Knight 2021, 56–7).

Applying the Damage Ranking System

These methodological considerations offer a framework for considering damage present on numerous different types of metalwork over a longer chronological period and across a large region. As such, I conclude this chapter by applying the Damage Ranking System to the metalwork from south-west Britain. Over 4200 pieces of metalwork are known

Table 2.8: Summary of criteria and considerations for applying the Destruction Indicators and Damage Ranking System to gold objects

Damage Ranking	*Destruction Indicator(s)*	*Criteria*	*Object type(s)*
0 Definitely not deliberate	All	Post-depositional/post-recovery processes causing damage (eg, ploughing, cleaning), informed by knowledge of context/post-recovery history	All
	Twisting	Present as part of 'decorative' function	Twisted penannular ornaments eg, bracelets, torcs
1 Probably not deliberate	Bending	Minor deformation (no parameter)	Sheet objects
		Associated damage, eg, dents & notches, that are seemingly modern/post-recovery	All
		Present in areas that might bend through use	Penannular ornaments eg, bracelets, rings
	Twisting	Minor deformation	Sheet objects
		Partial twist (<45°) possibly linked to use eg, opening/closing of a bracelet	Penannular ornaments eg, bracelets, torcs
	Crushing	Partial compression with single associated mark, eg, puncture, tool blow, probably accidental or caused through recovery	Hollow objects eg, lock rings
	Breakage	Patterns of breakage linked to use or structural weakness (eg, stress-bearing terminals) Casting/manufacture flaws	All
2 Probably deliberate	Bending	Deformation that would have hindered presumed functionality Associated damage, eg, tool marks, that are seemingly ancient	All
	Twisting	Extensive twisting or rotation (>45°)	Typically non-twisted ornaments
	Crushing	Ambiguous associated marks, but associated with similarly treated objects	All
	Breakage	Patterns of breakage unlikely to be linked to use or structural weakness (eg, bracelet terminals) Associated bending or twisting <45° Multiple broken pieces of different objects conforming to a similar size &/or weight within a single accumulation Frags & pieces associated with deliberately damaged material eg, frags in a plugged socket	All
3 Definitely deliberate	Bending / folding	Extreme plastic deformation	Sheet objects/ ornaments
		Creases in the surface indicating repeated bending/folding (aka rolling)	Sheet ornaments eg, strips, lunulae
	Twisting	Extensive rotation (>180°)	Typically non-twisted ornaments
	Crushing	Full compression of objects, with ancient tool marks Compressed with other objects	All

Damage Ranking	*Destruction Indicator(s)*	*Criteria*	*Object type(s)*
3 Definitely deliberate	Breakage	Multi-piece breaks (3+ pieces/ frags) Breaks with associated tool marks eg, chisel marks, hammer blows Associated with bending/twisting >45° Mid-section frag. indicating an object was once in 3+ pieces	All
Uncertain	–	Applied when damage to objects cannot be classed within ranking system & would be misleading to do so	All

from about 1500 findspots across this region (Pearce 1983; Knight *et al.* 2015). The corpus of material includes copper, bronze and gold weapons, tools and ornaments, which were deposited in a range of conditions and contexts. Previous work has highlighted the growing proportion of objects showing signs of deliberate damage, as well as the regional variations in metalworking traditions and depositional practices (Pearce 1983; Knight *et al.* 2015, 5–7). In this sense, the metalwork of south-west Britain offers a prime dataset for applying the DRS.

This requires first-hand study of the objects, and/or detailed recording, illustration and photography which will allow an accurate assessment of the object condition. Data collection was undertaken between February 2015 and March 2017 with the aim of sampling the following categories of metalwork:

- 'Weapons' (eg, daggers, swords, spearheads);
- Axeheads;
- Incomplete or broken objects, particularly those for which deliberate destruction has previously been suggested;
- Objects from hoards, funerary contexts, scatters,[2] or occupational contexts;
- Single finds with a known provenance held at the museums visited; and
- Finds with adequately detailed records on the Portable Antiquities Scheme online database.

From this sampling process, a catalogue of 1735 metal objects was compiled, documenting the condition of the object, as well as the circumstances of discovery and information about the findspot. This is available via the Archaeology Data Service: https://doi.org/10.5284/1090300. Approximately three-quarters of all weapons were analysed as well as more than half of single finds, and nearly 1300 broken/incomplete objects (Table 2.9). The sampled figure from hoards, funerary contexts, scatters and occupational contexts initially seems low but is significantly affected by two assemblages that were not studied: a hoard of 777 axeheads and fragments from Langton Matravers, Dorset; and the seabed assemblage of 420 metal pieces, mostly ingots, from Salcombe, Devon. The sampled number of axeheads was similarly affected by Langton Matravers. The total number of objects from these two sites accounts for nearly a third of all metalwork with a currently known location from south-west Britain.[3] These groups were not studied because both have seen dedicated research that can be drawn upon (Needham *et al.* 2013; Boughton 2015; Roberts *et al.* 2015; Wang *et al.* 2016; 2018). Indeed, whilst the compiled catalogue forms the main resource for analysis in the subsequent chapters, those objects of interest that were not available for study will be incorporated into discussion based upon published details. Overall, the sampled dataset covers a geographically diverse range and a good chronological spread (Fig 2.19; Table 2.10). The application of the DRS to this dataset allows us to observe broad trends in the treatment of objects.

Object analysis: completeness, Damage Ranking and Destruction Indicators

For each object, typology, chronology, condition and general completeness were recorded. Completeness was grouped under five categories: 0–25%; 26–50%; 51–75%; 76–99% and 100%, based on the presumed

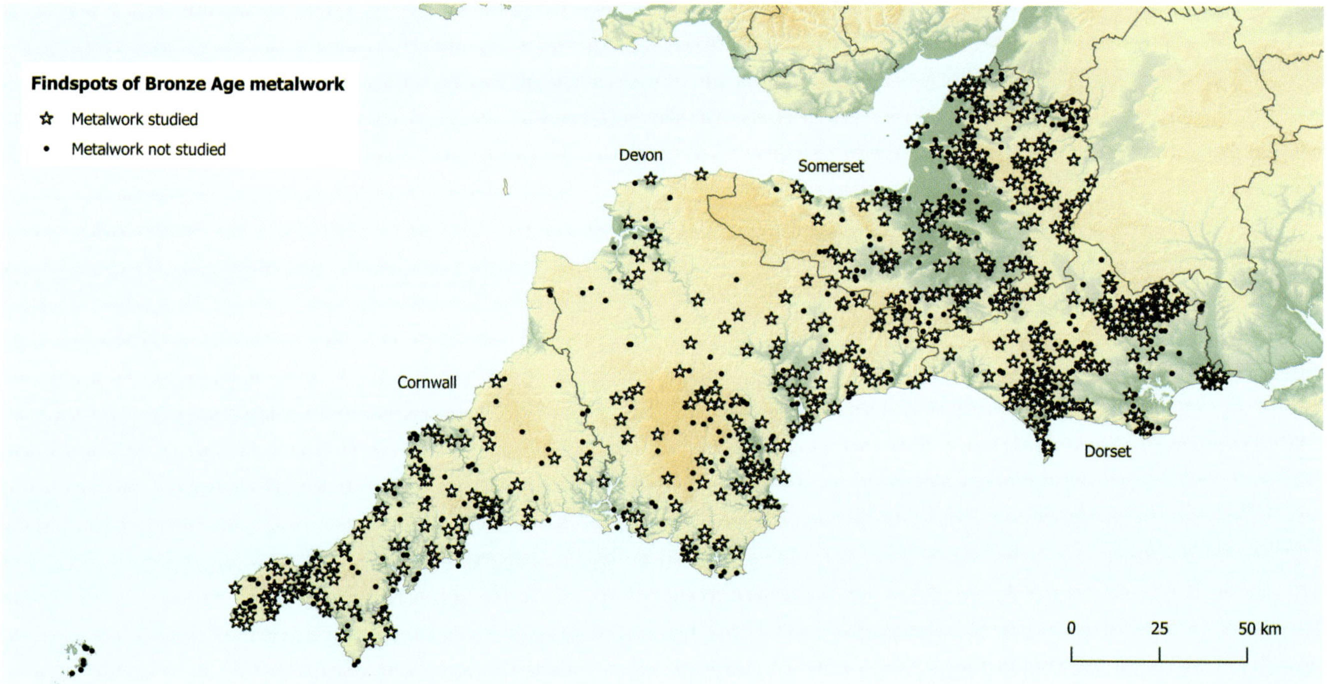

Figure 2.19: Findspots of Bronze Age metalwork from south-west Britain. Those marked with stars were studied as part of this research. Contains OS data © Crown copyright and database right 2021

Table 2.9: Metal objects from south-west Britain sampled in relation to the sampling criteria

Sampling criteria	*Overall total*	*Total with known location*	*Total sampled*	*% sampled (with known location)*
Weapons	533	452	335	74.1
Incomplete/broken objects (objects not ranked 100% or n/a completeness)	Uncertain	Uncertain	1290	–
Hoards/burials/scatters/occupational contexts	3227	2826	1161	41.1
Single finds (incl. weapons)	1083	941	555	59.0
Single finds (excl. weapons)	873	752	429	57.05
Axeheads	2020	1881	540	28.7
All objects	*c.* 4289	3808	1735	45.56

original form. Occasionally, two further categories were used: n/a (not applicable); or Uncertain. Metalworking material, such as casting jets and casting waste, generally fell under 'Not applicable' as it could not be considered part of any specific object; 'uncertain' applied to object fragments of an indeterminate type where an estimation of completeness could not be made.

Each object was assessed for evidence of production, preparation, use and pre-depositional treatment. Indicators of poor manufacture, lack of preparation or overworking may all have contributed to the final condition of the object. Any damage was documented, including both ancient and modern damage as well as accidental and deliberate, and interpretive descriptions were avoided to focus on the observable factors that might indicate the cause of the damage. Key features were noted (eg, the degree and direction of a bend) as well as any associated marks, casting flaws and effects of corrosion. Damage rankings were then attributed.

Most objects were deposited either as fragments or mostly complete with few objects falling within the 26–75% completeness categories (Fig. 2.20). These categories indicate the current state of the object rather than the deposited state because post-depositional processes have hindered the interpretation of whether some objects were deposited complete; it is thus likely that the number of objects deposited 100% complete was higher.

Almost all objects deposited between the Chalcolithic–Middle Bronze Age were 76% or more complete whilst nearly half of all Late Bronze Age objects were deposited 0–25% complete (Figs 2.21, 2.22), representing a shift over time from depositing complete objects to depositing more fragmentary material. Additionally, this later period contained the greatest number of casting jets and other metallurgical material (ranked 'not applicable'). In the Earliest Iron Age, more complete objects were more frequently deposited again; this reflects the broader depositional practices observed in Earliest Iron Age Britain (Boughton 2015).

This assessment of completeness, however, does not indicate the level of intent. Incompleteness could be the result of use, accident or post-depositional damage, whereas some objects may have been deliberately damaged but left overall complete. This is where the application of the Damage Ranking System to a large dataset becomes essential, as it enables us to quickly recognise and interpret trends in intentional or unintentional damage.

Over a quarter (456) of the objects studied showed signs of deliberate damage, and a further 193 objects were probably deliberately damaged (Fig. 2.23).[4] 348 objects were completely undamaged (ie, damaged-ranked n/a) and 598 objects presented only accidental, use-related or post-depositional/recovery damage. 140 objects had damage that could not be confidently categorised. Most objects ranked 2 or 3 were 0–25% complete whilst almost all of those ranked 0 were 76–99% or 100% complete, indicating fragmentation was often the result of intent rather than accident (Fig. 2.24). In contrast, few objects with a higher completeness rating showed signs of deliberate damage.

The highest number of objects ranked 2 or 3 occurred during the Late Bronze Age (Table 2.11; Figs 2.25, 2.26). When combined with the completeness data, we can begin to clearly observe the general trend towards depositing deliberately damaged, fragmentary metalwork over time. This trend has been noted elsewhere for areas of Bronze Age Europe, particularly during the Middle–Late Bronze Age (eg, Huth 1997, 149–50; York 2002; Maraszek 2006; Rezi 2011), but the present overview indicates the starkness of this shift across the whole of the Bronze Age, which must have been tied into changing social values surrounding metalwork, deposition and the role of deliberately damaged, incomplete objects.

Deliberate damage was recorded under the Destruction Indicators outlined above, though some were further sub-divided to allow greater specificity (Table 2.12). Each Destruction Indicator was observed on the metalwork of south west Britain at least once (Fig. 2.27). Fragmentation and breakage were most commonly observed, with bending and crushing of objects also frequent. This is unsurprising as the process of breaking objects often leaves associated plastic deformation such as crushing and bending, and hammer or chisel marks and cracking were frequently observed. Significantly, this associated damage reflects the method and tools used for fragmentation and allows us to understand the role of the

Period	Overall no. metal objects	Objects sampled	Overall no. findspots	Findspots sampled
Chalcolithic	18	9	17	8
EBA	303	126	232	87
E–MBA	15	8	14	8
MBA	1028	468	506	233
M–LBA	464	84	121	61
LBA	1112	853	406	251
LBA–EstIA	110	54	19	8
EstIA	947	53	49	18
Bronze Age/ uncertain	292	80	156	37
Total	*c.* 4289	1735	1520	711

Table 2.10: The number of metal artefacts and findspots sampled from south-west Britain

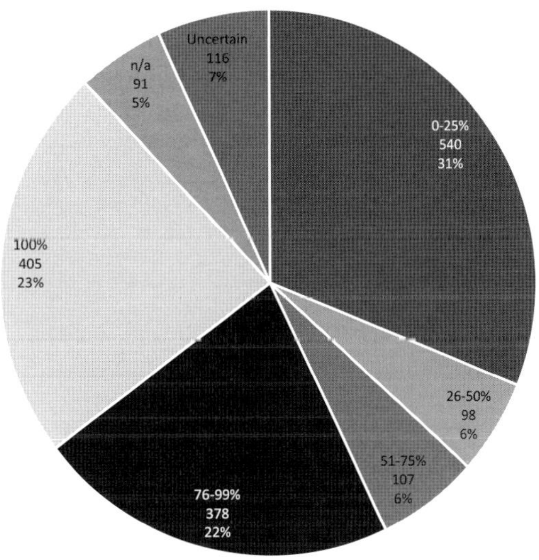

Figure 2.20: Relative proportions of metal objects studied within each completeness category (n=1735)

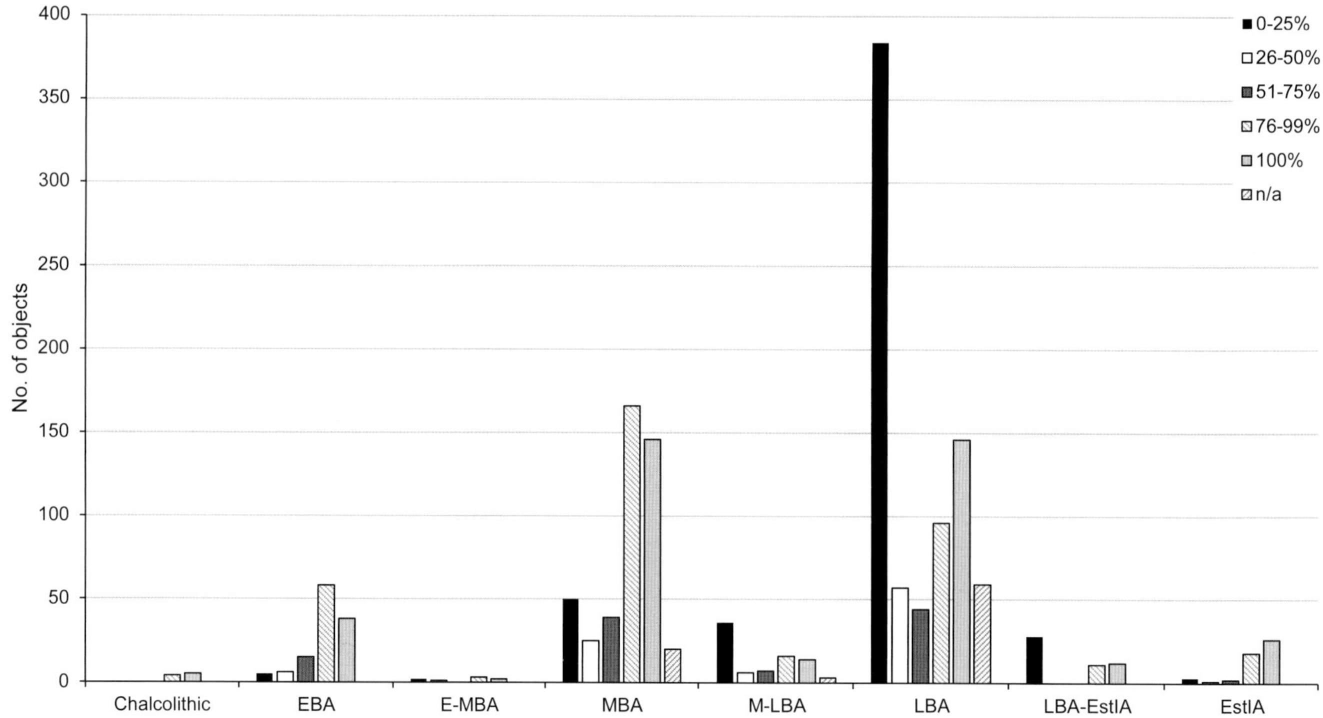

Figure 2.21: The completeness of the sampled metal objects across the Bronze Age (n=1550)
**Objects of 'uncertain' completeness or uncertain date have been removed for clarity*

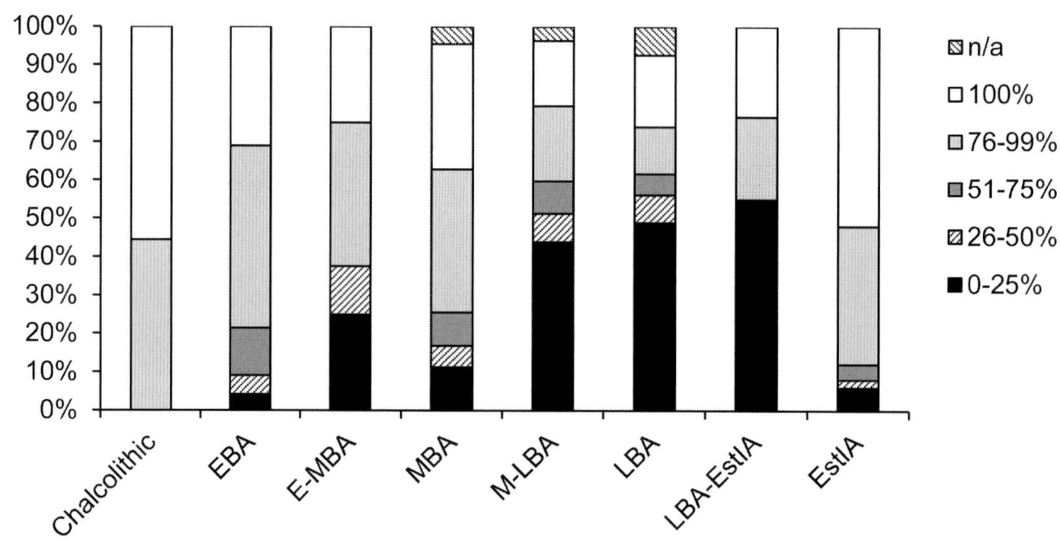

Figure 2.22: The proportions of object completeness within each chronological period (n=1550)
**Objects of 'uncertain' completeness or uncertain date have been removed for clarity*

person involved in destroying the objects. Large groups of fragmented objects may have required the involvement of a metalworker, for instance. Other damage, such as rolling, notching and plugged sockets, occurred infrequently but suggests more particular attention was paid to how objects should be destroyed. Whilst the fragmentation of many objects may have been part of the recycling process, for example, the folding/rolling of a single object or deliberately plugging a socket is a more considered act (Cahill 2005; Dietrich & Mörtz 2019). These are often linked to specific types of objects or sit within broader social practices, as we shall see in the following chapters. If we consider that each action was the result of individuals or communities operating within wider social ontologies, we can recognise that the ways in which objects were damaged relied on understanding what an appropriate treatment for different objects was; this was linked to depositional practices, the materials from which objects were made and the networks of which people were a part.

With the approach and framework outlined in this chapter we can begin to see how a rigorous study of damaged objects will allow us to understand *how* objects were damaged and how this may have been linked to either post-depositional or else intentional processes. The broad level application of the Damage Ranking System allows a useful overview and a structure for highlighting trends in prehistoric practices. Over the following three chapters, I will approach the dataset from south-west Britain chronologically and explore case studies to better address the intricacies of the relationship between people and the treatment and deposition of metalwork over time.

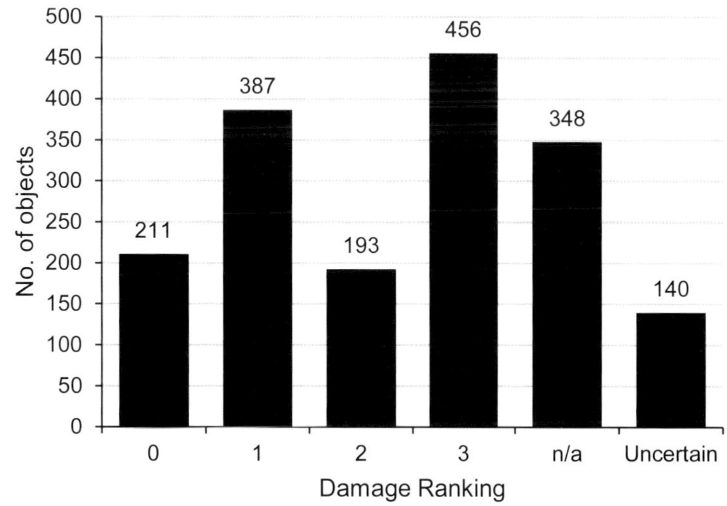

Figure 2.23: Number of objects within each Damage Ranking (n=1735)

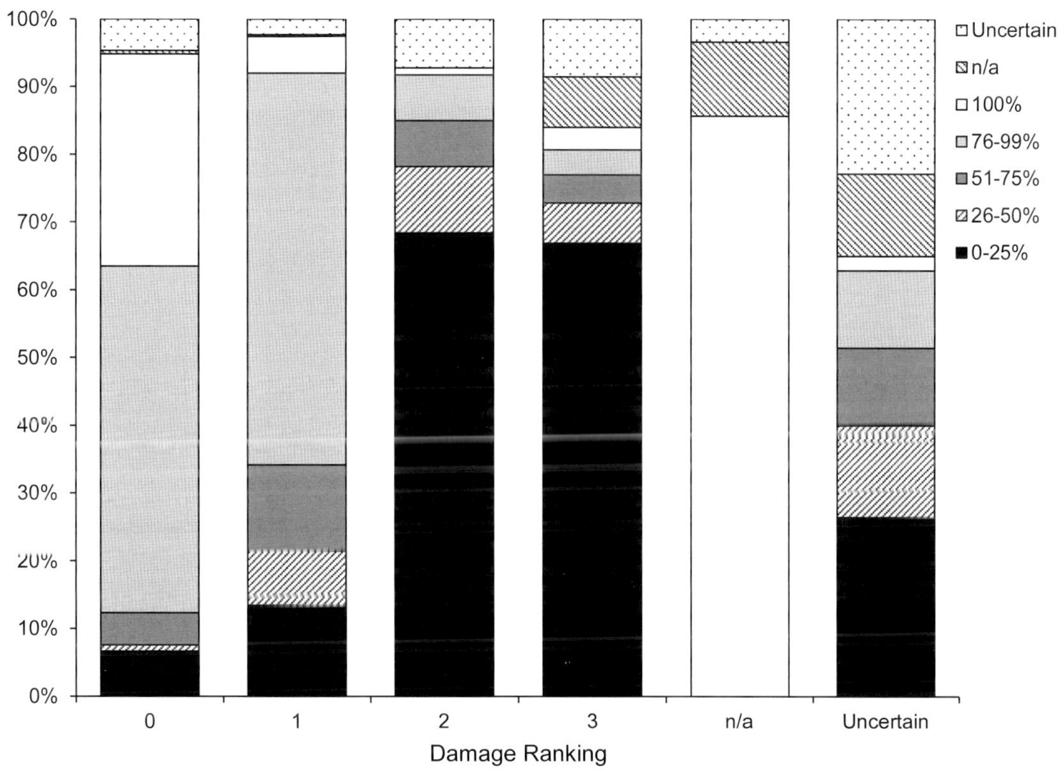

Figure 2.24: Relative proportions of completeness recorded within each Damage Ranking (n=1735)

Table 2.11: Number of sampled objects from south-west Britain within each Damage Ranking

Period	*Damage Ranking*						*Total*
	0	*1*	*2*	*3*	*n/a*	*Uncertain*	
Chalcolithic	2	1	–	1	5	–	9
EBA	37	49	6	6	19	9	126
E–MBA	3	2	–	–	2	1	8
MBA	98	149	32	46	104	39	468
M–LBA	5	30	16	10	11	12	84
LBA	51	120	111	364	150	57	853
LBA–EstIA	3	9	8	19	13	2	54
EstIA	9	16	1	–	24	3	53
Bronze Age/uncertain	3	11	19	10	20	17	80
Total	211	387	193	456	348	140	1735

Table 2.12: Destruction Indicators and sub-divisions applied to the sampled metalwork

Destruction Indicators	*Sub-divisions*
Bending/folding	Bent (longitudinal) Bent (transverse) Folded Rolled
Twisting/torsion	
Crushing	
Notching	
Breakage	Broken – multi-piece Broken – single piece Frag.
Burning	
Plugged sockets	Placed inside a socket Plugged socket
Stabbed/penetrated	

*Figure 2.25: Proportions of objects within each damage ranking across the Bronze Age (n=1655) *Objects of uncertain date have been removed for clarity*

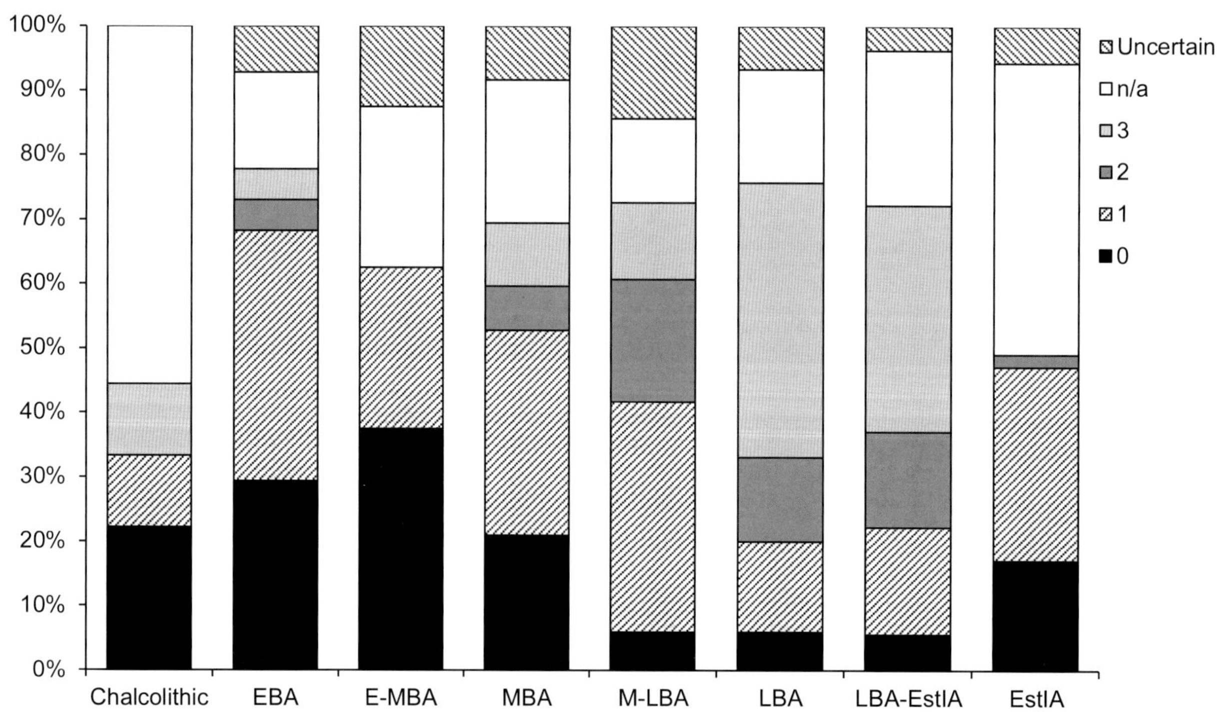

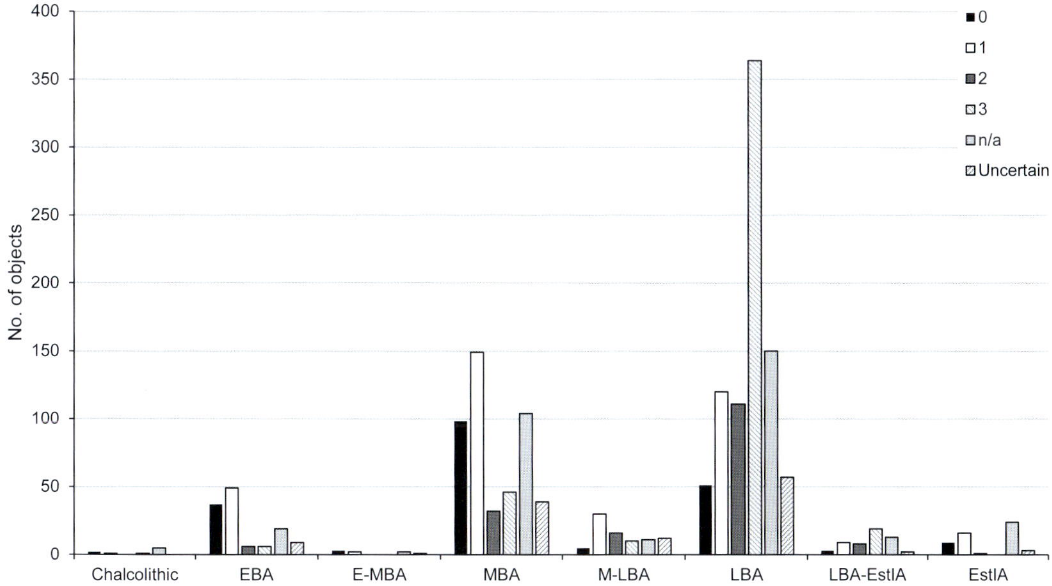

Figure 2.26: Absolute numbers of objects within each damage ranking across the Bronze Age (n=1655)
**Objects of uncertain date have been removed for clarity*

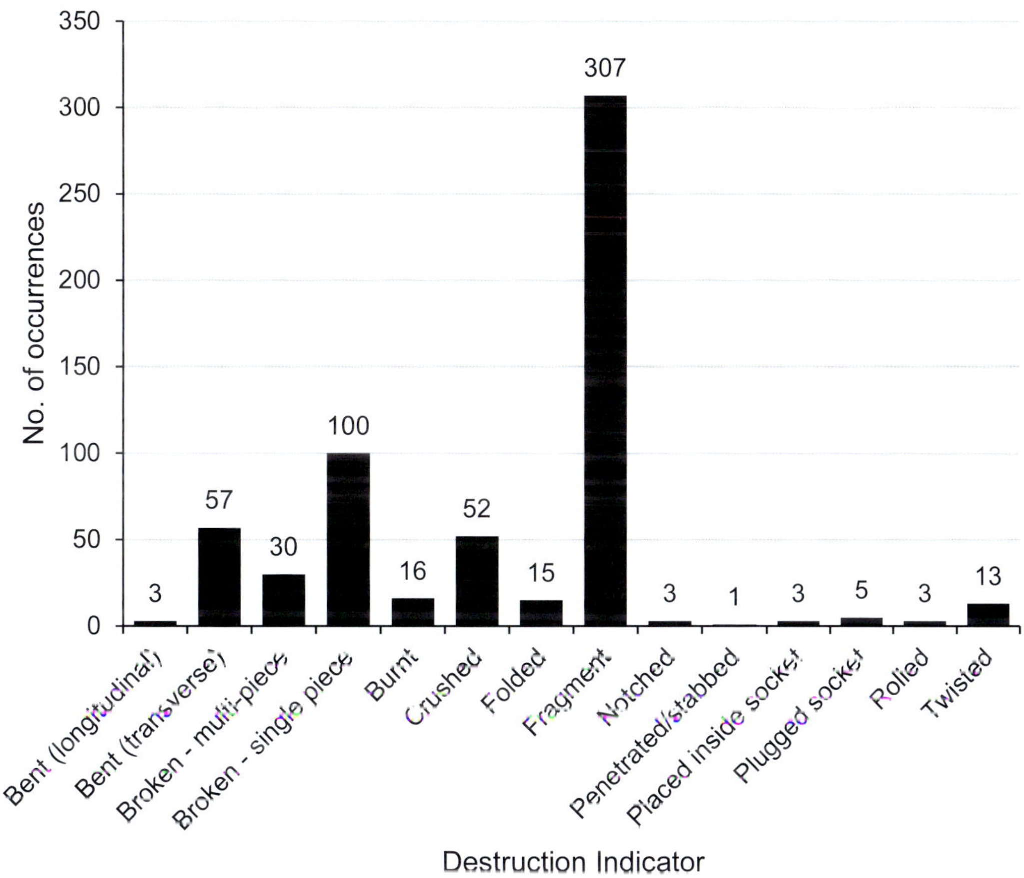

Figure 2.27: The frequency of destruction indicators recorded (n=653)
**Indicators recorded across 456 objects*

Notes

1 Alternatively termed *sharp notch* and *round notch* by Hermann *et al.* 2020a; 2020b.

2 'Scatters' were defined as groups of objects found within close proximity (eg, a field) and possessing a similar chronological span (cf. Knight 2018, 251–3).

3 At least 481 objects are lost, destroyed or in uncertain locations with no further details (Pearce 1983; Knight *et al.* 2015) and thus could not be sampled.

4 Although objects were often attributed multiple damage rankings, for simplicity each object is recorded only once here according to its level of damage, with deliberate damage taking precedent over accidental damage. This applies to the data displayed in Figures 2.24, 2.25, 2.26 and 2.27.

3

Burnt, broken and buried: the Chalcolithic–Early Bronze Age, *c.* 2450–1500 BC

The earliest metal objects in Bronze Age Britain included copper axeheads and knives and sheet gold objects; these were commonly deposited complete as single finds or in funerary contexts and occasionally in hoards. This remained the case, even as a greater variety of objects were produced towards the end of the third millennium and first half of the second millennium BC, though in some areas hoards became more common. The inception of metallurgy and circulation of metal objects occurred alongside a series of other changes in material culture and cultural practices, including funerary rites, ceramic styles and lithic production (Needham 2009; Parker Pearson *et al.* 2019, 15–16). Isotopic and aDNA evidence increasingly indicate these changes can be linked to the movement of people in and out of different parts of Britain from various parts of continental Europe over time (Olalde *et al.* 2018; Parker Pearson *et al.* 2019). During this period, we can observe a variety of practices linked with monumental and funerary constructions in the landscape, the treatment of the dead, and the way material culture was used and deposited.

The deliberate destruction of Chalcolithic and Early Bronze Age metalwork prior to deposition rarely forms the focus of discussion, no doubt because it is encountered relatively infrequently. The evidence from south-west Britain highlights this well. Of the 133 Chalcolithic–Early Bronze Age artefacts studied, only seven cases of deliberate destruction could be identified. To these, we can add six objects that were probably deliberately destroyed; this still only accounts for less than 10% of the material studied. Over three-quarters (77.4%) of objects were deposited complete or almost complete, including all-but-one of the Chalcolithic artefacts and some of those with signs of deliberate damage. The remaining objects were incomplete through ancient accidental damage or post-depositional processes. This suggests it was considered most appropriate to leave metal objects undamaged where possible. Of those that were deliberately damaged, all but one was found associated with funerary contexts. Metalwork deposited in funerary contexts was typically interred alongside other grave goods such as stone tools, ceramic vessels and objects produced from 'exotic' materials (eg, shale, amber and faience); the treatment of these objects is relevant for understanding whether the treatment of metal objects was distinctive or in keeping with other practices relating to portable material culture. We saw in Chapter 1 that the link between the destruction of objects and the death of people is well-established, and the examples from south west Britain offer the chance to directly consider the relationship between people and objects. In this chapter I will explore this link through a consideration of the few deliberately damaged metal objects deposited in graves in south-west Britain, and then go on to consider the treatment of other objects deposited as single finds and in hoards.

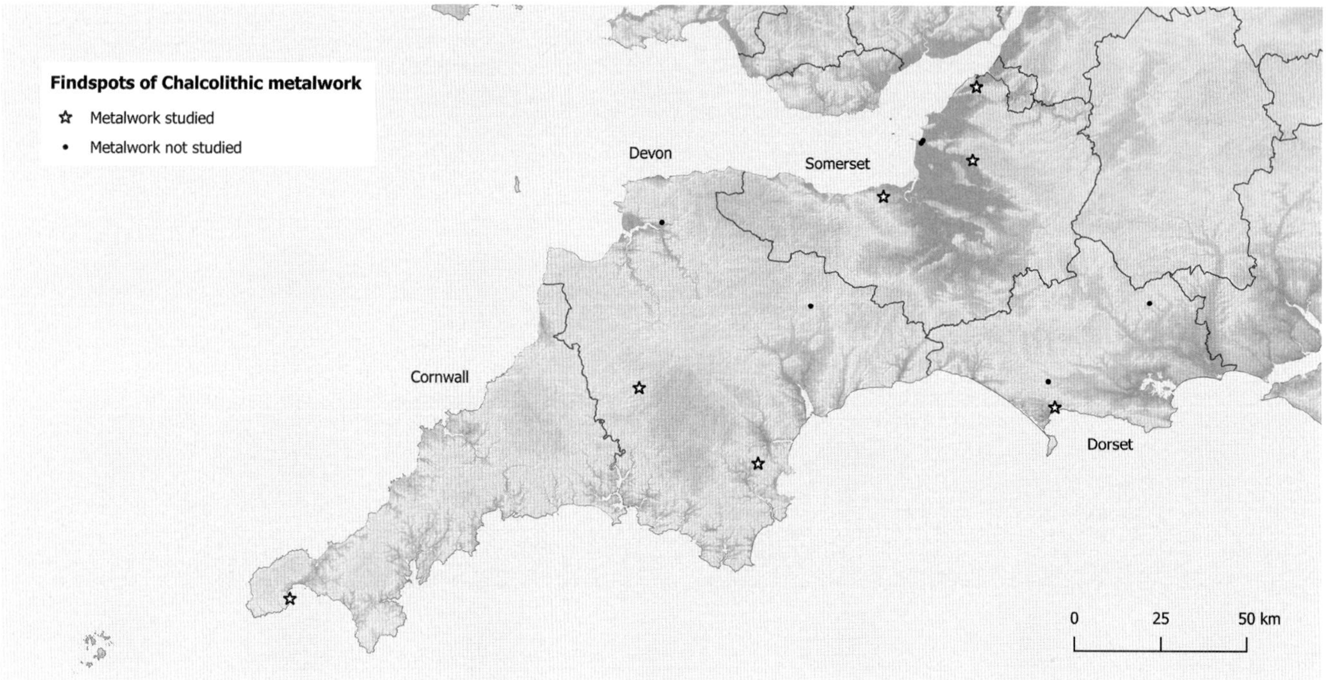

Figure 3.1: Findspots of Chalcolithic metalwork from south-west Britain. Those marked with stars were studied as part of this research. Contains OS data © Crown copyright and database right 2021

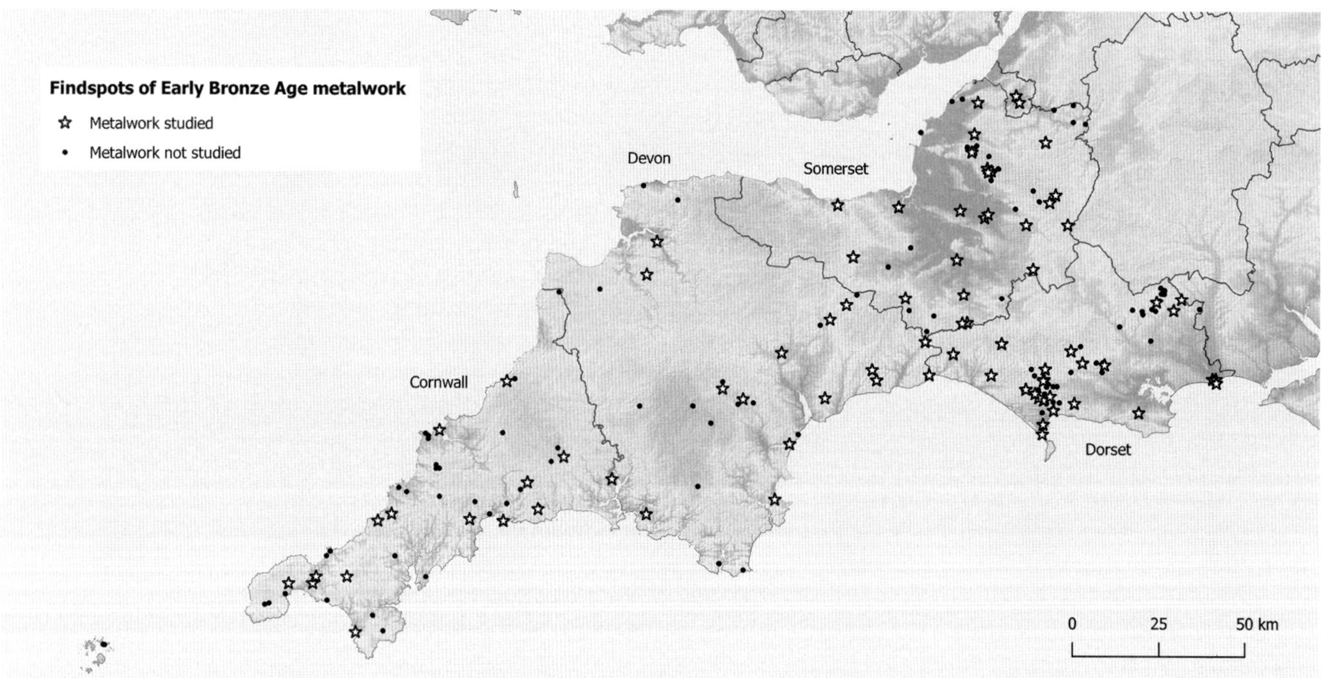

Figure 3.2: Findspots of Early Bronze Age metalwork from south-west Britain. Those marked with stars were studied as part of this research. Contains OS data © Crown copyright and database right 2021

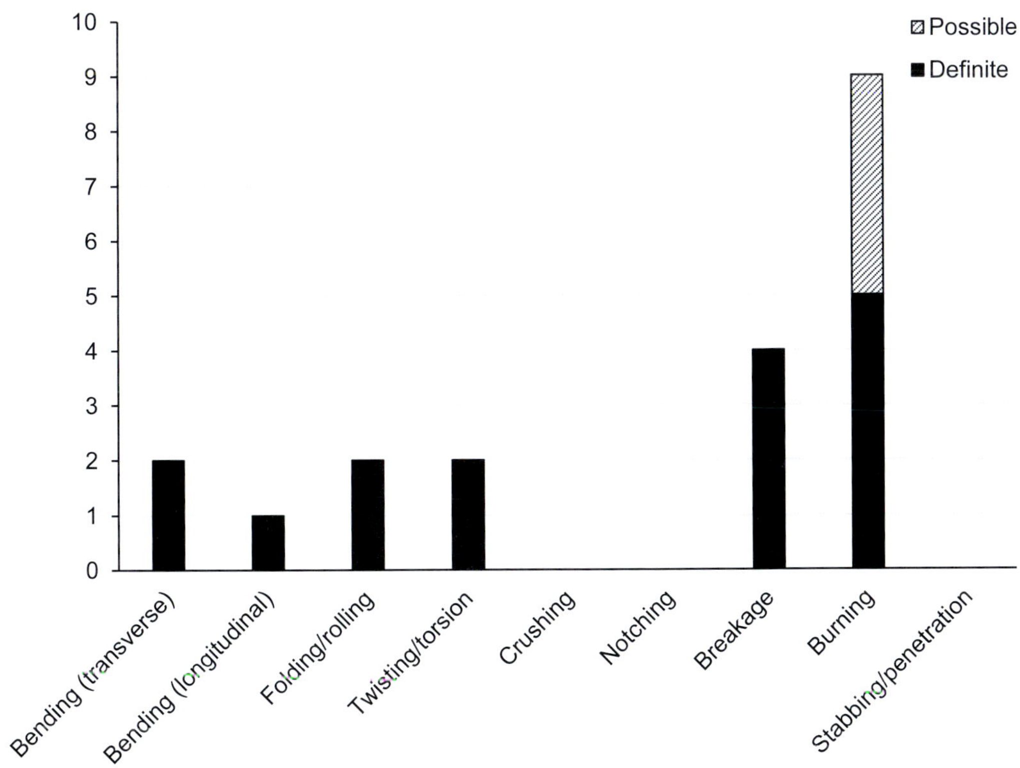

Figure 3.3: Destruction Indicators present on the Chalcolithic–Early Bronze Age objects studied

Assessing the evidence for Chalcolithic–Early Bronze Age destruction and deposition in south-west Britain

To begin with we might question why there is such a stark difference between the number of destroyed objects deposited in these earlier periods and those deposited in the later Bronze Age (Fig. 2.27). Firstly, although the Chalcolithic–Early Bronze Age covers a much longer span of time than the Middle and Late Bronze Age, fewer metal objects were deposited overall in south-west Britain (Figs 3.1 & 3.2). Indeed, a curious feature of the region is that despite potentially playing a pivotal role in early metal supply systems, very few copper and gold objects were deposited between 2450–2150 BC (Timberlake 2009, 100), which may suggest that either metal was not being deposited, or it was not being kept near its source. This latter situation seems to be particularly true of Cornish gold, which was used to produce large numbers of Chalcolithic and Early Bronze Age lunulae deposited in Ireland, whilst relatively few lunulae were deposited in Cornwall (Mattingly *et al.* 2009; Standish *et al.* 2015). Similarly, few early burials or other signs of activity are known.

The limited corpus of metalwork from throughout the earlier Bronze Age can also be linked to a significant absence of large groups of material, such as hoards, in the later 3rd and early 2nd millennium BC; most metal artefacts were instead deposited as single finds or individual inclusions in or around graves and burial monuments, a pattern reflected in other parts of Britain and Ireland (Needham 1988; Becker 2013). It is only around 1700–1500 BC that larger groups of material were deposited in south-west Britain, though these remain exceptional rather than the rule.

Regarding the damage observed, the most common Destruction Indicator was burning (Fig. 3.3). The nine possible and definite cases of burning recorded were all copper-alloy daggers associated with burials of cremated human remains or other burnt material, highlighting an important link between the treatment of the objects and the treatment of the deceased. Exposure to fire at low temperatures will not cause copper/copper alloys to burn; any observable charring evidence results from the formation of corrosion products when charred

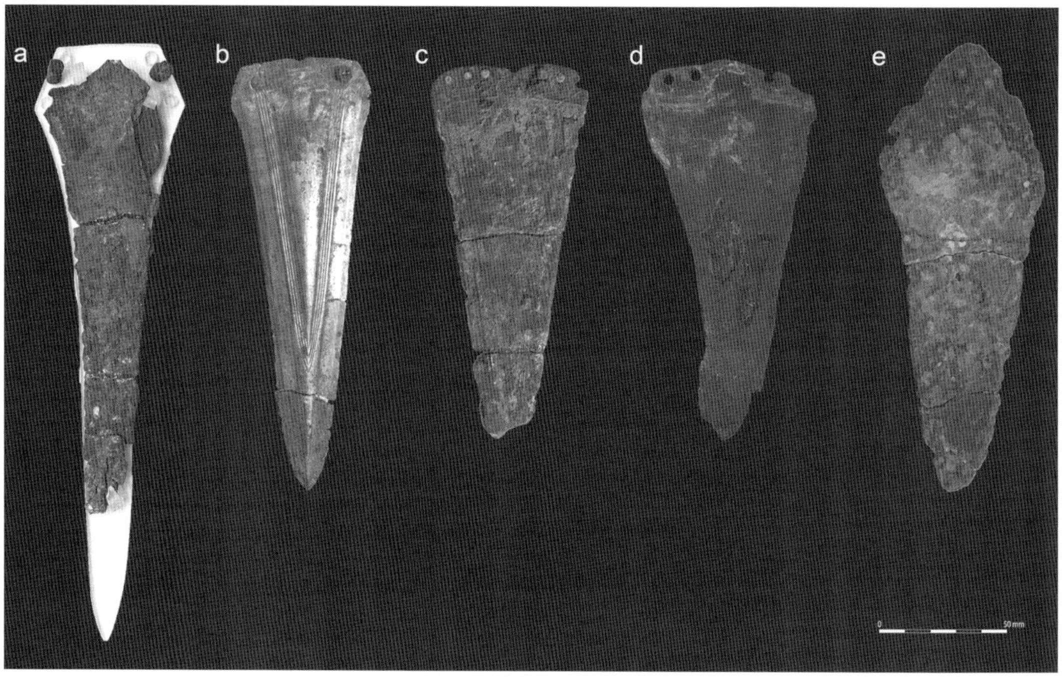

Figure 3.4: Five Early Bronze Age daggers demonstrating signs of burning: a) Angrouse I; b) Wall Mead I; c and d) Weymouth 8; e) Yettington (photo: author, courtesy of Bristol City Museum and Art Gallery (acc.no.E1779), Dorset County Museum, Royal Albert Memorial Museum and Art Gallery, Exeter, and the Royal Institution of Cornwall)

Figure 3.5: A warped and twisted fragment of the Yettington dagger, Devon (RAMM-F055) (photo: author, courtesy of the Royal Albert Memorial Museum and Art Gallery, Exeter)

organic materials, such as textiles, leather, or wood, are in contact with the object. Higher temperatures that bring the metals close to their melting points will cause deformation and melting. Experimental work exploring cremation practices indicates pyres will exceed temperatures of 1000°C and slighter pieces of metalwork (eg, pins) are also more likely to be obliterated in the process than more substantial objects (eg, daggers) (Sheridan 2010, 11; Marshall 2011). In Alison Sheridan's (2010) cremation experiments, for instance, she noted that a bronze awl and wooden handle were 'entirely consumed in the flames', leaving no trace, whilst the copper dagger 'had only superficial surface alteration'. This illustrates the circumstantial nature of the evidence: certain objects may have been completely obliterated meaning that surviving evidence could be an incomplete representation and some metal objects may have been burned, but the post-depositional conditions did not allow the survival of archaeological evidence. In this study, objects were not assessed as 'burned' unless it was macroscopically evident, though microstructural analysis may further this interpretation in the future. This latter point is crucial as 27 of the metal objects studied were associated with 17 cremation burials, but only five showed conclusive macroscopic burning evidence and a further four showed possible evidence. Similarly, in her survey of daggers from Britain, Sabine Gerloff (1975) noted only ten examples displaying signs of heat damage out of the 346 daggers found with burials, three of which are from south-west Britain.[1] However, in all cases, the heat-damaged daggers were associated with cremation burials and a range of grave goods, sometimes also displaying signs of burning. The surviving evidence of 'deliberately destroyed' metalwork therefore probably represents only a partial record.

Daggers in south-west Britain

The corpus of daggers and knife-daggers from Cornwall, Devon and Somerset is relatively small, with the majority buried after 2000 BC in funerary contexts or at monuments (Jones & Quinnell 2013). By contrast in Dorset, daggers and knives were more common inclusions in burials (Gerloff 1975; Pearce 1983), with examples known from the Chalcolithic onwards. Past studies have highlighted the range of conditions in which daggers and knife-daggers were deposited (Wall 1987; Woodward *et al.* 2005, 35–8; Jones & Quinnell 2013, 19), but although deliberate damage is often noted (eg, Ashbee 1960, 96; Needham 2000a, 44; Woodward *et al.* 2005, 35–8; Woodward & Hunter 2015, 27), the implications are rarely explored further.

Burning blades and bodies

Five south-western daggers were damage-ranked 3, all dating post-2000 BC (Table 3.1). Each dagger presented evidence of burning (Fig. 3.4) and the daggers from Angrouse I, Wall Mead I and Yettington were also intentionally bent, broken, twisted and/or cracked (Fig. 3.5). The Angrouse dagger is warped and distorted by heat around the heel, though it is possible the blade was deliberately bent (cf. Jones & Quinnell 2013, 19). If caused by burning, the distortion suggests it was exposed to a high heat, probably accompanying the body on the pyre.

Other non-conclusive damage, including breakage, was observable on all five examples. One dagger from Weymouth 8 (DCM-F043a), for instance, seemingly broke into multiple pieces because of corrosion rather than deliberate human action. The exception is the Wall Mead dagger, which broke near the tip into two pieces in antiquity, associated with longitudinal bending. The bend is about 5–10 degrees from straight and caused two cracks along the external edge and one along the internal edge of the bend. The two pieces do not refit neatly, with the tip fragment bending away from the main blade indicating the point of breakage, which is associated with minor material loss. Although there is a small casting flaw in the break, which would have caused a weak point for fracturing, it seems the dagger may have been struck against something to incur the bending and breakage, perhaps through violent use.

Four of the deliberately damaged daggers were deposited with cremated remains, suggesting they were burnt with the body. The bulb-headed pin, perforated pendant and ceramic cup associated with the Wall Mead dagger are intact however, suggesting that whilst the dagger was burnt with the body, other grave goods were included afterwards, or else survived the pyre relatively unscathed. The Angrouse dagger, conversely, was found with fragments of a Trevisker vessel, cremated remains and iron pyrites. The dagger survives in four fragments and the incomplete ceramic sherds may support the idea that the dagger was deposited fragmented too. The Yettington dagger was interred in a barrow with burnt wood and a broken stone battle axe, though no human remains survived, which may be the result of Devon's acidic soils. The wood and the condition of the dagger indicates that the objects were burnt. It is unclear whether the stone axe was broken intentionally or by accident, but the decision to include an already fragmented object indicates the intentional selection process behind interments.

The Weymouth 8 (Ridgeway 7) barrow context is more complex (Fig. 3.6). The two burnt daggers were found lying on top of a secondary interment of cremated remains (No.3) along with fragments of a third dagger, a low-flanged axehead and a sheet gold pommel. The pommel is largely complete and may have been associated with one of the daggers, and a small piece of textile is preserved on the flanged axehead suggesting it was wrapped upon deposition. Secondary Interment No.3 was deposited in the earthen mound of the barrow which covered a stone cairn which in turn covered a subterranean stone cist. The cist contained decayed human skeletal remains and two secondary interments had been made into the stone cairn above it. One of the secondary interments (No.1) also had an associated dagger (DCM-F042) that had no signs of deliberate damage. This interment consisted of incomplete skeletal remains of a 21 year old individual represented by 'almost all the upper jaw and teeth… seven broken bones, and the upper part of the skull', but none of the vertebrae (Cunnington in Drew & Piggott 1936, 21). The incomplete nature suggests a fragmentation of the body, with pieces of the skeleton deliberately selected

Table 3.1: Daggers studied from south-west Britain damage-ranked 2 and 3

No.	*Site*	*Dagger type*	*Relative date BC (approx.)*	*Destruction Indicators*	*Other damage*	*Damage Ranking(s)*	*Context & associated objects*
RCM-F001	Angrouse I, Cornwall	Camerton-Snowshill	1725–1500	Bent (transverse) Burnt Twisted	Broken (multi-piece) Corrosion Post-recovery Rivet holes broken	0,3	With cremated remains in stone-lined pit under barrow Biconical urn frags & iron pyrites
BCMAG-F015a	Wall Mead I, Somerset	Camerton-Snowshill	1950–1875	Bent (longitudinal) Broken – multi-piece Burnt	Cracked	2,3	With cremated remains in stone cist in chambered long barrow Complete bulb-headed pin (BCMAG-F015b), perforated whetstone/pendant & Aldbourne-type cup
DCM-F043a	Weymouth 8, Dorset	Armorico-British A	1875–1725	Burnt	Corrosion Post-recovery	0, 3	Barrow covering cairn containing 2 secondary interments, plus stone cist containing an inhumation Both daggers associated with secondary interment of cremated remains, complete flanged axe (DCM-F043c), dagger frags (DCM-F043d), & complete gold pommel (DCM-F043e). Other objects in barrow included pottery, stone & bone tools, & animal bones.
DCM-F043b	Weymouth 8, Dorset	Armorico-British A	1875–1725	Burnt	Hilt damage	3	
RAMM-F055	Yettington, Devon	Type Milston	2000–1900	Burnt Twisted	Broken (multi-piece) Corrosion Post-recovery	0,3	In barrow with no human remains Lump of stone, piece of burnt wood, & broken perforated stone battle-axe
RAMM-F009	Broad Down (Barrow D), Farway, Devon	Camerton-Snowshill	1725–1500	Burnt?	Broken (multi-piece)	0,2	In tree-trunk coffin with burnt bones in cist covered by flint cairn Kimmeridge shale cup found about 3 ft (*c.* 1 m) away
DCM-F008a	Cranborne 4 (Boveridge House), Dorset	Armorico-British (variant Winterborne Came)	1950–1875	Broken	Broken (refitting pieces) Hilt damage	1,2	Under a barrow, possibly with interment Dagger with broken rivet holes (DCM-F008b)

No.	Site	Dagger type	Relative date BC (approx.)	Destruction Indicators	Other damage	Damage Ranking(s)	Context & associated objects
BCMAG-F010	Green Barrow, Priddy, Somerset	Knife-dagger (Series 7B)	1950–1725	Bent/bowed (transverse)	Hilt damage Broken rivet holes	0,1,2	Barrow, possibly with secondary interment of cremated remains Crutch-headed perforated bone pin
ASH-F012	Sigwells II, Somerset	Camerton-Snowshill	1725–1500	Burnt?	Broken (single piece), Corrosion	0,2, Uncertain	In bark coffin within barrow; small frags burnt bone representing burial of cremated remains & flints
DCM-F045a	Winterborne Came 38, Dorset	Armorico-British C	1725–1500	Broken (multi-piece, refitting) Burnt?	Bent Hilt damage, rivet holes torn	1,2	Under barrow, probably with cremated remains Incomplete dagger (DCM-F045b) & knife-dagger (DCM-F045c), ring-headed bone pin, & other bone implements also possibly associated
DCM-F046	Winterborne St Martin 46, Dorset	Snowshill (variant Edington)	1950–1725	Burnt?	Broken (multi-piece, refitting), Corrosion damage	0,2	With secondary interment of cremated remains, enclosed by a ring of stones within barrow which also contained primary inhumation & bones of 3 infants. Dagger associated with incomplete incense cup

for deposition or else removed. Beneath this interment, a stone 'macehead', a polished flint axehead and a bone dagger pommel were recovered (Fig. 3.7); it is possible the pommel was associated with the dagger. Although the inhumation was unburnt and the dagger showed no signs of damage, the pommel showed traces of burning (Hardaker 1974, 16). Secondary interment No.2 comprised cremated remains with no associated finds. Other finds recovered from the cairn included animal bones, stone and bone tools and pottery.

The Weymouth 8 barrow thus presents multiple phases during which interments and other deposits were made, and there are several elements to consider. Most of the artefacts associated with the burials can be considered roughly contemporary but due to the broad nature of relative dating one cannot determine if the interments were made days, years or decades apart. Different treatments and levels of care are represented across the objects, with some wrapped, some complete, some burnt and some fragmented, which allows us to disentangle some of the different object-person relationships. The burnt daggers with secondary interment 3 may have been burned with the body, suggesting these could have been the possessions of the dead, whilst the wrapped flanged axehead may have been an offering by mourners. Similarly, the combination of both inhumations and cremations within the barrow, cairn and cist indicates changing practices and/or personal preferences towards interments as the monument was constructed and engaged with. The various objects found within the cairn but not associated with any of the individuals could have been incorporated during construction of the cairn and barrow or included later. The polished flint axehead is of particular interest as this was probably produced during the Neolithic period and thus may represent a curated object of some age; its deposition as part of the cairn material could have been a significant action connecting the past with the present. These repeated engagements over time may have been a form of veneration or ongoing interaction with the monument and the burial of people and objects were part of this active relationship. Set in its wider context, Weymouth 8 is part of a larger cemetery of barrows along the Dorset

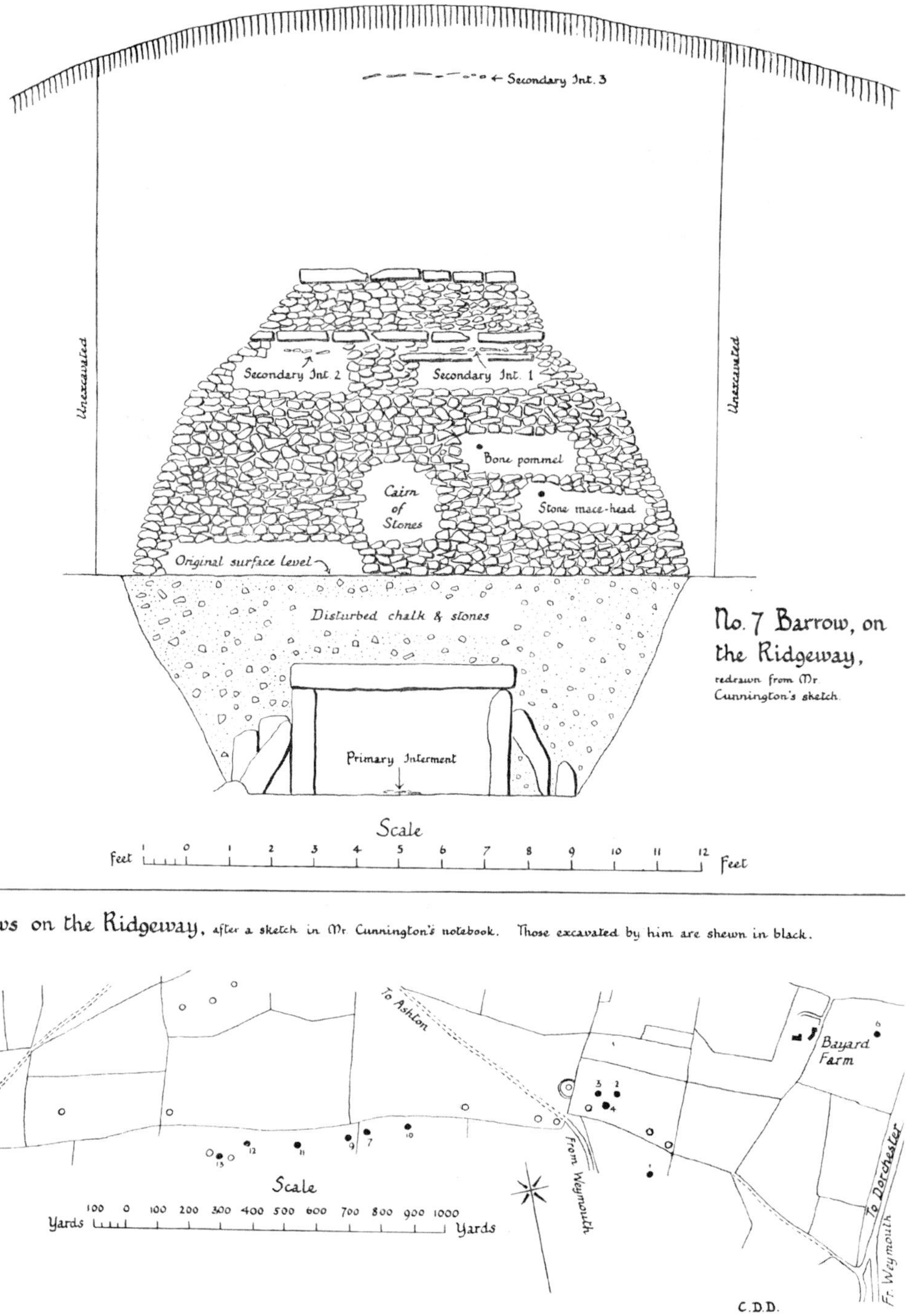

Figure 3.6: The internal structure of the Weymouth 8 (Ridgeway 7) barrow, Dorset (above) and map of barrows along the Ridgeway (below) (source: Drew & Piggott 1936, pl. iv. Reproduced by kind permission of Dorset Natural History and Archaeological Society)

Ridgeway, several with numerous interments, construction phases and various depositions. The overall complex was a significant arena for expressing social ideals.

These five dagger examples demonstrate that the destruction of Early Bronze Age metalwork associated with burials was part of a wider scheme of practices that cannot be generically summarised. The inclusion of damaged and incomplete objects, even where intent cannot be demonstrated, seems to have been a key part of burial practices. It is therefore important to consider all fragments, not just of metalwork, that have been deliberately chosen for interment with a burial. Daggers were linked, at least partly, to the cremation of

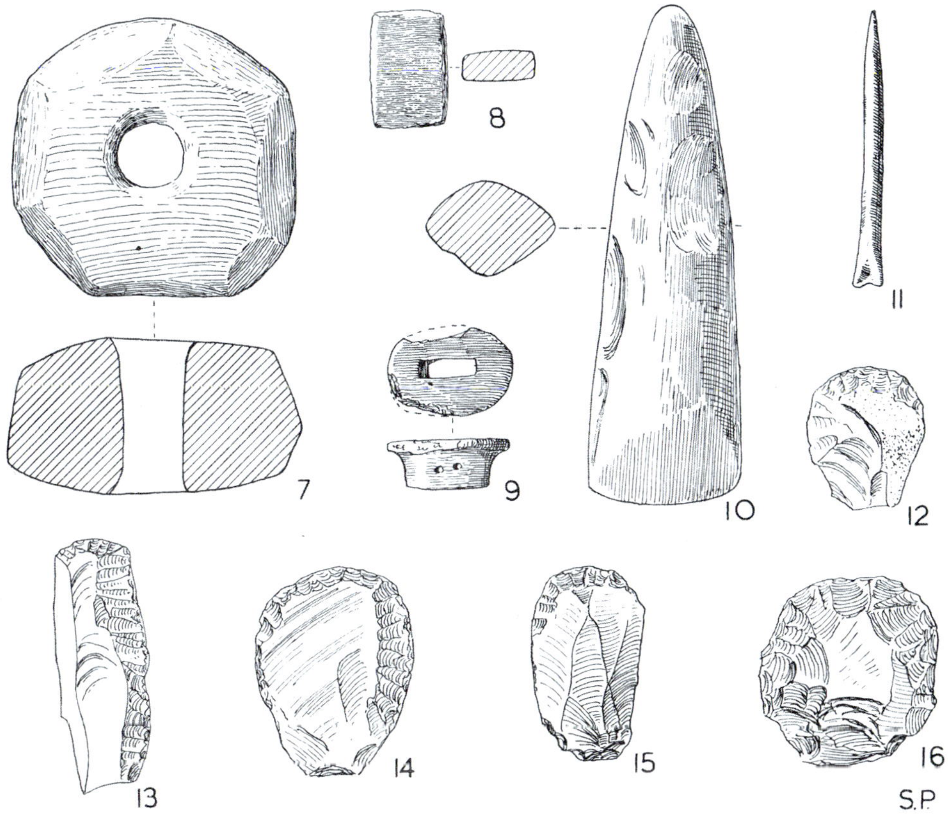

Figure 3.7: Non-metal artefacts recovered from the cairn of Weymouth 8 (Ridgeway 7) barrow. 7. Stone mace-head; 8. Sandstone tablet; 9. Bone pommel; 10. Flint axe; 11. Bone pin; 12–16. Flint and chert scrapers (source: Drew & Piggott 1936, pl. vi. Reproduced by kind permission of Dorset Natural History and Archaeological Society)

an individual though some daggers show no evidence of burning despite being associated with cremated remains (eg, Dewlish 8, Dorset: DCM-F009) illustrating the variation in the practices (cf. Jones & Quinnell 2013). Cremation served a transformative purpose ahead of burial and at least in some cases, it was important that objects went through the same transformation as the body.

Damage, wear and curation of daggers and other objects

Six other daggers were damage-ranked 2 showing possible signs of destruction, again linked with burning and fragmentation though this was obscured by corrosion and post depositional processes (Table 3.1). Most other daggers were included in burials in a complete condition or else broken through use or corrosion. Several daggers, such as from Wall Mead II (BCMAG-F016) and Shave Hill (TTNCM-F045), both Somerset, have worn or damaged blades and damaged hilts with broken rivet holes which probably relates to weak attachments to the handle; such damage is important though as it indicates these objects saw a period of extended use (or at least use until breakage) before entering the grave (cf. Woodward & Hunter 2015, 27ff.). Other daggers show signs of preparation, sharpening and wear along their edges and when included in a grave might suggest their significance to the deceased or their role with the living. Daggers are often considered symbolic of constructing a hunter or warrior identity or else as an object for the afterlife, though they may have also been part of the burial process and included for their involvement with the performance of death (Jones & Quinnell 2013, 21). In this scenario we might recognise more about the social value of the object and its association with the deceased individual, rather than necessarily inferring its role in construction of identity. Alternatively, if used to the point of damaging the object, such as breaking the handle (whether accidentally or deliberately), we can speculate that the object may have been damaged and deliberately not repaired but retained until the death of a person, or else damaged *because* the person died. Removal of a handle may have been part of destroying the object, though if done with sufficient care and precision would leave no identifiable traces archaeologically.

The treatment of other objects and also of the buried individuals becomes important here as it can highlight relationships between different aspects of the burial process and the importance of destruction, even where daggers are seemingly complete. This can be exemplified with three dagger-associated burials from Devon (Upton Pyne, Huntshaw G.2 and Fernworthy) and one from Dorset (Winterborne St Martin G.46). At Upton Pyne (barrow 4), a corroded, yet mostly complete, knife-dagger was recovered from a clay-lined cist below cremated bones, a fragmentary bronze pin and a composite necklace (RAMM-F047; Jones & Quinnell 2013, 7–8). The cremated bones and necklace were perhaps wrapped in a skin or cloth, fastened by the pin. The necklace, made from shale and encrinite beads (and possibly one made from amber), was probably accumulated over time with new and old beads included (Sheridan 2016, 112–4); whilst it may not have been 'new', there is little to suggest the dagger was of any significant age when deposited. At Huntshaw G.2, a largely complete dagger was placed on a bed of leaves and deposited with cremated remains that may represent small amounts of multiple people, perhaps suggesting curation of multiple individuals (RAMM-F025; Jones & Quinnell 2013, 19). At Fernworthy, Lydford, a knife-dagger with a damaged hilt was found with a shale button, a flint knife and three Beaker fragments, though with no evidence of surviving human remains (Gerloff 1975, 165, no.280; Jones & Quinnell 2013, 17). The limited quantities of human remains are a curious feature of burials in Cornwall and Devon, particularly for those cremated, suggesting these were not necessarily the primary focus of mortuary practices (Jones 2005; 2011; 2012a; Wickstead 2008, 120).

In Barrow G.46 at Winterborne St Martin, a secondary interment of cremated remains was associated with a dagger and incomplete incense cup (DCM-F046). This dagger was heavily corroded and fragmented, but the remains of a burnt sheath survive, indicating that the dagger was burned and buried while complete in its sheath. This cremation was enclosed by a ring of stones within a barrow that also contained a primary crouched male interment associated with a handled ceramic bowl, as well as bones of three infants with a smaller Food Vessel (Grinsell 1959, 154). This barrow thus echoes the complexities of burial arrangements and multiple interments observed at Weymouth 8. Furthermore, in these latter two examples, we may question where the rest of the ceramic vessels are and why they were deposited incomplete. Did the missing fragments continue in circulation allowing the living to enchain themselves with the dead?

Cups and connections

Many of these burials illustrate connections between the living and the dead but some inclusions also highlight localised access to resources as well as wider networks people were a part of. These may have related to how artefacts were treated. The possibly burned and fragmented dagger from Broad Down E (Farway 32), was found with cremated human remains in a possible tree-trunk coffin in a collapsed cist under a barrow (Kirwan 1870; Jones & Quinnell 2013). About 3 feet (*c.* 1 m) away a complete shale cup was recovered, found within the barrow and deposited in relation to, but seemingly not associated with, the burial (Needham *et al.* 2006, 102–3). Another shale cup was recovered from a nearby barrow deposited above a deposit of cremated remains and burnt layers of charcoal and flint, a possible pyre site (Kirwan 1870; Needham *et al.* 2006, 101–2). The condition of the cup suggests it was added afterwards and not burned. Another possible shale cup, now lost, was found with a tree-trunk burial under a barrow at Stoborough, Dorset (Needham *et al.* 2006, 103–4). The shale derives from sources at Kimmeridge on the Isle of Purbeck, Dorset; this material was extracted and circulated across Britain by the Late Neolithic/Chalcolithic period and used to produce fine objects (Denford 2000). In Early Bronze Age south-west Britain, it probably operated as a local prestige material, obtained from craftspeople operating in central southern England (Sheridan 2016, 111).

More broadly, these cups fit within the wider tradition of precious cups produced from 1900–1700 BC and were often deposited with the dead. These cups, made from amber, shale, gold and silver, comprised part of an Early Bronze Age 'maritime interaction network' (Needham 2009, 20) across the Channel and southern North Sea. At Rillaton, Cornwall a gold cup was deposited with skeletal remains in a cist below a barrow, associated with a dagger (broken upon recovery), pottery, pieces of 'ivory' and 'glass beads' (probably faience) (Smirke 1867; Needham *et al.* 2006, 84–7; Jones & Quinnell 2013). This appears to represent an accumulation of wealth, with the objects probably deposited complete (Jones & Quinnell 2013). Although fitting within broader traditions across northern Europe, the Rillaton cup may have been a locally produced artefact derived from local sources. The gold composition aligns with Borg's (2010) geochemical sub-group A3D type. Gold artefacts of this composition have been found across Germany and Denmark and, significantly, closely matches the gold from the Nebra Sky Disc, which is thought to derive from Cornish sources (Borg 2010; 2019, fig. 2, 40–1, 53–4). The Rillaton cup could therefore represent a rare example of gold that was extracted and deposited in Cornwall at a time when much gold was circulated further afield: this would have enhanced the social value of the object.

The final site to mention is the famous Clandon barrow, Dorset (Needham & Woodward 2008). Here, an amber cup was found in fragments, scattered amongst a flint cairn under a barrow; it may have been deliberately broken prior to deposition and it too was probably locally manufactured (*ibid.*, 31). A fragmented, possibly crushed, collared urn was found in the barrow, as well as fragments an accessory vessel, also scattered, though below the cairn (Cunnington in Drew & Piggott 1936, 19–20; Needham *et al.* 2006, 96). Fragments of a dagger were also recovered, though surviving pieces of the sheath suggest the dagger was probably deposited complete. The other objects, including a gold lozenge plaque cover and a jet macehead with gold-covered shale studs, were included complete. No evidence for human remains survived. Analysis of the artefacts deposited highlighted the diverse connections expressed by the Clandon Barrow material, assembled from networks that reached across the Channel to continental Europe and around Britain and Ireland (Needham & Woodward 2008). These materials and objects expressed cosmological significance, which may have motivated the decision to bury this material (*ibid.*). As Jones (2012b, 134) has argued, this assemblage 'articulates and performs a series of foreign connections and links'. The decision to treat them in certain ways adds to this dimension. Breaking the finely crafted amber cup, one of only two so far known in northern Europe, would surely have been a powerful, socially charged act, which contrasted with the treatment of other precious cups deposited in south-west Britain, which were generally deposited complete, sometimes after cremation events. Similarly, crushing or fragmenting and scattering the ceramic vessels, before and after constructing the cairn and barrow may represent layers of social interactions with this monument.

Differences in death

Overall, these burials exemplify individual elements of performance and ceremony associated with mortuary practices, with the objects accumulated and treated in particular ways. The burnt daggers presented above can be linked with cremation of the bodies with which they were associated; cremation offered a means not only of destroying the body but also the equipment that accompanied the individual on the funerary pyre (McKinley 1997, 130). The surviving archaeological record largely omits macroscopic indicators of burning on bronzes, or else destroys other associated materials, but the small dataset presented here shows that burning is occasionally observable and speaks to the transformative role fire occasionally played for making both the body and the artefacts suitable for burial. Moreover, we can envisage the sensory aspects of this occasion: cremation was an emotive and evocative process with fire contributing to the experience (Downes 1999; Wright 2021).

Fragmentation also played a role and unburnt broken objects highlight that different modes of destruction were appropriate at different times. Differences in wear, damage and the way burials were constructed offer us glimpses into the complexities of funerary practices. At Upton Pyne, the necklace, potentially an heirloom, may have symbolised connections that the deceased had in life; the cremation of multiple people buried together with the

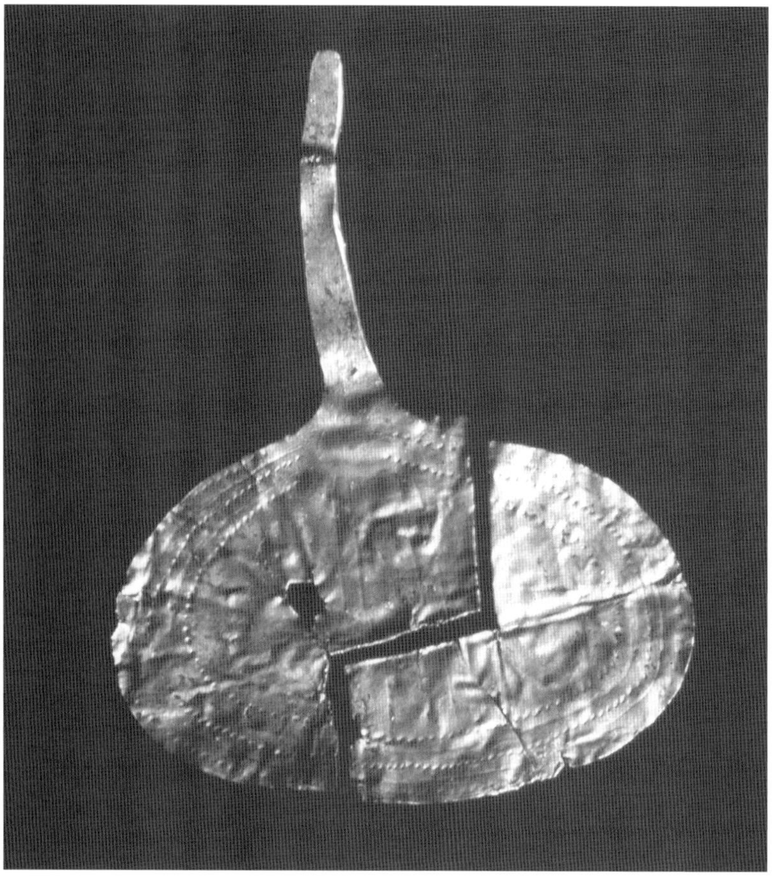

Figure 3.8: The basket ornament from Stogursey, Somerset (PAS-F253) © Trustees of the British Museum

dagger at Huntshaw infers aspects of social entanglement; and the individual components of different objects at Fernworthy (a single button, fragments of an incomplete Beaker) may serve to represent more complete objects, a *pars pro toto* practice. In support of this latter point, we can consider a burial from Boscawen-un, Cornwall, where rivets, but no dagger, were seemingly deposited in a barrow with cremated bone, suggesting this object was dismantled (Borlase 1872, 219; Jones & Quinnell 2013, 16). Jones and Quinnell (2013, 19) have particularly highlighted differences in wear across different objects within burials to suggest varying object biographies and by extension their varying relationships with people (both living and dead) prior to deposition (cf. Brück 2019, 71–90). The ways in which precious cups were treated similarly connected practices in south-west Britain to wider networks. This can be extended to the different treatments of the deceased individuals, and the repeated reopening and re-engagement with burial monuments over time. All of this related to perceived identities of the deceased and the associated social conventions surrounding mortuary practices.

Rolled gold

In 1999, a sheet gold basket ornament was found while metal-detecting at Stogursey, Somerset (Fig. 3.8; PAS-F253; Needham 2000b). The ornament was rolled tightly into five layers before deposition with the tang wrapped around the body or 'basket'. It was unrolled after recovery revealing punched dot decoration and a pressed groove adorning the circumference of the object. Additionally, there are the remains of creases adjacent to the direction in which it was rolled suggesting it may have previously been folded. The object has broken into pieces at two right angles splitting across weaknesses caused by the creasing. The ornament probably dates to the Chalcolithic period, *c.* 2450–2200/2150 BC, making it not only the earliest evidence of metalwork destruction in south-west Britain, but also one of the earliest deposits of metalwork from the region. Moreover, it fits into the broader tradition of basket ornaments produced around this time.

Basket ornaments are typically found in pairs and with burials (Needham 2011, 131–3) and over twenty examples are now known from 14 sites in Britain (following Needham 2011; Needham & Sheridan 2014; PAS data), though the Stogursey example is the only one currently known from south-west Britain. Although many were deposited in a 'rolled' state, giving them their distinctive basket shape, several basket ornaments were deliberately manipulated and/or damaged prior to deposition. One of the two ornaments found with the Amesbury Archer burial, Wiltshire, was 'severely crushed' and the tang had broken off (Needham 2011, 130). Single finds from the parish of Calbourne, Isle of Wight, and the Cholsey area, Oxfordshire, were both found crushed and folded (Basford 2005; Byard 2012) and a pair from Whitchurch, Hampshire, were found folded one inside another (Byard 2015a). These examples strengthen the idea that the Stogursey ornament had previously been folded.

The deliberate deformation of sheet gold objects has been observed relatively frequently during the later 3rd millennium BC. Gold lunulae, for example, although generally deposited complete, were occasionally rolled prior to or upon deposition. Mary Cahill (2005) noted 16 examples deposited in Ireland that showed signs of rolling or folding, and at least two further examples are known from Scotland, from Orbliston, Moray, and Auchentaggart, Dumfries and Galloway; the former was 'closely rolled up as a scroll' (Paton 1870, 32) and the latter was 'folded together and rolled up almost like a ball' (Gilchrist Clark 1880, 222). Of the five surviving lunulae from south-west Britain, none of the four from Cornwall shows signs of deformation (Mattingly *et al.* 2009), though Cahill (forthcoming) has suggested the example from Tarrant Valley, Dorset (PAS-F145), shows signs of folding. This remains uncertain as the lunula had also suffered plough damage, which seemingly fragmented it into three pieces, but of the two smaller fragments, one is folded and the other is twisted and distorted, which may represent deliberate manipulation.

Figure 3.9: The rolled gold band from Tom Tivey's Hole, Somerset (BCMAG-F014) © Bristol Culture (Bristol Museum & Art Gallery) Acc. no. F4290

Other gold objects were also folded or rolled. Neil Carlin (2018, 189) highlights that some gold discs (so-called 'sun discs') in Ireland show signs of folding similar to that seen on lunulae. A rolled clipped gold band from Tom Tivey's hole, Somerset (Fig. 3.9; BCMAG-F014), can be paralleled with examples associated with Beaker burials in France and Iberia and three additional sites in Britain: Pendleton, Lancashire; Kingsmead Quarry, Berkshire; and Chilbolton, Hampshire (Taylor 1994, 51–3; Barrowclough 2014; Wessex Archaeology 2014). Single finds of rolled gold bands were also found at Little Baddow, Essex (Richardson 2017) and Berwick St Leonard, Wiltshire (Smither 2020).

Gold objects are typically assumed to have held a 'personal' element, which is certainly supported by the numerous associations of pairs of basket ornaments with burials. The death of an individual may have necessitated a destruction of their possessions, or objects linked with them. The deliberate deformation of sheet gold objects was also quite an intimate process, certainly for these fragile ornaments. Folding and rolling is a practice that required care, skill and attention, and it seems to have been repeatedly undertaken in some cases. It may be that folding or crushing basket ornaments served as a metaphor for the ending of an individual's life (cf. Brück 2006a). However, many deformed gold objects were not found with individuals; this included the Stogursey ornament and extends to the lunulae and other sheet goldwork. The removal of these objects from circulation by burying them and the dis-association from their owner(s) may have been a physical expression of severed ties between individuals and objects. Alternatively, such objects may have been communal symbols, considered inappropriate for graves and thus deposited in landscapes relevant to communities (cf. Carlin 2018, 207–8).[2] Objects, such as lunulae, may have expressed certain rites, relationships, or life stages and if any of these ceased to be relevant it was necessary to remove this object from circulation. However, the form of destruction discussed is more complex than, for instance, the burning of daggers, because some of these gold ornaments could (and probably were) unrolled or unfolded. In this sense, deformation placed the objects into a suspended state where they could not have functioned for their original purpose, but such transitory destruction could be reversed should the occasion arise. Of course, those we find archaeologically represent instances where destruction and deposition were the final acts, and crushed examples indicate the damage was never intended to be reversed. Deliberate deformation and removal of functionality emphasised that the object(s) no longer served its original purpose, or that any object-person relationship had ended at that moment.

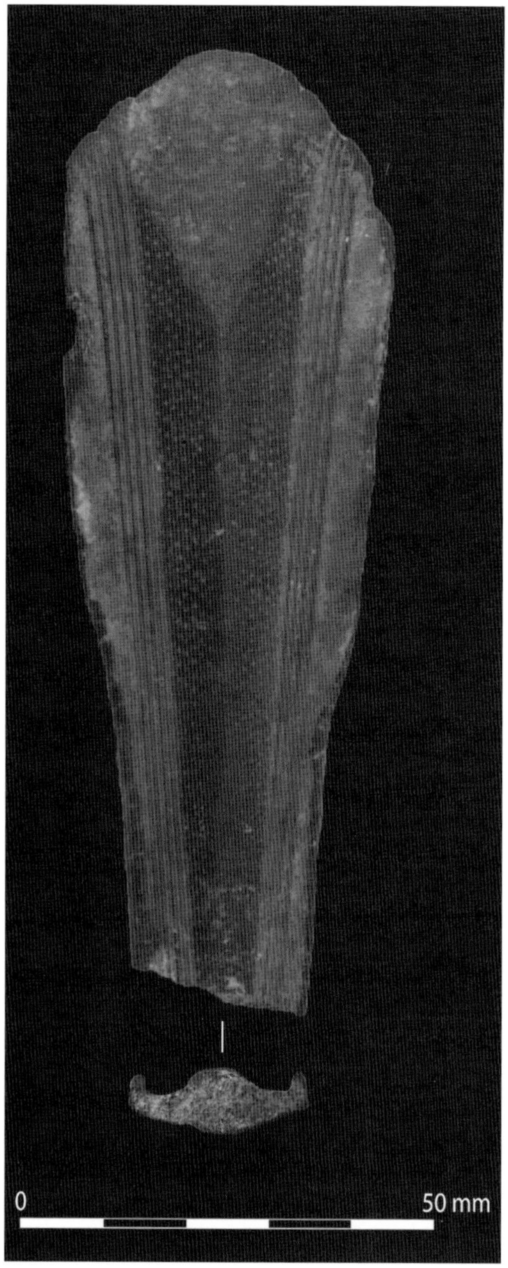

Figure 3.10: A reworked Early Bronze Age dagger from Gussage St Michael 2 South IV (PRIV-F024) (photo: author, courtesy of Martin Green)

Beyond breaking point

Some damaged or broken objects clearly continued in circulation post-damage. A broken Camerton-Snowshill dagger recovered from Gussage St Michael, Dorset (PRIV-F024), was reworked into what appears to be a flanged axehead form (Fig. 3.10). The dagger broke across the lower blade in antiquity; towards this end the dagger edges have been hammered up on one face to form low flanges. Additionally, the hilt end has been hammered and ground, removing the original shape and creating an uneven crescentic edge; this suggests the dagger piece was worked into a makeshift axe or chisel.

A dense concentration of Late Bronze Age and Early Iron Age metalwork has been found around Gussage St Michael, with the dagger representing one of the few pieces dating to the Early Bronze Age. Early Bronze Age barrows are known from the nearby area and the dagger is in keeping with what one might expect to be deposited in a funerary context. The dagger may thus represent an object reworked following breakage, or else a rediscovered deposit that was reworked, either during the Early Bronze Age or perhaps even as late as the Late Bronze Age. Earlier, rather than later, reworking is perhaps more probable as flanged axeheads were contemporary with this type of dagger and a fragment of one was found nearby (PRIV-F012). Regardless, it suggests that the original role of the dagger (usually accompanying the dead) was no longer remembered, recognised or considered important at the time of reshaping. Reworking the dagger also reworked its social role and in the process new relationships between people and objects were formed.

Individual flat axeheads found while metal-detecting in Landulph, Madron and Perranzabuloe, all Cornwall (PAS-F011; PAS-F013; RCM-F031), broke across the body in antiquity (Fig. 3.11). Casting flaws on the Landulph axehead suggest the break was accidental, perhaps through use, whilst the Madron axehead may have broken while incising grooved decoration. The cutting edges and breaking points on both axeheads are worn suggesting they potentially continued in use or circulation after breakage. Moyler's (2007) fragmentation experiments demonstrated that flat axeheads are difficult to break and consequently it may have been significant when material failure did occur. Metallographic analysis of the Perranzabuloe axehead showed it had been worked and annealed and the cutting edge is now blunt and chipped (Northover in Tyacke 2007). The butt broke off in antiquity, probably by accident, but it has been significantly reworked through extensive hammering on the end causing material displacement and some bending towards the butt (*c.* 10 degrees) (Fig. 3.11c). The extent of this deformation may even indicate the axehead was reused as a hammerhead.[3] The recurrence of broken axeheads is explored further below,

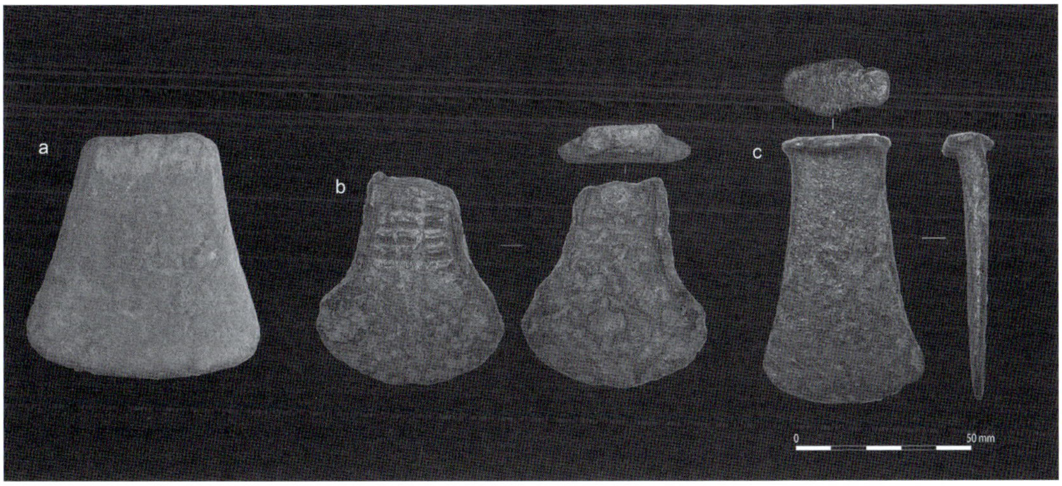

Figure 3.11: Broken Early Bronze Age axeheads from a) Landulph (PAS-F011); b) Madron I (PAS-F013); c) Perranzabuloe I (RCM-F031) (a: adapted image courtesy of the PAS/Trustees of the British Museum; b and c: author's photos courtesy of Royal Institution of Cornwall)

but clearly the breakage and damage did not always mean objects ceased to have a practical, or indeed symbolic, function. Instead, damage may have transformed their use.

This theory is supported by other evidence of object curation and the possibility of heirlooms. Amongst other criteria, Ann Woodward and John Hunter (2015, 472–3) suggest that heirloom objects might be recognised through their state of extensive wear and fragmentation, especially when compared with other objects within an assemblage. They identify worn and ancient breaks across Early Bronze Age grave goods in Britain including dagger pommels, belt and pulley rings, jet buttons and bone pins, which may all have continued in use or been retained for a period after the initial damage was sustained prior to deposition. At Mount Pleasant Henge, Dorset, it seems Beaker sherds were deliberately selected and accumulated for deposition in ditches (Woodward 2002), and analysis of the crutch-headed bone pin from Green Barrow, Somerset, indicated that it continued in use after breakage (Woodward & Hunter 2015, 177). This is not to imply that all broken objects held significance; rather it emphasises that breakage did not always diminish the importance of an object nor necessitated its immediate disposal. This is easier to interpret in funerary contexts where the extended wear of an object can be compared with the treatment of the deceased and other associated objects, but perhaps extended to single finds. Axeheads were rarely buried in graves in Britain (Needham 1988) so the exclusion of even worn and well-used forms accords with contemporary ideas about what was appropriate to bury with the deceased. Even if an object obtained significance to an individual over a long use-life, there were still certain social conventions about how it should be deposited. Regardless of context, worn and damaged objects continued to hold significance and importance to the individuals who owned them. As we shall see in the following chapter, this continued into the Middle Bronze Age.

Complete and incomplete axeheads

Overwhelmingly the metal objects most frequently deposited during the Chalcolithic and Early Bronze Age were axeheads (Needham 1983; 1988). This is unsurprising given the axe was already an established and useful object form across Neolithic Europe, with functional and symbolic meaning to societies; we can see the production and treatment of metal axes as a continuation of previous practices (Crellin 2020, 199f.). What is striking is that clear evidence for their deliberate destruction is completely lacking in Chalcolithic and Early Bronze Age south-west Britain, and indeed many other parts of Britain and Ireland (Needham 1983; Becker 2013), even though they were the most numerous metal objects deposited. Here we should be conscious of the timeframe under study, with the earliest axeheads around 2450 BC made from copper and almost certainly in circulation alongside some stone axeheads. Most examples studied here, albeit numbering few, showed signs of use, which accords with Rachel Crellin's wider study of copper axeheads from Britain which found they were often heavily used prior to deposition (2020, 213). However, due to the softness of copper it is unclear how long these axeheads were utilised as tools; an intensive period of use could have quickly reduced the functionality of the axe (Kienlin & Ottaway 1998). Limited signs of reworking or resharpening were observed on Chalcolithic axeheads from south-west Britain – again paralleling Crellin's results – and it is possible that there was limited understanding of how metal behaved, particularly in terms of recycling and recasting. This is supported by chemical analyses of early metal axeheads in Britain and Ireland that suggest that the very earliest copper/copper-alloy axeheads were often not recycled and metalworking skills and techniques took time to develop and refine (Bray 2012, 62–7; Crellin 2020, 213–4). All copper axeheads studied here, and indeed many later Early Bronze Age bronze axeheads, were deposited complete, suggesting that at least some of these early axeheads warranted deposition before they had ceased being potentially usable tools.

Studies of Neolithic stone axeheads reveal the complex ways these were deposited; they were often buried complete, used and as single objects (Edmonds 1995, 133; Walker 2018). The treatment of early metal forms broadly mirrors and probably continued established perceptions and appropriate depositional practices for axeheads. Edmonds (1995, 132–3) describes how processes of deliberate deposition and occasionally destruction of stone tools were communal performative events that served social functions, and copper/copper-alloy axeheads probably fulfilled similar roles, though they are only infrequently included in Chalcolithic–Early Bronze Age structured deposits. The wrapped example from Weymouth 8 is one of only a few deposited in a funerary context in Britain, though dates to the early 2nd millennium BC so it is unlikely this practice represented a continuation of Neolithic actions. Nonetheless, the remains of textiles adhering to the surface of the axehead indicates the care taken when depositing it.

From *c.* 2000 BC, axeheads were more widely produced, with greater variation in the forms and decoration, suggesting greater processes of individualising objects, perhaps linking them to certain people, places or traditions. Single deposits remained most common in south-west Britain, though hoards deposited 1700–1500 BC, such as those from Pilsdon, Dorset (DCM-F029), Trenovissick, Cornwall (RCM-F047), and Plymstock, Devon (BM-F006/RAMM-F039), demonstrate the importance of selecting and collecting complete axeheads, and sometimes spearheads and daggers, for deposition. These also fit within wider traditions along the southern British coast at this time (Needham *et al.* 2006, 78–9, fig. 38). Most notably, the Plymstock hoard contained 22 objects, including 16 complete and one incomplete flanged axeheads, three daggers, a tanged spearhead and a chisel/punch, and was deposited *c.* 1600–1500 BC under a heavy stone slab overlooking the River Plym estuary (Hawkes & Smith 1955, GB.9). The Plymstock axeheads encompass a range of sizes and were almost all complete when deposited; each seemed to be from an individual model or mould, individually worked after casting, and none appeared to be extensively used or worn. These were not objects that had exceeded their functional usefulness. By contrast, all three of the associated daggers had damaged hilts that would have prevented attaching a handle; the spearhead was also damaged with a broken tip and tang and bent and cracked along the blade. The act of gathering this diverse group of material, which would have required time and energy to coordinate, as well as the effort and spectacle of sealing the deposit with a large stone slab, implies the significance of the event. The objects within the hoard, much like those gathered for burial deposits, probably had a variety of pre-depositional functions in relation to the individuals/communities who owned them. There is a noticeable contrast between including complete usable axeheads alongside damaged blades in this deposit. We can observe and speculate that selecting and burying these objects in these varied conditions had greater value than keeping and maintaining usable objects in circulation.

The place in which such deposits were made was probably also significant. Like the Plymstock hoard, single finds of axeheads from Hengistbury Head (RHMG-F003), Padstow (PAS-F021b) and Smallmouth (DCM-F032) were also deposited at river estuaries or on coastlines, whilst other finds were deposited close to headwaters (eg, Kentisbeare: RAMM-F026), on hilltops (eg, Landulph: PAS-F011) or in bogs (eg, Glastonbury Turbaries: TTNCM-F054m). Deposition in these cases was undertaken in relation to aspects of the inhabited landscape and through these various examples, we can observe that much like their stone predecessors, metal axeheads also served a symbolic function in deposition linked to certain natural places.

Although most axeheads were deposited complete, 16 incomplete axeheads broken across the body were studied, either surviving as a fragment of the butt end, or as the lower blade and cutting edge (eg, Fig. 3.11). None shows macroscopic evidence of damage associated with breakage, such as hammer marks or chisel marks, meaning it would be inappropriate to consider them the result of intentional fragmentation. Indeed, some can be more confidently linked with use-related breakage, such as the axehead from Landulph. Others are less clear though, with few macroscopic indicators of poor casting or limited signs of use. Could some of these be the result of deliberate fragmentation? In support of this idea, we can consider that the heated fragmentation of an axehead would have been a relatively achievable task, certainly performed for recycling purposes. Elsewhere in Britain the deliberate fragmentation of Early Bronze Age axeheads prior to deposition was occasionally undertaken, most notably in parts of Scotland (O'Connor 1999, 181). Furthermore, a survey of Early Bronze Age axeheads reported in England and Wales through the Portable Antiquities Scheme identified 57 broken and incomplete flat and flanged axeheads out of the 266 recorded with images.[4] However, we currently lack experiments involving Early Bronze Age axeheads that might demonstrate what material failure through use would look like. Further investigations are clearly needed to conclusively understand the nature of this damage. Nonetheless, the practice of depositing incomplete axeheads is more widespread than has previously been recognised.

As observed elsewhere (eg, Crellin 2020, 187–224), the deposition of Chalcolithic and Early Bronze Age axeheads played a variety of roles in south-west Britain that transformed over time. The deposition of incomplete axeheads, whether accidentally or intentionally broken, seems to have been rare (though evidence is growing), with the emphasis on burying complete examples. However, the great majority were used prior to deposition and from this we may suggest that the history of the object, how it was used and who had owned it, may have contributed to how, where and why it was deposited.

Conclusions

Few Chalcolithic and Early Bronze Age metal objects in south-west Britain indicate conclusive evidence for deliberate destruction. Where it can be observed, it was most commonly daggers linked with the death of an individual. This was something that occurred infrequently and, of the case studies presented, all occurred after 2000 BC. This all suggests that destruction was the exception, not the rule. In some cases, the treatment of the body and objects was paralleled, ie, both were burned, and in others there were differences. Above everything else this reflects the complex nature of funerary practices. The destruction of objects was one part of a wider set of actions, which involved the construction of and engagement with the burial monument, the selection, gathering and treatment of various objects and the burial of the body, whether cremated or not. We can thus see destruction as part of a decision-making process that was linked to other social conventions and changes, probably influenced by the relationship between the objects, the deceased and the communities who were undertaking the burial ceremony.

As we have seen, the treatment of different objects before burial in a grave was in part linked to the history and connections of the objects, often indicated by their state of wear. Where these objects were deposited with people, it becomes easier to interpret their social significance, but even single unassociated finds may have functioned similarly. Several objects have been highlighted that were accidentally damaged or broken, but seemingly continued in circulation after their functional usefulness had ended. This was most notable for axehead fragments, which were then deposited in isolated circumstances, dis-associated from individuals, as was the custom for these objects. Importantly, the damage sustained did not make these objects null and void.

Of course, the incomplete objects form only a small part of the metalwork deposited during the Chalcolithic and Early Bronze Age. By far, the most important thing was depositing complete, undamaged objects, sometimes used, sometimes unused. It is only in the later periods that destruction of metalwork became more common.

Notes

1 Gerloff 1975, nos 45, 143, 201, 204, 209, 254, 289, 292, 303, 338.

2 I am grateful to Andy M. Jones for raising this point.

3 Many thanks to one of my reviewers for raising this interesting idea.

4 This follows a search of the Portable Antiquities Scheme online database (www.finds.org.uk) conducted on 02/12/2020 using the combined search terms 'Bronze Age' and 'flat axehead'.

4

Selective destruction: the Middle Bronze Age, *c.* 1500–1150 BC

From *c.* 1500 BC onwards, the production, use and deposition of weapons, ornaments, and tools across Britain increased. The majority were buried in hoards and as single finds or occasionally within occupational contexts; the association of metalwork with human remains and burial monuments that was prevalent in the earlier part of the 2nd millennium BC largely ceased, reflecting broader shifts in burial traditions towards cremation as the main mortuary rite, usually with no or few grave goods associated (Caswell & Roberts 2018).

In south-west Britain, we can clearly observe the changing practices relating to metalwork deposition over time (Fig. 4.1). No hoards from south-west Britain date to the Acton Park metalworking assemblage, aligning with much of the rest of the country (Needham *et al.* 1997, 56), but the deposition of two or more objects became increasingly widespread from *c.* 1400 BC. It is this shift towards hoarding that accounts for the sudden increase in metal objects recovered archaeologically and we may link this to broader social

Figure 4.1: Findspots of Middle Bronze Age metalwork from south-west Britain. Those marked with stars were studied as part of this research. Contains OS data © Crown copyright and database right 2021

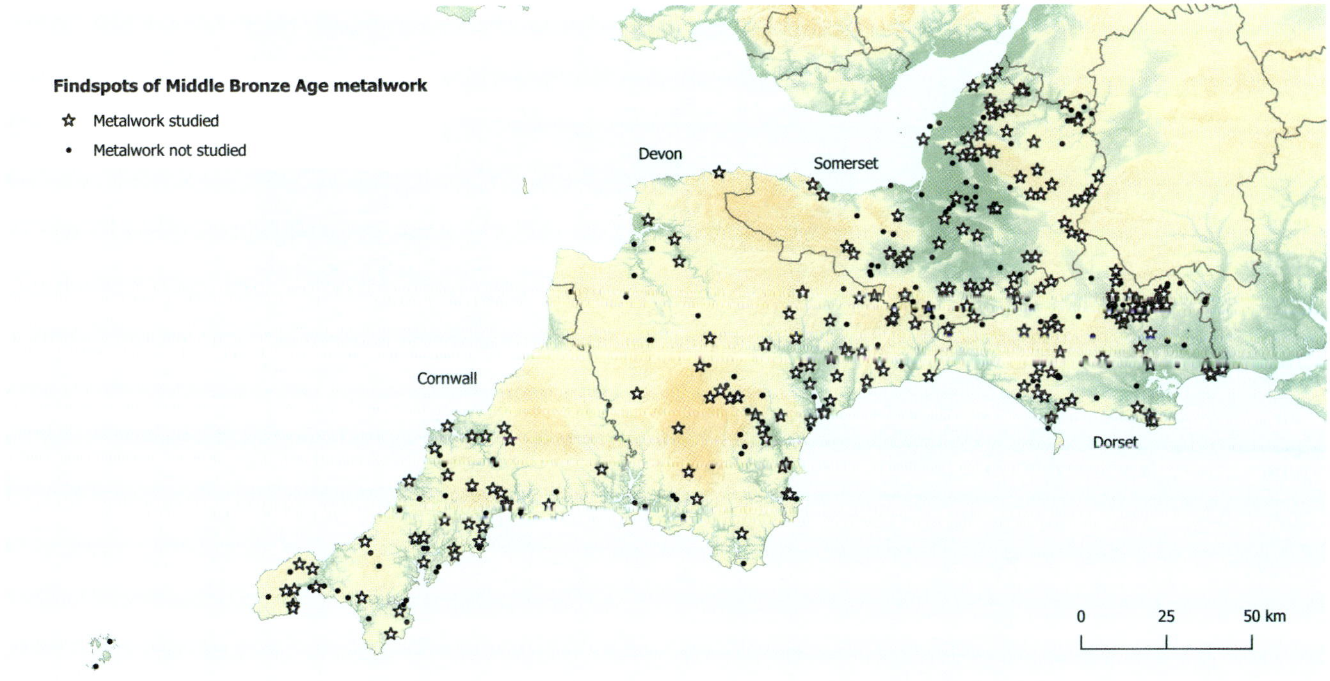

Figure 4.2: Frequency of Destruction Indicators recorded on the Middle Bronze Age metalwork studied (n=91)

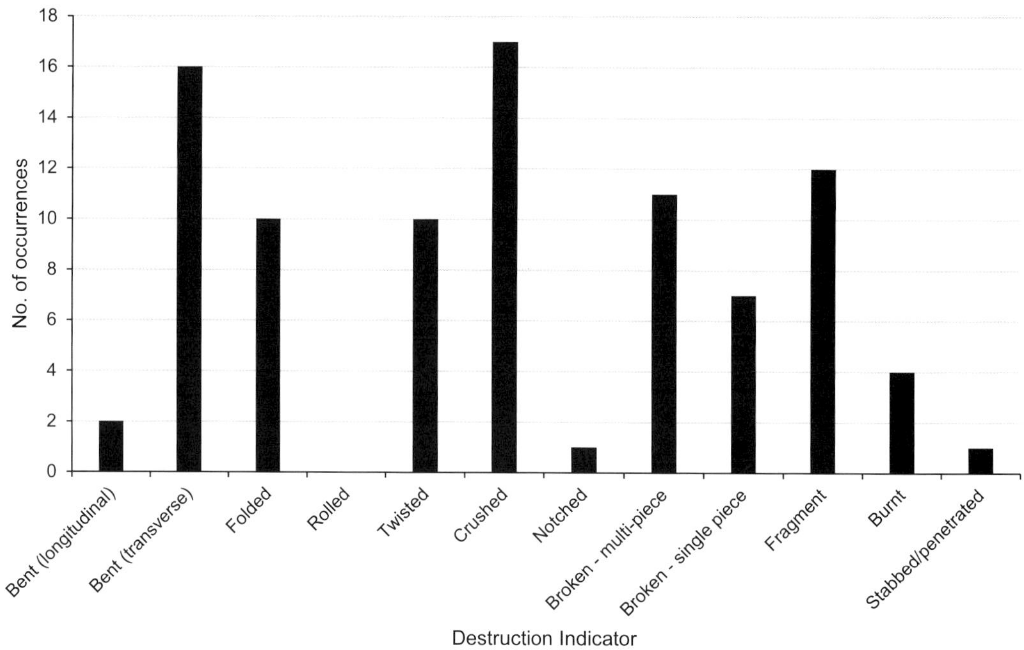

Figure 4.3: Proportional representation of Middle Bronze Age metalwork with (Y) and without (N) signs of deliberate damage (n = 433 copper-alloy objects and 35 gold objects)

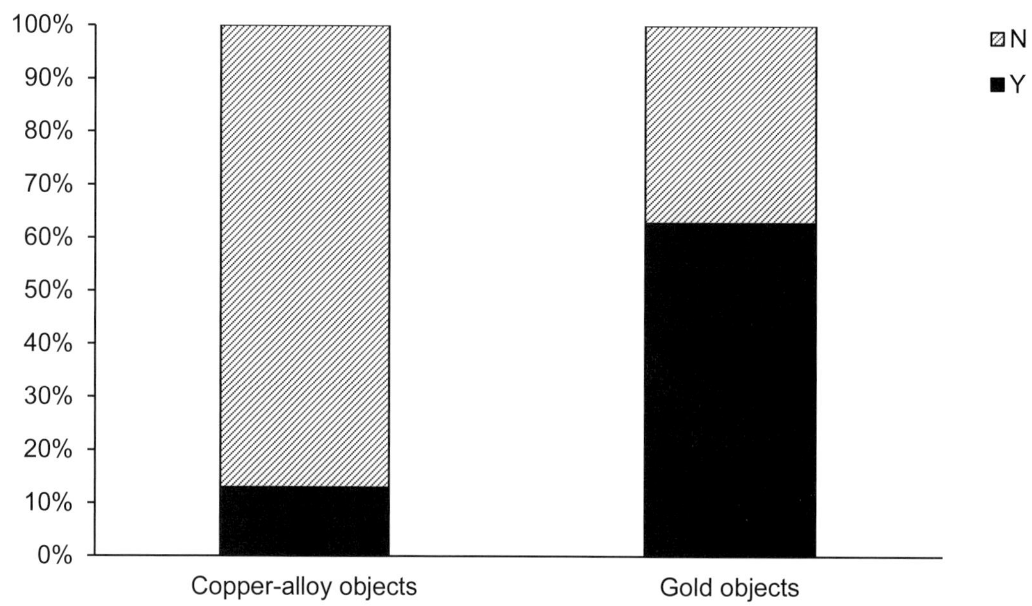

changes and connections. Hoards of palstaves and ornaments reflect connections across the Channel with France (O'Connor 1980; O'Connor *et al.* 2017; Nordez 2019) and although the Great Orme mine in Wales was a key supplier of copper between 1600–1400 BC, links with Continental sources became the norm by *c.* 1400 BC (Northover 1982b; Rohl & Needham 1998; Williams & le Carlier de Veslud 2019). The possible shipwreck assemblages at Salcombe Bay attest that material was coming in and/or out of the South West by *c.* 1275 BC at the latest (Needham *et al.* 2013).

Recognisable occupational contexts (including pit clusters, field systems, single farmsteads and 'villages') became more common from *c.* 1750 BC onwards, with relative conformity in settlement patterns seen in both southern Britain and northern France (Needham 2009; Brück & Fokkens 2013; Mordant 2013; Roberts 2013). Although broadly similar, there were regional differences in settlement organisation across south-west Britain. Circular structures, sometimes grouped in 'villages', and accompanied by granaries, ponds and fences, developed in Dorset and Wiltshire during this period (Fitzpatrick 2007, 117–8) whilst various stone structures and reave systems were built alongside roundhouses on the granite uplands of Devon and Cornwall (Johnson 1980; Fleming 1988; 2007). Hollow-set roundhouses in the Cornwall lowlands indicate a regional variation of a broader structural form; around twenty such structures are currently known (Jones & Quinnell 2011, 217–8; Jones 2015, 178; Andy M. Jones pers.comm.). In Somerset, however, evidence of occupational activity is largely limited to small enclosures, artefact scatters, ditches and pits (Fitzpatrick 2007, 118; Davies & Webley 2020, 50). These spaces provided specific arenas for deposition of the range of materials, including metalwork and metalworking debris.

Alongside these various changes, deliberately damaged objects were increasingly deposited, especially in comparison to the Chalcolithic–Early Bronze Age period (Fig. 2.27). Breakage, fragmentation, transverse bending, and crushing were the most recognised destruction indicators on Middle Bronze Age metalwork (Fig. 4.2). All seventeen crushed objects were from the Priddy hoard, Somerset (see below), but the remaining indicators were present on various objects and from different contexts and in combinations with other indicators. However, it remained most appropriate to deposit objects in largely complete conditions: of those studied, only *c.* 17% could be damage-ranked 2 or 3 (Figs 4.3, 4.4) with weapons and

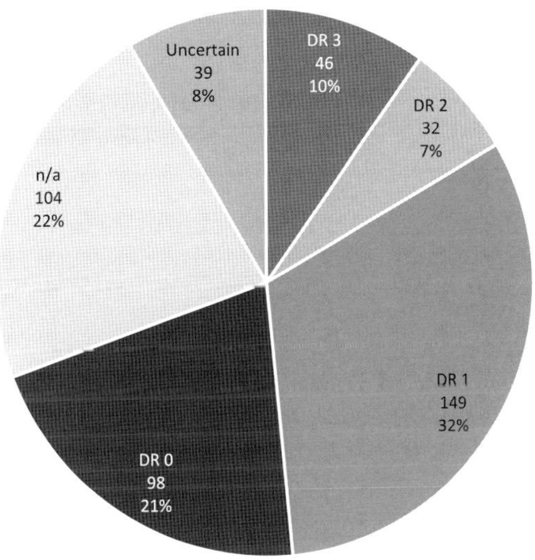

Figure 4.4: Relative proportions of Middle Bronze Age metal objects studied within each damage ranking (n=468). Each object was recorded only once, within the highest damage ranking taking precedent.

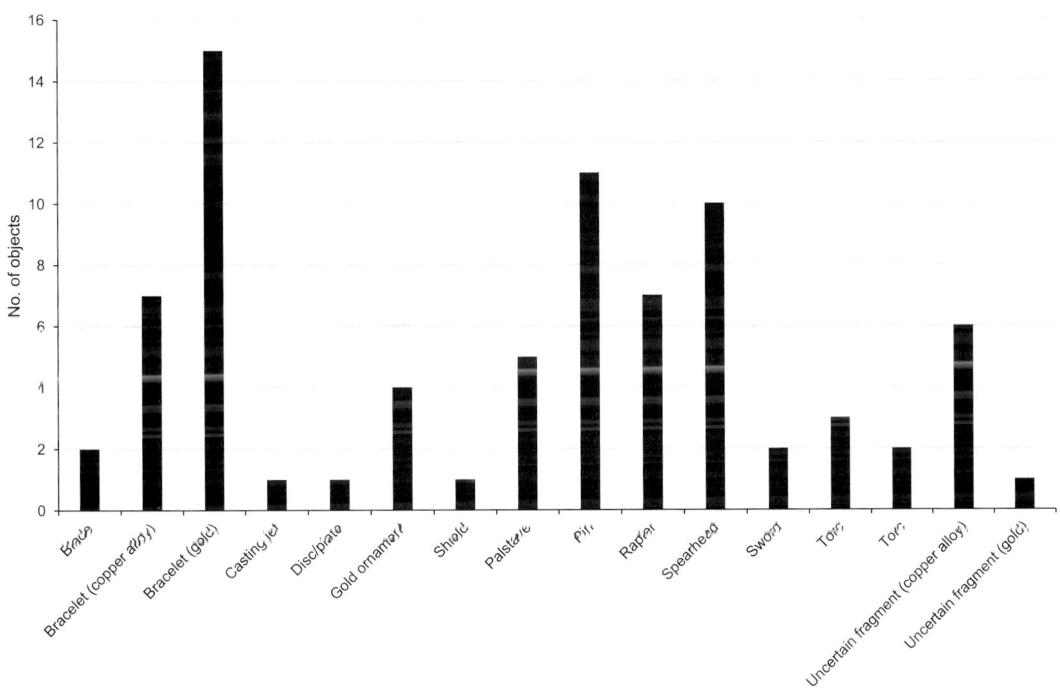

Figure 4.5: Object types showing signs of deliberate destruction (n=78)

ornaments most commonly presenting signs of intentional damage (Fig. 4.5).

That it became more appropriate to destroy objects during the Middle Bronze Age is not a new observation (eg, York 2002). However, there were nuances and selectivity to these practices, and this was related as much to the different types of objects being deposited as it did to individual object histories, contexts and regionalised ideologies. In this chapter I will pull out key objects and metalwork hoards from south-west Britain where destructive practices were associated with deposition, as well as considering the deposition of complete objects, such as palstaves, and the destruction and deposition of a range of materials in occupational contexts to highlight how we can recognise these practices as an expression of how people, objects, and places were related.

Ornaments and ornament hoards

The Middle Bronze Age was a period of increased production of copper-alloy and gold ornaments across Britain and these were deposited in various ways. In south-west Britain, ornaments, including torcs, bracelets and pins, most commonly displayed signs of deliberate damage, with 43 of the 104 artefacts studied damage-ranked 2 or 3. This included single finds as well as a significant proportion deposited in select hoards.

Ornament deposition has traditionally been studied through the lens of the 'ornament horizon', defined by Smith (1959a), encompassing the practice of depositing bronze and gold ornaments in hoards with tools and occasionally weapons in southern Britain. Recent studies have highlighted the chronological distinction within this 'horizon': hoards containing copper-alloy ornaments are a commoner feature of the Taunton metalworking assemblage in southern England (1400–1275 BC), whilst gold ornaments tend to feature across Britain during the Penard metalworking assemblage (1275–1150 BC) (Roberts 2007; Needham 2017; O'Connor *et al.* 2017; Wilkin 2017). Twenty-five ornament hoards are currently known from the South West, with the majority from Somerset and Dorset, often including tools such as palstaves (Fig. 4.6). Seventeen further hoards are known from the neighbouring counties (Gloucestershire, Hampshire and Wiltshire) (following Wilkin 2017, appendix 2), indicating a broader depositional tradition that aligns the communities of Somerset and Dorset closer with southern central England, rather than western end of the peninsula. This suggests regionalised approaches to deposition and the treatment of objects at play. This hoarding of ornaments is particularly relevant as many ornament hoards show signs of deliberate manipulation and organisation of objects, which included not only bending, crushing and fragmenting, but also threading, nesting, looping and complex spatial arrangements (Wilkin 2017, 29–34).

Indeed, of the south-western ornaments damage-ranked 2 or 3, 31 were from the hoards from Taunton Union Workhouse (TTNCM-F053) and Priddy (TTNCM-F040), both Somerset, and we can use these as a basis for exploring how destroying and depositing ornaments allowed people to manage their relationships. These hoards are of two distinctively different characters and belong respectively to the Taunton and Penard assemblages, thus each fitting within the broader chronological traditions. Here I consider these hoards in greater detail and highlight how destructive actions against ornaments may have helped manage identities and express social agencies in different ways.

The Taunton Union Workhouse hoard, Somerset (TTNCM-F053)

In 1877, a hoard of approximately 40 objects was recovered during work at the Taunton Union Workhouse (Fig. 4.7; Table 4.1; Pring 1880; Smith 1959b, GB.43). The hoard contained complete and incomplete objects largely consisting of palstaves and pins. Other object types were represented by singular inclusions (eg, a spearhead, socketed hammer, two sickles, and a bracelet). It is the largest hoard dating to the Taunton assemblage (1400–1275 BC) in south-west Britain and one of the largest in southern Britain. All damage rankings and seven destruction indicators are represented within this hoard; these objects were treated in a variety of ways.

Destruction of the objects

Fourteen objects were deliberately destroyed, and two were damage-ranked 2. An incomplete spearhead was probably deliberately hot-short, separating the blade and the socket (Fig. 4.8).

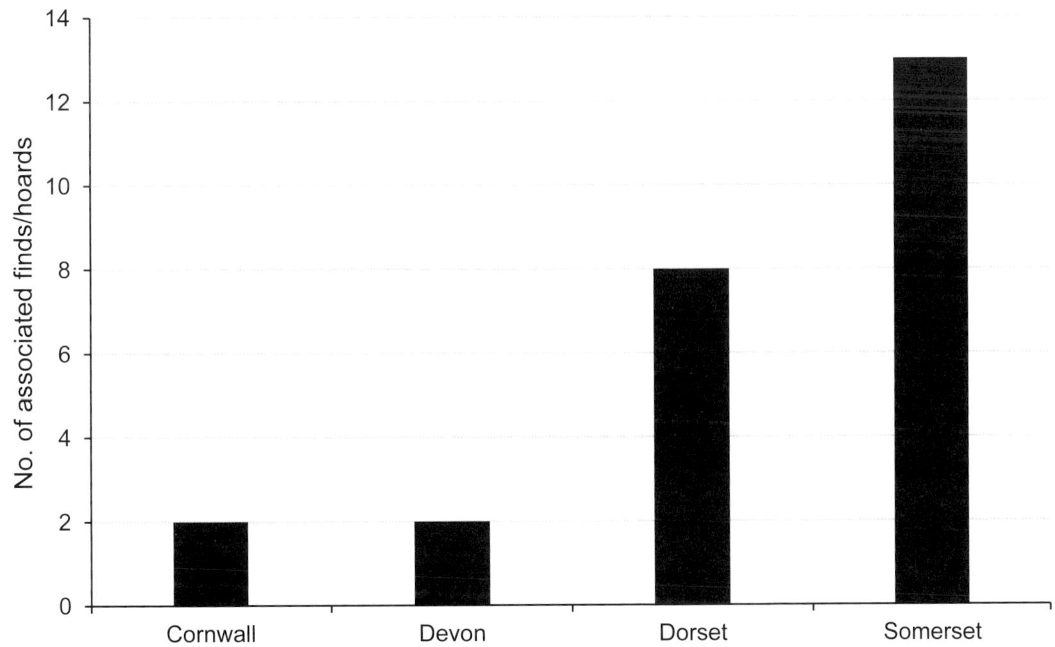

Figure 4.6: Number of Middle Bronze Age ornament/ornament-dominant hoards from south-west Britain (n=25)

Figure 4.7: Objects from the Taunton Union Workhouse hoard (photo: author, courtesy of Somerset Archaeological and Natural History Society and South West Heritage Trust, acc. nos TTNCM 36A-45B)

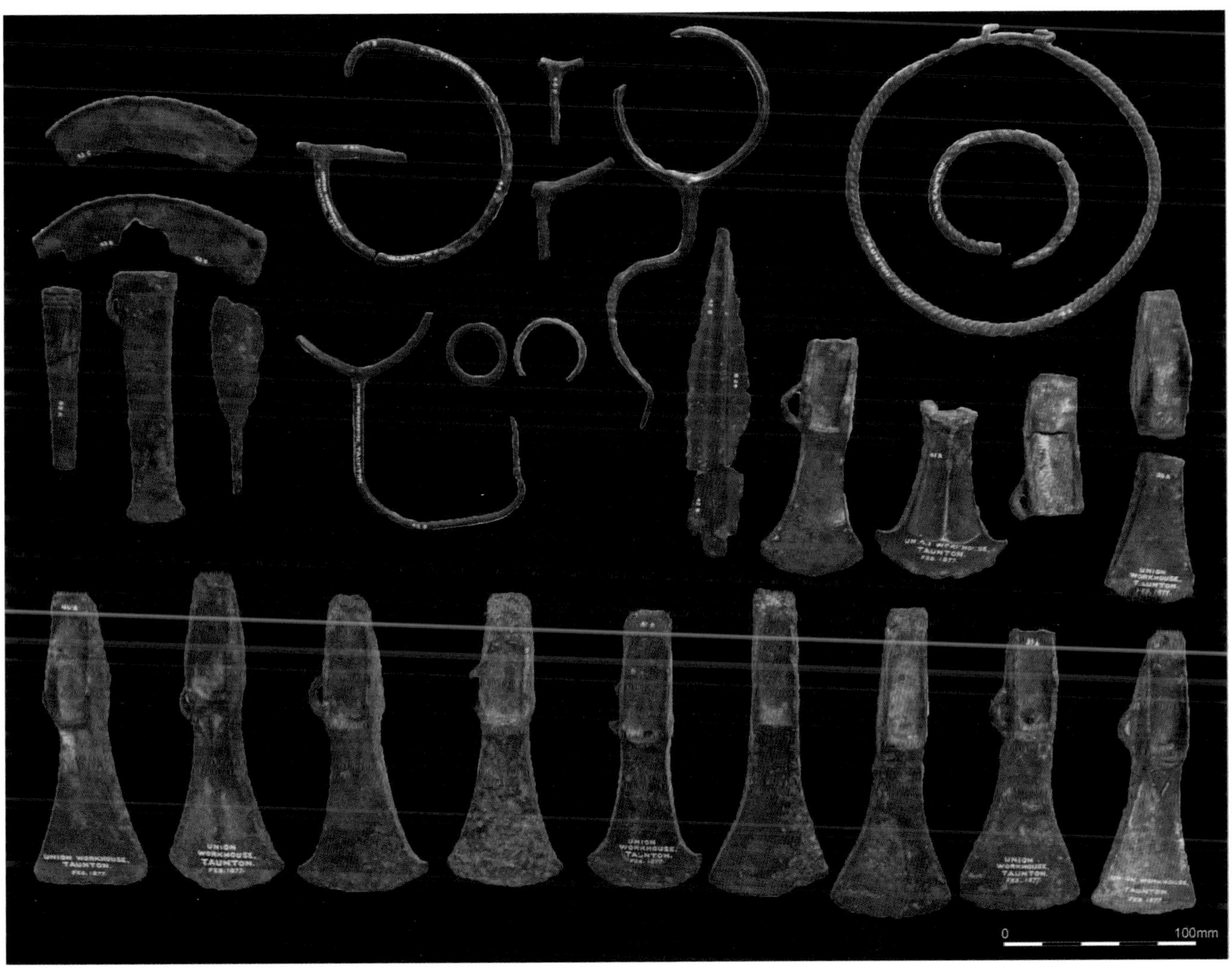

Table 4.1: The Taunton Union Workhouse hoard, Somerset

TTNCM-F053	*Object*	*Completeness %*	*Use evidence*	*Damage Ranking(s)*	*Destruction Indicators*
a	Spearhead	26–50	Y	0,3	Broken (multi); burnt
b	Socketed axehead	76–99	Y	Uncertain	None
c	Palstave	76–99	Y	0, Uncertain	Uncertain, poss. burnt
d	Palstave	76–99	Y	0, Uncertain	Uncertain, poss. burnt
e	Palstave	76–99	Y	0, Uncertain	Uncertain, poss. burnt
f	Palstave	76–99	Y	0,1, Uncertain	Uncertain, poss. burnt
g	Palstave	76–99	Y	0,1, Uncertain	Uncertain, poss. burnt
h	Palstave	76–99	Y	0,1, Uncertain	Uncertain, poss. burnt
i	Palstave	100	N	0, Uncertain	Uncertain, poss. burnt
j	Palstave	100	N	0, Uncertain	Uncertain, poss. burnt
k	Palstave	100	N	n/a	None
l	Palstave	76–99	Y	0,1, Uncertain	Uncertain, poss. burnt
m	Palstave	76–99	N	0,1, Uncertain	None
n	Palstave	26–50	Y	1	None
o	Palstave	0–25	N	0,1	None
p	Socketed hammer	76–99	Y	1	None
q	Sickle	51–75	Y	0,1	None
r	Sickle	51–75	Y	0,1	None
s	Torc	76–99	Y	0	None
t	Bracelet	51–75	Y	0,3	Broken (single)
u	Ring	100	N	n/a	None
v	Ring	76–99	N	0,1	None
w	Razor	51–75	Y	1	None
x	Pin	51–75	N	0,2	None
y	Pin	51–75	N	0,3	Bent (L + T); broken (single)
z	Pin	26–50	N	0,3	Bent (L); broken (multi)
aa	Pin	0–25	N	0,1	None
bb	Pin	0–25	N	1	None
cc	Pin	0–25	N	0,2	None
dd	Pin	0–25	N	3	Bent (T); fragmented
ee	Pin	Uncertain	N	3	Bent (T); broken (multi); fragmented
ff	Pin	Uncertain	N	0,3	Bent (T); broken (multi); twisted
gg	Pin	0–25	N	3	Bent (T); fragmented
hh	Pin	0–25	N	3	Bent (T); fragmented; twisted
ii	Rod	Uncertain	N	3	Bent (T); broken (single)
jj	Rod	Uncertain	N	3	Bent (T); fragmented
kk	Rod	Uncertain	N	3	Bent (T); fragmented
ll	Rod	Uncertain	N	3	Bent (T); fragmented
mm	Rod	Uncertain	N	3	Bent (T); fragmented
nn	12 × rod frags	n/a	N	Uncertain	Uncertain

(Y = Yes; N = No; (L) = longitudinal; (T) = transverse)

Figure 4.8: The incomplete spearhead from the Taunton Union Workhouse hoard (TTNCM-F053a) (photo: author courtesy of Somerset Archaeological and Natural History Society and South West Heritage Trust, acc. no. TTNCM 42B)

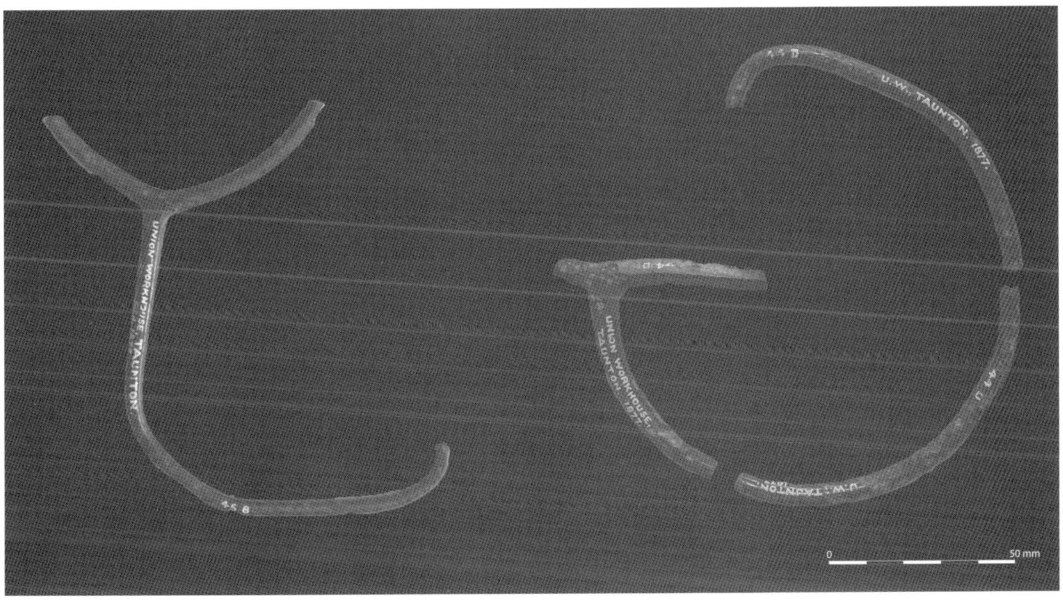

Figure 4.9: Bent and broken quoit-headed pins from Taunton Union Workhouse (TTNCM-F053y and TTNCM-F053z) (photo: author, courtesy of Somerset Archaeological and Natural History Society and South West Heritage Trust, acc. nos TTNCM 45B and TTNCM 41D)

A worn bracelet (TTNCM-F053t) survives in three refitting pieces, with one terminal broken off and the other incomplete: these breaks appear to be ancient and as neither terminal fully survives, one or both may have been deliberately removed to render the bracelet unusable. All pins in the Taunton hoard were incomplete and many were deliberately bent and broken. The shaft of a pin was bent into a u-shape; another was bent almost into a full circle towards the absent head (Fig. 4.9); these were very tactile actions. The plasticity of bronze means the shafts might have been easily bent by hand, though the removal of the heads may have required heating and striking the objects. Breakages across the heads and lower shafts (ie, removing the tips) again suggests a deliberate selection of a portion of the object. Other pin and rod fragments were broken at both ends and suffered varying degrees of bending and twisting.

The damaged objects contrast with the undamaged or accidentally damaged artefacts in the hoard, including a complete socketed axehead, a complete socketed hammer and two sickles with damage related to use and/or casting flaws. Eleven palstaves were deposited mostly complete, some with minor material loss or a broken side-loop. Two incomplete pieces of palstave were present, one represented by a hafting end broken above the stop ridge (TTNCM-F053o) and the other by the blade and cutting edge, also broken across the stop ridge (TTNCM-F053n). These two pieces have previously been illustrated as part of the same palstave (eg, Smith 1959b, GB.43(28), Pearce

Figure 4.10: Turquoise patina on a palstave from the Taunton hoard (TTNCM-F053g) (photo: author, courtesy of Somerset Archaeological and Natural History Society and South West Heritage Trust, acc. no. TTNCM 38B)

1983, 533, no.752bb) but are in fact from two different palstaves. Both pieces broke accidentally in antiquity, resulting from casting flaws and structural weaknesses. Significantly, though, the two pieces form a complete composite palstave, perhaps a symbolic representation of a complete artefact.

Despite displaying no obvious destruction indicators, the palstaves may have been decommissioned by removal of their hafts and were perhaps burned. Blue patina linked with burning has been observed on some bronze objects from Late Bronze Age hoards (Gwilt 2004, 121) informed by ongoing studies into the presence of this feature (Mary Davis pers.comm.). Although this may be affected by elements in the soil (Robbiola *et al.* 1998, 2094ff.), twelve of the Taunton palstaves and the spearhead bear turquoise corrosion of varying intensity. One palstave (TTNCM-F053l) bears dark grey and turquoise corrosion, whilst another (TTNCM-F053g) is covered in a dark brown patina across one face and pale turquoise patina across the opposite face (Fig. 4.10). Furthermore, this second palstave is slightly twisted and warped, which may be the result of intense heat. This is also observed on the socketed axehead and accounts for the high number of objects in this hoard with an 'Uncertain' damage ranking. That the pins, bracelet and spearhead in the Taunton hoard might have been broken through heating and striking could strengthen the idea the hoard was burnt or suffered fire damage.

The Taunton hoard in context

The Taunton Union Workhouse hoard was found about 3 feet below the modern surface, indicating it was probably in its original depositional spot. The area around and beneath the hoard was stained a dark colour, which Pring (1880, 94) attributed to corrosive decay of the objects though the corrosion of the objects is minor; a better explanation might be that the hoard was deposited in an organic container that has since decayed. The contemporary hoard of tools and ornaments from Edington Burtle was recovered from a peat bog in an oval wooden box, for instance (TTNCM-F015; Fig. 4.11; Stradling 1854; Smith 1959b, GB.44). The Taunton hoard findspot lies on a north facing slope overlooking the River Tone. Although waterways have undoubtedly altered since the Bronze Age, the position of the Taunton hoard is in keeping with a series of other Middle Bronze Age metalwork deposits along this stretch of the Tone Valley (Fig. 4.12; Pearce 1983, 160, fig.4.19).

At least five other sites of hoards or associated objects have been found nearby. The Sherford hoard (TTNCM-F047) consisted of six palstaves and a basal-looped spearhead but no ornaments and none of the objects showed signs of deliberate damage. This hoard was deposited two feet below the surface (Smith 1959b, GB.45) recovered close to a series of modern streams also in sight of the River Tone. Further up the valley another hoard, now lost, was found at West Buckland in the alluvium of the River Tone on the south side; it comprised two palstaves, a bar-twisted torc and an embossed armring (Sanford 1865–6; Taylor 1982); these objects were seemingly deposited complete and the original account indicates charcoal and burnt bone was associated, perhaps representing the remains

Figure 4.11: The Edington Burtle hoard, Somerset (TTNCM-F015) © Somerset Archaeological and Natural History Society and South West Heritage Trust, acc. nos TTNCM 24A-31B

of a cremation burial (Sanford 1865–6; Taylor 1982, 15–6). At Staplegrove, two complete palstaves were found, though little is known about this discovery (Rowlands 1976, 258, no.119)[1]; similarly two palstaves, both now lost, were found at Nynehead on a low hill called The Burrows (Pearce 1983, 521, no.699). Lastly, at least twelve objects were recovered from a ditch outside the Middle Bronze Age enclosure at Norton Fitzwarren hillfort; these included nine bracelets, two palstaves and one socketed axehead as well as corroded fragments and pottery sherds (TTNCM-F036; Needham 1989a, 29–39). Most of these objects were deposited complete, with the bracelets possibly 'in a bundle tied with a string' (*Current Archaeology* 1971, 120), though all have suffered extensive corrosion damage. Hoards linked with occupational contexts are rare, and although the Norton Fitzwarren hoard was deposited outside the enclosure, it was no doubt buried in relation to the people who owned the objects and lived in this place. Indeed, its position in the enclosing ditch may have served to legitimise any claim to the place. Apart from a possible Middle–Late Bronze Age enclosure at Monkton Heathfield (Somerset HER 22049), Norton Fitzwarren is currently the only known certain settlement near the Taunton hoard and is one of the highest points

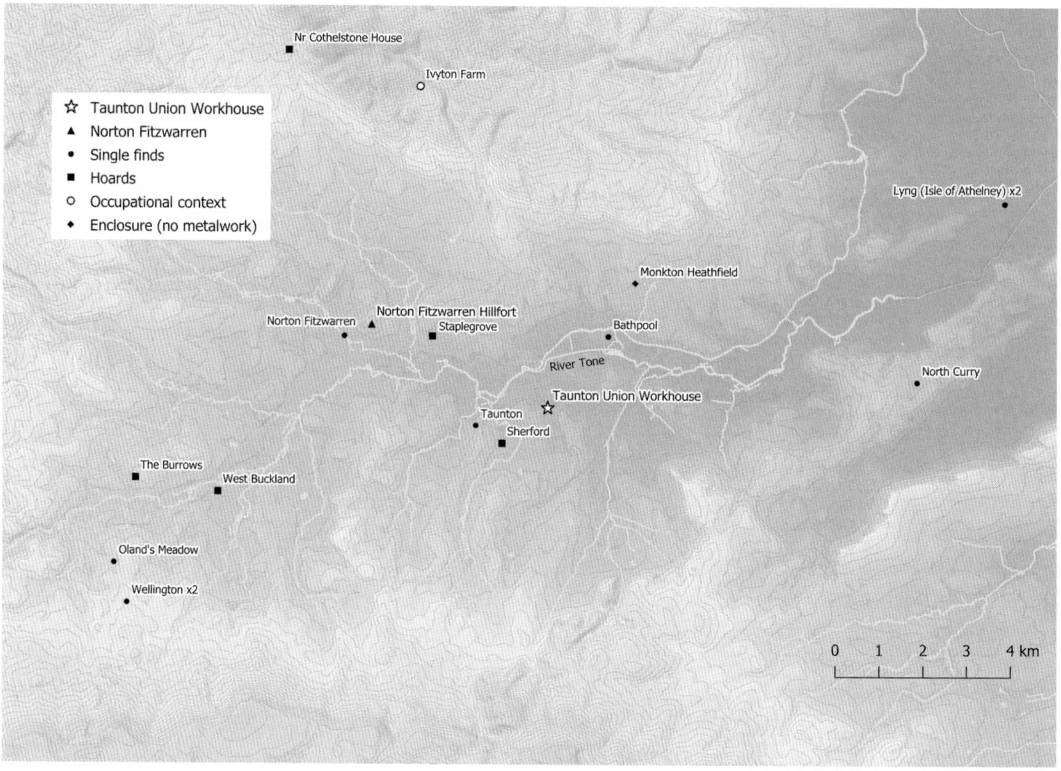

Figure 4.12: The Taunton Union Workhouse hoard in its immediate landscape context with contemporary sites and metalwork deposits marked. Contains OS data © Crown copyright and database right 2021

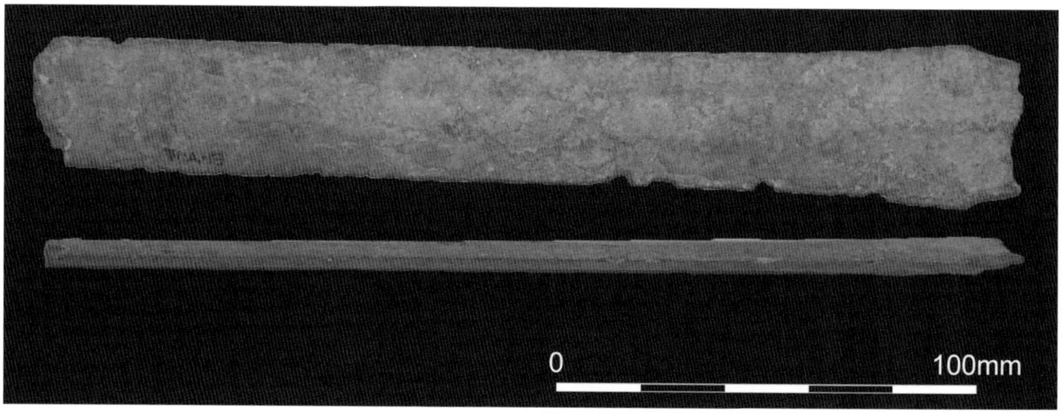

Figure 4.13: A broken sword from Bathpool, Somerset (TTNCM-F002) (photo: author, courtesy of Somerset County Council and South West Heritage Trust, acc.no. TTNCM 1.A.15)

in this area; the hill is surrounded by streams and brooks that feed into nearby rivers, most noticeably the convergence of two tributaries into the River Tone to the south.

Single finds of Middle Bronze Age metalwork include a used and deliberately broken sword from Bathpool (Fig 4.13; TTNCM-F002), a mostly complete dirk with modern repairs from Norton Fitzwarren (Burgess & Gerloff 1981, 10–1, no.37) and a complete and undamaged palstave from the Taunton area (Pearce 1983, 534–5, no.754). However, of these only the palstave is broadly contemporary with the Taunton hoard, the dirk dating slightly earlier and the sword slightly later. Nonetheless, the position of these findspots within and along the River Tone valley imply a long-lived depositional locale with some significance for where deposits were made. Waterways often formed focal points for depositing Middle and Late Bronze Age metalwork (eg, Yates & Bradley 2010a; Dunkin *et al.* 2020), though there was probably a variety of reasons for this. For instance, the River Tone may have formed a natural boundary for communities in the area; alternatively, deposits may have referenced the role of the Tone as part of a trade route or as a means for mobility, linking with the River Parrett to the east (cf. Pearce 1983, 160). The Taunton hoard must be understood in relation to this landscape and the nearby deposits. This hoard was deposited in a relatively unspectacular location, at one of the lowest points in the Tone valley, yet it contained many objects. From this, we may consider that any communal significance of this place is now lost to us, but the size and character of the hoard allows insights into the nature and social scale of the event.

The social role of the Taunton hoard

Most ornament hoards deposited in southern England contained six or fewer objects (Wilkin 2017, 18), and we can envisage that gathering two or three tools and ornaments for a deposit might be the work of a small group, but the forty artefacts of the Taunton hoard suggest a more communal effort. Similarly-sized and larger hoards from Monkswood, Somerset, Near Lewes, East Sussex, West Ashling, West Sussex, and Wylye, Wiltshire, also contained complete and damaged objects as well as indicators of structured deposition (Smith 1959b, GB.42; O'Connor *et al.* 2017). The timescale over which depositions of this nature were undertaken is unknowable but the event of gathering, damaging and depositing the material would have been a significant and probably memorable event, designed to have long-lasting impact. Neil Wilkin (2017, 28–9) highlighted that over a quarter of all ornament hoards across southern England had equal numbers of tools/weapons and ornaments, which may relate to processes of 'expressing and creating balance or imbalance in the symbolic force represented by object types'. In the South West this seems to be a trait of Somerset hoards, with equal numbers of torcs and palstaves deposited at Weare, Spaxton and Wedmore (Wilkin 2017, 28–9), and from Dorset we can add a hoard of two armrings and two palstaves from Eglesham Meadow (Pearce 1983, 468, no.372) and a spearhead and armring found together at Bryanston 1 (BM-F013; Pearce 1983, 466, no.356). Brück (2019, 107–8) has suggested such balanced deposits may have been buried to symbolise marriage partnerships (see also Needham 2001, 292). Although ornament hoards in Britain were rarely or never associated with human remains, elsewhere in Europe swords, spearheads and axeheads were regularly deposited in male burials, and pins and neck rings were often associated with females, though there was a degree of overlap for certain armrings and occasionally daggers (Bergerbrant 2007, 8–9). If, however, we consider that gendered object associations transcended continental European burials to hoards from southern Britain, it is possible these deposits also had a gendered component and thus referenced the identities of those depositing the objects (Wilkin 2017, 29; Brück 2019, 107–8). Where we see imbalance in these deposits (eg, more tools than ornaments as in the Taunton hoard), we may speculate this reflects some form of imbalance in a relationship. This is not a wholesale explanation for these hoards – indeed it does not account for hoards comprising only tools or ornaments, nor single deposits – but it allows us to conceptualise how Bronze Age social relationships and ontologies may have been expressed, enacted and maintained through such depositions, with objects representing or embodying identities (cf. Needham 2001).

The history and treatment of artefacts was probably integral to this. For instance, if we follow the idea that the deposition of a roughly equal number of complete tools and ornaments symbolised a partnership or alliance, the fragmentation of objects could in this scenario represent the end of a partnership or death of an individual within that relationship (cf. Brück 2019, 107). In the context of Taunton, the deposition of deliberately damaged objects was an unusual feature, with most other ornament hoards from Somerset deposited with complete ornaments and tools, such as at Norton Fitzwarren. However, destructive actions were present in other Taunton-assemblage hoards from south-west Britain, including Edington Burtle, Monkswood, and Pinhoe, Devon (RAMM-F037). We may consider destruction was a selective act, undertaken in particular circumstances, rather than a wholesale approach to deposition. Significantly, many deliberately damaged ornaments showed signs of use, both in hoards and as single finds. The removal of bracelet terminals, for instance, was possibly inflicted upon penannular ornaments with a longer use-life, as indicated by the worn Taunton bracelet (cf. Roberts 2007, 148). The hoards from Pinhoe and Monkswood included

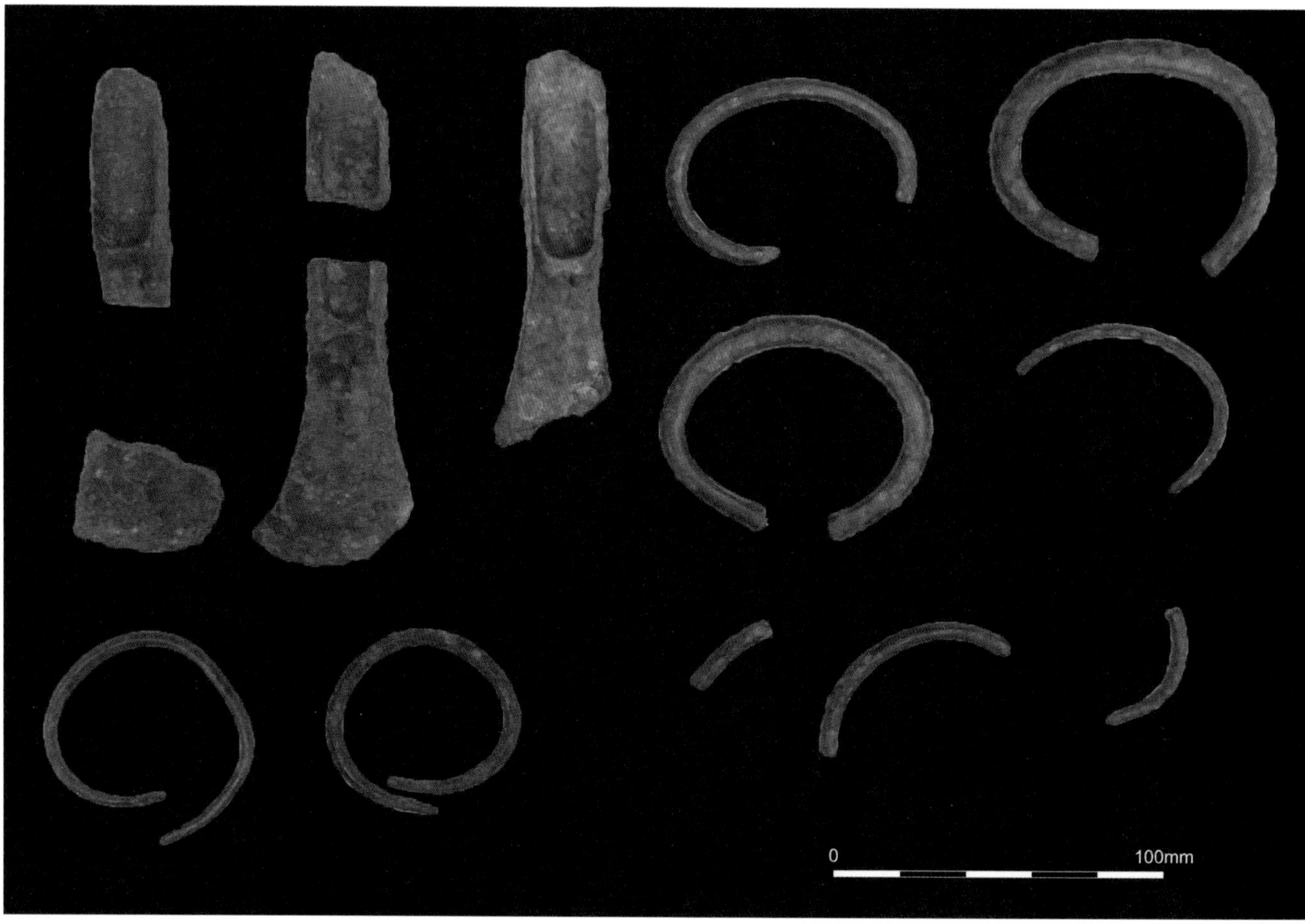

Figure 4.14: The Pinhoe hoard, Devon (RAMM-F037) (photo: author, courtesy of Royal Albert Memorial Museum and Art Gallery, Exeter)

split bracelets, bracelets without terminals and torc terminal fragments deposited alongside complete and damaged weapons and tools (Fig. 4.14). A worn bar-twisted torc from the Edington Burtle hoard similarly lacked terminals (TTNCM-F015k) and another bracelet was missing one terminal; a further bracelet was threaded with two interlinked rings, one of which was produced from a torc terminal (Fig. 4.11). Single finds of bronze torcs from near Sherborne, Dorset (PAS-F137), and Pen Pits, Somerset (SM-F004), also lack both terminals. The severe deformation of the Taunton pins is matched by comparable examples of bent and/or broken quoit-headed pins in hoards from Monkswood (Smith 1959b, GB.42), Wylye (Ellis *et al.* 2013), and Bix, Oxfordshire (Byard 2015b; 2016), and as individual finds from north Dorset (PAS-F178) and Witton, Norfolk (Robbins 2008). This was not exclusive to Britain: contemporary deposits in Ireland and France likewise contained ornaments occasionally showing signs of wear and were manipulated and/or fragmented in particular ways (Becker 2013, 230–1; Nordez 2019, 199–202). Comparisons across these deposits suggest wider ideas within the ornament hoard tradition about how to damage and destroy ornaments (Wilkin 2017), most notably by removing ornament terminals or severely bending pin shafts. If these were connected with or owned by certain people, symbolising certain aspects of their relationships and indeed their identity, destruction would have been a significant performative action to remove the object from the social realm as well as physically expressing changes to relations.

This may extend to the tools and weapons seen in these hoards. Burning and fragmentation has already been noted for the Taunton spearhead and palstaves. Similar evidence was observed on palstaves in the Pinhoe hoard; the spearhead, two of the knives and one of the sickles in the Monkswood were also broken and/or missing their tips. Even

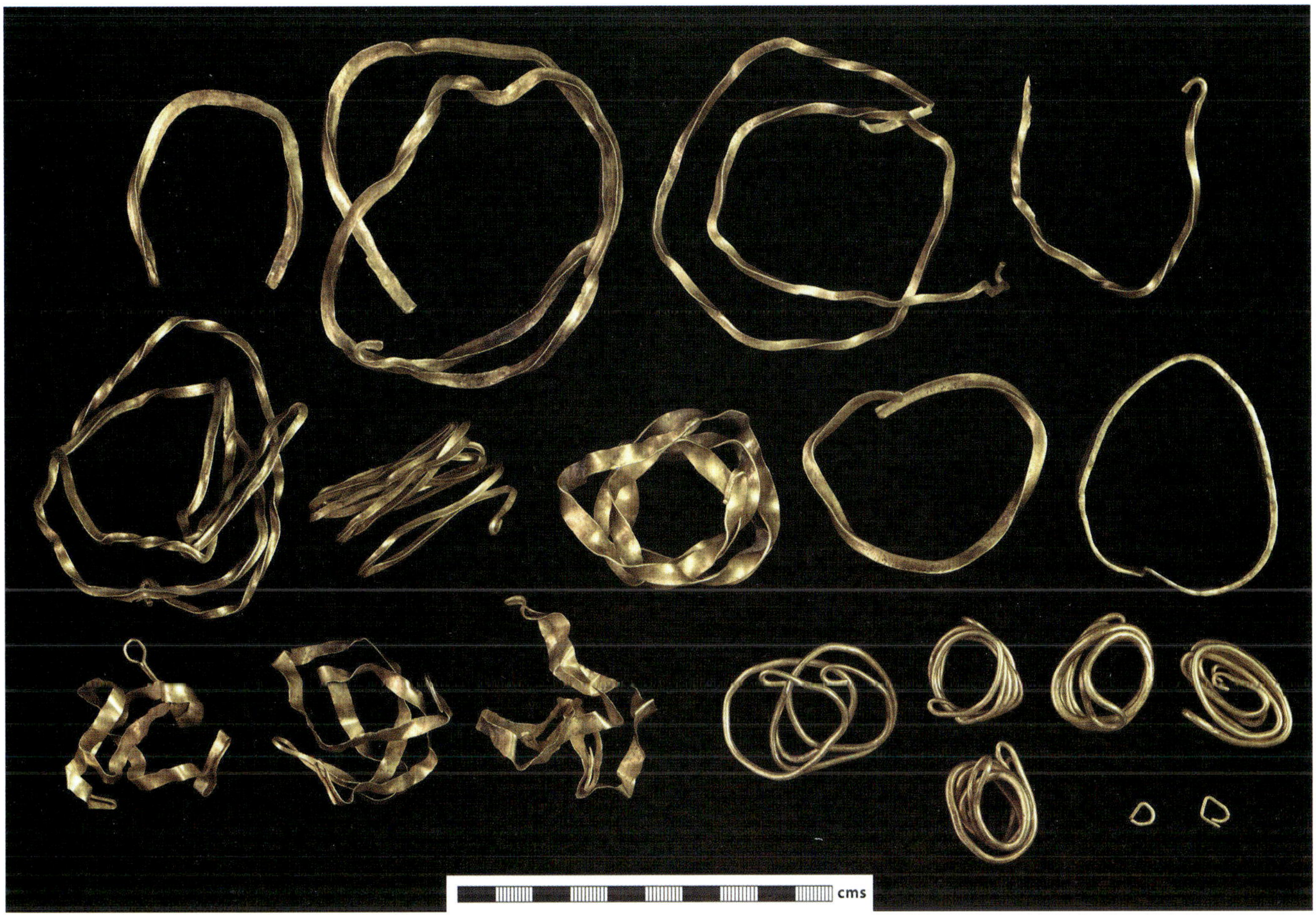

Figure 4.15: The Priddy hoard, Somerset (TTNCM-F040) © Somerset County Council and South West Heritage Trust, acc.no. TTNCM 46/2007

where tools survive complete and seemingly undamaged, such as the palstaves and sickles in the Edington Burtle hoard, these may have been decommissioned by the removal of their organic components; the containment of the Edington Burtle metalwork in a wooden box suggests that any organic hafts for the tools were removed prior to deposition, potentially a form of temporary destruction as with the rolled gold ornaments discussed in Chapter 3. The possibility that the Taunton hoard was also in a decayed organic container suggests these palstaves were also deposited without their hafts. These various actions made the objects suitable for deposition.

From this analysis, we can conclude that the Taunton Union Workhouse hoard was a deposit brought together by one or more social groupings incorporating a variety of practices in an important locale. This was undertaken in relation to a wider understanding of how ornament hoards were structured. Clearly it was necessary to damage or destroy some of the material, which could be linked to the corresponding histories of the objects, the perceived and accepted ways they should be treated prior to deposition, and/or the identities and relationships the objects symbolised. The possibility that some of the hoard was heated and broken before deposition implies at least one, if not several, events in which fires were set and objects were damaged. The skills involved in these destructive acts need not have been particularly great, nor the acts spectacular, but the practices were significant, deliberately selecting portions of the objects to be involved whilst excluding others and reinforcing social beliefs through repeated actions. The character of the hoard is in keeping with what we might expect from the area, and this may have been part of maintaining and establishing, or conversely breaking, relationships. However, this was not universal. The Taunton hoard has largely been set in the context of Somerset, where

Figure 4.16: The two palstaves found near the Priddy hoard (TTNCM-F040q, r) (courtesy of the PAS/Trustees of the British Museum)

Table 4.2: The Priddy hoard, Somerset

TTNCM-F040	*Object*	*Completeness %*	*Damage Ranking(s)*	*Destruction Indicators*
a	Bar-twisted bracelet	76–99	3	Broken – multi-piece; crushed; twisted
b	Bar-twisted bracelet	100	3	Crushed; twisted
c	Bar-twisted bracelet	100	3	Crushed; folded
d	Ribbon-twisted bracelet	100	3	Crushed; twisted
e	Bar-twisted bracelet	100	3	Crushed; twisted
f	Type 5D bracelet	100	3	Bent (transverse); crushed
g	Doubled-and-hooked ribbon bracelet	100	3	Crushed; folded; twisted
h	Doubled-and-hooked ribbon bracelet	100	3	Crushed; folded; twisted
i	Doubled-and-hooked ribbon bracelet	100	3	Crushed; folded; twisted
j	Doubled-and-hooked ribbon bracelet	100	3	Crushed; folded
k	Doubled-and-hooked bar bracelet	100	3	Crushed; folded
l	Doubled-and-hooked bar bracelet	100	3	Crushed; folded
m	Doubled-and-hooked bar bracelet	100	0,3	Crushed; folded
n	Doubled-and-hooked bar bracelet	100	3	Crushed; folded
o	Ring ornament?	100	3	Crushed
p	Ring ornament?	100	3	Crushed
q	South-western-type palstave (Cu alloy)	100	0	None
r	Gr.IV palstave (Cu alloy)	100	0	None
s	Bar twisted bracelet	76–99	3	Broken – multi-piece; crushed; twisted

similarly composed deposits were also buried. Contemporaneous examples from Devon and Cornwall are scant and ornament hoards in Dorset typically only contained ornaments, with tools/weapons rarely included. This suggests ornaments and ornament hoards were an important part of managing social lives in the Somerset region (cf. Needham 1989a, 38), whilst communities across south-west Britain may have used other mechanisms for which the deposition of ornament hoards was not always integral.

The Priddy hoard, Somerset (TTNCM-F040)

The Priddy hoard, comprising seventeen gold bracelets/torcs in nineteen pieces, was found while metal-detecting in 2005 and probably dates to the Penard assemblage (*c.*1275–1150 BC) (Table 4.2; Fig. 4.15; Minnitt & Payne 2012). The ornaments were deposited in a 'tight ball' but were disentangled by the finder before the find was reported to the Portable Antiquities Scheme (*ibid.*, 109). An archaeological excavation and geophysical survey revealed no further contextual information. Two complete palstaves were later found separately about 50m from the hoard (Fig. 4.16). It is unclear whether these palstaves were associated with the hoard. However, they date to the Taunton or early Penard assemblage and no other Middle Bronze Age metalwork depositions are known within the area, so it is possible the palstaves formed part of the overall depositional practice (Minnitt & Payne 2012, 109). The Priddy ornaments were largely complete and included finished and unfinished forms, though were deliberately crushed into a ball for deposition.

The properties of gold and thin nature of the ornaments means this deformation could have been undertaken with little effort, perhaps by hand. This is seen across other Middle Bronze Age gold ribbon ornaments. At Ellesborough, Buckinghamshire, two folded and coiled ribbon bracelets were found (Tyrell 2009), and a broken bracelet or ring from Freshwater, Isle of Wight, was folded over prior to deposition 'with a bundle of compressed gold ribbons wedged within the fold' (Basford 2014). At Winterhay Green, Ilminster, Somerset, an incomplete hooked ribbon torc, now lost, was reportedly found 'rolled up into a knob' alongside two palstaves and a broken bronze bracelet (Dobson 1931, 89; see ASH-F013). Rolled gold bracelets were also recovered from the Salcombe Bay assemblages (British Museum acc. nos 2010,8032.4, 2010,8032.7, 2010,8032.8, 2010,8032.9)[2] and the Burton hoard, Wales (Gwilt *et al.* 2007); such rolling and folding recalls Early Bronze Age deformation practices. Of note, the Heyope hoard, Powys, comprised three ribbon torcs that were also deposited in a tangled ball (Fig. 4.17; Savory 1958, 7–8, 55–6), a comparable practice to that performed at Priddy. The Capel Isaf hoard, Powys, may also have conformed to this pattern; a ribbon torc fragment and four armlets were deposited in a 'tight mass' and 'wrapped round each other' (Savory 1977, 37); Wilkin (2017, 32) took this to imply the objects were nested though there is no reason why it might not imply a greater entanglement. Because the Priddy hoard was disentangled, we can tell that individual ornaments within the hoard were clearly tightly coiled before they were crushed into the larger ball. This particularly relates to the thin bar bracelets and suggests a series of manipulation events prior to the final compression.

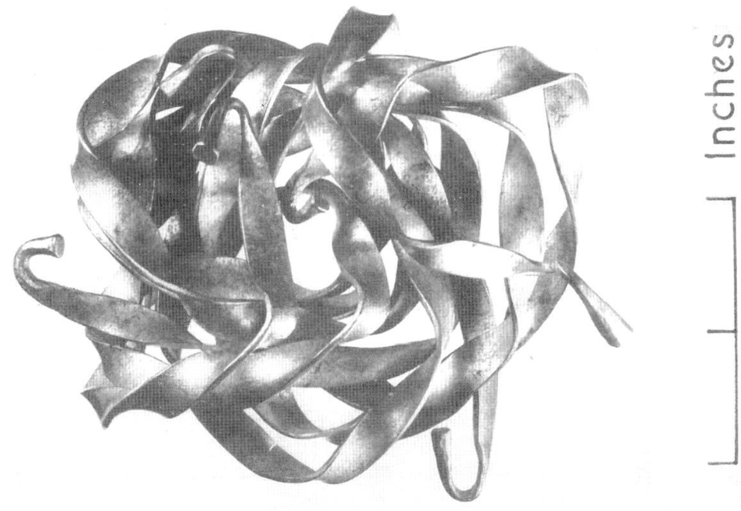

Figure 4.17: The Heyope hoard, Wales, as found (source: Savory 1958, pl. ii C. Reproduced with kind permission of the Cambrian Archaeological Association)

Minnitt and Payne (2012) present the deposit as that of an individual burying personal items. However, the number of bracelets and various styles might more accurately indicate a variety of participating individuals or communities with the overall hoard indicating a collective deposition as part of a specific event. Compressing the ornaments into a tight ball prior to deposition was a key part of the performance of deposition and in a scenario involving multiple individuals, we can envisage a symbolic element to this action.

However, we should also consider a prosaic aspect to the deposit. The compression of gold ornaments, such as at Priddy, appears to lack a certain degree of care and we may suggest their destruction was part of a recycling process and thus involved a goldworker. We can see this clearly in an example of three gold torc fragments melted and fused together at Ancaster, Lincolnshire (Daubney 2011). A search of the Portable Antiquities Scheme database also highlights large numbers of deliberately cut and bent torc fragments from across southern England. From the South West, examples are known from 'West Dorset' and Powerstock, both Dorset (PAS-F145; PAS-F179), Paul I and Camborne I, Cornwall (PAS-F022; RCM-F013), Horton, Somerset (Shoemark 2016), and Salcombe Bay (Needham *et al.* 2013, 86). The Salcombe Bay examples also indicate that gold was being transported in its manipulated and fragmented form. Hoards from Cirencester, Gloucester (Needham 2007b), and Fittleworth, West Sussex (British Museum acc. no. 1996,0902), contained a minimum of 38 and 42 gold objects respectively, including torcs, bracelets and rings, many of which had been deliberately bent, coiled and/or cut. Complete bracelets and broken gold bars threaded with gold beads were also illustrated in the Beerhackett hoard, Dorset (Ouvry 1850, 64–5). Compression at the ends of many of these torcs and bracelets suggests definite cutting actions using tools, perhaps reducing the objects for recycling in a crucible and requiring certain equipment.

Unfinished objects in the Priddy and Cirencester hoards (Needham 2007b, 29–30) also suggest a goldworker was integral and/or contributed to the deposit. In the Dundry hoard near Bristol, an unworked coiled gold bar and hammered gold fragment were deposited alongside two palstaves and copper-alloy metallurgical waste (BCMAG-F008), which has similar connotations. Even when destructive acts were not conducted, we can also glimpse some involvement of a person with material knowledge: for instance, the Towednack hoard, Cornwall (BM-F003), contained nine undamaged gold objects including finished and unfinished torcs and bracelets (Hawkes 1932); these objects fit within a graded weight system, suggesting these might have been the wares of a goldsmith. This does not necessitate a purely functionalist interpretation for this material: as Needham (2007b, 30–1) argues, the fragmentation of the Cirencester objects goes beyond that necessary for recycling, and the discovery of the Towednack hoard describes the 'smaller pieces neatly arranged within them [the larger torcs]' (Hawkes 1932, 179), ie, a structured deposit. At Priddy, the deposition of two complete palstaves may have been undertaken in relation to the known location of gold objects. However, the destruction and deposition observed of many gold objects dating to the Penard metalworking assemblage clearly served a rather different purpose to that undertaken on bronze ornaments in the preceding Taunton assemblage, which targeted certain parts of ornaments. The wearing of gold ornaments still played roles in constructing identity during the period 1275–1150 BC, but when they were removed from circulation for deposition, many were deliberately deformed in such a way that their original form and function and by extension association with certain people could no longer be recognised. The Priddy ornaments, crushed into a ball, meant individual components and relations were indistinguishable. The event of deposition no doubt remained important, but pre-depositional destruction served to sever social relations with individual ornaments rather than create them. Instead, the collection, deposition and removal of gold from circulation may have symbolically established and communicated a broader communal ideology whereby the sacrifice of gold was more important than keeping it in the social sphere.

Rapiers, spearheads and places

After ornaments, many of the deliberately damaged objects studied were weapons, including dirks, rapiers and spearheads. Two rapiers from Shillingstone, Dorset (PAS-F148; Fig. 4.18), for instance, were bent and fragmented; most pieces were still present for one rapier and all the pieces were present for the second. This second rapier was thus deposited complete yet incomplete. This contrasts not only with complete rapiers deposited elsewhere (eg, Badbury Rings, Dorset: BM-F009; Talaton I, Devon: BM-F007/RAMM-F049; Pen Pits, Somerset: SM-F004), but also individual pieces or fragments (eg, North Crofty, Cornwall: RCM-F026; Gussage St Michael 8, Dorset: PRIV-F039). Although traditionally one might interpret fragments as pieces for recycling and complete examples as votive offerings, the deliberate damage of a rapier whilst also leaving it largely complete implies a more complex process at play, regardless of whether the intended end result was sacred or profane. This is further illustrated by a complete palstave and complete but folded rapier found while metal-detecting at Henstridge, Somerset (Fig. 4.19; Wilkin 2019). The careful folding of the

Figure 4.18: The two broken rapiers from Shillingstone, Dorset (PAS-F148) (courtesy of the PAS/Trustees of the British Museum)

rapier without breaking it would have been a difficult task, requiring knowledge of the material to achieve this: it cannot be explained through purely practical rationales yet required the involvement of a specialist. Whatever the reason for bending the Henstridge rapier or fragmenting the Shillingstone rapiers, damaging the objects before deposition was inherent to the process and destroying them would have been important for transforming the objects into a suitable state for deposition.

Of course, Middle Bronze Age rapiers and blades were prone to bending and breaking if used incorrectly (eg, Molloy 2007; Faulkner-Jones 2016). As suggested for broken Early Bronze Age axeheads, however, it is possible that even accidental or use-related damage contributed to the significance of an object. Damage communicated the life and history of the object and rather than repair it, it was

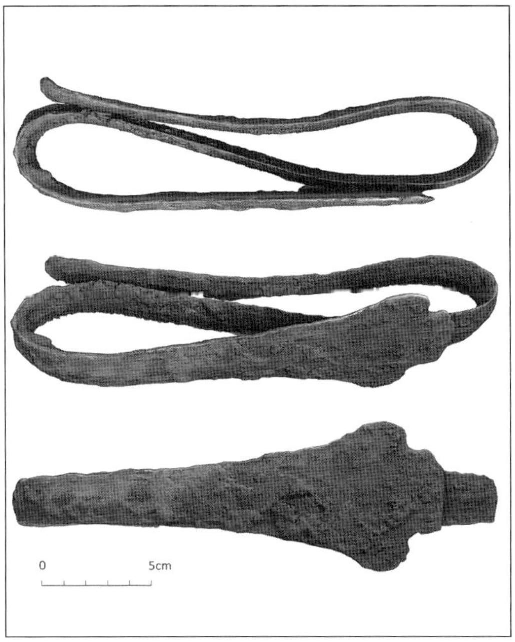

Figure 4.19: The folded rapier from Henstridge, Somerset (courtesy of the PAS/Trustees of British Museum, amended by Craig Williams)

Figure 4.20: The notched spearhead from Glastonbury Turbaries, Somerset (TTNCM-F054b) (photo: author, courtesy of Somerset Archaeological and Natural History Society and South West Heritage Trust, acc.no. TTNCM 35B)

appropriate to bury it instead. An example of this could be the bent and broken rapier from Broadsands, Devon (TOR-F004), which was buried close to a Neolithic passage tomb overlooking the coastline of Tor Bay (Sheridan *et al.* 2008; Knight & Chandler 2018).

The same might be argued for damaged spearheads. We have already observed the deliberate breakage of the Taunton Union Workhouse spearhead. A spearhead from Tarrant Monkton I, Dorset (BM-F026a), appears to have broken by accident resulting from casting flaws, but further intentional damage was then inflicted. Both examples were found with complete palstaves, paralleling the relationship between the damaged rapier and complete palstave from Henstridge, and highlighting a difference in the perception of how object types should be treated.

This extends to various locales in which multiple individual depositions were made over time. Thirteen objects spanning the Early–Late Bronze Age were recovered while peat cutting in the Glastonbury Turbaries, Somerset (TTNCM-F054). Of these, ten date to the Middle Bronze Age and included spearheads, blades and palstaves. Whilst the palstaves were deposited mostly complete and with minimal signs of use, the spearheads were deposited with signs of extensive wear or else with casting flaws; a dirk was possibly deposited missing its tip (TTNCM-F054j) and a sword may have been deposited with a damaged hilt (TTNCM-F054l). Of note, one of the spearheads (TTNCM-F054b) was deposited complete apart from a series of significant notches along the blade edges creating an irregular serrated effect (Fig. 4.20). The notches are all broad, deep, and U-shaped, indicating they were sustained by repeated strikes from a thick blade, perhaps that of an axe. This was damage designed to render the object unusable and this is the only instance of such extreme notching from south-west Britain. Weapons, of course, imply conflict and the involvement of weapons in physical actions against other individuals, literally becoming a matter of life and death, may have heightened their importance and affected how they should be treated prior to deposition, especially compared to tools such as axeheads, which had a less aggressive function. We might thus ask an unknowable question: what was the history of the Turbaries spearhead that necessitated such devastating hacking?

The depositional landscape of the Glastonbury Turbaries finds – and the place of the Broadsands rapier mentioned above – raise another important consideration, which is that there were clearly certain places that were socially suitable for depositing metal objects, even if the condition of the object varied. In both examples, this could be linked to the temporality of the place: an ancient tomb at Broadsands and a long-term depositional landscape at Turbaries. Both complete and undamaged examples were deposited in similarly significant locales. A complete but bent rapier was recovered from just outside the later hillfort at Badbury Rings, Dorset, in an area overlooking the confluence of two rivers in an established landscape of Bronze Age barrows (BM-F009). The depositional site may have thus referenced the natural and/or the man-made landscape, but also indicates a place of long-term significance that became more established in the Iron Age. The bending of the rapier is probably related to its use, and thus to its history as an object of combat; it would have been relatively simple to repair, but preserving the damaged condition was important and intrinsic to the decisions made about how and where to deposit it. Similarly, complete but used examples of Middle Bronze Age spearheads, dirks and rapiers are known from wetland locations, including bogs, moorlands and rivers, such as at Avonmouth, Bristol (BCMAG-F001), Weston-in-Gordano, Somerset (PAS-F264) and Pitney Moor II, Somerset (TTNCM-F039). A hoard of six rapiers showing signs of use were possibly deposited in a bog at Talaton I (Tucker 1867, 110–2; Burgess & Gerloff 1981, 60). Like waterways, wetlands were long-lived focal points for depositions of Bronze Age metalwork, particularly weapons, from *c.* 1400 BC onwards.

In Cornwall, deposits of used objects in watery places may have also been linked to the streaming of tin and possibly gold, ie, collection of alluvial ores from rivers and streams. In 1757, a reworked rapier was recovered from streamworks at Paramoor with a broken rivet hole and bent tip, probably damaged through ancient use (ASH-F004; Borlase 1769, 311; Burgess & Gerloff 1981, 37, no.254). At Roche, two complete spearheads, both now lost, were found deep in streamworks, and at Benallack,

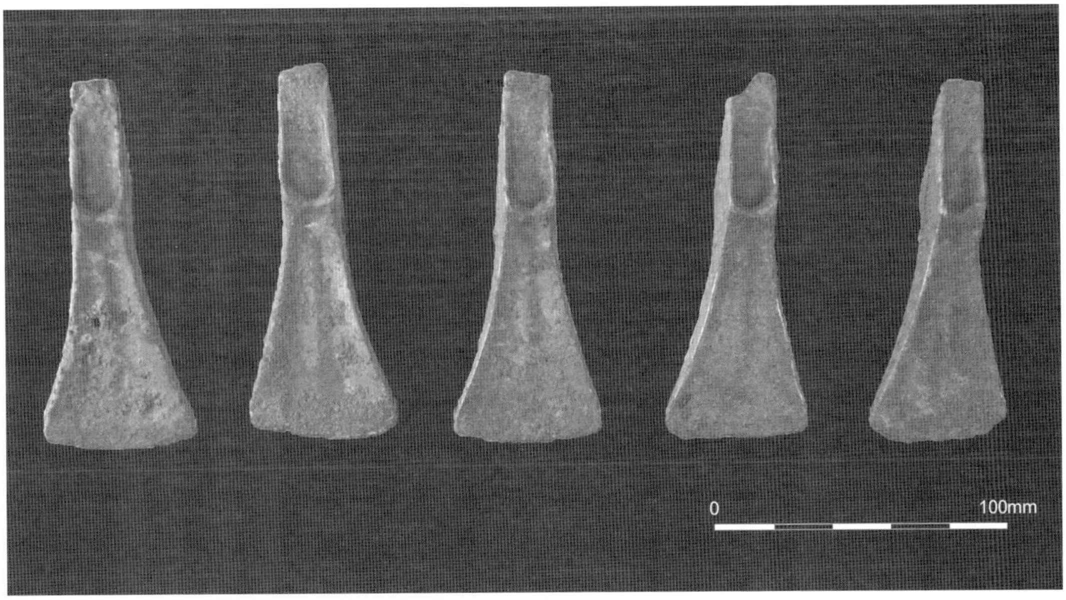

Figure 4.21: The five surviving palstaves from the Bournemouth Hospital hoard, Dorset (PM-F001) (photo: author, by kind permission of Poole Museum)

a notched rapier with broken rivet holes was recovered as well as a palstave (Penhallurick 1986, 175, 198–9; 1997, 29). Other metalwork from the Early Bronze Age to the medieval period is known from streamworks (Hencken 1932, 164–6; Penhallurick 1986, 173–224; 1997; Jones & Kirkham 2019, 116–8), and here, it seems objects were repeatedly deposited in watery locations in relation to the means of obtaining material resources (Jones & Kirkham 2019, 116–8; cf. Hencken 1932, 164). These deposits provide proxy evidence that tin and possibly gold was acquired during the Bronze Age from Cornish streams, but these also represent special deposits, perhaps offerings that reciprocated the material obtained (cf. Penhallurick 1997; Jones & Kirkham 2019, 116–8).

Palstaves and palstave hoards

In contrast with ornaments and weapons, palstaves were overwhelmingly deposited in complete conditions as single finds and in hoards. Even when broken, palstaves rarely showed signs of intent but instead clear indicators of accidental breakage: for instance, a palstave broken across the stop ridge from a scatter at Ottery St Mary, Devon presented several casting flaws (RAMM-F035a). The desire to deposit palstaves complete is exemplified by the complementary pieces from two different palstaves in the Taunton Union Workhouse hoard. More commonly, palstaves were deposited as-cast (eg, the Bournemouth Hospital, Dorset: PM-F001; Fig. 4.21) or with minimal signs of preparation and/or wear (eg, the Truro hoard, Cornwall: RCM-F051). They also highlight aspects of regionality and insularity – the distinctive high-flanged south-western palstave was common in palstave-only hoards of Devon and Cornwall and mixed tool-ornament hoards of Somerset, with few signs of external influence (O'Connor 1980, 56; Knight 2018, 220–2). By contrast, relatively few palstaves were deposited in Dorset, though the greatest number comprised continental-style examples that reflected connections across the Channel. At Marnhull, 89 complete and one incomplete Breton and Norman-style palstaves were deposited (Lawson & Farwell 1990); the Dewlish hoard of six palstaves contained four Norman palstaves (O'Connor 1980, 437–8); and a hoard from Bere Regis contained three British-style palstaves alongside a possible French import (Trevarthen 2016). Palstave-only hoards such as these are known across southern Britain (Rowlands 1976; O'Connor 1980, 49) and northern France (Gabillot 2003) and represent commonly held ideals across the Channel at this time, even when undertaken with insular styles. These large deposits of palstaves are commonly interpreted as hoards of industrial production or commodities that were never recovered (eg, Rowlands 1976; Fontijn 2020, 94–8).

Whilst it is undeniable that such deposits may have served this purpose, we must question

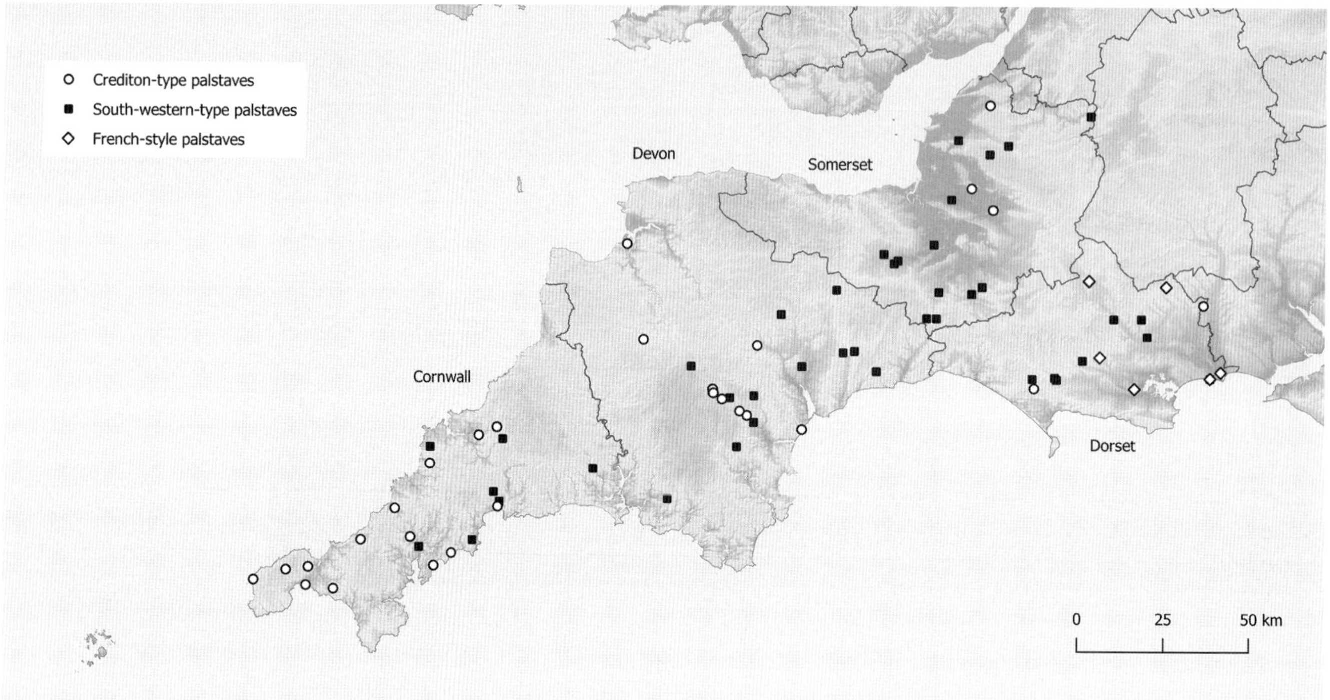

Figure 4.22: The distribution of distinctive palstave forms in south-west Britain. Contains OS data © Crown copyright and database right 2021

that if this material was intended for economic exchange, why was so much left in the ground (Fontijn 2020, 87)? Contextual information for deposits, where available, suggests there was a structured aspect to the deposits. At St Tudy, Cornwall (RCM-F042), nine palstaves were deliberately stacked, four or five on top of the others, and the Bournemouth Hospital hoard, Dorset, was probably deposited in a pit (PM-F001; Champion & Jarvis 1992). In many cases, palstaves were clearly deposited without their hafts. This is supported by other examples from Britain and France, such as five palstaves deposited in individual closely related pits near Canterbury (Chestnut & Wilkin 2014), and 14 different palstaves were placed in a ceramic bowl at Birchington (Powell-Cotton & Crawford 1924), both Kent. At Chappelle-du-Bois-des-Faulx, Normandy, France, two hoards of palstaves were deposited stacked and in bundles in two closely related pits (Verney 1991); similarly, palstaves were tightly packed into a pit at Gatteville, France (Le Carlier & Marcigny 2011). Packing into pits may represent aspects of convenience or formalisation of the burial process, but elsewhere this was clearly done in relation to already ancient places or landscapes with meaning. Five palstaves were deposited in relation to the Neolithic chambered tomb at Mulfra Quoit, Cornwall (Pearce 1983, 415–6, no.88), and a large hoard of up to 100 objects, probably palstaves, was inserted into an earlier barrow at Lovehayne, Devon (RAMM-F028; Jones & Quinnell 2008, 41–2). Lastly, the Marnhull palstaves were found packed into a small pit, some flat, some on end, seven in a rough crescent on top of pit (Lawson & Farwell 1990, 131). This hoard, located along the Stour Valley, may have been deposited in relation to the route along which it was imported from Normandy (O'Connor 2009, 274). These structured arrangements, as well as their depositional locations referencing specific locales and places echoes that seen in the ornament hoards and we can suggest this was integral to the appropriate deposition of many palstaves.

In some cases, the place chosen or the arrangement in the ground may have been driven by practical choices for storing the objects or rediscovering them later, which also assumes that such material was intended for retrieval (cf. Needham 2001). Here I follow David Fontijn (2020, 106; Fontijn & Roymans 2019) in suggesting that at least some of this material was never intended to be recovered. Deposition in this case removed the objects from potential circulation and transformed the palstaves from objects for trade and exchange into something inalienable (cf. Fontijn 2008a). Bloch and Parry (1989) argued that every society has different methods for acquiring and converting commodity objects into locally acceptable forms; this can be supported ethnographically by the destruction of wealth seen in the potlatch ceremonies of the Pacific north-west coast (Mauss 1990) or historically in the sacrifice and deposition of parts of objects at Roman and Greek temples (Needham 2007a, 288; Hansen 2016, 185–6; Fontijn & Roymans 2019, 181). Drawing on this economic theory, Fontijn (2008a) argued that the deposition of a 'trader's hoard' from Voorhout in the Netherlands may represent this process. The Voorhout hoard consisted of metalwork foreign to the Netherlands that might have been viewed as polluted; to make the material acceptable for recycling a portion had to be sacrificed in *pars pro toto* style. He recently argued similarly for a hoard of ten imported palstaves from Hoogeloon, the Netherlands, comprising nine French 'Normand' types and one British type; these were deposited in a pool and thus unlikely to have been intended for retrieval (Fontijn & Roymans 2019).

There are, however, significant differences between the Middle Bronze Age hoards of south-west Britain and that from Voorhout or Hoogeloon. Firstly, many of the deposits in the South West comprise regionally distinctive forms of palstaves and secondly, south-west Britain is a metalliferous region whilst the Netherlands is not. However, the main supplies of metal were sourced from continental Europe at this time. Breton and Norman palstaves deposited in Dorset and elsewhere along the south may have been part of the process of making the imported material socially acceptable, though the scale of the Marnhull hoard suggests a large sacrifice of economic potential that was perhaps intended to be retrieved but was lost or forgotten. In Somerset, east Devon and Dorset, a regionally distinct high-flanged 'south-western' form of palstave was produced and deposited in hoards and as single finds (Smith 1959a; Schmidt & Burgess 1981, 141–3); a variant of this, known as the 'Crediton' type, has a complimentary distribution in Cornwall and west Devon (Fig. 4.22). This suggests communities living in the western peninsula produced forms that captured aspects of their regionality and identity, before then treating and depositing these objects in widely accepted ways. Like importation, manufacture of objects may have also required token deposits, so a certain proportion of objects produced were consigned to the ground.

However, this still remains only a partial explanation. The ornament hoards mentioned above highlight that palstaves could function differently in different social spheres. The *pars pro toto* interpretation only accounts for some of the palstave hoards and may also explain some single finds, but what of palstave hoards made up of eclectic forms and different types of wear? Around 1830, a hoard of eight palstaves were recovered from Plumley, Devon (RAMM-F038; Way 1869, 346). Accounts vary but at least four of the eight palstaves deposited at Plumley were deposited in an upright position under a boulder, whilst the other four may have been found under another boulder or were scattered nearby (Croker 1852, 186; Tucker 1867, 119; Way 1869, 346). Moreover, they were reportedly found in the same field as six stone hut circles, which were destroyed shortly after 1836 for building materials (Anon. 1925, 51). Of the four that survive, at least three are south-western-type palstaves produced from three different moulds and showing varying signs of wear. Like the ornament hoards, I would argue here we are again observing a deposit selectively gathered by individuals and/or communities to express or solidify certain relations with people, objects and/or the place of deposition. The deliberate placement of the Plumley palstaves, potentially associated with a settlement, suggests this was a deposit with social meaning beyond a purely economic purpose. For these acts, destruction was not deemed appropriate prior to deposition (though removal of organic hafts may have served to remove the functionality of the objects) and it remained largely understood that palstaves should be deposited complete. Through palstaves we can observe how a single object form may be treated and deposited in varied ways, serving a variety of roles in managing the Bronze Age social world.

Destruction and deposition in occupational contexts

The areas where people lived were some of the most dynamic spaces for carrying out depositions directly related to daily life and

Table 4.3: Middle Bronze Age metal objects studied from occupational contexts

Findspot/No.	*Object(s)*	*Context*	*Completeness %*	*Damage Ranking(s)*	*Evidence of use*	*Other damage*
			Hambledon Hill, Dorset			
BM-F020	Palstave	Iron Age hillfort, uncertain context	26–50	0,1	Uncertain	Broken at stop ridge and blade; corrosion damage
DCM-F017	Spearhead	Iron Age hillfort, uncertain context	76–99	0	Y	Hafting damage
			Kites Farm, Dorset			
BTM-F001	Palstave	Uncertain	100	n/a	Y	None
			Boden Vean, Cornwall			
RCM-F003	Knife	Post-hole of roundhouse	76–99	0	Uncertain	Corrosion damage
			Tredarvah, Cornwall			
RCM-F043a	Flanged axehead	Scattered domestic layer	100	n/a	Uncertain	None
RCM-F043b	Spearhead	Scattered domestic layer	76–99	0, Uncertain	Y	Broken (multi); broken blade; some post-recovery damage
RCM-F043c	Knife	Scattered domestic layer	51–75	0, Uncertain	Uncertain	Broken (multi); broken tip & hilt; burning; some post-recovery damage
RCM-F043d	Blade	Scattered domestic layer	Uncertain	0, Uncertain	Uncertain	Broken (multi); broken blade; some post-recovery damage
RCM-F043e	Pin	Scattered domestic layer	0–25	0,1	Uncertain	Broken (multi); corrosion damage
RCM-F043f	Pin	Scattered domestic layer	76–99	0,1	Uncertain	Broken (multi); corrosion damage
RCM-F043g	Uncertain	Scattered domestic layer	Uncertain	0	Uncertain	Broken (multi); corrosion damage; fragmented
RCM-F043h	Pin	Scattered domestic layer	Uncertain	0	Uncertain	Broken (multi); corrosion damage
RCM-F043i	Pin	Scattered domestic layer	Uncertain	0, Uncertain	Uncertain	Corrosion damage; fragmented
			Trethellan Farm, Cornwall			
RCM-F048a	Spearhead	Bronze Age land surface	51–75	0,1	Uncertain	Broken (multi); broken tip; socket damaged; corrosion damage
RCM-F048b	Socketed point	Ritual hollow	Uncertain	0, Uncertain	Uncertain	Broken (single); socket damaged; corrosion damage
RCM-F048c	Blade	Bronze Age land surface	Uncertain	2	Uncertain	Broken (single); broken blade; tip broken
RCM-F048d	Bracelet	Floor of roundhouse	26–50	1	Uncertain	Broken (single)
RCM-F048e	Cu-alloy rod	Bronze Age field system	Uncertain	Uncertain	Uncertain	Broken (single)
RCM-F048f	Cu-alloy object	Roundhouse	Uncertain	Uncertain	Uncertain	Broken (single)
RCM-F048g	Stone mould	Ritual hollow	Uncertain	1	Y	Broken (single)

Findspot/No.	Object(s)	Context	Completeness	Damage Ranking(s)	Evidence of use	Other damage
			Cadbury Castle, Somerset			
TTNCM-F007k	Spearhead	Late Iron Age pit, with Late Bronze Age pottery	0–25	2	Uncertain	Mid-blade frag.
TTNCM-F007oo	Spearhead	Pit; found with 4 pieces metal-lurgical waste (TTNCM-F007jj)	0–25	2	Uncertain	Mid-blade frag.
TTNCM-F007rr	Pin	Trench of cruciform church; found with F007bb (LBA disc-headed pin)	76–99	1	Uncertain	Broken (refitting pieces/frags); shaft broken
			Ham Hill, Somerset			
TTNCM-F020c	Sickle	Iron Age hillfort, uncertain context	51–75	0,1	Uncertain	Broken blade (refitting pieces/frags); corrosion damage; some post-recovery damage
TTNCM-F020d	Sickle	Iron Age hillfort, uncertain context	26–50	0,1	Uncertain	Broken blade (single piece); casting flaws; corrosion damage
TTNCM-F020m	Palstave	Iron Age hillfort, uncertain context	76–99	1	N	Blade edges damaged; some post-recovery damage; use-damage
			South Cadbury (Milsom Corner), Somerset			
TTNCM-F031	Shield	Ditch of enclosure	76–99	0,3	Uncertain	Corrosion damage; stabbed/penetrated
			Norton Fitzwarren Hillfort, Somerset			
TTNCM-F036a	Bracelet	Pit in enclosure ditch	76–99	0	Uncertain	Broken (multi); corrosion damage
TTNCM-F036b	Bracelet	Pit in enclosure ditch	0–25	0	Y	Broken (multi); corrosion damage
TTNCM-F036c	Bracelet	Pit in enclosure ditch	76–99	0	Uncertain	Broken (multi); corrosion damage
TTNCM-F036d	Bracelet	Pit in enclosure ditch	0–25	0	Uncertain	Broken (multi); corrosion damage
TTNCM-F036e	Bracelet	Pit in enclosure ditch	51–75	0	Uncertain	Broken (multi); corrosion damage
TTNCM-F036f	Bracelet	Pit in enclosure ditch	76–99	0	Uncertain	Broken (multi); corrosion damage
TTNCM-F036g	Bracelet	Pit in enclosure ditch	76–99	0	Uncertain	Broken (multi); corrosion damage
TTNCM-F036h	Bracelet	Pit in enclosure ditch	76–99	0	Uncertain	Broken (multi); corrosion damage
TTNCM-F036i	Bracelet	Pit in enclosure ditch	76–99	0	Uncertain	Broken (multi); corrosion damage
TTNCM-F036j	Palstave	Pit in enclosure ditch	76–99	0	Uncertain	Corrosion damage
TTNCM-F036k	Palstave	Pit in enclosure ditch	51–75	0	Uncertain	Broken (single); broken blade; corrosion damage
TTNCM-F036l	Socketed axehead	Pit in enclosure ditch	76–99	0	Uncertain	Broken (single); broken blade; corrosion damage; cracking
TTNCM-F036m	Uncertain	Pit in enclosure ditch	n/a	n/a	Uncertain	Corrosion damage

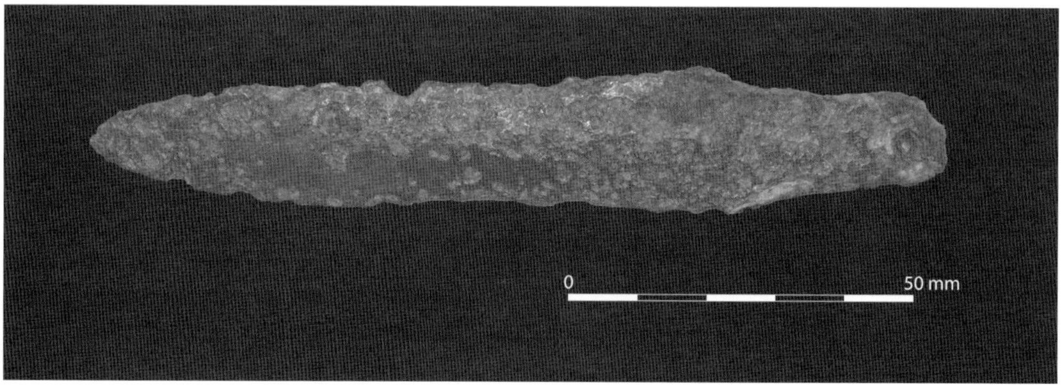

Figure 4.23: A copper-alloy knife from a posthole within a roundhouse at Boden Vean, Cornwall (RCM-F003) (source: author, courtesy of the Royal Institution of Cornwall)

important social events. Across Britain, the deposition (and occasional destruction) of metal objects, stone tools, ceramics, animal bones, human remains and a range of other substances and materials was a regular practice that has been related to various activities including the construction and deconstruction of structures, delineating boundaries, subsistence practices or craftworking on site (eg, Brück 1999b *inter alia*; Gerritsen 2003). South-west Britain was no exception.

Damaged metalwork

Damaged metalwork has been recovered from a variety of occupational contexts but few of those studied could be considered deliberate (Table 4.3). At Trethellan Farm, Cornwall, a blade fragment from a Bronze Age land surface was damage-ranked 2 (RCM-F048c). Two probably deliberately damaged fragments of Middle Bronze Age spearheads from Cadbury Castle, Somerset were recovered from later Iron Age/Roman contexts making it difficult to interpret the age of the damage. The remaining material studied largely presented a combination of use-related and post-depositional damage and was predominantly found scattered within occupational layers rather than as structured deposits. Nonetheless, complete and broken metal objects served a variety of functions.

At Rowden, Dorset, a copper-alloy knife fragment was recovered from a hut wall, whilst an incomplete copper-alloy arrowhead was found with flints, loomweight fragments and faunal remains in the infill of the same hut (Gingell 1991, 104). Similarly, a ribbed bracelet fragment was found in a roundhouse at Bestwall Quarry, Dorset, and another fragmentary bracelet was recovered from a pit associated with a burnt mound (O'Connor 2009). Fragmentary and incomplete metalwork was also recovered from infill deposits of roundhouses and ditches at Ivyton, Somerset (Roffey *et al.* 2004), and Tremough, Cornwall (Jones & Quinnell 2015). These objects appear to have broken accidentally but the various infills and deposits with which they are associated have been linked with abandonment processes and the overall lifecycle of roundhouses (cf. Brück 1999b; 2006a; Nowakowski 2001). At Penhale Moor, Cornwall, a broken spearhead was found at a 70° angle, tip down in the upper layer of a roundhouse indicating it may have been thrust in to 'kill the house' (Nowakowski 1998, 237–8; 2001, 145). Postholes of a roundhouse at Boden Vean, Cornwall, contained a used knife (RCM-F003; Fig. 4.23) and two perforated clay weights, which were again linked to the process of abandonment (Gossip 2008; 2013).

Breaking quernstones

Metalwork deposits did not occur in isolation and many infills also contained fragmentary stone and ceramic objects, which served a variety of functions. The objects deposited can be linked to activities we might envisage as part of 'daily life' at a farmstead or village. The material from which an object was made was not necessarily important – the treatment of the object was. We may take the quernstone as just one example of an object that was frequently deposited both complete and incomplete at Middle Bronze Age sites in south-west Britain, often in structured deposits (Watts 2014).

Quernstones were essential objects for food production and their destruction and deposition marked the removal of important objects of subsistence from circulation as well as serving to manage social practices. House 7 at Bestwall

Quarry was closed with a deposit of a complete but broken quernstone placed in a pit with fragments of pottery and animal bone, and the remains of the structure were 'sealed by an ashy deposit containing large amounts of burnt flint, worked flint and pottery' (Ladle & Woodward 2009, 84). A complete quern was also found at House 2, and two complete querns, one of which was broken, was deposited in a pit (Ladle & Woodward 2009, 369). At Scarcewater, Cornwall, a Middle Bronze Age pit contained six stone rubbers of different materials and an adjacent stone-lined pit contained a saddle quern split in two with a rubber and several other stone fragments; furthermore, two halves of a deliberately broken muller were found in neighbouring roundhouses (Jones & Taylor 2010, 28, 115; Watts 2014, 90ff.). At Gwithian, a quernstone fragment, mussel shells, a cow's molar and a fragment of animal bone were found in a posthole associated with an Early–Middle Bronze Age structure (Sturgess & Lawson-Jones 2006, 388). Additionally, a 'gully' on one side of this structure was partially lined with broken querns and contained finds including 'a pottery ring, a bronze awl and a dog whelk which had been pierced many times' (*ibid.*, 20). Quernstone fragments were also built into the walls of a structure at Shaugh Moor, Devon (Wainwright & Smith 1980). If we consider the symbolic nature of quernstones, as a tool for food production and thus having life-giving capacities (cf. Watts 2014), we can envisage the social significance of selecting, incorporating and even breaking these objects as part of the wider suite of deposits. Work by Kerri Cleary (2018) suggests that quernstones were more likely broken deliberately, rather than by accident or through use; the decision to deposit incomplete quernstones thus represents a conscious premeditated action. Fragmentation events may have been part of closing structures and settlements alongside other processes.

Remains of metalworking

Metalworking debris deposited at settlements likewise forces us to consider how the symbolic function of material may have been a key motivation for its deposition. The fragmentation of clay moulds to remove the metal object is inherent to the production process and scatters of this material were found at Tremough, Cornwall (Pearce 2015) and at the slightly later site at Sigwells, Somerset (Skowranek 2007, 109–11). At Sigwells, however, Richard Tabor suggested the mould fragments 'were far more fragmentary than necessary to extract the finished product' (2008, 67); in other words, these were subjected to intentional breakage after extracting the finds. Similarly, Andy Jones (2015, 189–95) has convincingly argued that the incomplete, worn and, in some cases, reused moulds found associated with Roundhouse 1 at Tremough were incorporated as part of a formalised process for abandoning the structure, perhaps representing personal possessions of the people who occupied the house.

These various deposits emphasise the complexities of practices at occupational contexts in south-west Britain, and indeed are reflected across Britain, involving the full suite of available material culture. Incomplete objects, whether deliberately broken or not, were gathered for a range of purposes and are of a different character to that collected for contemporary hoards. In some cases, objects, including metalwork, formed part of refuse layers; elsewhere they were integral deposits or infills. The various caches of deliberately selected material presented above suggest that depositional acts conveyed social significance, and the utilisation of broken objects linked the community and different structures within a settlement. Across these sites, we can envisage the conscious processes of dismantling structures, digging pits, breaking some objects, while leaving others intact, as well as a series of burning events, all serving as social ceremonies linked with occasions, which may relate to closing houses or celebrating key points in the lives of the inhabitants (cf. Ladle & Woodward 2009, 369f.). People used these events to establish themselves, their lives and their sense of place in the world. Where we have detailed excavations we can even begin to construct what I will term here a *biography of destruction*; this not only focuses on reconstructing the act of destruction and deposition but also sets it in its cultural sphere. This is particularly clear in the case of the destruction and deposition of the South Cadbury shield.

A biography of destruction: the South Cadbury Shield (TTNCM-F031)

In 1997, a bronze shield was found during archaeological excavation in the upper fills

Figure 4.24: The South Cadbury shield, Somerset (TTNCM-F031) © Somerset County Council and South West Heritage Trust, acc.no. TTNCM 110/1998/1

of the junction of two boundary ditches of a Middle–Late Bronze Age enclosure at Milsoms Corner, South Cadbury, Somerset (Fig. 4.24; Coles *et al.* 1999; Needham *et al.* 2012). This is the only shield known from the South West. Upon deposition, this shield was positioned face down in the ditch, with the central boss set into a stakehole. It was then penetrated three times from the back with a blunt, non-metal object, possibly a wooden stake (Coles *et al.* 1999, 38–9, 45–6). This destructive act occurred *in situ*, indicated by bronze fragments that were carried into the soil below the shield (*ibid.*). The shield rim was also damaged, perhaps hammered upon deposition (Needham *et al.* 2012, 479), but it could be accidental or combat-related.

The shield is a 'Yetholm' type, dating to the Penard metalworking assemblage (1275–1150 BC); compositional analysis confirmed that the bronze was consistent with production during this period (Needham *et al.* 2012; Uckelmann 2012, 49). However, the shield was deposited in contact with a red deer or cattle hip bone, which produced a Late Bronze Age radiocarbon date (2810±80 BP; 1060–840 cal BC (1σ) or 1210–810 cal BC (2σ)) suggesting that the shield may have been in circulation and/or curated for up to two hundred years prior to deposition (Coles *et al.* 1999, 37; Needham *et al.* 2012; Knight forthcoming a). Therefore, the destruction of the shield may have been linked with ending its long use-life.

We can explore this through three avenues;

1. The manufacture and social role of the shield;
2. The wider context of shield depositions; and
3. Other activities at the enclosure.

Manufacture and social role of the shield

Bronze shields represent impressive feats of craft. The main body of the South Cadbury shield was hammered from a single piece of bronze to about 0.4–0.6mm thick, and adorned with 25 concentric ribs, alternating with 25 rows of *c.* 6030 bosses; a handle was riveted onto the back (Uckelmann 2012, 45, no. 45, pls 68–69). Manufacture of this object was highly skilled and required repeated sessions of coldworking and annealing to reduce the strain on the metallic microstructure and limit the risk of unwanted fragmentation (Neil Burridge pers.comm.); this process is supported by a metallographic analysis of the Cadbury shield (Needham *et al.* 2012, 484). This was a spectacular object, difficult to make, and to date only 24 are known from Britain, plus seven reported in literature but now destroyed or lost (Uckelmann 2020, 270). Not everyone would have had access to one and it may have been an import into the region. This in turn would have increased the social value of such an object. Uckelmann (2011; 2012) argued that shields served three core functions – defence, display and dedication – with the purpose of shields transforming over time because of their social involvements. Intrinsic to this, we can consider the sensory aspects of shields. In terms of form and size, the object type has no bronze parallels, and the bright and reflective bronze colour would have made for an impressive and mnemonic object (Knight forthcoming a). The ribs and bosses may have functionally strengthened the shield (Molloy 2009), but the décor is similar to some contemporary ribbed and bossed bracelets (eg, at Norton Fitzwarren). If intended for display purposes the Cadbury shield may have been reserved for certain ceremonies or rites of passages, incorporating these sensory elements; alternatively, knowledge of the shield may have been restricted with only limited access to certain people within the community. The potentially extended period over which the shield was retained, indicates that it was a treasured object within the community. It may have become inalienable to the community in which it was situated, a powerful symbol.

The wider context of shield depositions

In the wider context of other shield depositions, the South Cadbury example stands out. Almost all other Yetholm-type shields were buried in watery locations, such as bogs, except for a recent discovery from Woodstock, Oxfordshire (Uckelmann 2020). Often, shields were deposited in specific ways: for instance, at Beith, North Ayrshire, five or six shields were deposited on edge in a circle in a bog (McCulloch 1864, 165; Coles 1960, 106–7). However, few show signs of deliberate destruction, and none to the extent of South Cadbury. This suggests that the South Cadbury shield was not deposited according to broader concepts of how shields were being deposited elsewhere. Somerset is after all not short of wetland locations, so the decision to deposit the shield in an enclosure ditch suggests that the wider understanding was unimportant, or perhaps forgotten from social memory if the shield was of some age.

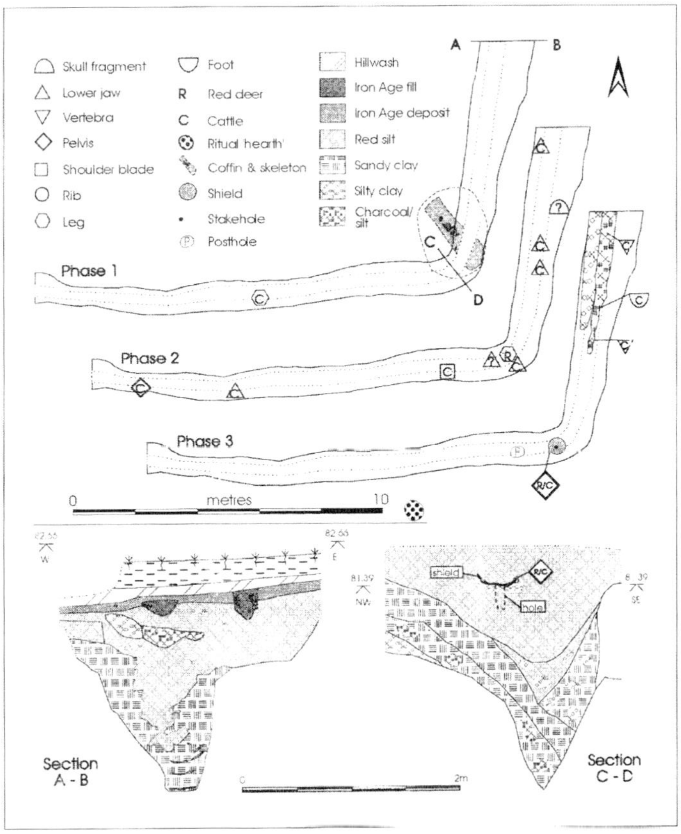

Figure 4.25: A plan of the Milsoms Corner Bronze Age enclosure ditch, showing the various depositions. Phases 1 and 2 date to the Middle Bronze Age, whilst Phase 3 dates to the Late Bronze Age (image courtesy of Richard Tabor)

Other depositional activities at Milsoms Corner

The shield deposition should not be viewed in isolation. The enclosure ditches went through two phases of enlargement and infilling over the course of 400–500 years, with the shield deposited in the final phase (Phase 3) (Fig. 4.25). Initial construction of the enclosure ditch cut an Early Bronze Age burial pit that contained at least two individuals, in the process removing the lower half of one skeleton (Coles *et al.* 1999, 35–7). The lower leg bone of this skeleton was found in a Late Bronze Age posthole packed with burnt stones approximately one metre west of the stakehole over which the shield was set (*ibid.*, 37). It has subsequently been suggested that the depositions in the posthole and stakehole, and the destruction of the shield, were linked (Tabor 2008, 91). This also suggests that this leg bone was retained, curated and circulated from the time of its discovery until its point of deposition in the Late Bronze Age alongside the shield. Communities were active in this area over this period, as indicated by repeated depositions in the ditches, mostly of selected faunal elements, eg, cattle mandibles in Phase 2.

In Phase 3 contemporary areas of burnt stones were identified in and near the ditches. The stones packed with the lower leg bone were burnt blue stones (Tabor 2008, 91), which have also been highlighted as sealing other deposits in and around the ditches. However, burnt red stones lined the base of a contemporary 'scoop' south of the enclosure, which was covered by a charcoal-rich deposit, a single burnt flint, a bowl sherd, and a single cattle rib 'snapped into two roughly equal halves' (Tabor 2008, 84–5). The stones were carefully selected for their specific colours and the act of burning is inherently destructive and transformative. The selection of specifically coloured stones was also observed at the nearby enclosure at Sigwells (*ibid.*, 90). The range of evidence has led Richard Tabor (*ibid.*) to suggest that the Phase 3 actions at Milsoms Corner, including the destruction of the shield, were all broadly contemporary, perhaps occurring within a matter of days and linked to feasting activities.

The function of destruction

The destruction of the shield thus forms part of a tradition of deposition within the ditches but also forms one of several selective and destructive acts. The hip bone of the red deer/cattle found underneath the shield and the human leg bone represent the fragmentation of animals and humans and the deliberate selection of specific pieces, even if the leg bone may have been found inadvertently during ditch construction. The performance of shield destruction in the Milsoms Corner ditch was probably a public action observable by a wide audience and therefore might be considered an open expression of a set of beliefs or changing circumstances. The lifecycle of the shield may have been widely known; its potentially long life means the deposition and destruction of the shield could have been an act of transformation linked with a kinship or communal identity metaphorically ending the identity of the shield. The public performance can be seen both as a mnemonic act, establishing a memorable event, and also a process of forgetting ending the life of the object and any relations attached to it (Knight forthcoming a); the destruction of *Malanggan* art in Melanesia serves a similar function (Küchler 1987; 2002). Following destruction, the shield was left *in situ* though it is unclear whether it was immediately covered up or allowed to bury naturally. It is possible that its position was preserved in social memory and thus achieved a mythological status.

The combination of all these features offers a rich case study that emphasises a sequence of destructive and depositional events of a variety of objects and materials in relation to a landscape with a long history. This demonstrates the potential for establishing *biographies of destruction* whereby destruction and deposition can be understood in their wider cultural contexts as socially-situated processes. The shield, an object atypical for the region, had inalienable qualities emphasised by its aesthetics and display function. The long length of time over which it was kept indicates its role as a communal symbol, perhaps with an heirloom status. The destruction of this object could thus be linked with the end of a certain set of beliefs or the death of a lineage; the destruction of the shield was a constructed event situated in a settlement boundary alongside a variety of other coordinated practices. It is possible to envisage an accompanying feasting event (cf. Tabor 2008) with a public ceremony that severed the relationships between the people and the object whilst also serving to establish a prolonged memory, thus enabling construction of a communal personhood.

Conclusions

Although the destruction of metalwork was not widespread in south-west Britain, it was clearly a growing practice during the Middle Bronze Age. There is relatively limited evidence until *c.* 1400 BC and even then we only catch glimpses in the archaeological record, such as in the Taunton hoard. Indeed, the clearest evidence in the region comes almost entirely from Somerset with links to activities elsewhere in the country; metalwork depositions in Cornwall, Devon and Dorset, by contrast, rarely incorporated destruction. This suggests a highly selective practice with regards to how objects should be treated with regionalised approaches undertaken in reaction to specific circumstances. Although for some communities, destruction of objects was appropriate for deposition and a way of managing certain events and relationships, elsewhere the practice of burying objects was enough. In the case of palstave hoards, this may have been part of managing the Bronze Age economic system of imports from elsewhere or production of local forms. When destruction did occur, only certain objects were seemingly eligible, most notably weapons and ornaments, whilst others, such as tools, were destined to be buried complete.

Deposition, and the associated actions, did not occur in isolation. They took place in significant landscapes and were socially situated events. Destruction heightened the significance of the deposit, serving to enforce wider understandings and create mnemonic events through dramatic actions. The evidence from contemporary occupational contexts, where destructive actions were undertaken on a range of objects, suggests that deposits were regularly integral to managing the social world at settlements (cf. Brück 2006a). Unlike hoards, this was widespread across the South West and, in some cases, can be linked to the abandonment and decommissioning of roundhouses, which necessitated deposits of complete and deliberately damaged material. However, whilst the ideology was widespread, decisions around which objects and materials were varied.

That we can observe regionalised trends with hoards, and no distinct 'pattern' in what objects were deposited where, how and when across different contexts, implies that although there are broader concepts at play in terms of what was or was not appropriate, it was a localised choice. It was important that objects were deposited, and that some of these were left complete or alternatively broken, but communities chose how best to construct their deposits depending on the social situation.

Notes

1 Pearce (1983, 530, no.743) also lists a dagger with these palstaves but original donation records do not indicate they were found together (Anon. 1875, 70; Gray 1932, lxxv).

2 Accessible via: https://www.britishmuseum.org/collection/

5

Mass destruction and minor destruction: the Late Bronze Age–earliest Iron Age, *c.* 1150–600 BC

When one considers the deliberate destruction of Bronze Age metalwork, it tends to be the Late Bronze Age that attracts most attention. The period from *c.* 1150–800 BC represents an era of mass deposition of metalwork across north-western Europe in a range of contexts; much of this material was buried in worn-out or fragmented conditions, frequently with various destruction indicators (Huth 1997; Maraszek 2006; Turner 2010a). In Britain, this was particularly the case in the south, and south-west Britain fits within this trend. Over time, the more 'selective' approach towards destruction that we observed in the Middle Bronze Age gave way to a period where deliberately destroying objects was very common. The large volume of metalwork deposited around this time has typically been viewed as scrapped material or else the abandonment of bronze as an economically viable material by the end of the period (Coles 1960; Burgess 1979; Thomas 1989), though it is clear that at least some was the result of deliberate symbolic depositional action (Bradley 1998; Fontijn 2002; Needham 2007a; Mörtz 2018); destruction of metalwork was a common feature within both types of deposit, though in the chapter I will emphasise that such a strict distinction is not necessarily appropriate.

During the Earliest Iron Age (800–600 BC), metalwork continued to be deposited in relatively large quantities, but it was of a different general nature, with hoards typically comprising complete, unbroken axeheads, and single finds of a more limited range of material, such as socketed axeheads, swords and razors (O'Connor 2007; Boughton 2015). In south-west Britain, metalwork deposited during this period is almost exclusively undamaged axeheads and small tools in localised regions.

I have chosen to address both periods within this chapter because, firstly, it emphasises the starkness of the contrast in the metalwork depositional traditions, and secondly it allows us to examine the transformation of how and why communities deposited metalwork. As we shall see, although the production, treatment and deposition of metalwork was undertaken according to broader ideas, it also related to regional and interregional networks and reflected individual approaches.

Mass destruction: the Late Bronze Age *c.* 1150–800 BC

853 Late Bronze Age metal objects were studied from south-west Britain, over half of which (*c.* 57%) showed signs of intentional destruction (Fig. 5.1). This occurred in a similar array of contexts as in the preceding centuries, but deliberately destroyed objects were more common in certain contexts than others (Fig. 5.2). This can, in part, be attributed to the numbers of objects recovered from different contexts – more metal objects were deposited in hoards than occupational contexts for instance – but it is also related to the type and variety of metal objects produced, circulated and deposited.

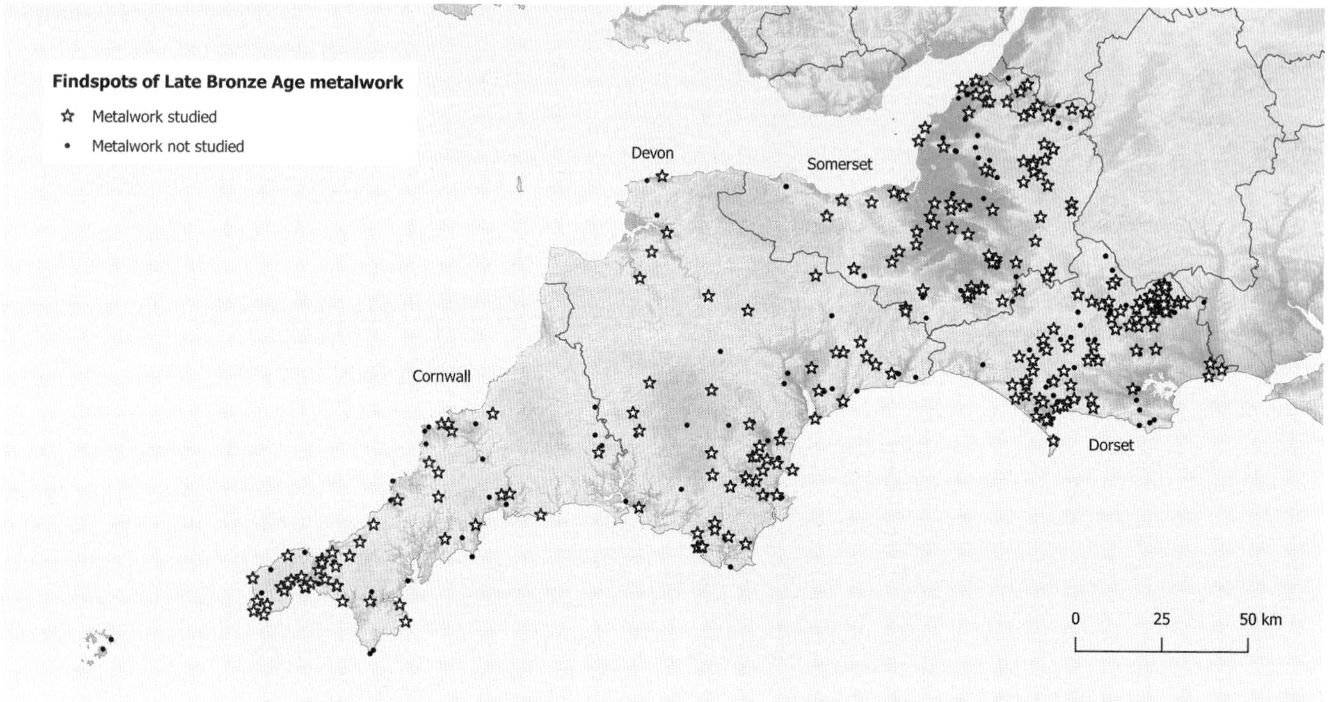

Figure 5.1: Findspots of Late Bronze Age metalwork from south-west Britain. Those marked with stars were studied as part of this research. Contains OS data © Crown copyright and database right 2021

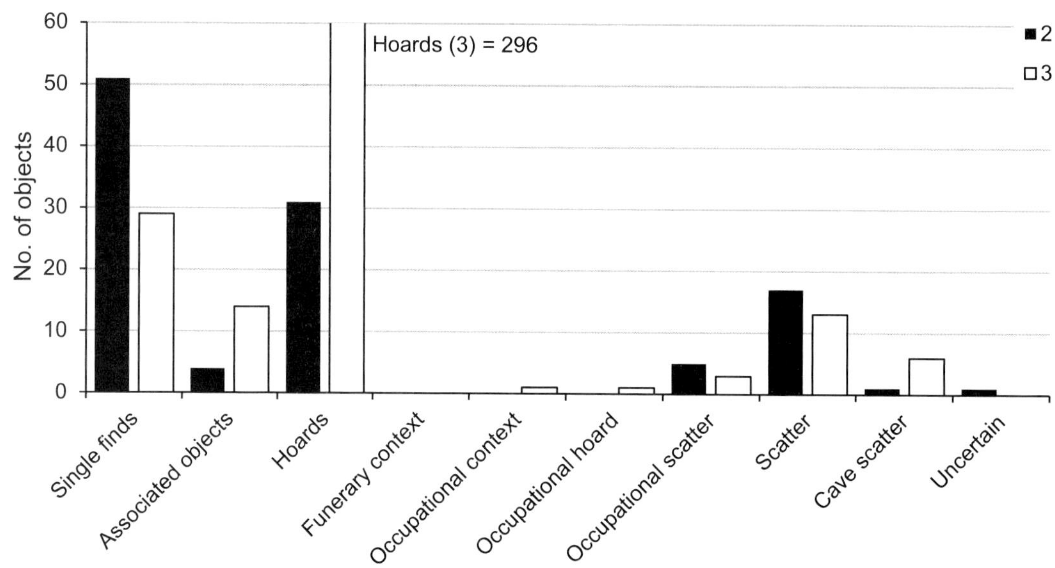

Figure 5.2: Frequency of Late Bronze Age metalwork from south-west Britain damage-ranked 2 or 3 divided by context (n=473)

Almost half of all objects studied were copper/copper-alloy ingots, which were almost all deliberately fragmented; other objects commonly displaying signs of deliberate destruction included socketed axeheads, swords, and spearheads (Fig. 5.3). These objects were frequently deposited singly or in hoards. By contrast, several object forms, including small tools and ornaments, showed limited or no damage; these were objects most commonly recovered from occupational areas or scatters, but rarely from hoards.

Deliberately damaged objects were most frequent in Cornwall, where over three-quarters of the metalwork studied were probably or definitely destroyed (Fig. 5.4). A similarly high percentage of deliberately damaged metalwork was deposited in Devon; there was a greater proportion of complete and/ or accidentally damaged finds from Dorset.

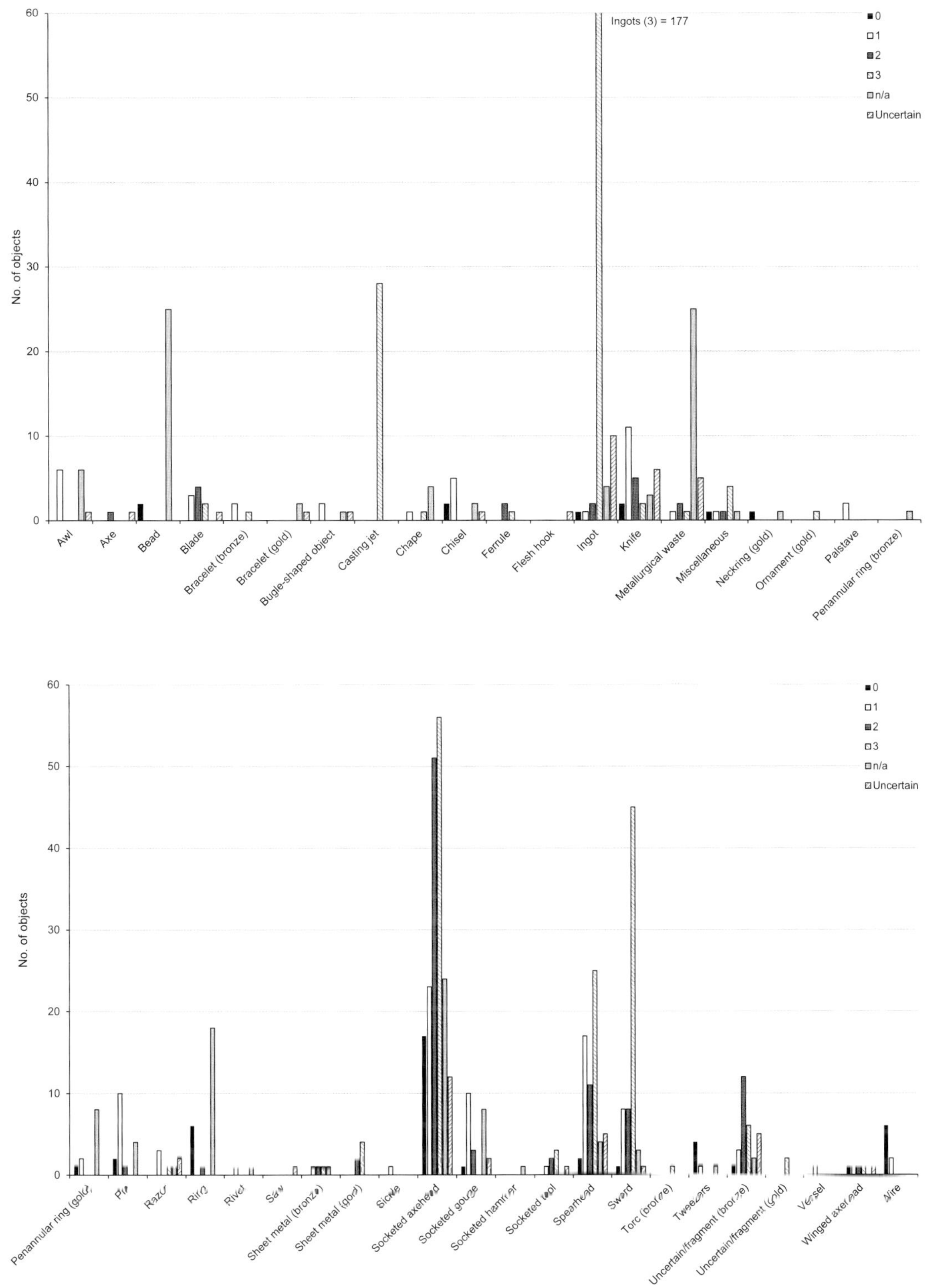

Figure 5.3: Late Bronze Age metalwork studied from south-west Britain divided by object type and damage ranking (n=853)

From Somerset, deliberate destruction initially appears relatively common, but this is skewed by the inclusion of a large hoard of deliberately fragmented metalwork from Stogursey (see below); excluding this hoard, the proportion of remaining metalwork damage-ranked 2 or 3 drops to 25%. Additionally, although there is an almost equal number of findspots where deliberately damaged metalwork has been found, findspots of undamaged metalwork are far fewer in Cornwall and Devon, especially when compared to Dorset

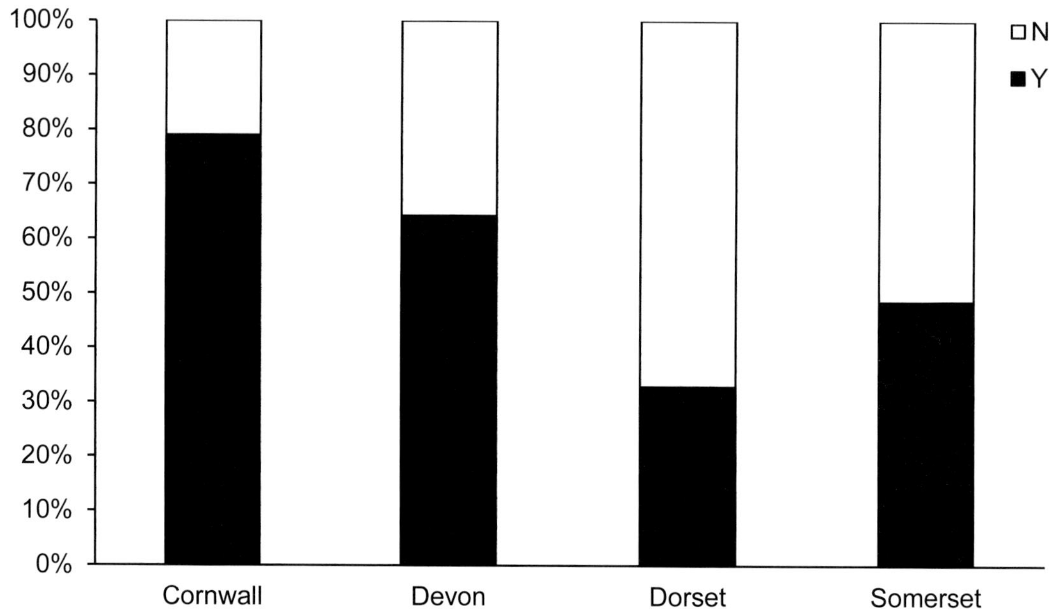

Figure 5.4: Proportional representation of objects showing signs of deliberate damage divided by county

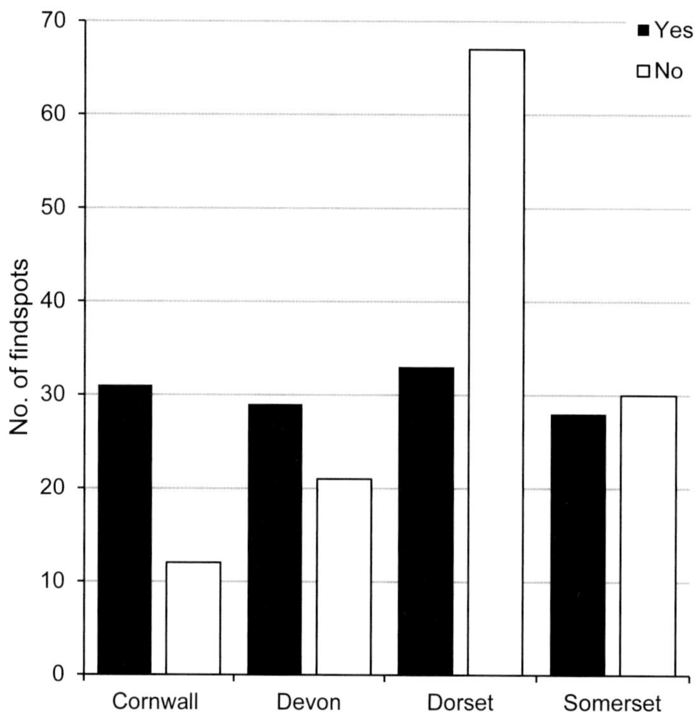

Figure 5.5: Frequency of findspots containing deliberately destroyed objects (Yes) and those containing no deliberately destroyed objects (No) divided by county (n=251)

(Fig. 5.5). Whilst this may reflect a distribution relating to recovery bias, these trends indicate regionalised approaches to the destruction and deposition of metalwork; in some areas deliberate destruction prior to deposition was clearly more common. An analysis of different contexts and individual case studies illustrates this further.

Late Bronze Age associated finds and hoards

More than 45 findspots with associated finds and hoards have been recovered from south-west Britain, with many containing mostly or solely deliberately destroyed metalwork. The majority date to the Ewart Park metalworking assemblage (*c.* 920–800 BC), the period in

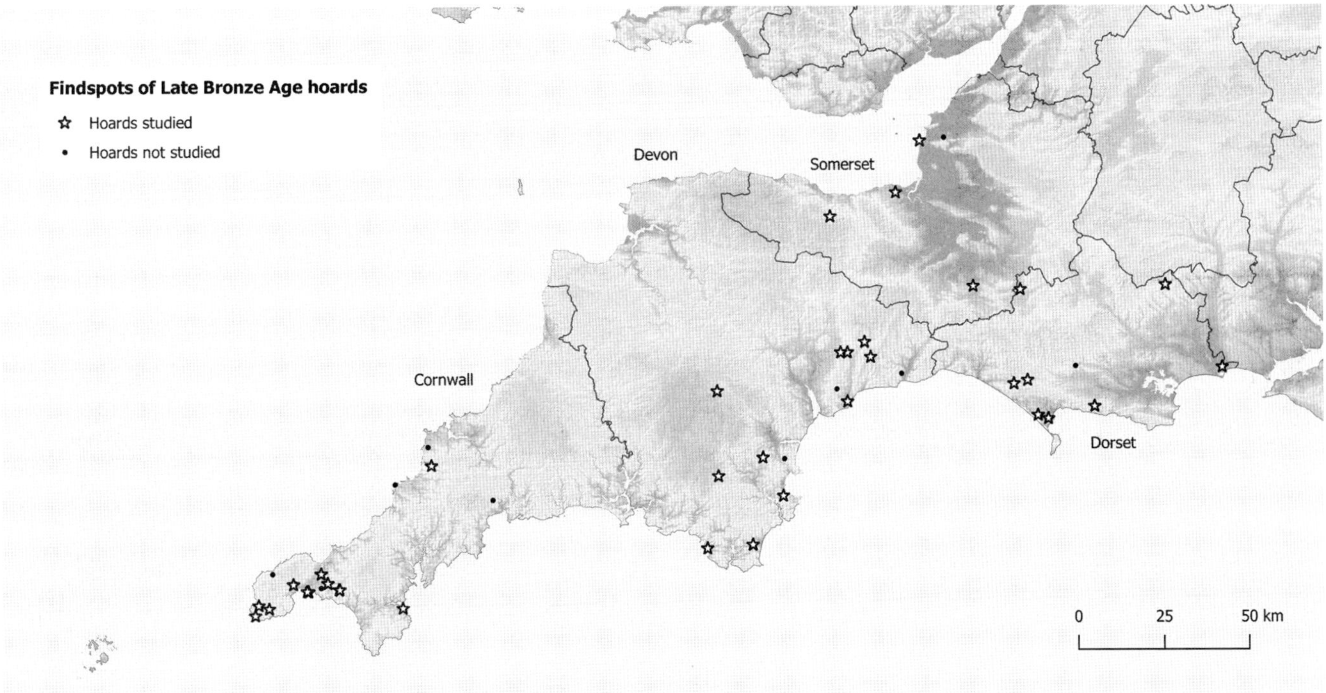

Figure 5.6: Findspots of Late Bronze Age metalwork hoards and associated finds from south-west Britain. Those marked with stars were studied as part of this research. Contains OS data © Crown copyright and database right 2021

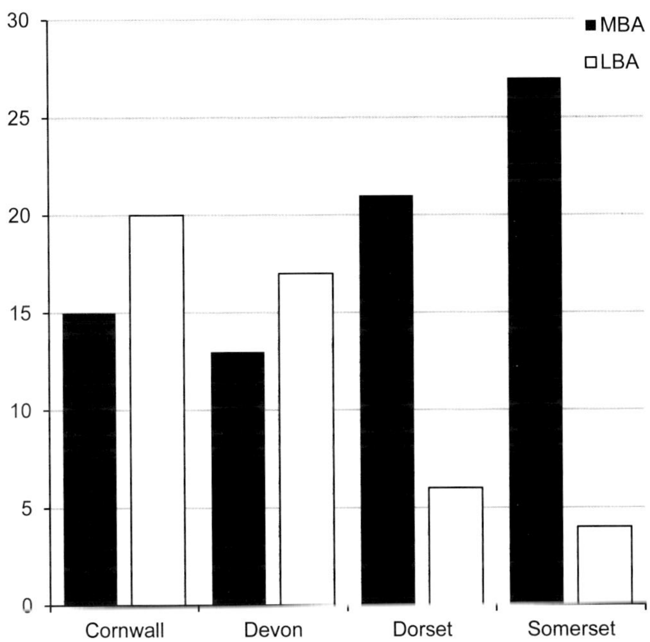

Figure 5.7: Comparison of number of Middle and Late Bronze Age associated finds and hoards from south-west Britain

Britain when most fragmentary hoards were deposited, though at least one hoard – the Bloody Pool hoard – dates to the earlier Wilburton-Blackmoor assemblages (*c.* 1150–920 BC). The concentration of south-western hoards in the 9th–8th centuries BC allows us to examine similarities and differences in hoarding practices across the region within a relatively confined timeframe. Most were deposited on the south coast, though clustered in certain areas (Fig. 5.6). Whereas hoards were relatively infrequent in Devon and Cornwall during the Middle Bronze Age, these are now the areas with the highest concentration of associated deposits; the inverse is true of Dorset and Somerset (Fig. 5.7), which reflects changing social attitudes and preferences towards deposition over time. Differential preferences are also captured in the varied content within the hoards, which suggests limited uniformity across the region in terms of what was and was not appropriate to deposit (Table 5.1). Different deposits allowed people to express broader ideas through localised practices.

The Bloody Pool hoard, Devon

This is clearly highlighted by the Bloody Pool hoard of spearheads and ferrules that we encountered at the beginning of the book. It was found in 1854 while digging in a swampy marsh on south Dartmoor (RAMM-F005; Tucker 1855, 84–5). The spearheads were broken into multiple fragments, not all of which survive, and the large, barbed spearheads within this hoard indicate it was deposited *c.* 1020–920 BC.

Missing pieces of the spearheads may have been deposited and subsequently lost, but many other contemporary examples of broken spearheads also lack the upper blade. Of the 78 barbed spearheads from Britain listed by Richard Davis (2015, 181–91), 50 were either broken across the blade or survive only as blade or socket fragments, supporting the idea that the Bloody Pool spearheads were deliberately deposited without their upper blades. The tips were thus either retained, recycled, or deposited elsewhere.

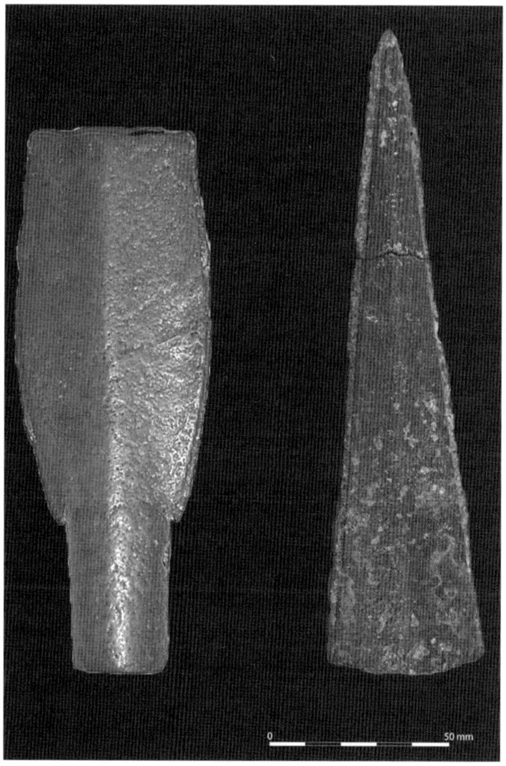

Figure 5.8: Two broken spearheads from Thurlestone, Devon (left: PAS-F087; courtesy of the Portable Antiquities Scheme/Trustees of the British Museum; right: PCMAG-F005a; photo: author, courtesy of The Box Plymouth)

The deposition of the Bloody Pool hoard falls within broader trends of destroying and hoarding weapons in Britain during the 10th century BC (Burgess *et al.* 1972; Coombs 1975; Mörtz 2018). Barbed spearheads were often deposited intentionally, either singly or in hoards, in or close to watery locations, such as rivers, lakes and bogs (Davis 2015, 190). Tobias Mörtz (2018) highlights a number of large weapon hoards deposited around this time (comprising more than 25 weapons), though smaller weapon deposits were also deposited across Britain. Nonetheless, the Bloody Pool hoard is a conspicuous westerly outlier in the context of similar deposits in Britain.

To date, barbed spearheads in south-west Britain have only been recovered from south Devon and Somerset (Table 5.2). One complete example was found near Godney, Somerset (Pearce 1983, 516, no.672), whilst the rest comprised fragments typically within larger assemblages. Five fragments were deposited in the Stogursey hoard, recovered from a possible wetland context (see below). From Thurlestone Beach, two deliberately broken spearheads, one of them barbed, have been found at different times in different locations; one of these pieces was associated with a complete pegged spearhead (Fig. 5.8; PAS-F087; PCMAG-F005). A recently discovered hoard of 17 copper-alloy objects, also from Thurlestone, primarily comprised deliberately destroyed spearheads, including some barbed examples, and small fragments of other objects (PAS-F088). At the time of publication, this hoard was going through the legal process for treasure in England and Wales and had yet to go to the coroner's inquest so it cannot be discussed in detail here.[1] However, it represents the second weapon-dominant hoard known from south-west Britain and is of a similar nature to the Bloody Pool hoard; alongside the single finds it reinforces the idea that communities in south Devon held a specific relationship with weapons that necessitated their intentional destruction prior to deposition.

The limited number of barbed spearheads and contemporary weapon hoards from south-west Britain suggests a wider ideological understanding of how depositions of these objects should be enacted. It does not appear that these objects were in wide production

Table 5.1: Late Bronze Age associated finds and hoards recovered from south-west Britain

No./Ref.	*Findspot*	*No. of pieces/ frags*	*Objects*	*Landscape location*	*Notes*
			Cornwall		
RCM-F002	Beacon Field	3	Swords	Uncertain	2 swords in 3 frags
RCM-F005	Breage I	24	Socketed axeheads; sword; knife; bracelet; ingots; casting waste	Hilltop	Fragmentary; found close to Breage II
RCM-F006	Breage II	7	Socketed axeheads; swords; ingots	Hilltop	Fragmentary; found close to Breage I
RCM-F012	Gillan, St Anthony-in-Meneage	4	Socketed axehead; ingots	Coastal, Stream bank, Wetland	Fragmentary; ingots found together & axehead close by in boggy ground
PAS-F014	Madron II	2	Swords	Coastal, Confluence, Hillslope	Non-refitting frags found associated
PAS-F029	Sennen	3	Socketed axehead; ingots	Coastal	All found in same field; ingots associated
RCM-F035	St Buryan	12	Socketed axeheads; ingots; flint flake	Coastal, Headland, Hilltop	Fragmentary
RCM-F037	St Erth hoard I	27	Sword; socketed axehead; gouge; ingots; casting waste	Hilltop, river valley	Fragmentary; 22 objects in 27 pieces; found near St Erth II and 2 pieces of gold
RCM-F038	St Erth hoard II	17	Winged axehead; ingots	As above	Fragmentary; found near St Erth I and two pieces of gold
PHGM-F002	St Erth I	2	Socketed axeheads	Uncertain	One complete, one deliberately broke; reportedly found together
PAS-F036	St Levan	53	Socketed axehead; winged axehead; sword; knife; razor; casting jet; ingots	Hilltop, Overlooking coast	Fragmentary; buried in a container in a pit
NT-F001	St Michael's Mount	47	Socketed axeheads; knife; sword; chape; buckle; gouge; disc/plate; ingots; casting waste	Hillslope, Tidal island	Fragmentary; buried in a cavity under a boulder
Knight *et al.* 2015, no. 15	Kelsey Head	3	Ring; buttons	Coastal, Headland	Possible hoard
Pearce 1983, no. 82	Lelant / Lanant	8+	Ferrule; swords; socketed axeheads; casting waste	Uncertain – near river estuary	Number of socketed axeheads unknown
Penhallurick 1986, 199	Luxulyan	3?	Cauldron	Tin stream?	1 complete, 1 incomplete, 1 fragmentary
Knight *et al.* 2015, no. 40	Rosemorran Farm, Madron	3	Gold bracelets	Uncertain – close to coast	Deposited interlinked
Penhallurick 1986, 216; Herring 2000, 106	Marazion Marsh	Uncertain	Weapons, spearheads & axeheads	Uncertain	Found *c.* 1540, reportedly wrapped in linen. No surviving material
Pearce 1983, no. 107	Morvah (Carne	6	Gold bracelets/armrings	Coastal	Deposited complete; circumstances of deposition uncertain

No./Ref.	*Findspot*	*No. of pieces/ frags*	*Objects*	*Landscape location*	*Notes*
Knight *et al.* 2015, no. 60	Porthcothan, St Eval	*c.* 9	Ingots, metallurgical waste, ceramic vessel	Hilltop, river valley, view of coast	Bronze material buried in vessel
Pearce 1983, no. 67	St Hilary	Uncertain	Knife	Uncertain	Originally part of a hoard weighing 80 pounds but melted down.
			Devon		
RAMM-F001	Ash Farm	11	Ingots	Uncertain	Fragmentary
PAS-F045	Awliscombe I	3	Sword	River valley	1 sword in 3 sword fragments
RAMM-F005	Bloody Pool	9	Spearheads; spear ferrules	Bog, Upland	6 objects in 9 fragments
BM-F004	Chagford I	2	Spearheads	Hillslope, river valley	Both complete; possibly associated
RAMM-F022	Gittisham Barrow	4	Ingots	Hilltop	Inserted into a barrow
PAS-F073	Lower Frittiscombe	2	Gold rings	Uncertain	Complete
PAS-F074	Newton Abbot I	7	Ingots	Hilltop	Fragmentary; all deliberately broken
PAS-F076	Otterton I	7	Ingots	Coastal	Fragmentary; all deliberately broken; found near Otterton II
PAS-F077	Otterton II	12	Ingots	Coastal	Fragmentary; all deliberately broken; found near Otterton I
PAS-F082	Stoke Gabriel I	2	Ingots	Overlooking coast	Two fragments
RAMM-F050	Talaton II	12	Socketed axehead; gouges; ingots; casting waste	Hillslope, near natural springs, near water-ways	Fragmentary; all deliberately broken
PAS-F088	Thurlestone	17	Spearheads; socketed axehead; blade	PAS protected	Deliberately damaged objects; further details restricted
Knight *et al.* 2015, no. 124	Churston Ferrers (Lupton Park)	3	Ingots	Overlooking coast	Fragmentary; all deliberately broken
Northover & Salter 1990	Coffinswell	*c.* 15	Ingots	Hillslope	Fragmentary; scattered hoard
Knight *et al.* 2015, no. 125; Taylor 1999	Colaton Raleigh	4	Gold bracelets; clipped gold fragment	Heathland	Found nested
PAS DEV-0D2AA0	Colyton	2	Sword	PAS protected	Two non-refitting blade fragments
PAS SOM-81B00C	"Near Dawlish"	17	Ingots; gold bracelets	PAS protected; possible bog	13 ingot fragments found together near 4 folded gold bracelets; possibly multiple deposits
			Dorset		
PAS-F109	Chickerell I	2	Gold bracelets	River valley	Interlinked
DCM-F024	Long Bredy	6	Sword; spearhead; gouge; razor	Hillslope, Overlooking river	4 or 5 objects in 6 pieces; some deliberately damaged
DCM-F025	Lulworth	23	Sword; socketed axehead; spearheads; decorated plaque; flesh-hook; rings; bugle-shaped object; pins; bracelet; casting jet	Dry valley, Hillslope	18 objects in 23 pieces; some deliberately damaged

No./Ref.	*Findspot*	*No. of pieces/frags*	*Objects*	*Landscape location*	*Notes*
ASH-F007	Near Weymouth I	2	Spearhead; sword	Uncertain	Both deliberately damaged; found together
PAS-F140	Overcompton	2	Socketed axeheads	Uncertain	2 frags found while metal-detecting
RHMG-F007	Somerford	2	Socketed axehead; gouge	Uncertain	Said to be part of disturbed hoard
			Somerset		
TTNCM-F005	Brean Down II	3	Gold bracelets	Coastal settlement	Occupation midden layer also containing ceramic, bone, & shell frags
PAS-F227	Martock	2	Blade; socketed axehead	Hillslope, near natural spring	Deliberately broken
TTNCM-F023	Fayne	4	Flat axehead; palstaves; socketed axehead	Low on hillslope, tributary valley, edge of Exmoor	Possible multi-period hoard
TTNCM-F058	Stogursey	146	Socketed axeheads; palstaves; swords; spearheads; gouge; sword chape; knife; casting jet; ingot; casting waste	Low-lying dryland?	Large proportion of deliberately broken objects

and circulation in the South West, but when deposited, they were buried with an understanding of how such objects should be treated. The function of barbed spearheads remains subject to debate, and although they may have been thrusting weapons (cf. Knight 2019a, 255, 258), they are most commonly considered to have been aggrandised, ceremonial martial objects (Burgess *et al.* 1972, 227–8; Fox 1973, 120; Davis 2015, 182; Mörtz 2018, 177–8). Removal of these from circulation would have been important, especially considering their seemingly limited circulation within the South West.

The process of destruction and deposition, involving heating, breaking and a marshy context, conveys a symbolic nature of the act; indeed, Aileen Fox interpreted the find as 'a votive offering to the spirit of the pool' (1973, 120). Tom Greeves (2019) highlights over 40 similar pools across Dartmoor, frequently close to other prehistoric features and monuments. He emphasises their potentially sacred nature, their mythological connotations, and their practical function as watering holes for livestock or gathering places within the designed prehistoric landscape; through this lens it becomes easy to envisage Bloody Pool as an important location where an offering was made. The destruction and deposition of these weapons served as a localised ceremony in a specific place, while also connecting communities with wider systems of depositional performance.

Ingots and ingot-dominant hoards in south Devon

Whilst the Bloody Pool hoard stands out in south Devon, single finds and hoards of deliberately broken ingots, occasionally with fragments of other objects, are more common. Nine associated finds and hoards have so far been discovered as well as single ingot finds and those in scatters, concentrated along the south coast or along river valleys (Fig. 5.9). Many of these have been found since 1998 and their distribution now provides useful insights into the value and movement of raw material in the region. For instance, there is a significant concentration of ingot deposits along the Otter valley, as well as around Tor Bay; to a certain extent this may be recovery bias, but the Salcombe Bay assemblages strengthen the idea that these deposits are linked to the

Table 5.2: Barbed spearheads from south-west Britain

No./ref.	*Findspot*	*No. barbed spearheads*	*Associated objects*	*Context*
RAMM-F005	Bloody Pool, Devon	3	1 pegged spearhead 2 ferrules	Bog/moorland
PCMAG-F005	Thurlestone Beach I, Devon	1	1 pegged spearhead	Beach/coast
PAS-F087	Thurlestone Beach II, Devon	1	–	Beach/coast
PAS-F088	Thurlestone, Devon	*c.* 6	Hoard of *c.* 17 objects	Details restricted
TTNCM-F005	Cadbury Castle, Somerset	1	Multi-period settlement assemblage of 47 objects	Hilltop/hillfort
TTNCM-F058	Stogursey, Somerset	5	Hoard of *c.* 146 objects	Possible wetland
Pearce 1983, no. 672	Godney, Somerset	1	–	Uncertain

trade and exchange of raw metal, with the large natural bays and river estuaries of south Devon providing entrance points into south-west routeways (cf. McGrail 1993; Bradley 2019, 259–60). At present it is unclear whether this represents material coming into or out of Britain.

All ingots studied in these hoards were deliberately broken though none refits, and many contained large casting hollows; these fragments represent the remains of larger pieces probably broken for casting or recycling. Those that have been analysed are of unalloyed copper, including one from Ottery St Mary III (PAS-F081), two from Gittisham (RAMM-F022), a hoard of 15 from Coffinswell (Northover & Salter 1990), and 280 ingots from Salcombe Bay (Wang *et al.* 2018). Pure copper is very ductile even at high temperatures and difficult to fragment, especially at the thickness of many plano-convex ingots. Future experimentation will help determine how this might be achieved, but it probably required heating the copper close to melting point.

Apart from the Salcombe Bay assemblages, which contained both Middle and Late Bronze Age material, only two ingot-dominant hoards from Devon contained other object types: Talaton II (RAMM-F050) and 'near Dawlish' (Burnett 2017). The Talaton II hoard contained seven ingot fragments, fragments of two socketed gouges and a socketed axehead, and metallurgical waste. The objects are all heavily worn, and the overall character suggests a very mundane function, perhaps discarded as scrap. Similarly, the 'near Dawlish' hoard contained 11 ingot fragments, two deliberately fragmented socketed axeheads and a fragment of a sword blade (Fig. 5.10). Four gold bracelets were also found with or near the hoard. The associated objects allow us to date these hoards to the Late Bronze Age, which can be broadly applied to the other ingot deposits presented here, as well as by their comparison with other ingot hoards in southern Britain (eg, Turner 2010a).

The production and use of ingots were inherently destructive necessitating the smelting of ores or the reduction of other objects into an ingot form, as well as a transformation process from the ingot into another object, which may have heightened their perceived social value. Even when fragmentation was purely functional, the places in which pieces and fragments were deposited suggests a deliberate and considered activity. Hoards and other deposits were often positioned in relation to the coast and waterways, referencing the means by which raw material was moved in and out of the areas. Locally sourced or imported material could have necessitated a *pars pro toto* offering, burying objects of economic value. The possible association of folded gold bracelets with fragments of ingots and other objects near Dawlish suggests that we cannot easily draw a line between what material might be considered functional or symbolic – many might interpret the deposition of gold bracelets as a symbolic depositional act sacrificing objects of identity and wealth; ingots were also a form of wealth and could be viewed similarly. Ingot fragments alongside a range of other Late Bronze Age material at Kent's Cavern suggests the use of the cave for multiple crafts activities and a place that became important over time (BM-F005/TOR-F010); deposition here referenced the place. Finally, four ingots were buried beside or

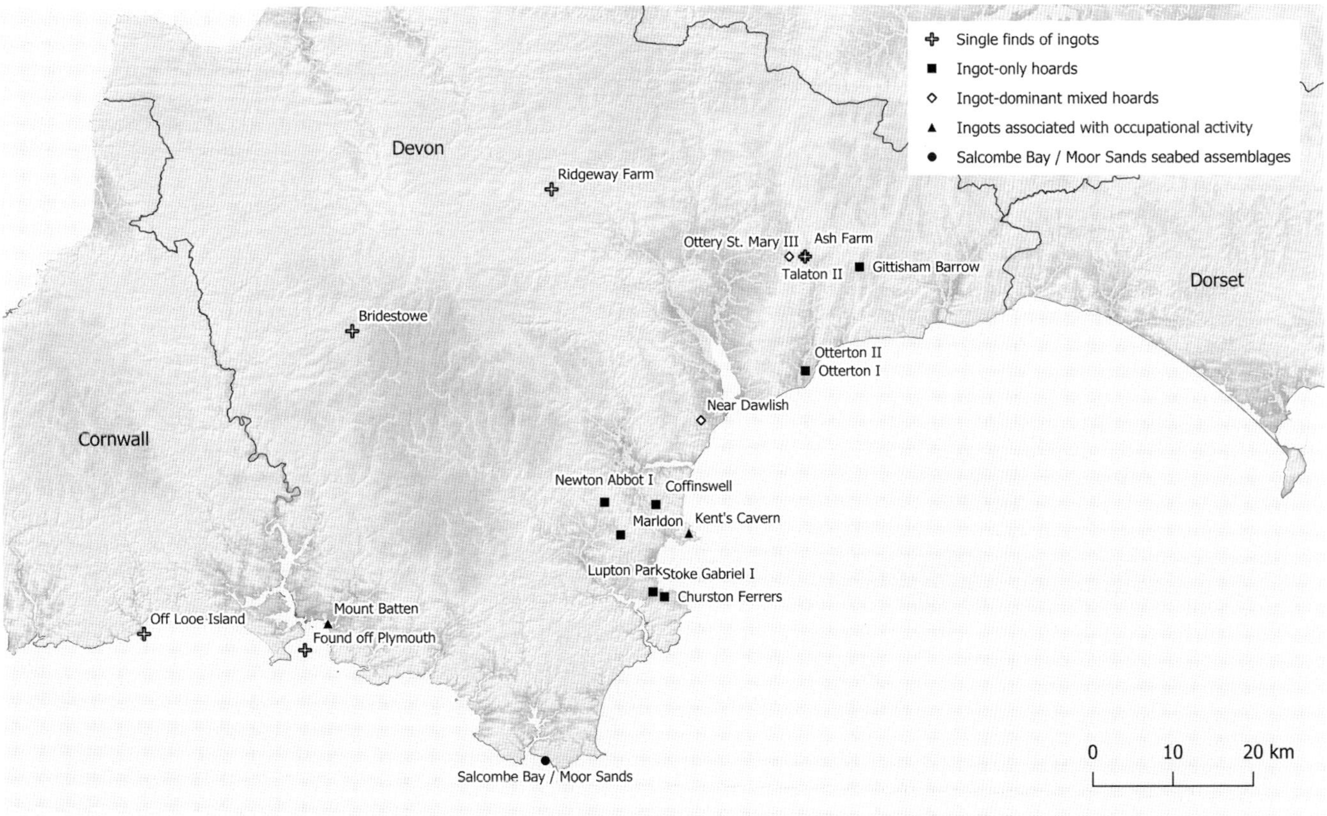

Figure 5.9: Findspots of Late Bronze Age ingots in south Devon. Contains OS data © Crown copyright and database right 2021

under a stone that was part of a ring around an Early Bronze Age cairn at Gittisham (RAMM-F022). This was one of several later Bronze Age metalwork deposits placed into earlier monuments in and around Gittisham Hill, incorporating and perhaps referencing the already ancient funerary landscape (Jones & Quinnell 2008, 47–8). These case studies illustrate how seemingly functional material, such as ingots, may gain significance or express certain aspects of society through their place of deposition.

A carp's-tongue/Boughton-Vénat complex in Cornwall?

In 2009, a Late Bronze Age hoard was found on the north-west slope of St Michael's Mount, a tidal island situated in Mounts Bay (NT-F001; Fig. 5.11). Approximately 50 objects were recovered, the majority from a cavity underneath a rock and overlying boulder. This hoard largely comprised fragments of ingots associated with various objects, including complete and incomplete socketed axeheads, fragments of swords, a hog's-back knife, a bag-shaped chape and a unique decorated fitting, possibly a fastener or buckle (Table 5.3). Almost all objects in this hoard were deliberately damaged prior to deposition, including heated and broken sword fragments and blocked socketed axeheads. The hoard is certainly more diverse than the ingot hoards from Devon, and the character of material closely compares with the fragmentary hoards of the carp's-tongue/Boughton-Vénat complex buried in south-eastern England and Atlantic France *c.* 900/875–800/775 BC (Briard 1965, 199–239; 1991; Burgess 1968; Coffyn *et al.* 1981; Boulud & Fily 2009; Turner 2010a; Brandherm & Moskal-del Hoyo 2014). The St Michael's Mount hoard thus hints at the influx of this depositional practice from across the Channel.

This theory is strengthened by the growing number of similar hoards from Cornwall. Of the 20 Late Bronze Age hoards, at least 12 largely comprised axeheads, ingots and/or casting waste (see Table 5.1) and six of these also contained incomplete swords and occasionally a knife or razor. Most have been recovered since 1998, but historic discoveries from St Hilary (Pearce 1983, 410–1, no.67), Lelant

Figure 5.10: The 'near Dawlish' hoard, Devon © Royal Albert Memorial Museum & Art Gallery, Exeter

(Pearce 1983, 413–4, no.82) and Marazion Marsh (Penhallurick 1986, 216; Herring 2000, 106), highlight large accumulations of similar material that are now lost. We can also add an assemblage from Kenidjack Castle, St Just-in-Penwith, which comprised 20–30 copper pieces, three axeheads, a casting jet and a piece of tin in the foundation of a small square hut (RCM-F018). Some of these hoards and assemblages contained objects characteristic of the carp's-tongue complex, such as winged axeheads from St Levan (PAS-F036), St Erth II (RCM-F038) and Kenidjack Castle, a carp's-tongue sword fragment from Breage II (RCM-F006; Fig. 5.12), and seven possible or definite examples of hog's-back knives within these hoards or as single finds. Although this material is not a dominant part of the hoard deposits, the character fits with what is expected of the carp's-tongue/Boughton-Vénat complex (Brandherm & Moskal-del Hoyo 2014). These objects were clearly part of the material culture repertoire and deposited in ways that suggest communities in these areas were connected and had similar ideas about how it should be treated. Furthermore, material indicative of influence from north-western France is increasingly found in south-west Wales, such as hoards from Manorbier (Gwilt *et al.* 2011) and Marloes and St Brides (Gwilt *et al.* 2014), both Pembrokeshire. Through the distribution of these hoards we can envisage material travelling across the Channel, around the Cornish peninsula and into the Bristol Channel.

Carp's-tongue/Boughton-Vénat hoards often present the full range of destruction indicators with heavily fragmented and worn-out artefacts, plugged socketed axeheads, bent weapons and tools, and pieces of ingots and casting waste. They have typically been interpreted as the result of scrapping activities (ie, material intended for disposal), perhaps linked to a collapsing bronze industry or the growing use of iron (eg, Burgess 1979; Thomas 1989). This seems unlikely. As Anthony Harding (2000, 356–7) has noted, this interpretation only applies to a specific temporal period and does not account for the high number of bronze objects deposited during the preceding

Figure 5.11: The St Michael's Mount hoard, Cornwall (NT-F001) © Jim Parry, National Trust

Wilburton metalworking assemblage; large numbers of fragmentary bronze objects were deposited across Europe between 1300–800 BC and this cannot be explained by the growing use of iron or a collapsing industry (*ibid.*). Recent approaches have instead advocated for the accumulation of different processes brought together for deposition as indicating something beyond reduction practices for recycling or mundane disposal (Boulud & Mélin 2009, 256–8; Turner 2010a, 92; Adams 2017, 60–1; Bordas & Boulud-Gazo 2018, 29–33).

Certainly, when we consider the hoards deposited in Cornwall various practices were undertaken with objects deposited in a range of conditions and subjected to diverse practices. Eight destruction indicators were recorded, with deliberate fragmentation overwhelmingly common (Fig. 5.13). Of the 116 ingots studied within these hoards, 112 were deliberately fragmented, with some formed by the remelting of other objects. Some of the objects were hot-short, whilst others were fragmented using a chisel (Fig. 5.14); moreover, fragments range in size from 10 mm to over 130 mm, and in weight from 2 g up to 966 g, suggesting that not all objects were fragmented in the same manner or indeed at the same time. This is further supported by the presence of blocked socketed axeheads in the hoards from Breage 1 and St Michael's Mount, both of which required the initial fragmentation of other objects first. This also indicates fragmentation may have been a controlled and possibly skilled process rather than an ecstatic event (*contra* Nebelsick 2000). If one considers that at least 47 objects are represented in the St Michael's Mount hoard, of which only fragments survive, one can envisage substantive destruction events. A large fire or hearth was required in which all objects were

Table 5.3: A summary of the St Michael's Mount hoard, Cornwall

NT-F001	Object	Completeness %	Use evidence	Damage Ranking(s)	Destruction Indicators/associated marks
a	Socketed axehead	76–99	N	0,1	None
b	Socketed axehead	26–50	P	3	Broken; hammered; plugged socket
c	Socketed axehead	26–50	N	3	Broken (single piece); crushed; plugged socket
d	Socketed axehead	0–25	N	3	Chisel marks; crushed; hammered
e	Socketed axehead	0–25	P	3	Crushed; hammered; fragmented
f	Socketed axehead	0–25	N	2	Broken (single piece); fragmented
g	Knife	26–50	P	2	None
h	Socketed gouge	26–50	N	Uncertain	None
i	Sword	0–25	N	3	Bent (transverse); fragmented
j	Sword	0–25	N	3	Fragmented
k	Blade	0–25	N	3	Fragmented
l	Sword	0–25	N	3	Fragmented
m	Uncertain	0–25	N	2	None
n	Chape	100	N	n/a	None
o	Miscellaneous decorated fitting	76–99	N	1	None
p	Disc/plate	Uncertain	Uncertain	2	None
q	Disc/plate	Uncertain	Uncertain	2	None
r	Uncertain fragment	0–25	Uncertain	2	None
s	Uncertain – copper cake?	0–25	n/a	2, Uncertain	None
t	Socketed axehead	0–25	N	3	Fragmented; hammered
u	Metallurgical waste	n/a	n/a	n/a	None
v	Casting jet	n/a	n/a	3	Broken (single piece)
w	Uncertain	n/a	n/a	0	None
x	Ingot	Uncertain	n/a	0,3	Broken (single piece)
y	Ingot	0–25	n/a	0,3	Fragmented
z	Ingot	0–25	n/a	0,3	Fragmented
aa	Ingot	0–25	n/a	0,3	Fragmented
bb	Uncertain	Uncertain	n/a	Uncertain	None
cc	Ingot	0–25	n/a	3	Fragmented
dd	Ingot	0–25	n/a	3	Fragmented
ee	Ingot	0–25	n/a	3	Fragmented
ff	Ingot	0–25	n/a	3	Fragmented
gg	Ingot	0–25	n/a	3	Fragmented
hh	Metallurgical waste	n/a	n/a	n/a	Uncertain
ii	Ingot	0–25	n/a	3	Fragmented
jj	Ingot	0–25	n/a	3	Broken (single piece)
kk	Ingot	0–25	n/a	3	Fragmented
ll	Ingot	0–25	n/a	0,3	Fragmented
mm	Ingot	0–25	n/a	0,3	Fragmented
nn	Ingot	0–25	n/a	3	Fragmented
oo	Ingot	0–25	n/a	3	Fragmented
pp	Ingot	0–25	n/a	3	Fragmented
qq	Ingot	0–25	n/a	3	Fragmented
rr	Ingot	0–25	n/a	3	Fragmented
ss	Ingot	0–25	n/a	0,3	Fragmented
tt	Ingot	0–25	n/a	3	Fragmented
uu	Ingot	0–25	n/a	3	Fragmented
vv	Uncertain	Uncertain	n/a	Uncertain	None

(Y = yes; P = possible; N = no)

Figure 5.12: The Breage II hoard, Cornwall (RCM-F006) (photo: author courtesy of the Royal Institution of Cornwall)

heated, broken and removed, or alternatively a series of smaller processes after which various fragments were accumulated for a single deposit. There also appears to be a selective element to the objects that were fragmented, with an overall limited range of object types present: small tools are rarely present and spearheads and ornaments are conspicuously absent. This suggests that some objects were more appropriate for inclusion in these hoards than others. In some hoards, complete usable objects were deposited alongside the destroyed material, including an axehead from St Erth II, an axehead, buckle and chape from St Michael's Mount, and a hog's-back knife from St Levan. Interestingly, these objects are representative of those defining objects of the carp's-tongue complex and may have been deliberately left intact for their recognisably foreign character.

These complete objects are nonetheless in the minority, and the reduction of the rest of the material, although unnecessarily extensive in some cases, does not imply selective ways of fragmenting the material, especially when compared, for instance, to the patterned breakage of the Bloody Pool hoard. The fragmentation and accumulation of these hoards are instead better framed in an economic sense, linked with the supply, production and recycling of metal as a material, though deposition may have been governed by certain rules about what should and should not be included. Like the ingot hoards from Devon, the Cornish hoards were probably the result of incoming metalwork as part of an exchange system, but the treatment of the metalwork reflected broader understandings. This has been suggested for the carp's-tongue hoards elsewhere (Brandherm & Moskal-del Hoyo 2014, 38–41) and can be explored further here through consideration of landscape locations.

Similar hoards in south-east England and north-west France were concentrated primarily in coastal locations and on hilltops (Boulud & Fily 2009, 285, fig. 1; Turner 2010a, 47, fig. 2), a pattern reflected among the Cornish hoards (Fig. 5.15). Fifteen of the 20 hoards deposited in Cornwall (including those not of carp's-tongue character) were deposited in western Cornwall and seven of these were buried on either hilltops or hillslopes. In Brittany, hoards were occasionally concentrated in certain areas, such as the multiple deposits at Gouesnac'h

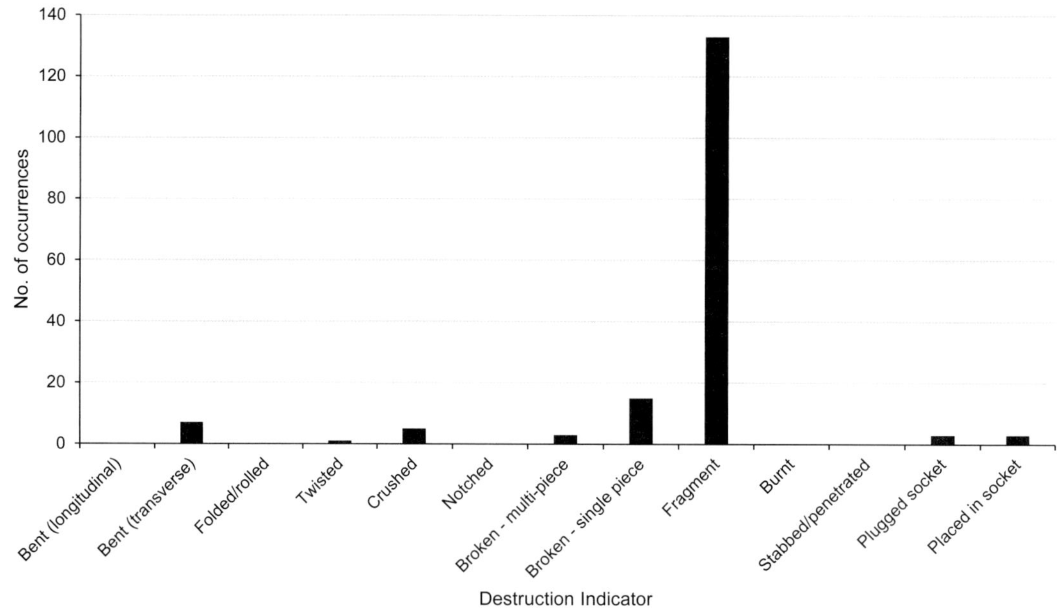

Figure 5.13: Frequency of Destruction Indicators recorded on Late Bronze Age metalwork from hoards deposited in Cornwall (n=170) (148 objects represented)

Figure 5.14: A chiselled sword fragment from the Breage I hoard (RCM-F005c). The arrow points to the chisel mark (photo: author courtesy of the Royal Institution of Cornwall)

(Boulud & Fily 2009), and the same is true for the Breage and St Erth parishes, both of which have produced two closely associated hoards on hilltops. Although the number and size of the Cornish hoards are much smaller than those from north-west France and south-east England – which sometimes contained several hundreds of objects – it appears that hoards deposited in Cornwall were governed by similar rationales. Moreover, their concentration in western Cornwall may be significant, as this contains one of the main tin- and copper-bearing lodes in south-west Britain (Pearce 1983, 97); proximity and access to raw materials may explain why there is such a concentration here.

The Stogursey hoard, Somerset: influences from the North, South, East and West

The hoard from Wick Park, Stogursey, is the largest hoard from the South West, containing 146 bronze objects (TTNCM-F058; Table 5.4; Figs 5.16 & 5.17; McNeil 1973). It was found in 1870 during drainage operations in a field under a flat stone, about 2 feet down in the clay, contained within a space of about 1 cubic foot (0.028 m^3) (Fig. 5.18; Hood 1873; Gray 1908, 60). This hoard comprised complete and broken socketed axeheads, as well as fragmentary spearheads, swords and casting material; it dates to the late Wilburton or early Ewart Park assemblage *c.* 950–900 BC. One hundred artefacts (*c.* 68%) showed signs of deliberate destruction. As with the Cornish hoards, this material was probably damaged over multiple events and in a variety of ways. Small fragments of axeheads and swords from Stogursey match those produced through destruction experiments involving heating and fragmentation (Knight 2017; 2019a; Fig. 5.19). By contrast, some spearhead fragments in the hoard may have been broken while cold, suggesting multiple events, perhaps undertaken by people with variable access to skills, tools and resources (Fig. 5.20).

Out of the 146 objects only two pieces refit, meaning that either pieces were deliberately selected for inclusion or multiple objects were accumulated and removed over time until almost no refitting pieces and fragments survived. We may apply a similar economic rationale to that presented above, but the diverse character of this hoard means we can explore alternative

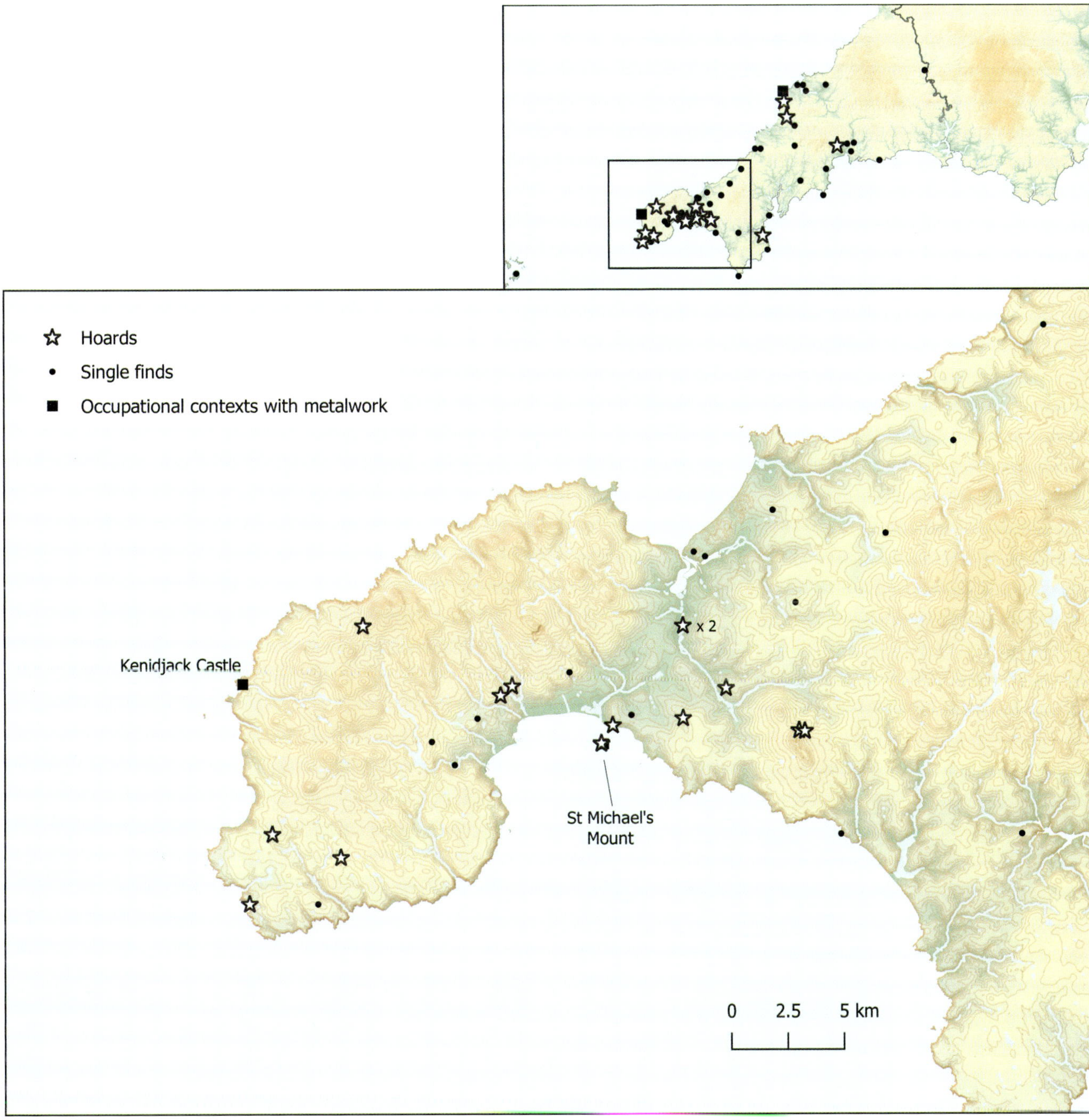

Figure 5.15: Late Bronze Age metalwork deposits in western Cornwall. Contains OS data © Crown copyright and database right 2021

ideas of selection by examining the portions of the objects which are represented. Cutting-edge fragments of socketed axeheads, for instance, occur more frequently than other axehead portions (eg, sockets) and represent a minimum of 22 axeheads – many deliberately damaged – plus 24 complete or mostly complete examples (Fig. 5.21). Although this may constitute randomised accumulation (cf. Wiseman 2018), the recurrence of specific portions of objects is notable and suggests the metalwork may have been gathered from a limited or deliberately selected range of material. The choice of cutting edges specifically may be a symbolic reference to the functional aspect of the axehead.

The complete or mostly complete axeheads represent diverse forms, including Yorkshire, Meldreth, Croxton and Welby types, which derive from manufacturing traditions in Wales, northern and eastern England, but

Figure 5.16: A selection of complete and fragmentary axeheads and casting waste from the Stogursey hoard (photo: author, courtesy of Somerset Archaeological and Natural History Society and South West Heritage Trust)

have limited currency in south-west Britain. The nature of these objects led McNeil to portray Stogursey as 'a key hoard, drawing together influences from the North, South, East and West' (1973, 52), situating Stogursey as a coming together of several traditions. In this sense, the hoard provides an insight into the different connections and interactions of communities living in north Somerset; we can consider this further through the presence of South Welsh-type axeheads.

Forty-eight such axeheads are currently known from south-west Britain of which 13 (27%) were recovered from the Stogursey hoard. However, South Welsh-type axeheads are most common in south-east Wales and there are around 250 examples known as single finds and in hoards across Wales (Gwilt 2004; Adam

Figure 5.17: A selection of complete and fragmentary objects from the Stogursey hoard, including swords, spearheads and ingots (photo: author, courtesy of Somerset Archaeological and Natural History Society and South West Heritage Trust)

Gwilt pers. comm.). Only two hoards in Britain contain more South Welsh-type axeheads than Stogursey: the St Mellons and 'near Cowbridge' hoards, both Vale of Glamorgan (Stanton 1984; Lodwick & Gwilt 2002). The number of South Welsh-type axeheads in the Stogursey hoard, alongside its atypical nature in the South West and its proximity to the south coast of Wales, suggests it represents an intrusion from south Wales. In support of this, the diverse and fragmentary character of the hoard has no parallels in Somerset but closely aligns with the composition of other south Wales hoards (cf. Gwilt 2004). The St Nicholas hoard, Vale of Glamorgan, for instance, contained 39 objects also including socketed axeheads, swords, spearheads, casting jets and ingot fragments (Fig. 5.22; Gwilt 2003a).

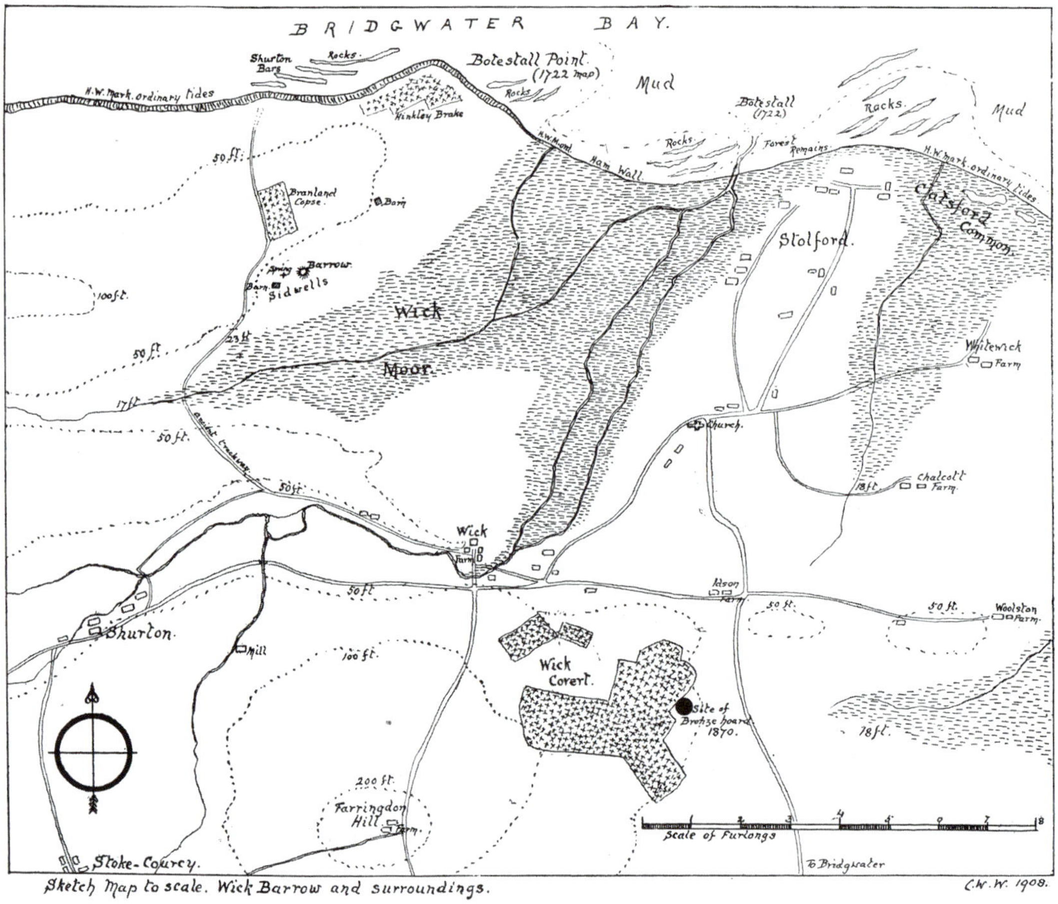

Figure 5.18: Sketch map of area around Wick, Somerset, including marking of hoard. No contemporary Late Bronze Age deposits are known nearby. 8 furlongs = 1 mile / 1.6 km (adapted from Gray 1908, pl. 11, reproduced by kind permission of the Somerset Archaeological and Natural History Society)

Figure 5.19: A comparison of a heated and fragmented axehead replica (left) with fragments of axeheads from the Stogursey hoard (right) (photo (right): author, courtesy of Somerset Archaeological and Natural History Society and South West Heritage Trust)

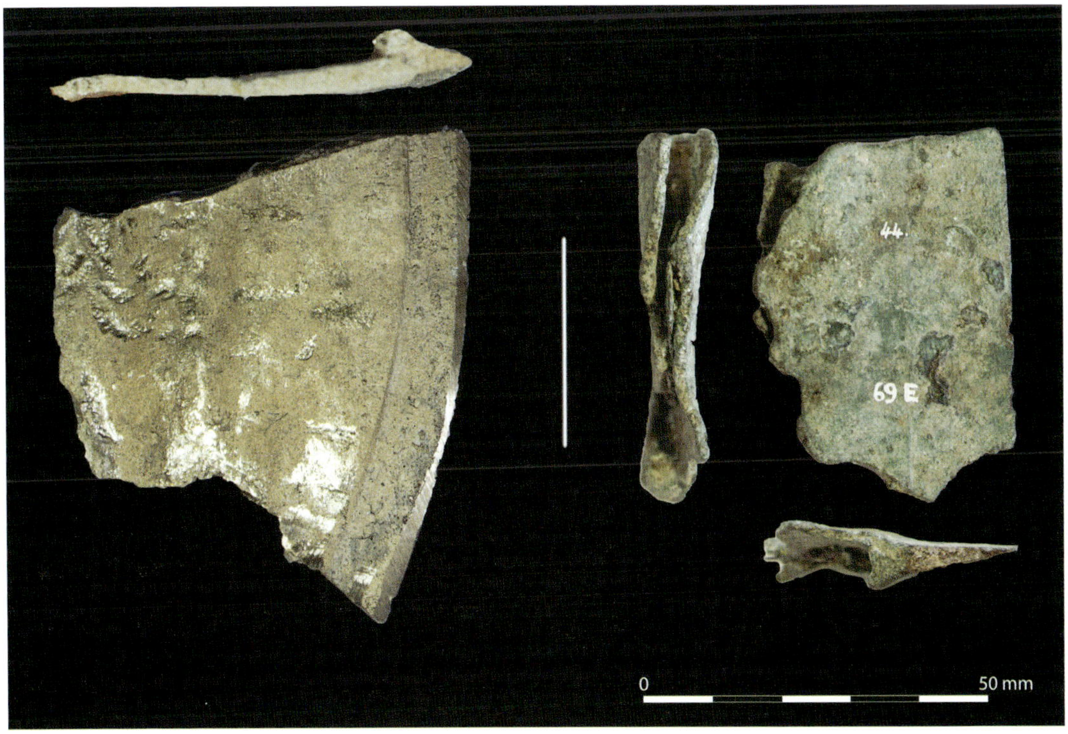

Figure 5.20: A comparison of a fragment of an unheated and broken spearhead replica (left) with a fragment of a spearhead from the Stogursey hoard (right) (photo (right): author, courtesy of Somerset Archaeological and Natural History Society and South West Heritage Trust)

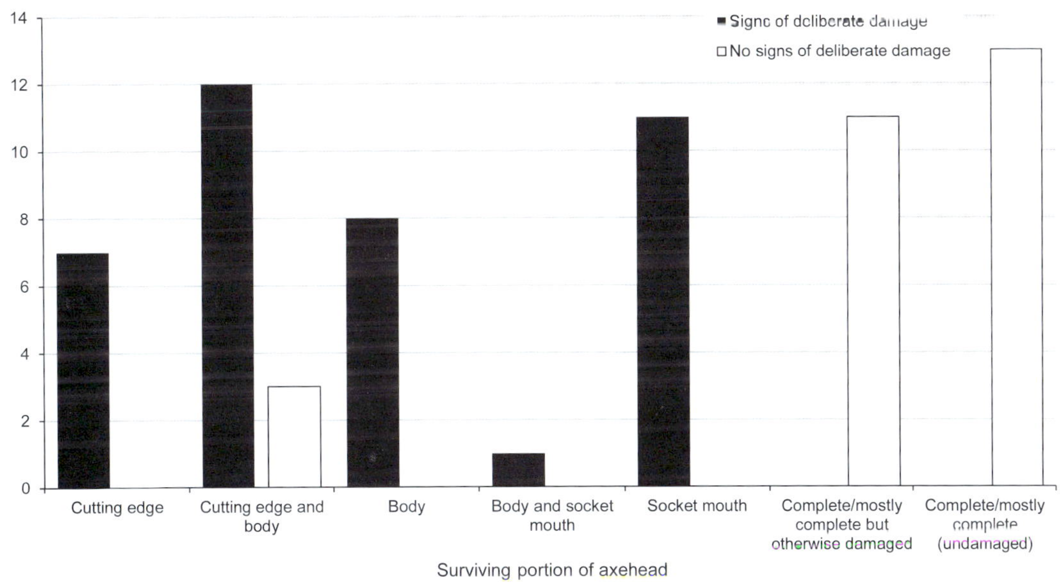

Figure 5.21: Portions of socketed axeheads recovered from the Stogursey hoard, Somerset, divided by whether they show deliberate damage or not (n=66)

Hoards with a similar character are known elsewhere, including Glascoed and Llangwm, both Monmouthshire, and Llancarfan 1, Vale of Glamorgan (Lodwick 2002; Gwilt 2003b; Gwilt & Lodwick 2005).

The Stogursey hoard therefore specifically relates to accumulation and depositional practices more common across the Bristol Channel. The combination of casting material and as-cast objects may indicate that some artefacts were produced close to the depositional site, meaning this hoard could have been a store of material: the deliberately damaged objects were a functional reduction of material for the crucible and recasting (McNeil 1973; Pearce 1983, 244ff.). However,

Table 5.4: A summary of the Stogursey hoard, Somerset

Object	*No.*	*Completeness %*						*Use evidence*		*Deliberate damage*		*Destruction Indicators/associated damage*
		0–25	*26–50*	*51–75*	*76–99*	*100*	*n/a*	*Y*	*N*	*Y*	*N*	
Socketed axehead												
Three-ribbed	12	6	–	1	3	2	–	1	11	6	6	Bent; crushed; hammered; fragmented
South Welsh-type	13	–	1	1	4	7	–	–	13	3	10	Cracked; crushed; fragmented; hammered; broken
Yorkshire-type	2	1	–	–	1	–	–	1	1	1	1	Crushed; fragmented; hammered
Croxton-type	1	–	–	–	–	1	–	–	1	–	1	–
Welby-type	1	–	–	–	–	1	–	1	–	–	1	–
Plain/ribbed/uncertain	31	29	–	–	2	–	–	7	24	28	3	Crushed; fragmented; hammered
Meldreth-type	4	–	–	–	4	–	–	2	2	–	4	–
Faceted	2	1	–	–	1	–	–	1	1	1	1	Fragmented; hammered
Socketed axehead total	66	37	1	2	15	11	–	13	53	39	27	
Late-type palstave	2	–	–	1	1	–	–	–	2	–	2	
Socketed gouge	1	–	–	–	1	–	–	–	1	–	1	
Thorndon-type socketed knife	2	–	–	–	2	–	–	–	2	1	1	Bent (transverse); broken; crushed; hammered
Sword												
Ewart Park-type	4	3	1	–	–	–	–	–	4	3	1	Bent (transverse); broken; fragmented
Possibly Ewart Park-type	8	8	–	–	–	–	–	1	7	8	–	Bent (transverse); blade edges removed; burnt; fragmented
Carp's Tongue	1	1	–	–	–	–	–	–	1	1	–	Bent (transverse); fragmented
St Nazaire-type	1	1	–	–	–	–	–	1	–	1	–	Fragmented
Uncertain	8	8	–	–	–	–	–	4	4	8	–	Bent (transverse); broken (single and multi–piece); fragmented; hammered
Sword total	22	21	1	–	–	–	–	6	16	21	1	
Tongue-shaped chape	1	–	–	–	–	1	–	–	1	–	1	
Spearheads												
Pegged (type 11)	9	2	–	4	2	1	–	4	5	6	3	Bent (transverse); broken; cracked; crushed; fragmented; hammered
Pegged, with fillets (type 13)	1	1	–	–	–	–	–	–	1	1	–	Fragmented; hammered
Barbed (type 15A)	5	5	–	–	–	–	–	1	4	5	–	Crushed; fragmented; hammered
Uncertain	3	3	–	–	–	–	–	–	3	3	–	Fragmented
Spearhead total	18	11	–	4	2	1	–	5	13	15	3	
Casting jet												
Casting jets for South Welsh-type axeheads	7	–	–	–	–	–	7	–	7	7	–	Broken
Other	8	–	–	–	–	–	8	–	8	8	–	Broken
Casting jet total	15	–	–	–	–	–	15	–	15	15		

Object	No.	Completeness %						Use evidence		Deliberate damage		Destruction Indicators/associated damage
		0–25	26–50	51–75	76–99	100	n/a	Y	N	Y	N	
Ingot												
Plano-convex	6	5	–	–	–	1	–	–	6	5	1	Burnt; fragmented
Other	2	2	–	–	–	–	–	–	2	2	–	Fragmented
Ingot total	8	7	–	–	–	1	–	–	8	7	1	
Casting waste	11	2	–	–	–	–	9	–	11	2	9	Broken
Overall total	146	78	2	7	21	14	24	24	122	100	46	

this becomes difficult to reconcile alongside the complete, usable objects and the seemingly deliberate selection of object portions for inclusion. Additionally, there is a combination of as-cast, worn and broken elements, which could represent a conscious choice to include the full cycle of object production, use and destruction (cf. Turner 2010a). Such interpretations are difficult to prove, and Wiseman's (2018) analysis of 'scrap' hoards instead suggests that similar fragmentary hoards represent a random accumulation of material over time, deposited with the intention of recovery and recycling. Objects were thus added and removed periodically and this certainly conforms to the evidence for multiple fragmentation events across objects within the hoard. A utilitarian function for the Stogursey hoard whilst in circulation seems a probable explanation, though the surviving elements indicate that the hoard was gathered from far-reaching networks and gives us a glimpse of the overall circulation of different object forms. That the most complete, surviving objects are those that encapsulate those networks suggests that even if the hoard was randomly accumulated over time, there was some process of selection inherent in what was or was not collected and fragmented and a more symbolic element to its deposition. Moreover, the seemingly south-Welsh character of the hoard allows us to recognise that this deposit represents an imported ideology and/or material or else is the result of the actions of an individual or community travelling from south Wales to Somerset. Accumulating, fragmenting and depositing a hoard with a specific regional character served as a way of expressing how individuals and groups considered hoard deposits should be constructed and allowed them to establish meaning through deposition.

The (not-so-)scrap hoards of Dorset

Late Bronze Age associated objects and hoards from Dorset tend to comprise metal-detected discoveries of two or three scattered fragments of axeheads or tools. Only two more substantial Late Bronze Age copper-alloy hoards have been recovered from Dorset, both dating to the Ewart Park metalworking assemblage.[2] These hoards each contained fragmentary material, which may suggest a utilitarian function. However, they are of distinctly different

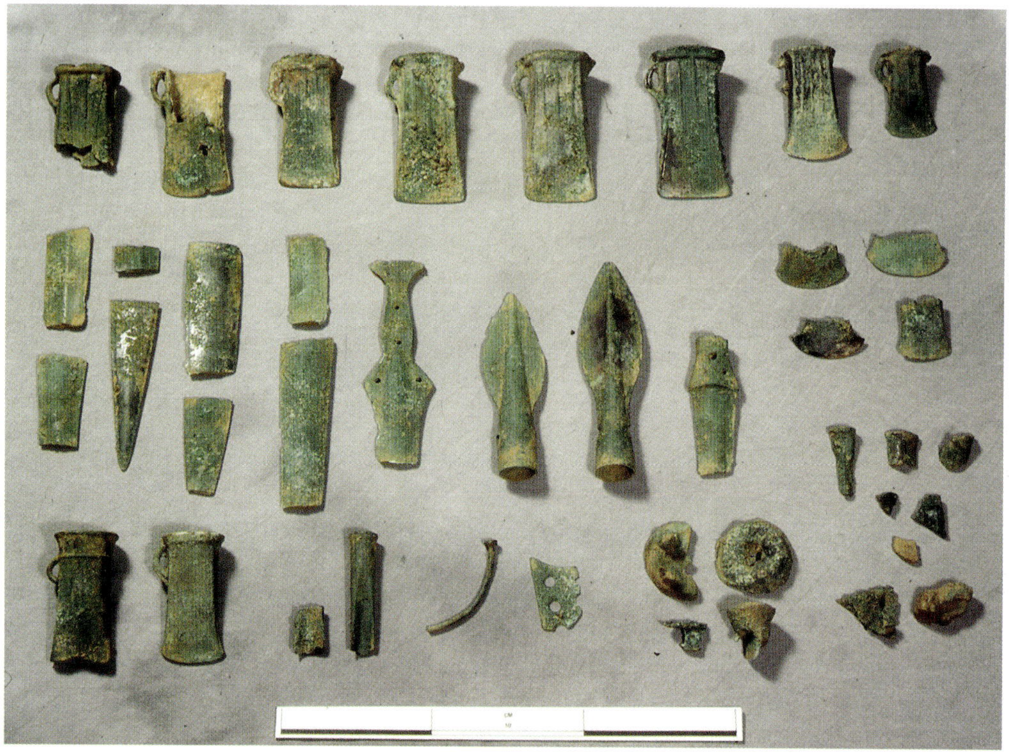

Figure 5.22: The St Nicholas hoard, Wales © Amgueddfa Cymru - National Museum Wales

characters to those hoards discussed so far, and instead, a close consideration of their character makes it possible to interpret them as assemblages collected for other reasons.

The Long Bredy hoard

The Long Bredy hoard, found while metal-detecting in 2009, contained a spearhead, socketed gouge, razor and three pieces of at least one sword (DCM-F024; Fig. 5.23; Table 5.5). The sword was deliberately bent and broken, and the tip of the razor was bent over. Damage to the spearhead was probably use-related and the socketed gouge is intact. Both the spearhead and gouge retain a piece of wood in the sockets which may suggest they were deposited with broken hafts; this could have been a method for rendering these objects unusable.

A hoard of this nature would typically be classed as 'scrap'. However, the ways in which the objects were damaged suggests that although the destruction of some or all of these objects was an inherent part of deposition, it was not necessarily undertaken with a utilitarian aim. The bending and breakage of the artefacts was probably achieved while the objects were cold; similarly if the hafts of the spearhead and gouge were broken prior to deposition this would not have required heat. Thus, unlike the other Late Bronze Age hoards discussed so far, the Long Bredy assemblage does not imply the involvement of a fire or even specific skills, merely the desire to damage the objects.

Associated weapons and tools within a hoard such as this are not uncommon at this time, but they are rare in Dorset. The Long Bredy hoard lacked the ingots and casting debris seen in other hoards and the small but diverse nature of this hoard is hard to parallel. This is an eclectic combination of objects that covers various aspects of Bronze Age life. Functionally, the gouge suggests crafts activities, whilst the razor was an item for personal grooming. The sword and spearhead have martial connotations, though the spearhead may also have been a hunting implement; use-damage implies these were well-used objects. A parallel can be drawn with sets of metalwork found within individual houses from Must Farm,Cambridge, which included combinations of axes, spears, sickles, chisels/gouges, razors and occasionally broken swords (Wiseman 2018, 46–7; Knight 2021). The Long Bredy hoard captures a similar breadth of metalwork and may have been the repertoire of a single individual. In this sense,

Figure 5.23: The Long Bredy hoard, Dorset (DCM-F024) (photos courtesy of PAS/Trustees of the British Museum, adapted by author CC BY-SA 4.0)

Table 5.5: A summary of the Long Bredy hoard, Dorset

DCM-F024	*Object*	*Completeness %*	*Damage Ranking*	*Preparation/use evidence*	*Deliberate damage/associated marks*
a	Ewart Park-type sword hilt	0–25	3	Bevelled edges	Broken (multi-piece); transverse bending (*c.* 70°)
b	Ewart Park-type sword blade (refitting with above)	0–25	3	Bowed edges; notches	Broken (multi-piece); transverse bending (*c.* 70°)
c	Ewart Park-type sword blade	0–25	3	Bowed edges; notches	Broken (single piece)
d	Socketed gouge	100	n/a	Hafting/riveting evidence; striations (sharpening/working)	None
e	Pegged spearhead	76–99	1	Bowing; hafting/riveting evidence; notches	None
f	Razor	76–99	3	Hammering	Tip transversely bent 115°

the deposition of this hoard could have been a very personal action.

The Lulworth hoard

The hoard from Lulworth, Winfrith Newburgh, is similarly eclectic with surviving elements including a sword, two spearheads, an axehead, a range of tools and ornaments and a flesh-hook (DCM-F025; Table 5.6). Damage on some of the objects means it has typically been considered a scrap hoard (eg, Needham & Bowman 2005), though at least some of the damage probably occurred post-recovery. The hoard was found in 1903 and stored at Lulworth Castle where a fire broke out in 1929 causing damage to the objects, (Oliver 1936, 28), the extent of which is unclear. For instance, only a sword tip fragment now survives but Oliver notes that 'when found the sword was complete although the point was broken off' (*ibid.*). The rest of the sword was thus destroyed or lost and it is uncertain whether the tip breakage represents ancient or modern damage. Similar notes on the completeness before and after the fire were not made for the remaining objects, but we cannot consider the current character or condition of the hoard exactly as it was when deposited, though there are no indications that additional objects were found and no longer survive.

Other damaged objects included two broken spearheads, one having been bent and crushed, perhaps in prehistory. Nine fragments of multiple incomplete decorated sheet plaques may represent accidental damage, but deliberately damaged examples are known from other Late Bronze Age hoards from Britain (eg, Coombs 1979, 208, fig. 11.6; Adams 2017, 52, fig. 9).

Like Long Bredy, the objects in the hoard are typical of the Ewart Park metalworking assemblage but atypical within Dorset and represent a range of activities, including personal ornamentation, crafts and combat. Furthermore, individual objects indicate the influence of other regions. Flesh-hooks, indicative of feasting, are typically found in northern Ireland, eastern England and the Atlantic façade of France and northern Iberia (Needham & Bowman 2005); the Lulworth example is the only known example from south-west Britain. These objects are occasionally found in 'scrap' hoards, whilst isolated complete finds were often deposited in bogs (*ibid.*, 119, table 3). The complete Lulworth example is not indicative of scrap material and its presence in a region outside the normal distribution may have been significant. Similarly, the surviving sword fragment, decorated plaques and bugle-shaped object are suggestive of influence from the cross-Channel carp's-tongue complex discussed above. Unlike Cornwall, though, the Lulworth hoard and the carp's-tongue objects do not appear to be part of a wider uptake of the depositional practices of south-east England and Atlantic France. Instead, we may suggest that these objects were considered unusual to the person or group that accumulated

Table 5.6: A summary of the Lulworth hoard, Dorset

DCM-F025	*Object*	*Completeness %*	*Damage Ranking*	*Preparation/use evidence*	*Deliberate damage/ associated marks*
a	Carp's-tongue-type sword	0–25	0	Bevelled edges; polished; striations (sharpening/ working); tip sharp	None
b	Pegged spearhead	51–75	3	Bevelled edges; casting material prepared/removed; dents; flattening; grinding; polished	Broken (single piece)
c	Pegged spearhead	0–25	3	Uncertain	Bent (transverse); broken (single piece); crushed; hammered
d	South Welsh-type socketed axehead	100	n/a	Casting material prepared/ removed; hammering	None
e	Socketed gouge	100	n/a	Casting material prepared/ removed; chips; polished	None
f	Bugle-shaped object	26–50	1, Uncertain	Polished	None
g	Wire finger ring	100	n/a	Uncertain	None
h	Swan's neck pin	100	0	Uncertain	None
i	Twisted wire bracelet	Uncertain	1	Uncertain	None
j	Wire	Uncertain	1	Uncertain	None
k	Sheet metal	Uncertain	1	Decorated; hammering; polished	None
l	Decorated plaque	Uncertain	3	Decorated; hammering; polished	Broken (multi-piece)
m	Decorated plaque	Uncertain	3	Decorated; hammering; polished	Broken (multi-piece)
n	Decorated plaque	Uncertain	3	Decorated; hammering; polished	Broken (multi-piece)
o	Decorated plaque	Uncertain	3	Decorated; hammering; polished	Broken (single piece)
p	Casting jet	n/a	3	Casting/metallurgical waste	Broken (single piece)
q	Disc-headed pin	100	2	Uncertain	None
r	Class 3 flesh-hook	100	Uncertain	Uncertain	None

and deposited the hoard, perhaps with connotations of wider connections. In this sense it is more like the Stogursey hoard. The largely complete nature of many of the Lulworth objects with relatively inconclusive evidence of deliberate damage suggests that the 'scrap' interpretation of this hoard is not valid. The decision to destroy only the spearheads and possibly the plaques, while leaving other objects complete, may have related to more widely understood notions of how such objects should be treated or else to personal choice upon burying the hoard. The combination of production material, used objects and destroyed artefacts, all with a diverse range of uses and functions, may indicate that this, like Long Bredy, was a hoard designed to capture a range of connections, processes and aspects of Bronze Age social life.

Late Bronze Age associated finds and hoards summary

There was no single cohesive practice of the treatment of hoards across south-west Britain. A study of the character of the objects, the destructive methods undertaken and an overall analysis of individual findspots indicates regional trends and highlights how hoards might be viewed within their contemporary landscapes and in relation to broader traditions elsewhere. There was an influx, adoption and

Table 5.7: Single finds of Late Bronze Age swords from south-west Britain

No./ref.	*Findspot*	*Portion of sword*	*Completeness %*	*Damage Ranking(s)*	*Findspot location*
ASH-F004	West Cornwall	Complete apart from 1 hilt tip	76–99	1	Uncertain
ASH-F006	Devon I	Complete apart from hilt butt	76–99	1	Possibly bank of the River Tamar?
BCMAG-F005	Bristol Bridge, Bath Street, Bristol	Tip & lower blade	26–50	0 3	Close to, possibly in, the River Avon
BM-F016	Cranborne I, Dorset	Complete apart from tip	76–99	1	Uncertain
BM-F017	Cranborne II, Dorset	Complete apart from 1 shoulder tip	76–99	1,2	Uncertain, possibly wetland
BM-F033	River Avon, Bath, Somerset	Complete	100	n/a	River
DCM-F001	Abbotsbury, Dorset	Shoulders & blade	76–99	2	Uncertain
DCM-F040	Westham Bridge, Weymouth, Dorset	Complete, apart from hilt terminal	76–99	2	River
DCM-F044	Weymouth Backwater, Dorset	Mostly complete but missing hilt & tip	76–99	2	River/estuary
PAS-F005	Camborne II, Cornwall	Mid-blade frag.	0–25	3	Uncertain
PAS-F018	Marazion I, Cornwall	Tip frag.	0–25	1	Hilltop, view of coast
PAS-F027	Polperro, Cornwall	Mid-blade frag.	0–25	2	Hill overlooking estuary/ coast
PAS-F040	St Winnow, Cornwall	Mid-blade frag.	0–25	3	Overlooking River Fowey estuary
PAS-F042	Tregoney I, Cornwall	Tip frag.	0–25	1	Confluence of waterways, hillslope, river valley
PAS-F064	Holne, Devon	Mid-blade frag.	0–25	3	Hill in Dartmoor overlooking River Dart
PAS-F138	Okeford Fitzpaine, Dorset	Mid-blade frag.	0–25	2	Hillslope in River Stour valley
PAS-F166	West Knighton, Dorset	Mid-blade frag.	0–25	2	Hill overlooking River Frome
PAS-F201	Chedzoy II, Somerset	Mid-blade frag.	0–25	3	Uncertain
PAS-F205	Chilcompton II, Somerset	Mid-blade frag.	0–25	3	Hillslope
PAS-F227	Martock, Somerset	Mid-blade	0–25	2	Hillslope, near natural spring
PAS-F237	Otterhampton I, Somerset	Mid-blade frag.	0–25	2	Near marshlands, close to coast
PAS-F250	South Petherton III, Somerset	Hilt & upper blade in 2 refitting pieces	0–25	Uncertain	Lowland, minor water valley
PCMAG-F001	Brent Tor, Devon	Hilt, shoulders & upper blade	26–50	3	Volcanic outcrop on Dartmoor, near natural pools
RAMM-F040	Pole Sands, Devon	Complete	100	0,1	Beach/coastal
SM-F007	Weymouth II, Dorset	Lower blade & tip	26–50	2	Uncertain, possibly watery context
TTNCM-F029	Midsomer Norton, Somerset	Complete	100	n/a	Hilltop, overlooking River Somer
TTNCM-F038	Pitney Moor I, Somerset	Shoulders & blade	76–99	0,1	Moorland
WEL-F005	Rodney Stoke, Somerset	Lower blade & tip	51–75	Uncertain	Hillslope, on edge of moorland (Stoke Moor)

No./ref.	*Findspot*	*Portion of sword*	*Completeness %*	*Damage Ranking(s)*	*Findspot location*
The following swords have not been studied first-hand, so Damage Rankings have not been attributed. Completeness assessed from images.					
Knight *et al.* 2015, 39, no. 113	Bishopsteignton, Devon	Blade frag. (further details unknown)	0–25?	–	Uncertain
Knight *et al.* 2015, 36, no. 70, pl. 26	St Sampson, Cornwall	Mid-blade frag.	0–25	–	Uncertain
Pearce 1983, 487, no. 475a, pl. 105	Weymouth Backwater, Dorset	Complete, apart from hilt terminal	76–99	–	River/estuary
Pearce 1983, 487, no. 476, pl. 105	Weymouth Backwater, Dorset	Complete, apart from tip of 1 shoulder	76–99	–	River/estuary
Pearce 1983, 493-4, no. 517, pl. 105	Woodlands, Dorset	Complete, apart from tip of 1 shoulder	76–99	–	Stream
Pearce 1983, 537, no. 771, pl. 93	Wellington, Somerset	Blade piece (modern damage)	*c.* 26–50	–	Uncertain

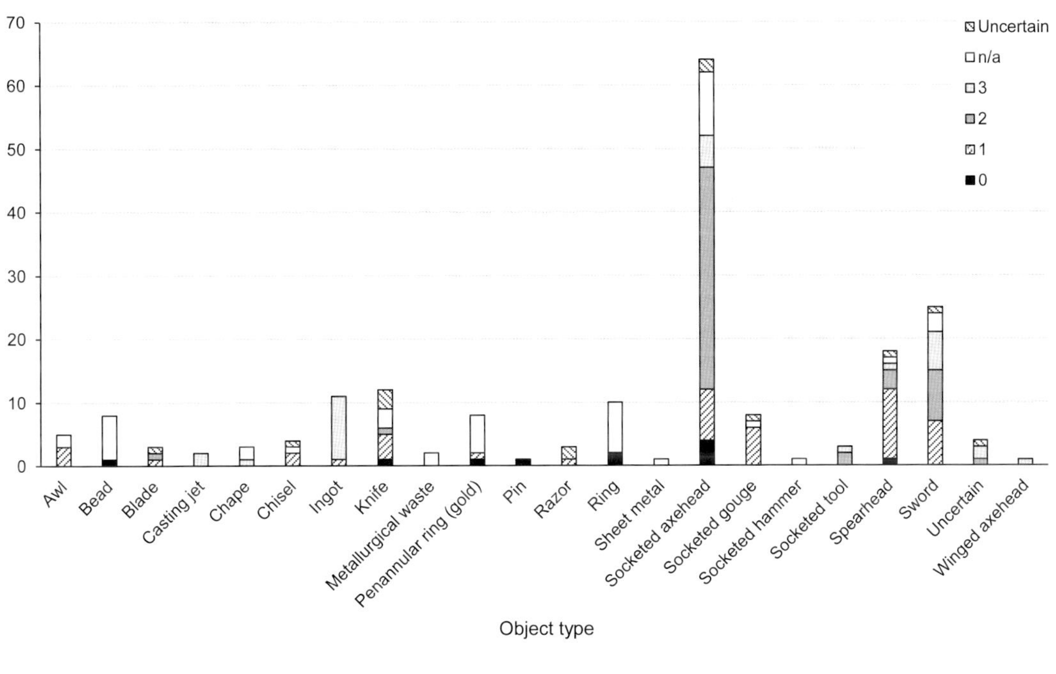

Figure 5.24: Summary of damage rankings on Late Bronze Age single finds of metalwork (n=197)

adaptation of ideas, perhaps linked to the movement of people, into all areas of the South West; the accumulation, destruction and deposition of objects was a reflection of interregional connections. The combinations of complete, worn and damaged objects, often with a variety of connotations, mean simplistic definitions of hoarding traditions (eg, votive offerings or 'scrap') fail to capture the localised nuances of the actions undertaken.

Late Bronze Age single finds

In her study of Irish Bronze Age metalwork, Katharina Becker (2013) suggested that single finds should be considered as part of the spectrum of depositional practice alongside hoards and burials. By analysing the associations of different artefact types and where they were deposited in the landscape, she was able to show that single finds of the same types of artefacts displayed similar depositional

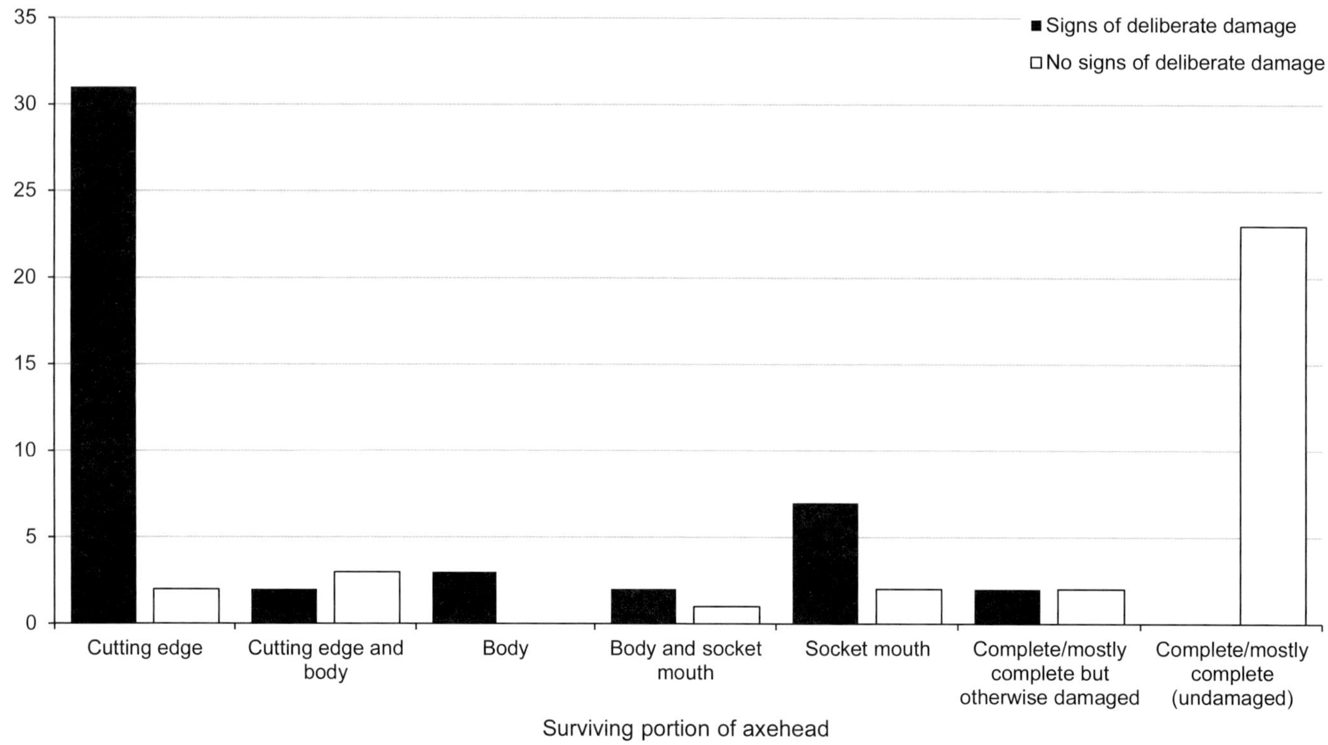

Figure 5.25: Portions of socketed axeheads found as single finds divided by whether they show deliberate damage or not (n=80)

patterns and thus were governed by similar rules of deposition. This approach is adopted here, though with an additional focus on the treatment of single isolated finds.

A total of 206 Late Bronze Age single finds were studied, of which 86 were probably or definitely deliberately damaged; most of these damaged finds were socketed axeheads, swords and casting material (eg, ingots, casting jets) (Fig. 5.24). Many of the remaining objects, including awls, beads, chisels, gouges, palstaves and pins, presented use-related damage (eg, bent tangs, chipped cutting edges), though almost a quarter displayed no damage at all. This suggests that certain objects required certain treatments, which is supported by the overall trend for the Late Bronze Age in south-west Britain (Fig. 5.3), as well as the hoards presented above. The treatment of single finds prior to deposition thus accords with the overall character of associated Late Bronze Age metalwork.

We can examine this further. The damaged single finds offer the opportunity to identify trends in the levels of completeness or portions of objects recovered. The advantage of this is that one can investigate the most recovered portions of damaged objects which might then be compared with objects from a known context (eg, a hoard) to assess the possibility that fragments were the result of intentional selection rather than accidental loss; thus we might identify deliberate depositional practices linked to single finds. Here I focus on swords and socketed axeheads specifically as objects commonly deposited in south-west Britain as single finds. These occur in sufficiently large numbers that trends can be confidently identified.

For both object types, complete and incomplete single finds are known across the South West. Mid-blade sword fragments are frequently recovered (Table 5.8), which must result from deliberate reduction events producing numerous fragments. Given that many blade fragments may be produced from a single sword, it is unsurprising that these would be most encountered as they have the highest chance of entering the archaeological record through discard, loss or deliberate deposition. These are also the pieces commonly encountered within hoards.

Regarding socketed axeheads, more than 140 have been recovered from south-west Britain, of which 80 were studied and 47 showed signs of intentional damage. A comparison of those

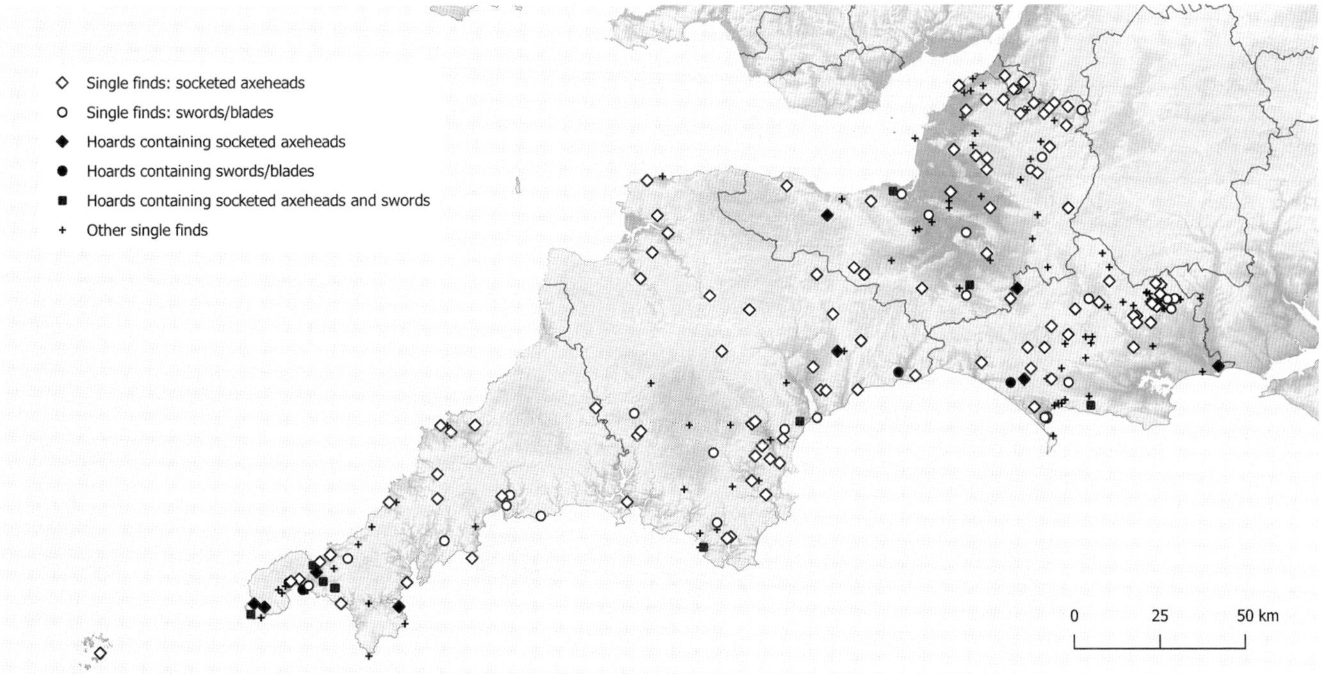

Figure 5.26: Findspots of Late Bronze Age socketed axeheads and swords/blades from south-west Britain. Contains OS data © Crown copyright and database right 2021

displaying signs of deliberate damage and those that did not reveals the high proportion of deliberately fragmented cutting edges, which is in stark contrast to the high number of complete axeheads (Fig. 5.25). Destruction experiments have demonstrated that hot fragmentation of an axehead produced multiple small fragments of the body and socket mouth, whilst the density of the cutting edge makes it more likely to survive as a single piece (Knight 2017), which probably explains their general survival and recovery. The more substantial fragments may also have been more easily retained and selected for deposition following fragmentation.

Individual sword and socketed axehead fragments were predominantly recovered on hilltops and in coastal and/or riverine locations across the South West in similar places to fragmentary hoards (Table 5.7; Fig. 5.26). By contrast, complete or mostly complete swords were almost exclusively recovered from wetland locations, including moorlands and rivers, which aligns with depositional practices for swords elsewhere (cf. York 2002). In south-west Britain, though, these finds are relatively few; an exception is a concentration of swords around Weymouth, Dorset. Depositing fragmented swords in dryer locations was more common. For instance, a deliberately broken sword was found near Brent Tor on Dartmoor, an upland area with rocky outcrops and surrounded by multiple natural pools (Fig. 5.27; PCMAG-F001; Greeves 2019).

The same rationales were broadly true of axeheads. Three axeheads, for instance, were found in the River Frome valley, where sword fragments were also recovered. Six findspots of socketed axeheads are distributed along the Bristol Avon, including three complete axeheads, and three deliberately broken fragments; from the river two swords have been recovered: a complete example from Bathford and a burnt and broken sword piece from Bristol. Like swords, the findspots of the complete socketed axeheads in these areas (and elsewhere) were more closely associated with wetland locations and watery features, including natural springs and bogs; fragmented axeheads were more commonly found in drier locations. This suggests there was a link between the pre-deposition treatment of the objects and their eventual depositional location. Single finds of deliberately damaged objects were not necessarily located randomly and cannot be readily attributed to accidental loss.

The reduction of swords and axeheads to small fragments suggests destruction of single finds related to a functionalist aspect (eg, to fit in a crucible). However, that so many of the deliberately damaged objects show a cohesive placement in landscape, typically in

Figure 5.27: A Late Bronze Age sword from Brent Tor, Devon (PCMAG-F001) (photo: author, courtesy of The Box, Plymouth)

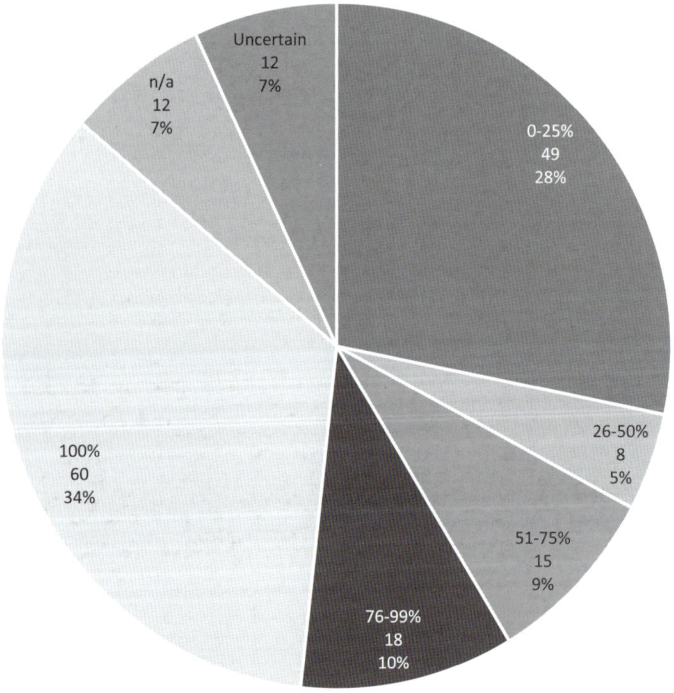

Figure 5.28: The completeness of Late Bronze Age metalwork recovered from occupational contexts and scatters (n=174)

view of a waterway, suggests an understanding about where such objects should be placed, or perhaps where fragmentation events were taking place (cf. Knight 2017, 218). As with ingots, these objects may have been remnants of functionalist practices that necessitated a token deposit in these locations. Like Becker's (2013) assessment of the Irish metalwork, it is probable that at least some single finds in south-west Britain were part of the same depositional spectrum and actions as larger accumulations of material. Moreover, recognising that they represent the vestiges of deliberate actions helps us consider these fragments within wider practices and processes and links them with agency.

Late Bronze Age occupational contexts and scatters

Overall, 208 metal objects were studied from 26 occupational contexts and scatters; 59 artefacts were damage-ranked 2 or 3 across 15 findspots, typically found on the same sites from which accidentally damaged and intact objects were also recovered. Many objects lack a detailed context other than that they were recovered from an 'occupational layer' and, in the case of the scattered objects, the context is implied from the collective association spread across an area. Objects were typically recovered mostly complete or highly fragmented (Fig. 5.28) and all deliberately damaged metalwork, including gold and bronze objects, was fragmented, as well as bent, crushed, or folded.

At Greylake, Somerset, several deposits were made near to a timber platform, including 12 fragments of Late Bronze Age pottery, two sheep jaw bones, two human bones and a crushed, melted and broken socketed axehead (Fig. 5.29; TTNCM-F019; Brunning 1997; 1998). This was an area of low-lying marshland and one of the few cases in Late Bronze Age south-west Britain where fragmented metalwork was possibly associated with a human burial; here, objects and bodies were treated in very similar ways. Fragmentation of objects, animals and people was a necessary precursor to deposition in a performative way. Similar situations in relation to wooden trackways and wetland locations are known elsewhere in southern Britain (Brück 1995, 249–50, 276–7).

Most of the metalwork from occupational contexts and scatters in south-west Britain, comprised fragments and casting waste, however, occasionally associated with ceramic refractories. The treatment of this material after fragmentation (ie, largely deposited in pits) is significant for indicating how such material was viewed (Table 5.8). The association of slag and metallurgical waste with the refractories found at Higher Besore, Cornwall (Gossip in press), and Dainton, Devon (Needham 1980), for instance, could indicate that these were deposits of waste. The objects could no longer be used and were consequently buried. However, the accumulation of sword moulds, crucibles and casting waste at Dainton was buried in a pit near to a series of cairns, one of which contained human skeletal remains, and probably related to nearby field systems (Silvester 1980). The refractories probably represent at least six phases of casting episodes (Needham 1980), and Robert Johnston (2021, 195) has suggested that there may have been

Figure 5.29: The crushed, burnt and broken axehead from Greylake, Somerset (photo: author, courtesy of Somerset County Council and South West Heritage Trust, acc. no. TTNCM : 95/1997/1)

a selective element to what was accumulated, transported and buried in a pit at this site. At Norton Fitzwarren, Somerset, fragmentary sword moulds were also collected, as well as ceramic jars, and buried in a pit near the entrance of the enclosure (Needham 1989b). In both cases, moulds were probably buried not long after their final castings and their careful deposition was perhaps related to marking their respective places, or else to the significance of metalcasting itself and the appropriate ways to treat such material (cf. Mörtz 2014; Webley *et al.* 2020, 113).

Although at least some of the casting debris may have held significance in deposition, almost all deposits of metal objects in closed contexts were seemingly waste products and other objects were typically found loose in occupational layers or scatters. Deliberately damaged ingots and casting jets were largely retrieved from scatter sites, which may indicate evidence of ephemeral occupation or activity relating to casting and recycling, such as at Kent's Cavern, Devon, Kenidjack Castle and Sennen, Cornwall (PAS-F029). On St Michael's Mount, a deliberately reduced copper ingot fragment was found within a probable Late Bronze Age structure in the same layer as a saddle quern and pottery sherds. The users of the structure possibly had some involvement in the use and trade of metalwork alongside other craft activities (Herring 2000, 46–7); alternatively, this may have been part of an abandonment process expressing a connection with metalworking nearby (Jones & Knight forthcoming). The mixture of stone, clay and metal waste material in these contexts

Table 5.8: Metalwork and metalworking material associated with Late Bronze Age occupational in south-west Britain

Site	*County*	*Character of the site*	*Metalwork and metalworking material*	*Depositional context*	*No./Key reference(s)*
Gwithian	Cornwall	Multi-period occupation site	4 frags of clay moulds for possible blade; 2 frags stone mould for socketed axehead; 3 fragmented pins	Finds from across the site in general occupation layers; 2 refitting frags of stone mould deposited in adjacent structures	Needham in Nowakowski 2007, 66
Higher Besore & Truro College, Threemilestone	Cornwall	4 Late Bronze Age post-hole structures	Clay sword mould; whetstone frags; slag; 4 ingot frags	Mould, whetstone & slag from pit [6500] alongside 56 pottery sherds. Ingots frags in topsoil	Gossip 2005, 16; in press
Kenidjack Castle	Cornwall	Small square hut outside promontory hillfort	Lumps of metal waste; casting jet; winged & socketed axeheads	Found in hut; Middle–Late Bronze Age metalwork also found nearby	RCM-F018; Pearce 1983, 411–2, no.72
Poden	Cornwall	Roundhouse	Knife; copper-alloy frags	Recovered during excavation of a roundhouse	Knight *et al.* 2015, 34–5, no. 49
St Michael's Mount	Cornwall	Probable Late Bronze Age structure	Copper ingot frag.	Within structure, in same layer as saddle quern & pottery sherds	Herring 2000; Jones & Knight forthcoming
Tremough	Cornwall	Ditched enclosure containing pits & post-hole structures	1 clay mould frag. for tip of a blade; 15 frags possible moulds	Found in pit [124] associated with Late Bronze Age Enclosure 1	Jones 2015, 202–25; Pearce 2015
Dean Moor	Devon	Nine stone huts in enclosed settlement	Lump of tin ore & tin slag	Found associated with huts	Fox 1957; Knight 2014, 32–3
Marldon	Devon	Possible scatter	Blade frag.; 3 ingot frags	Each found in same field but several years apart	RAMM-F030
Mount Batten	Devon	Late Bronze Age–Earliest Iron Age midden	Metallurgical waste & ingot frags	Found within general midden with fragmented Late Bronze Age–Earliest Iron Age metalwork	PCMAG-F004; Northover 1988
Stoneycombe Quarry (Dainton)	Devon	Occupation site & field system	43 clay frags of 3 crucibles; 150+ mould frags for swords, spearheads & possible rings; some bronze pieces	Mould & crucible frags found in & around pit near Late Bronze Age pot frags, possibly associated with cairn & burial	Needham 1980; Silvester 1980
Bestwall Quarry	Dorset	3 'farmsteads' comprising 7 structures & associated field systems	2 crucible & 3 mould frags, incl. socketed axehead & palstave moulds; socketed axehead frag.; socketed gouge	1 crucible frag. from pit; remaining refractories from another pit; socketed gouge placed at entrance to building with socket downwards	Ladle & Woodward 2009; Needham & Woodward 2009
Chalbury Camp	Dorset	Iron Age hillfort	Frags. bracelet, ring, rivets, & copper/copper-alloy piece	Recovered during excavations at Iron Age hillfort – could date to earlier Iron Age	Whitley 1943; Pearce 1983, 464, no. 346
Chickerell I	Dorset	Late Bronze Age hut	2 gold neckrings	Found interlinked close to Late Bronze Age hut	PAS-F109; Woodward 2000
Chickerell II	Dorset	Possible Late Bronze Age scatter	3 socketed axehead frags	Recovered from same field while metal-detecting but relationship to each other is uncertain	PAS-F110
Eldon's Seat	Dorset	Late Bronze Age–Earliest Iron Age midden	Chisel; frags bronze sheet & bronze rod	Chisel recovered from Late Bronze Age–Earliest Iron Age layer	Cunliffe & Phillipson 1969

Site	*County*	*Character of the site*	*Metalwork and metalworking material*	*Depositional context*	*No./Key reference(s)*
Everley Water Meadow	Dorset	Paleochannel near possible burnt mound	Frag. copper ingot, stone axehead mould, & clay plug	In a palaeochannel; copper ingot from unspecified context	Mercer & Healy 2008, 439; Webley *et al.* 2020, supplementary material
Gussage St Michael 2 & Gussage St Michael 5	Dorset	Scatter	More than 110 pieces Late Bronze Age metalwork, incl. metallurgical waste & casting jets	Scattered across 2 fields	PRIV-F019; PRIV-F035
Knighton House School	Dorset	Occupational layer	Disc-headed pin	Recovered from settlement context with prehistoric pottery	BTM-F002
Poundbury	Dorset	Ditched & palisaded enclosure with post-hole structures	Possible crucible frag.	Occupation layer	Skowranek 2007, 105
Sheepsleights, Worth Matravers	Dorset	Late Bronze Age–Iron Age settlement	Razor	Recovered from pit associated with wheat, Iron Age pottery & sheep bones; other pits from the site have yielded Bronze Age pottery	Pearce 1983, 494, no. 520
Tinney's Lane, Sherborne	Dorset	Late Bronze Age roundhouse settlement	Refractory material & *c.* 19 possible clay mould frags, incl. spearhead moulds; copper-alloy objects incl. 3 awls, 2 rings, 1 pin, 1 socketed axehead frag.	Mould frags recovered from 12 different features, incl. 10 pits. Copper-alloy objects found scattered onsite	Best & Woodward 2012
Valley bottom area, near Hambledon hillfort	Dorset	Occupational layer?	Stone mould for axehead; copper-alloy slag	Layered fill of watercourse contained pottery & mould frag.; slag recovered from near a pit packed with charcoal & calcined flints	Pearce 1983, 553, no. 870
Banwell	Somerset	Pit	*c.* 180 frags clay moulds & other refractory ceramics, incl. matrices for pins, rings, possible spearhead or ferrule, & possible socketed axehead & chisel	From a pit	Young 2013
Brean Down	Somerset	Late Bronze Age midden	2 gold bracelets & a gold frag.; copper-alloy bracelet & wire frags	Gold objects recovered from ditch with ceramic sherd; copper-alloy objects from general midden layers	TTNCM-F005; TTNCM-F006; Bell 1990
Cadbury Castle	Somerset	Iron Age hillfort; limited evidence for round structures, fencelines, & banks	44 pieces of copper-alloy & gold metalwork, spanning Early Bronze Age–Earliest Iron Age, incl. axeheads, pins, bracelets, tweezers, & awls, & metallurgical waste	General scatter from across the site, some from pits, ditches or later contexts	TTNCM-F007; Barrett *et al.* 2000
Ham Hill	Somerset	Iron Age hillfort	25 pieces copper-alloy metalwork, including pins, razors, chisels, & blades, & 2 frags stone mould for axeheads	Objects scattered across the hillfort; moulds date to the Earliest Iron Age	TTNCM-F020
Norton Fitzwarren	Somerset	Late Bronze Age enclosure ditch	*c.* 70 clay mould frags for swords	In a pit within the ditch	Needham 1989b
Sigwells	Somerset	Enclosure & round structure	*c.* 879 clay moulds for swords, spearheads, chapes, ferrules, socketed axeheads, & pins; *c.* 117 clay mould frags representing at least 8 objects	Larger assemblage of moulds from several trenches within enclosure & associated round structure; possible stone/ bone metalworking tools also recovered but not associated with moulds; remaining 117 mould frags from a single pit to NNW of the enclosure	Skowranek 2007, 109; Knight *et al.* 2015, 70, no. 428; Richard Tabor pers. comm.

Figure 5.30: A selection of material from Gussage St Michael, Dorset (photo: author, courtesy of Martin Green)

rarely represents an entire process, ie, it is rare to find all pieces of a mould or complete metalworking tools. It may be that certain parts of objects were deposited and others were reused or recycled into other objects in much the same way that metalwork hoards often comprised incomplete objects.

Other 'waste' material, including fragments of gold and copper-alloy sheet and five casting jets, was recovered through metal-detecting at Gussage St Michael, Dorset. Here, *c.* 117 of predominantly Late Bronze Age objects have been found from a series of fields alongside 610 g of casting waste (Fig. 5.30).[3] The scattered material remains and character of the material, including small and deliberately damaged objects, suggests this might represent a midden or metalworking site; however, no associated context (eg, a pit or hearth remains) has been identified. A small fragment of a stone axehead mould was recovered from Gussage Cow Down 5 II (PRIV-F015) though no other recognisable refractories (eg, crucibles) have yet been found nearby. A Late Bronze Age–Early Iron Age enclosure has been identified at Home Field to the north-east of the site (Green 1986; Ellis 2012); if related to the spread of metalwork and casting debris, this could represent a deliberate segregation of practices with metalworking taking place away from the settled area (cf. Knight 2014). This site also lies within the long-lived prehistoric landscape of Cranborne Chase (Barrett *et al.* 1991) so this scatter must surely relate to wider interactions in this landscape.

As in the Middle Bronze Age, deposits at occupational sites were also important social practices that expressed broader ontologies and marked certain events. At Brean Down, Somerset, two interlinked gold bracelets and a gold fragment were possibly deposited in a ditch associated with a ceramic rim sherd

(Fig. 5.31; TTNCM-F005; Bell 1990, 6). Both bracelets were complete though the fragment had been deliberately clipped and broken on three edges. Bell (1990, 72) suggested this may have been a dedicatory deposit aimed to establish boundaries or alternatively a 'founder's hoard' as indicated by the gold fragment. In the context of other gold deposits in south-west Britain, this was probably a deliberately structured deposit.

At Chickerell, Dorset, two interlinked 'neck-rings' were deposited in a possible enclosure (PAS-F109; Woodward 2000) and at Colaton Raleigh, Devon, three gold bracelets were nested one inside the other, associated with a small gold fragment (Fig. 5.32; Taylor 1999). Little is known about the context of the six complete gold bracelets from Carne near Morvah, Cornwall, but they represent insular and Irish styles, and it seems probable these were related to wider networks and deposited in a structured fashion (Cornish 1906, 357; Hencken 1932, 92–3; Hook & Needham 1989). By contrast, gold fragments of probable Late Bronze Age date were recovered from the Gussage St Michael scatters (PRIV-F035a), and fragments of a deliberately chiselled gold bar and a broken gold bracelet terminal were found at Cadbury Castle (Fig. 2.19; TTNCM-F007a, c). When compared with the fragmentary gold deposits, the Brean Down deposit, and others in south-west Britain, were carefully constructed depositions that acted as a way of expressing and managing the world. That so few deposits of gold bracelets have been discovered suggests this was a rare practice, reserved to fulfil significant purposes and events within the lives of people in these places. A complete socketed gouge deposited blade up in a pit at the centre of the entrance to one of the roundhouses at Bestwall Quarry, Dorset (Ladle & Woodward 2009, 374), suggests bronze objects may have occasionally fulfilled similar roles, though such examples are similarly rare in south-west Britain.

The destruction and deposition of other materials at occupational contexts greatly outweighs the number of metal objects, however, suggesting these were the main means by which people managed and organised their settled lives. We should also consider here that material distinctions were probably unimportant when it came to depositions around occupational areas. Late Bronze Age pits at Higher Besore Truro College, Cornwall contained numerous stone tools including mullers, rubbers and saddle querns in various states of use and re-use produced from different materials and, in the case of

Figure 5.31: The Brean Down gold bracelet hoard, Somerset (TTNCM-F005) (source: author, courtesy of Somerset County Council and South West Heritage Trust, acc.no. TTNCM 84.AA.67)

Figure 5.32: The Colaton Raleigh hoard, Devon © Royal Albert Memorial Museum & Art Gallery, Exeter

the querns, fragmented (Watts 2014, 90ff.; Gossip in press). These deposits have been linked with abandonment processes with the breakage of querns seemingly an integral component (Watts 2014). At Eldon's Seat, Dorset, a group of pot sherds, refitting to form three complete vessels, and six other ceramic fragments were found in a pit within huts 2 and 3; these were unweathered and probably deliberately broken for deposition (Cunliffe & Phillipson 1969, 199; Woodward 2009, 265). Roundhouses at Eldon's Seat were repeatedly rebuilt and the deposit may have been linked to a reconstruction phase. Similarly, three vessels were broken and 'crushed' *in situ* in three separate pit and gully contexts at Brean Down (Bell 1990, 70). At Bestwall Quarry, fragments of Late Bronze Age pots were deposited in a series of pits close to the roundhouses, some also containing burnt flint and charcoal (Woodward 2009, 247–51). At least some of this material may represent the destruction of a community's inventory, linked with the closing of houses or settlements, as has been suggested for deposits at Broom Quarry, Bedfordshire (Brück 2007, 29–30). In many cases at Bestwall, mostly complete and fragmented ceramics were deliberately selected for their size and fabric, forming part of a series of important social practices possibly linked to feasting (Woodward 2009, 262–5).

At Gwithian, Cornwall, two refitting fragments of a stone mould for a socketed axehead were deposited in two neighbouring houses (Burgess 1976a). This mould may have broken following extensive use allowing the potential for the object to gain significance through its longer lifespan. Significantly, the time and energy required to produce a stone mould can be as much as 20 hours (Barbieri & Cavazzuti 2014). One can thus envisage a situation in which the mould was not owned by a single person or household but rather an object produced, owned and valued by a community. The deposition of two fragments in neighbouring houses may have been a physical manifestation of an enchained relationship between these two households (cf. Chapman 2000), perhaps representing joint ownership of the mould. This does, however, raise the question of where the other half of the mould was deposited. It is rare to recover both halves of Bronze Age stone bivalve moulds (eg, Needham 1981) suggesting that the two pieces were deliberately separated after use of these objects had finished. The other half of the Gwithian mould may have been deposited elsewhere linked with another connection between people or the events in which the mould was involved. As in the Middle Bronze Age, the occasional deliberate destruction and deposition of a range of Late Bronze Age objects allowed people to express broader ideas in localised, selective ways that reflected their immediate relations. The social necessity of destruction and deposition outweighed the practical usefulness of the objects involved.

Late Bronze Age conclusions: networks of practice

In analysing Early Iron Age burials across the Low Countries and Central Europe, Sasja van der Vaart-Verschoof (2017; van der Vaart-Verschoof & Schumann 2020) highlighted the importance of recognising 'networks of practices', ie, similar practices undertaken across wide areas, as a way of understanding how prehistoric communities were connected. This seems an entirely appropriate way of viewing the Late Bronze Age data from south-west Britain. There were significant regionalised variations in the practices undertaken, and this was commonly linked to access to and influence from different areas, such as the Stogursey hoard or the hoards deposited in Cornwall. Moreover, some areas had no or very little evidence of Late Bronze Age hoarding and metalwork deposition. Although there was a dense concentration in western Cornwall and south Devon, few deposits were made in east Cornwall or north Devon. For whatever reason, hoarding was seemingly not a practice undertaken in these areas, or else any hoards deposited were subsequently recovered; the same can be said generally of Somerset and Dorset where so few hoards are known.

This highlights an important point. Although broadly the analysis of the material from south-west Britain accords with what one might expect from a region of Late Bronze Age Britain – metalwork was gathered and deposited in a range of contexts with deliberate destruction a frequent feature – it was clearly more complex than this. Applying overarching ideas about deposition across the whole region is not applicable; if superficially similar deposits

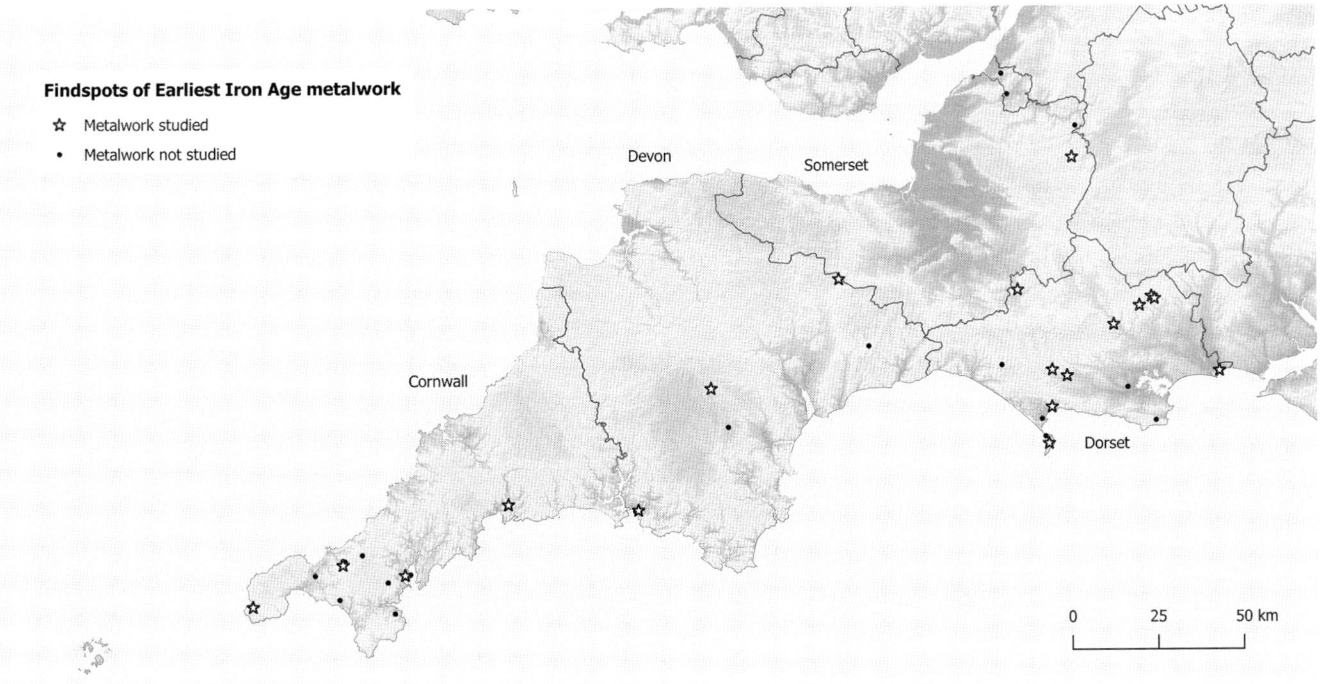

Figure 5.33: Findspots of Earliest Iron Age metalwork from south-west Britain. Those marked with stars were studied as part of this research. Contains OS data © Crown copyright and database right 2021

were undertaken for the same reason, such as fragmented hoards, we might expect the same widespread character. However, decisions around how and where to bury hoards were varied. Individual deposits were clearly an expression of different social relationships and the movement of ideas undertaken at a localised level, regardless of the intended function of the deposit. What we see archaeologically are snapshots of this.

This was also a scaled activity, with similarities in the findspot locations and treatment of single finds suggesting these were part of the same underlying structures that governed hoarding (cf. Becker 2013). Understanding and recognising the deliberate destruction of single finds, as well as trends in their depositional locations, means it is possible to situate these within selective depositional practices, as well as recognising the trajectories of these objects prior to ending up in the ground.

Finally, this accumulation and deposition of deliberately fragmented metalwork stands in contrast to the treatment of the same material in occupational contexts in the South West. As in earlier centuries, selective and carefully structured deposits of a range of artefacts continued to be integral to managing the social world at settlements, but stone tools, ceramics and metalworking debris were most common whilst the deposition of metalwork, damaged or undamaged, remained limited. This suggests that deliberately damaging and depositing metalwork was something predominantly undertaken away from these settled areas and more closely related to natural places. At settlements, objects such as ceramic vessels and quernstones were deemed more appropriate as deposits to mark significant events, such as founding or abandoning a structure. These were symbolic actions undertaken across the South West.

Minor destruction: earliest Iron Age *c.* 800–600 BC

At the turn of the 8th century BC there was seemingly a stark shift in the ways in which metalwork was selected, treated and deposited in south-west Britain. The diverse, fragmentary hoards of the preceding Ewart Park assemblage were replaced by axehead-dominant hoards of typically complete objects during the Llyn Fawr metalworking assemblage (or Earliest Iron Age). One of the most striking aspects is the complete lack of diversity in the metalwork, with fewer types of objects buried; axeheads and small tools make up most metalwork recovered from this period and deposits of goldwork ceased entirely (Figs 5.33 & 5.34).

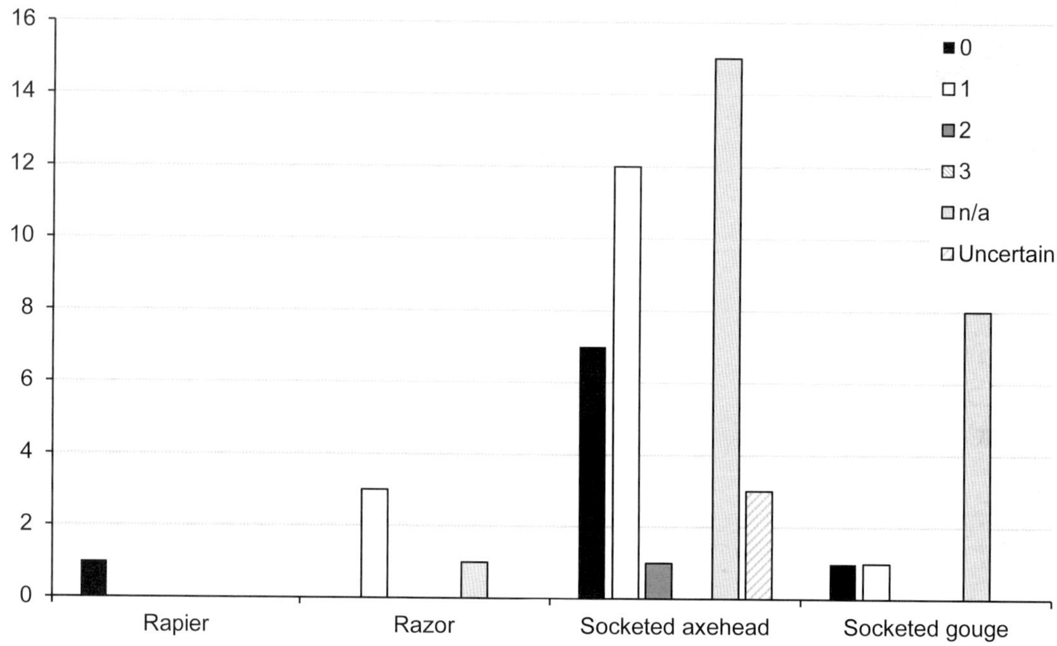

Figure 5.34: Earliest Iron Age metalwork studied from south-west Britain divided by object type and damage ranking (n=53)

Such changes occurred across much of Britain around this time (Needham 2007c; O'Connor 2007) and have traditionally been interpreted as representing the collapse of the bronze industry and the abandonment of bronze as a material (eg, Burgess 1979; Thomas 1989). These theories are now considered inadequate: shifts in how deposition was undertaken were probably related to broader social and cultural changes and the changing role of bronze in society (Needham 1990b, 130–40; 2007c; O'Connor 2007; Cunliffe 2015, 11ff; Knight *et al.* 2021, 24). Around this time, the first iron objects were produced as well as new styles of decorated pottery. The character of settlement remained largely consistent with the Late Bronze Age, but large midden accumulations occurred in southern Britain, comprising high volumes of fragmented pottery, butchered animal bones and a range of other material culture, occasionally including bronze objects (McOmish 1996; Waddington 2009; Waddington *et al.* 2019). Midden sites in south-west Britain tend to be smaller than those elsewhere but are known at Mount Batten, Devon (Cunliffe 1988) and Brean Down, Somerset (Bell 1990) as well as a cluster of eight possible middens on the Isle of Purbeck, Dorset (Ladle 2018, 291–5). These were sites where people gathered, exchanged and deposited objects as well as undertaking a range of communal activities, including craftworking, feasting and occasionally metalwork production (Ladle 2018; Waddington *et al.* 2019). Although the range was not as diverse as in preceding periods, new forms of copper-alloy objects were produced, circulated and deposited as single finds, in hoards, and at midden sites, including axeheads, swords, chapes, horse fittings and vessels (O'Connor 2007). Similarly, elsewhere in Europe elaborate bronze objects continued to be produced and deposited in burials during this period (van der Vaart-Verschoof & Schumann 2020).

The deliberate destruction of metalwork prior to deposition occurred less frequently and in south-west Britain such evidence is limited. Of the pieces studied, most intentionally damaged artefacts derive from the disturbed midden site at Mount Batten, spanning the Late Bronze Age–Earliest Iron Age periods (PCMAG-F004; Northover 1988). The fragmentation pattern of axeheads, sickles and blades suggest these were deliberately broken while hot (Fig. 5.35), and fragments of sheet vessels, probably cauldrons, were deliberately cut, torn, reduced and manipulated. These destructive practices are present on the chronological span of objects. Complete bronze objects dating from 1000–600 BC, including axeheads and knives, were also recovered from the site as well as sherds of pottery. At Cadbury Castle, a deliberately hammered and fragmented Late

Figure 5.35: Fragments of axeheads from Mount Batten, Devon (photo: author, courtesy of The Box Plymouth)

Bronze Age–Earliest Iron Age bucket base was found (TTNCM-F007ii) and a fragment of an Earliest Iron Age socketed axehead was recovered while metal-detecting at Hemington, Somerset (PAS-F215). These seem to represent isolated losses. To these examples, we can add a hoard of deliberately damaged metalwork from Kings Weston Down, Bristol (see below), but overall, it was no longer widely appropriate to destroy metalwork as part of making it suitable for deposition.

Most objects were instead deposited more complete (Fig. 5.36), often with limited signs of wear. Objects were buried unused and frequently as-cast and, although there are a few instances recovered from middens and occupational contexts (eg, O'Connor 2018), the majority were deposited either singly or accumulated into hoards. These will be the focus here.

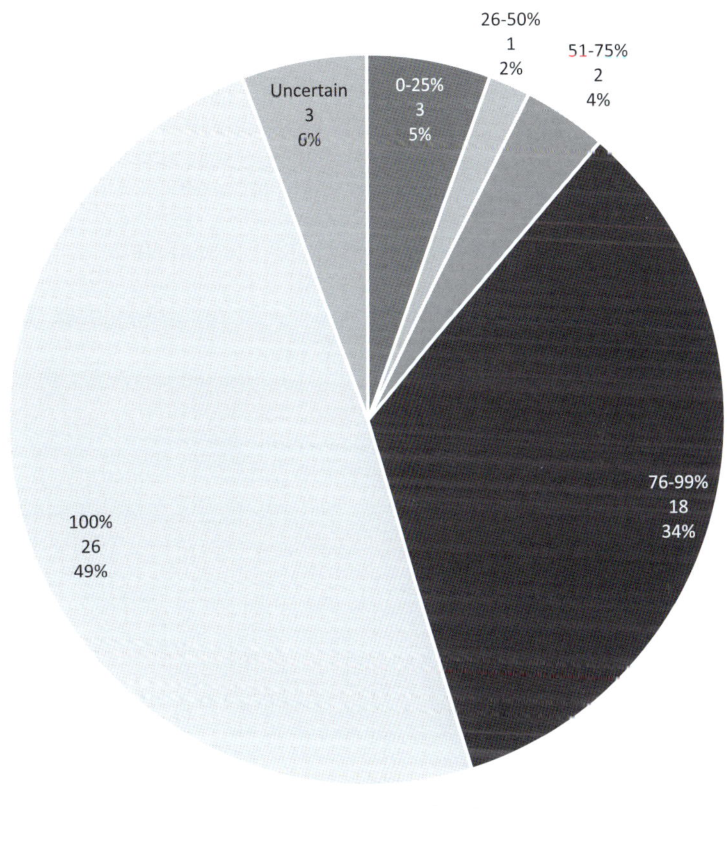

Figure 5.36: The proportions of object completeness within the Earliest Iron Age metalwork (n=53)

Earliest Iron Age token axeheads and axehead hoards in Cornwall and Dorset

Over 95% of Earliest Iron Age metalwork from south-west Britain comes from associated finds and hoards; the great majority of this material is axeheads. In south-west Britain, there were two distinct regionalised hoarding traditions in Dorset and Cornwall, both comprising different forms of afunctional axeheads.

Dorset

In Dorset, Portland- and Blandford-type linear-faceted axeheads were deposited in hoards and as single finds, and were rarely circulated or deposited outside the region (Boughton 2015).

Figure 5.37: The Langton Matravers hoard (photo: George Wickham, by kind permission of Ann Woodward)

They were occasionally associated with small slender socketed gouges, and associations range in size from three axeheads found near Weymouth (Pearce 1983, 487, no.478) to the accumulation of 373 complete and broken socketed axeheads and 404 additional axehead fragments at Langton Matravers (Fig. 5.37; Roberts *et al.* 2015).

In all cases, the socketed axeheads and socketed gouges were deposited as-cast, often with clay plugs still in the sockets, and have a silvery appearance, which results from a high-tin and high-lead composition of the copper alloy (Roberts *et al.* 2015). This composition makes the objects extremely brittle and unworkable as functional objects; many fragmented post-casting or post-deposition as a consequence. The as-cast condition further suggests these axeheads and gouges were never intended to be used and perhaps produced solely for deposition (Roberts *et al.* 2015, 387–9).

There is unfortunately little surviving information about the structure and context for most of the Dorset finds, but it appears depositions were undertaken in specific ways or places. At Eggardon Hill, seven socketed axeheads were recovered from a possible 'mutilated' barrow or mound from which a flint scraper and burnt pottery was also recovered (Grinsell 1959, 102). Circumstances of eight axeheads and five socketed gouges recovered at Thorney Down III (DCM-F037) are uncertain, but museum records indicate that four socketed gouges were found inside four of the axehead sockets. A hoard from Tincleton (DCM-F038), originally comprising 12 or 18 axeheads, was recovered during ploughing from a high point in an area of water meadows and marshy land, with multiple barrows and two natural springs nearby (Fig. 5.38). Axehead deposits from Weymouth, Portland and Langton Matravers occupy coastal locations with a view of the Channel and the latter hoard was deposited on the Isle of Purbeck in a landscape of dense settlement activity, which included several midden and craft production sites (BM-F023; Pearce 1983, 253; Roberts *et al.* 2015, 381–4, fig. 1). Moreover, the Langton Matravers axeheads were deposited across four pits and Roberts *et al.* suggest it drew inspiration from hoards of Armorican-type axeheads in north-western France, which comprised very large numbers usually buried in pits (2015, 384–6; cf. Briard 1965, 241–82). Occasional finds of Armorican-type axeheads in Dorset strengthen the idea of these cross-Channel links (Taylor 1980; O'Connor 2018). The structure and location of these deposits suggests connections with traditions of the Late Bronze Age, with a continued focus on natural features, coastlines, high locations and links with watery places.

Cornwall

We can observe similar extensions of Late Bronze Age practices in Cornwall. Again, the majority of metalwork deposited between 800–600 BC comprised socketed axeheads, though of a different nature. A hoard of 33 Sompting-type axeheads were deposited blade down in a ceramic vessel at Mylor (Bruns & Needham 2008; Knight *et al.* 2015, 35, no.54). These axeheads were deposited as-cast and unused at a findspot overlooking Mylor Creek, which leads out to the Channel. Like the Dorset hoards, the findspot bears similarities with Late Bronze Age practices in the region and the Mylor hoard may have been placed in reference to transport and exchange routes.

More commonly, undamaged Armorican-type axeheads typical of north-western France were deposited in Cornwall, with the examples

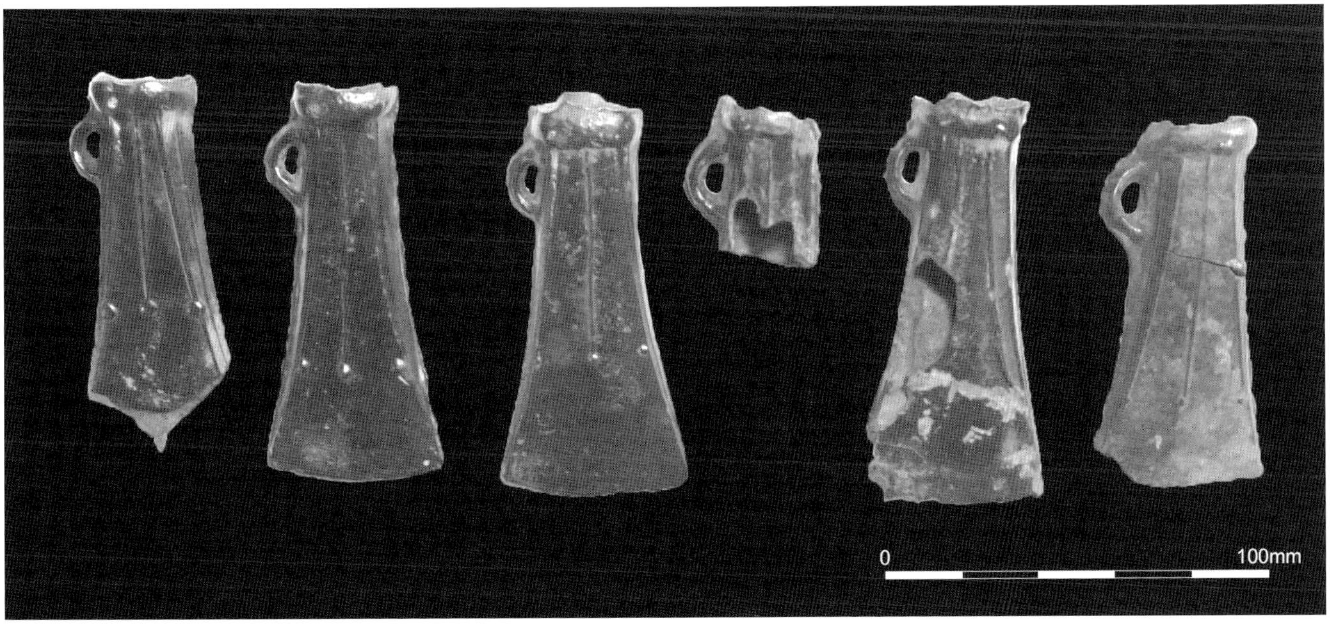

Figure 5.38: The Tincleton hoard, Dorset (photo: author, courtesy of Dorset County Museum)

known including an association from St Erth (Pearce 1983, 406, no.44), the remnants of a hoard from the multi-period site at Carn Brea, Redruth (Borlase 1769, 281), and single finds. Armorican-type axeheads broadly date to the Llyn Fawr assemblage, though their production and use probably began during the 7th century, continuing into the Early Iron Age (O'Connor 2007; Gomez de Soto *et al.* 2009; Gomez de Soto 2015; Cabanillas de la Torre & Gomez de Soto 2020). Like the Blandford/Portland-type axeheads, Armorican-type axeheads were usually deposited as-cast and many were probably afunctional, often produced with a high lead content (Briard 1965, 241–82; Boughton 2015, 45, 139–42). At Higher Roseworthy, Gwinear-Gwithian, forty to fifty socketed axeheads were found together in a pit beneath a large rock (Anon. 1881, 74; Cornish 1906, 356; Pearce 1983, 408–9, no.60); these axeheads were mostly fragmentary but appeared to have been laid in rows and deposited close to an Iron Age round known as The Hood. Surviving images of these axeheads indicate at least some were Armorican-type axeheads. It is unclear whether the fragmentation was deliberate or not, but extensive corrosion is noted for many. The location of this latter hoard is close to single finds of a complete Armorican-type axehead recorded from Barripper (BM-F001) and an incomplete example from Penponds (Pearce 1983, 403, no.24); all lie close to a small watercourse called the Red River, so-named for the extensive deposits of tin nearby giving it a distinctive colour.

There are two important points here. The first is that the presence of Armorican-type axeheads in Cornwall suggests a continued connection with north-western France from the Late Bronze Age but expressed through contemporary manufacturing and depositional traditions. As with the Late Bronze Age material, Armorican-type axeheads are concentrated around the western peninsula of Cornwall with few finds from Devon and Dorset, though there is another concentration of Armorican-axehead hoards in Hampshire and the Isle of Wight (Boughton 2015, 140, fig. 5.55). These hoards are of a much smaller scale than those in France though, which often comprised hundreds and sometimes thousands of Armorican type axeheads (Briard 1965, 241–82; 1987). The second point to raise is again the possible link between the deposits being made in Cornwall and accessibility to tin. The hoards from Carn Brea and Higher Roseworthy, as well as the single finds, all fall within a relatively close proximity in an area with a productive tin resource and this may have driven depositional practices in this region.

The function of token axeheads

The as-cast, afunctional axeheads deposited in Dorset and Cornwall represent two different manufacturing traditions but fit within a broader practice that can be observed in north-western Europe at this time whereby accumulations of afunctional axeheads were deposited together (Huth 2003, 44–9). The dense concentration of high-lead Armorican-type axeheads in north-western France has already been noted, and to these we can add the Geistingen-type axeheads of the Low Countries with unusually high levels of arsenic, antimony, silver and nickel (Butler & Steegstra 2003, 303–9; Nienhuis *et al.* 2013), and high-lead, as-cast palstaves deposited in northern Iberia (Delibes *et al.* 2016; Montero-Ruiz 2016; Parcero-Oubiña *et al.* 2019). Deposits of these axeheads almost always excluded functional axeheads that were also in circulation and deposited elsewhere and thus represent a selective practice (Fontijn 2020, 102). Armorican, Geistingen and Portland/Blandford-type socketed axeheads and as-cast palstaves from northern Iberia have all previously been considered forms of ingots for exchange (eg, Briard 1965, 271–2; 1987; Pearce 1983, 120–1, 253–6; Huth 2003, 44–9), but, as with the palstave hoards of the Middle Bronze Age, why were so many deposited and not recovered? The abandonment of material is typically linked to a collapsing bronze industry (eg, Burgess 1979; Pearce 1983, 120–1, 253–6; Huth 2003, 48), but these are better interpreted as deliberate social acts. For the Portland/Blandford-type axeheads, these required individually produced clay moulds, as well as access to large stocks of tin, lead and copper, and many were deposited with clay cores still in place. For a depositional event such as at Langton Matravers, this represents an intensive production event of several hundred axeheads, seemingly followed immediately by their deposition; Roberts *et al.* (2015) have highlighted that in the context of Isle of Purbeck, this deposit represents a deliberate social act amongst an active set of communities settled in the landscape. The same could be said of Armorican-type axeheads, which, in Cornwall, may have been deposited in connection with tin extraction and connected with more extensive accumulation practices across the Channel. For these afunctional axeheads, it seems that they took on a symbolic role as models, or tokens, of functional axeheads (Fontijn 2020, 98–103). Their production and deposition were important social events that referenced various connections and other activities, as well as expressing localised preferences and actions. Once placed in the ground it seems there was little intention of retrieving the material, and instead this acted as performative conspicuous consumption (Roberts *et al.* 2015).

The Kings Weston Down hoard, Bristol

One final hoard warrants attention here. The Kings Weston Down hoard was found while metal-detecting in 1980. It was discovered on a ridgeway just outside a Late Iron Age hillfort (Rahtz 1956) and at the other end of the Down four possibly Early Iron Age barrows had previously been excavated (Tratman 1923; 1926). Unlike the hoards from Cornwall and Dorset, the Kings Weston Down deposit consisted of one complete socketed axehead and approximately 27 fragmentary objects including axeheads, casting jets, a sickle and casting waste (Everden, date unknown; Locock 2001, 126; Boughton 2015, Appendix A, no.56), making it the most varied Llyn Fawr-assemblage hoard in south-west Britain. Many of the Kings Weston Down objects were worn and deliberately fragmented prior to deposition; associated damage included hammer blows, bowing and tearing. A fragment of a Blandford-type axehead positions the hoard chronologically in the Llyn Fawr metalworking assemblage, as well as suggesting links with contemporary manufacturing traditions in Wiltshire and Dorset, but three Transitional-type axeheads suggest a depositional date close to 800 BC. Moreover, the fragmentary character of the hoard indicates practices of the Ewart Park assemblage but at a slightly later date (cf. Boughton 2015, 214). As with some of the Late Bronze Age hoards, the fragmentation was possibly linked with processes of recycling, perhaps undertaken in a specific place in the landscape. Fragmented components of Llyn Fawr hoards are generally uncommon, but are increasingly recognised (O'Connor 2007, 64), with hoards from: Poolewe, Highland (Knight *et al.* 2021); Tower Hill, Oxfordshire (Coombs *et al.* 2004); Stockbury, Kent; Hindon, Wiltshire; and two from Arreton, Isle of Wight, all containing clear evidence for deliberate fragmentation (Hinds 2011; Basford *et al.* 2014; Raposo & Wilkin 2019). As a deposition early in the 8th century BC, the Kings Weston Down hoard can be situated in a period of changing approaches to the deposition of metalwork, where fragmented metalwork continued to play a role in hoarding as it became more common to bury objects complete and as-cast.

Earliest Iron Age conclusions

Earliest Iron Age metalwork was generally treated very differently to that deposited in the Late Bronze Age. The shift towards largely depositing as-cast axeheads stands in stark contrast to the practice of burying heavily fragmented hoards at the turn of the 1st millennium BC. This was true even in regions where fragmented hoards were previously common, such as Cornwall. This was also a period where practices were very regionalised, with most of the material deposited in south-west Britain from concentrated areas in Dorset and Cornwall and little in-between. This in turn suggests that either access to metal was in decline in certain areas and not others, or metalwork deposition was no longer a mechanism by which some communities managed and expressed their beliefs. Evidence from midden and settlement sites across southern Britain indicates that communities continued to thrive during the 800–600 BC period (Brück 2007; Roberts *et al.* 2015; Waddington *et al.* 2019) and new forms of bronze objects indicate that the material continued to be produced and used (O'Connor 2007). This means changes to depositional practices can be linked with broader social shifts and perceptions (Needham 2007c). However, when metalwork deposition did occur, some of the governing principles of the Late Bronze Age appear to have remained in the collective memory. Similar places were chosen, such as coastlines and hilltops, and they continued to express forms of localised practices, as well as representing wider connections. From about 600–400 BC, very little closely datable metalwork can be identified, and it seems the widespread practice of depositing bronze genuinely did cease.

Notes

1 I am grateful to Ian Richardson and Lucy Shipley for allowing me to mention its discovery here.

2 A socketed axehead and gouge from Somerford were supposedly once part of a larger disturbed assemblage (RHMG-F007), which may indicate an additional hoard, but further details are unknown.

3 See PRIV-F013–F022, F025–F031, F033, F035–F037, F040–F041

6

Destruction and deposition of metalwork in south-west Britain in its wider context

The analysis of Bronze Age metalwork from south-west Britain highlighted how practices of destruction and deposition manifested themselves in diverse ways. The earliest metalwork produced was only infrequently damaged before deposition, unless associated with the dead. By the Middle and Late Bronze Age, more selective and varied practices occurred, with regional and chronological variations in what was deposited, how and why. Metalwork deposited in the Earliest Iron Age was infrequent and focused on depositing complete, often afunctional, objects. Throughout we have observed that the ways metalwork was treated and the contexts in which it was buried are fundamental for allowing us to understand and recognise its role in Bronze Age social life. In this chapter, I draw on evidence beyond south-west Britain to situate the role of destruction and deposition in its wider context and in relation to specific themes. I conclude the chapter by considering how different aspects of deposits allow us to recognise and interpret their meaning.

Reduction and production of metalwork

The production of bronze objects required complex processes of crushing ore, smelting, melting, alloying and eventually casting into a stone, bronze, ceramic or sand mould (Carey *et al.* 2019; Webley *et al.* 2020). Although stone and bronze moulds have a relatively long durability (Wang & Ottaway 2004; Webley & Adams 2016), ceramic and sand moulds require irreversible destruction to remove the cast object. If recycling older material, objects were deliberately broken and included in the crucible, with their original form obliterated in the process, a truly destructive act. These are transformative processes during which destruction was integral to creation.

There are two aspects to consider here. Firstly, the destruction of materials and objects as part of metalcasting is necessary and serves a 'functional' purpose. Metalcasting involved constructing a fire and required skilled metalsmiths who understood technological processes; these were the people involved in destructive actions. Ores must be crushed and smelted, and weapons, tools and ornaments (in whatever condition) need to be fragmented and melted for new objects to be produced. This link between destruction and creation can be observed through other productive processes in prehistory, such as the felling of trees to clear land and construct structures, reductive stone tool technologies, and the crushing of shells, stones and ceramics for use as temper in pottery (cf. Brück 2006b).

However, this ignores the social dimension in which such activities take place, which leads to a second point: reductive and productive technologies operated within a social world and held connotations for those engaged with the processes, be that the craftsperson or the individuals/communities contributing and receiving objects. Metalworking is often seen as a cyclical or regenerative process (eg, Brück

2006b, 302–5; 2019, 101; Turner 2010a; Helms 2012) and the reduction and production of objects allowed people to express and enact certain ideas. For instance, if one considers that at least some objects were important because of their specific biographies or histories then the transformation into a new object may have served to extend and regenerate that biography (Brück 2006b). Needham (2007a, 282–3) suggests that an analogy might be drawn between the transition of a deceased individual to ancestral status and the impact of recycling objects in cementing their significance. Certain individuals or societies might recall the properties, qualities, and actions of the former object and in this way transformation of the object served to commemorate it within oral traditions, in much the same way people were remembered after death (*ibid.*). Knowledge of the origins of the material prior to destruction could have impacted how people related to recycled material; metal from a distant source may have held mythological connotations (*ibid.*, 283). Likewise, ingots or new objects formed from a variety of sources might come to represent a series of relations, offering a metaphor for the connections by which the material was acquired (*ibid.*). Similar ideas have been suggested for the reuse of pottery as grog in new pots (Woodward 2002, 1041; Brück 2006b, 304; Johnston 2021, 36, 190). We can catch glimpses of the meanings assigned to the origins of materials and objects in the ways and places they were deposited, such as the comparable treatment of Early Bronze Age objects in burials across Wessex and Armorica (Needham 2000c) or parallel Late Bronze Age hoarding practices in Atlantic France and south-eastern Britain (Brandherm & Moskal-del Hoyo 2014). In each case, it seems the original connotations of the objects and metal were preserved in social memory so warranted treatment that captured these origins of material through practice. This cannot have always been the case though, and in some cases, the recycling of material served to end any previous connotations by destroying its original form: some imported objects, such as Middle Bronze Age French-style palstaves or winged axeheads, rarely feature in deposits and were probably transformed into locally acceptable forms soon after arriving in Britain (Needham 2007a, 282; Needham *et al.* 2013, 153–4).

The treatment and deposition of material after the metalcasting event also indicates how it became involved in expressing ideologies and relations. Webley *et al.* (2020, 186–7) highlight that much metalworking material was deposited at liminal locations, such as ditches, field boundaries, watery locations, and caves; these were not necessarily the areas where metalworking took place and thus used refractories and metallurgical debris were transported there after the casting event, suggesting the importance of a place (cf. Brück 2019, 96–100). Evidence from Sigwells, Norton Fitzwarren and Springfield Lyons, Essex (Needham & Bridgford 2013) indicates ceramic moulds were sometimes extensively fragmented beyond what was necessary and deposited in specific areas associated with settlements and structures. At Gwithian, we observed an act of social enchainment through the deposition of refitting pieces of a broken stone mould in two adjacent structures (Chapter 5); elsewhere, deliberately broken bronze moulds were deposited in the hoards from Isleham, Cambridgeshire, and Grays Thurrock, Essex, alongside other deliberately destroyed material (Webley & Adams 2016). The role of moulds in transforming artefacts from one form to another, as well as the highly performative aspects of the metalcasting event, may have imbued these metalworking objects with significance that was then reflected in their special depositional treatment (Brück 2019, 98).

What we may draw from this is that the transformative destruction of objects, and the associated material involved (eg, moulds), served not only the very practical application of producing new objects, but also symbolic purposes in the management of memories, social relations and potentially the regeneration of ideologies as well as objects. Significantly, metalworking involved people who understood the material, and the destruction and production of objects was part of their embodied knowledge (Kuijpers 2013). By extension, these processes enabled the reproduction of social structures and meanings through repeated practices.

Exchanging fragments

Fragmentation was essential to metalworking and recycling, but it also served a variety of other roles. The debate about how metal objects, and particularly fragmented objects, may have been circulated and exchanged is long-standing with much discussion about whether objects and fragments functioned as social currency through interpersonal gifts or served a more commoditised role in trade networks (eg, Bradley 1985; Barrett & Needham 1988; Chapman 2000; Needham 2001; Barrett 2012; Brück 2015; 2016; 2019, 231–5; Brandherm 2018; Wiseman 2018; Rahmstorf 2019; Fontijn 2020, 86–107; Ialongo & Lago 2021; Kuijpers & Popa 2021). Objects may of course be both, circulating as alienable commodities that become inalienable when engaged in social exchanges and acquiring meaning through their use and relationships with people, as Fontijn (2002, 253–5) has convincingly argued for socketed axeheads (cf. Bloch & Parry 1989; Weiner 1992). Fragmentation and eventual deposition were processes by which this transformation was facilitated: breaking a sword, for instance, may transform it into a commodity or an item suitable for supernatural exchange (Barrett & Needham 1988, 138; cf. Bradley 1985; Needham 2001). Other objects were fragmented to be circulated and exchanged as part of social relations (Chapman 2000; Brück 2006b). This latter scenario is exemplified by the much-cited case of two refitting sword fragments in Staffordshire, which had divergent histories following breakage but were deposited on two intervisible hills (Bradley & Ford 2004). This suggests that the known biographies of objects were intrinsic to how some metals circulated. Other objects broke accidentally, perhaps through use or material failure, but nonetheless entered the archaeological record, as with some incomplete Early Bronze Age axeheads. All these potential pathways for fragmented metalwork were simultaneous throughout the Bronze Age. They occurred prior to deposition, which returns us to an important point made in Chapter 1: the events of fragmentation and subsequent trajectories of the fragments must be considered apart from their eventual burial in whatever context from which we draw our interpretations (cf. Brandherm 2018, 48).

Although the exchange of metalwork between people and/or specific places may have had symbolic connotations (Bradley 1985; Brück 2006b; 2019, 226–9; Johnston 2021, 114–5) – and we shall explore this further below – the circulation of all metal cannot be explained in this way; a large proportion of complete and fragmented metalwork that was circulated and exchanged was destined to be recycled (Northover 1982b; Bray & Pollard 2012; Wiseman 2018). Individual fragments enchained some social relationships, but the accumulation of material, especially in large hoards to and from which material may have been repeatedly added or taken away (Needham 2007a; Wiseman 2018), probably blurred specific associations. Over time, fragments and recycled metal would have become dissociated from original meanings, though they may have gained new meanings along the way, and social relations and social meanings behind objects were only active whilst the objects were in circulation, their forms were preserved or their eventual deposition remained in social memory. Shifts in metal supply networks probably also affected this as new networks were established and old ones fell out of use. Between *c.* 1600–1400 BC, for instance, most copper was sourced from the Great Orme mine in Wales (Williams & Le Carlier de Veslud 2019), but from 1400 BC onwards, supplies from continental Europe were the predominant source (Northover 1982a). Such shifts necessitated changes in interpersonal exchange systems and relationships with the material.

The system(s) by which metal was circulated and exchanged remains unclear (Harding 2013), but metal moved in recognisable object forms as well as fragments. In an important piece of work, Christoph Sommerfeld (1994) suggested that the large numbers of as-cast, unused sickles in some Central European hoards represented standardised values that may have operated as a form of proto-currency, produced and circulated *en masse*. During the early 2nd millennium BC, sickles were just one of several as-cast objects that appear to conform to relatively standardised forms and weights in circulation in northern and Central Europe; other objects included *Ösenringe* (ring ingots), axeheads and *Rippenbarren* ('ribs'). Several authors have highlighted that the shape and perception of these objects may have been important for standardising the circulation of metal and these may have been an early form of alienable commodity or exchange object (Sommerfeld 1994; Pare 2013; Fontijn 2020, 89–91; Kuijpers & Popa 2021). Such objects do not appear in Britain, though it is possible that at least some of the imported palstave hoards in southern Britain served this function, and possibly some of the Earliest Iron Age axehead hoards.

Recognisable objects raise the possibility that people may understand the origins of metalwork through its form but by at least the later Bronze Age, metalwork transported across the Channel arrived as amorphous ingots and complete and fragmentary objects, as exemplified by the probable shipwrecks at Salcombe Bay and Langdon Bay, Kent (Needham *et al.* 2013); the specific origins of this material may have been unknown and these chance discoveries highlight the distinction between where metalwork was destroyed and where it was eventually deposited. Once acquired, some or all of the material occasionally required certain practices to make the metal socially acceptable (Fontijn 2008; Vandkilde 2017; Fontijn & Roymans 2019). This may involve destruction and/or deposition, as discussed for Middle Bronze Age hoards in Chapter 4; alternatively, objects may be simply recycled into locally-acceptable forms (Bray & Pollard 2012). Fragmentation of bronze ingots or other artefacts has been suggested as a method for converting objects into a form of currency in other parts of Europe (eg, Sommerfeld 1994; Primas 1997) and recent work by Nicola Ialongo and Giancarlo Lago (2021) has analysed the statistical properties of fragments in Late Bronze Age Italy and Central Europe to suggest fragmentation conformed to standardised weight systems similar to hack-silver in the ancient Mesopotamia. However, these analyses do not provide comprehensive answers applicable to all fragments (Pare 2013), so it is probable that weight systems were not rigorously used everywhere. Evidence for standardised weight systems in Britain and Ireland, for instance, remains lacking.

The large fragmentary 'scrap' hoards deposited in lowland southern Britain during the ninth century are often used to infer aspects of the role of metal, either as caches of material for recycling or as evidence for a collapsing economy (eg, Burgess 1979; Huth 1997). However, these represent just one manifestation of a system at a specific time and are a relatively confined practice in lowland Britain and Atlantic France (cf. Barrett & Needham 1988, 137–8). Large numbers of contemporary fragmentary hoards are uncommon in central and northern Britain, for instance. Moreover, as discussed in Chapter 5, the suggestion that these hoards were deposited because bronze ceased to have value as an industry during the ninth centuries is unlikely to be the case as large fragmentary hoards were deposited in the centuries preceding this period (Harding 2000, 356–7). In the succeeding periods, new forms of bronze objects continued to be produced and deposited in parts of Britain and mainland Europe, such as the large hoards of token axeheads in Atlantic Europe (Roberts *et al.* 2015), or the elaborate bronze objects included in Hallstatt burials in the Low Countries and Central Europe (van der Vaart-Verschoof & Schumann 2020).

Crucially, when we engage with this debate and consider processes of exchange, we are left to draw conclusions from the surviving archaeological record, which is largely governed either by what was selectively deposited in burials, certain locales, settlements and hoards, or by what was abandoned (ie, deemed no longer significant) or lost/forgotten. Essentially, we are studying the material that did not get recycled or continue in circulation (Needham 2001; Becker 2013, 230; Fontijn 2020, 22–3). As such our understanding of Bronze Age exchange and circulation is chronologically and geographically varied as a result of human agency, and the practices under study must have been the exception, not the rule (Needham 2001, 282–4; Brandherm 2018, 48–9; Wiseman 2018; Fontijn 2020). In addressing this, Fontijn (2020) argued for an overarching system of depositional rules that governed practices across time and space in Bronze Age northern Europe; this applied not only to more specialised 'ceremonial' objects, but also seemingly alienable objects that may have been commodities. After some form of exchange, deposition was an appropriate process for transforming and enhancing the value of complete and incomplete objects, be that for later recovery or for permanent deposition. The social value of depositing material outweighed any intrinsic material value it may have had in circulation (Fontijn 2020).

The point of this discussion is not to suggest a single function or mode for the exchange of metal fragments, but rather to emphasise that the fragmentation, circulation and occasional deposition of metalwork was undertaken both for and because of interpersonal *and* economic exchanges within any social sphere depending on the situation. I have concentrated here on the potential of fragmentation in relation to broader systems of metal exchange, but as I have stressed in previous chapters, deposition was undertaken at localised levels within these broader structures often because of social relations. I turn now to the specific depositional contexts with which metalwork destruction is associated.

Death and destruction

Death is a transformative process. The treatment of the body and objects and the associated mortuary practices facilitate this. Artefacts and people were often treated in similar ways and when deposited together, objects helped construct or deconstruct the identity of the deceased, as well as establish and express relations between the living, dead and objects (Barrett 1994, 113–9; Brück 2004; Fowler 2004). Moreover, metaphorical links can be made between objects and bodies (Tilley 1999). If one considers the potentially animate or embodied nature of objects during a funerary process, as is evident in many ethnographic situations (eg, Grinsell 1961; Barley 1994; Küchler 2002), the death of an individual necessitated the 'killing' of their objects; the lifecycle of some objects was intertwined with that of an individual. A key expression of this was the mortuary practice itself. Burial practices shifted across the Bronze Age with inhumation being the primary practice in the earliest stages of the Bronze Age, followed by a mixture of inhumation and cremation practices before cremation became the dominant rite from about 1700 BC onwards (Caswell & Roberts 2018). The dead were initially placed in cists and barrows and later in cremation cemeteries, though over time human remains were incorporated into a range of contexts. The treatment of objects often paralleled the treatment of the dead.

For instance, in the Chalcolithic and Early Bronze Age it is now well-recognised that bodies were occasionally deposited incomplete, or the grave was later reopened and skeletal remains were manipulated, disarticulated and circulated (Petersen 1972; Brück 2004; 2006a; 2019, 24–7; Gibson 2004; Appleby 2013; Gibson 2013a; Fowler 2013; Booth & Brück 2020). Such practices indicate that it was acceptable for people to be curated after death, perhaps as part of social memory in preserving links with the dead (Fowler 2004, 72–6; Brück 2006a; Booth & Brück 2020). This occurred at the time when objects such as necklaces and ceramic vessels were also disassembled, fragmented, curated, and circulated (Woodward 2002; Frieman 2012).

From around 2000 BC, the evidence from south-west Britain indicated that the fiery destruction of metal and non-metal objects was most associated with cremation burials; this was broadly the case across Britain and Ireland (Brück 2004, 319–22; 2019, 71–6; Johnston 2021, 79–81). The act of cremation involves burning and destroying the body, the pyre and any adorning objects (McKinley 1997). It requires a range of socially situated practices, technologies and ultimately human agency, as well as a set of preparations, including the collection of fuel, building of a pyre and preparation of the body (Appleby 2013; Thompson 2015). Fire was transformative, as well as being highly sensory and spectacular (Downes 1999, 28; McKinley 2006; Quinn *et al.* 2014; Thompson 2015; Wright 2021), and cremation may have served to transform identities, transport people from this world to the next, or sever ties between the living and the dead (Quinn *et al.* 2014, 14, table 1.2). The inclusion and destruction of bodily adornments, jewellery, clothing and other material culture on the pyre, such as daggers, served to transform these as well (Brück 2004).

The simultaneous burning of objects and bodies created an inalienable link and entangled the dead with the associated artefacts. Examples of this are common, but there were no widespread prescribed associations for cremations; the inclusion of artefacts was reliant on human action and served to express what was or was not considered important. For instance, although daggers were commonly buried with inhumations and cremated remains in Wessex (Wiltshire and Dorset), eastern Scotland and Yorkshire (Gerloff 1975; Woodward & Hunter 2015), burials in north-western Wales typically contained dagger pommels, often burnt, but no blades (Lynch 1991, 164; Crellin *et al.* 2020, table 1). At Bedd Branwen, Anglesey, a broken burnt bone pommel was deposited with a burnt bone bead and unburnt jet and amber beads with two cremated young adults (burial H) under an inverted collared urn in a cist under a stone cairn (Lynch 1971, 24–6). A second burnt bone pommel was recovered with another cremation and a hone stone deposited in an inverted Enlarged Food Vessel urn at the edge of the cairn (Burial B) (*ibid.*, 26). In each case, the pommel was deliberately detached from the dagger and included on the pyre, along with other objects. The dagger was dismantled and the pommels became part of the funerary process, whilst the blade continued in circulation, was deposited elsewhere, or was perhaps recycled. This represented a sequence of destructive practices.

These pyre goods represent only one set of relations, though; those added to the burial afterwards held their own significances. Objects deposited with the body after cremation represented expressions of the social belief of the afterlife, as well as the mourners' own views of appropriate gifts; the memory and identity of the dead was thus constructed by the living (Barrett 1994, 113ff.; Brück 2004; 2009; 2014; Woodward *et al.* 2005; McKinley 2006, 82). The amber and jet beads deposited with Burial H at Bedd Branwen were added after the cremation event, laid on top of the urn before it was inverted (Brück 2004, 314–6). Likewise, whilst the burnt dagger at Wall Mead I discussed in Chapter 3 was included on the pyre with the deceased, the stone pendant, ceramic cup and bulb-headed pin, none of which show signs of deliberate damage, were probably offerings from the living to accompany the dead, enabling the upkeep of social values and beliefs through practice.

Incomplete objects also fulfilled this role. Objects may be accidentally or intentionally fragmented but their inclusion in a closed mortuary context is undoubtedly deliberate; by extension, the decision to remove or exclude parts of the objects was intentional. Where, for instance, is the other half of the stone battle-axe buried in the Yettington barrow or the remainder of the biconical urn at Angrouse? Incomplete vessels are particularly common in Devon and Cornwall where few complete examples have been recovered from burial contexts (Quinnell 2003; Jones 2005; Jones & Quinnell 2008, 49), in contrast with other areas. Incomplete inclusions in mortuary contexts across Britain, such as ceramic vessels and jet, amber and composite necklaces, raise similar questions (eg, Woodward 2000, 58–60; 2002; Sheridan & Davis 2002; Sheridan 2008; 2016; Frieman 2012). At the Early Bronze Age barrow cemetery at Lockington, Leicestershire, a small pit in the ring ditch of a barrow contained two incomplete ceramic vessels, a copper-alloy dagger and two gold armlets (Hughes 2000). The dagger was deliberately hammered and deformed (Needham 2000a, 27, 44) and the two broken vessels were possibly already old when deposited; one was set inside the other and inverted over one of the gold armlets (Woodward 2000). The structured nature of the deposit indicates its intent, but also highlights that the objects were deliberately deposited damaged and incomplete. Variable wear patterns and states of completeness have been repeatedly noted for Early Bronze Age jet necklaces buried in Britain and these represented assemblages of beads that were disassembled and recombined, with beads in circulation for different lengths of time prior to deposition (eg, Barrett 1994, 121–2; Sheridan & Davis 2002; Frieman 2012). Whilst pieces remained in circulation, individual components and fragments of objects were a mechanism for connecting kin with the dead, with objects maintained and curated as relics or heirlooms (Barrett 1994, 121–2; Woodward 2002; Brück 2004; Frieman 2012).

The dead also served this purpose, as highlighted by the manipulation of earlier inhumations. Surviving cremated remains often do not represent the full remains of an individual (McKinley 1997), especially in south-west Britain. This suggests that there was a degree of loss in collecting and burying cremated remains or that some was retained, and token deposits were made (McKinley 1997; Brück 2006a; Appleby 2013). This continued over time, with token cremation deposits common in the Middle and Late Bronze Age (McKinley 1997), indicating a range of treatments were appropriate for the dead. In southern England, Middle Bronze Age cremations were often deposited urned and unurned in cemeteries, though there is less evidence for this in Wales and northern Britain (Caswell & Roberts 2018). By the end of the 2nd millennium BC, formal funerary practices were uncommon and incomplete human remains (burnt and unburnt) were placed in pits, postholes and ditches at settlements instead, as well as in watery locations, caves and liminal spaces (Brück 1995; 2006a; 2006b; 2017; 2019, 48–61; Warden *et al.* 2016). At the Earliest Iron Age enclosure at Pimperne Down, Dorset, an intact femur was found in a structured deposit in a ditch along with ash and sealed with a flint capping; skull fragments were also found nearby and in postholes (Harding *et al.* 1993, 19–21; Brück 1995, 271). The various artefacts and human remains recovered at the Greylake platform, Somerset, suggest that here only incomplete objects and remains were appropriate for deposition perhaps as token offerings. Similar evidence can be observed at Brigg, Humberside (May 1976, 112–4) and at Flag Fen and Bradley Fen, Cambridgeshire (Pryor 2001; Knight & Brudenell 2020), where partial human remains were deposited alongside other artefacts associated with post alignments and trackways. At Milsoms Corner, it is likely the Early Bronze Age burial was discovered accidentally during later ditch construction, but the subsequent retention and redeposition of the human leg bone in the liminal location of a ditch indicates the objectification of human remains associated with a range of destructive activities (see Chapter 4). Elsewhere, the burial of human remains was part of legitimising new constructions or reusing already ancient places. At Na Clachan Aoraidh, Perth and Kinross, for instance, an unurned Late Bronze Age cremation was inserted within the hollow of a tree throw and a 'four poster' stone circle was constructed around this (Ellis & Ritchie 2018). At Whitton Hill Henge 2, Northumberland, the cremated remains of at least 24 individuals dating to the later 2nd millennium BC were deposited in a stone-capped pit within a Late Neolithic henge (Miket 1985, 144–7; Warden *et al.* 2016, 158, 163, table 11.1). The fragmentation, manipulation, circulation and eventual deposition of human remains in these cases helped legitimise, define and renegotiate places, finalise previous practices, and allow new events to take place (Brück 1995). As Brück argued: 'the dead became strong symbols of such concepts as liminality, continuity, identity, and renewal' (*ibid.*, 264). In many cases, human remains were deposited incomplete, suggesting the original body had been 'fragmented' in much the same way as objects (cf. Brück 2006a) and they were often deposited in similar places as metalwork (Burgess 1976b; Brück 1995; Johnston 2021, 110–12). The deposition of human remains alongside and in similar places as artefacts indicates that the fragmentation and deposition of artefacts fulfilled comparable roles. We could interpret this as the objectification of humans and/or the personification of objects.

The death of a person is an evocative and emotive event. Mortuary practices were important occasions where the relationship between the living and the dead could be negotiated, social memories could be managed, and social identities could be transformed through specific actions (cf. Johnston 2021, 65, 81). This frequently involved the removal and retention of cremated remains or body parts. The same was true of objects, which show signs of curation, selective inclusion and deliberate destruction. As we saw in Chapter 3, metal objects were often integral to this and the decision to treat different artefacts in different ways was related to the type of object and the meanings they conveyed: daggers were particularly the focus of destructive treatments, whilst ornaments were less often damaged. Similarities in the treatment of bodies and artefacts throughout the Bronze Age highlights that many objects were inalienable and the social impact of death necessitated such actions. Fragments of bodies and objects, some of which were deposited, some of which were circulated, helped people establish and preserve various social relations (cf. Brück 2019, 74–6).

Destruction close to home

The spaces people occupied were key arenas for managing their lives and beliefs. As well as human remains, a range of objects and materials was deposited at settlements from *c.* 1600 BC onwards, often in a fragmentary state. Metalwork, metalworking material, stone tools, pottery and querns were all incorporated into specific places for a variety of reasons. This has often been linked to abandonment processes, as we saw with the material from south-west Britain. The spearhead thrust into a structure at Penhale Moor at its closing is one example of this (Nowakowski 1998, 237–8; 2001, 145); the bracelets buried at Bestwall Quarry are another (Ladle & Woodward 2009). The deposition of objects was just one aspect of abandonment, however, which also required the dismantling and/or burning of a structure; this latter process was usually considered and coordinated with inherently performative aspects.

Dismantling structures

At Scarcewater, Cornwall, Roundhouse 1100 was decommissioned after less than a century of use *c.*1500–1400 BC, with the superstructure and walling demolished, possibly followed by the burning of one of the posts (Jones & Taylor 2010, 75–6). The interior was then infilled with a rubble layer, including fragments of ceramics and worked stone. Roundhouse 1250 on the same site underwent a similar process, though it was in use for perhaps a century longer, and pottery, worked stone and quern fragments were placed within several postholes on the western side of the building. The wall was then demolished and pushed inside the structure hollow and the interior infilled with pottery and worked stone. Two postholes were then dug into the infilled interior and posts erected. The site was thus 'marked', perhaps to signal the end of the structure's lifecycle while also memorialising the site (*ibid.*, 76). At both Broom, Bedfordshire, and Broomfield, Essex, structures were systematically dismantled, with posts on the left side of the building deliberately removed whilst those on the right side were left intact (Webley 2007, 138–9). In both cases, a range of material, largely comprising pottery, was deposited in association with the parts of the building left standing. At Broomfield, pottery, flints, stones, charcoal and daub were seemingly burnt in a pair of postholes/pits *in situ* after the house had passed out of use (Atkinson 1995, 6; Webley 2007, 139). At Trevisker, Cornwall, at least one of the Middle Bronze Age buildings was burned down (House A) and Structure B on the same site was sealed by a layer of silt and stone rubble, which also contained two rubbing stones, part of a saddle quern and a burnt bronze knife fragment (ApSimon & Greenfield 1972). Structures were also possibly deliberately burnt down at Halls Hill, Northumberland (Gates 2009, 50–1) and Mile Oak, East Sussex (Russell 2002); at Kintore, Aberdeenshire, five of the 13 Middle–Late Bronze Age houses were burnt prior to abandonment (Cook & Dunbar 2008, 338, 342–4). These various structures were then generally infilled with deposits of material culture. Just as fire was important for transforming people and objects, the same was occasionally true of buildings (Johnston 2021, 155). There was thus a degree of performance to ending the use of structures; the spectacles of dismantling buildings, pushing in walls, burning posts and so on would have been mnemonic events coordinated and enacted by the community. Depositions were part of the process and fragmenting objects helped to close structures. As Fokke Gerritsen (2003, 95–6) has pointed out, however, closure or abandonment of a structure did not necessarily mean abandonment of a settlement and in this way the significant event of dismantling or burning a house was part of the continued life of a settlement and its inhabitants, which was renegotiated and transformed in meaning over time.

'Event-marking'[1] *and curated objects*

Abandonment was of course not the only occasion during which deposits were made and practices performed. The construction and foundation of a house, delineating boundaries, harvests, and events in the lives of people, such as births and formalisation of partnerships, were all important social occasions in which objects served a purpose (Brück 1999b; 2006b; Gerritsen 2003). Late Bronze Age–Earliest Iron Age midden accumulations, for instance, often represent the remnants of communal gatherings and feasting events as well as sealing earlier settlements (eg, Lawson 2000; McOmish *et al.* 2010; Gwilt *et al.* 2016). Numerous fragmented copper-alloy vessels suggest this may have been the case at Mount Batten, though there were relatively limited faunal remains and Cunliffe (1988, 101) suggests this may have instead been a local community with a focus on metalworking during the Late Bronze Age–Earliest Iron Age. Selective deposition of metalwork and faunal remains has been observed at the Earliest Iron Age midden accumulation at Llanmaes, Vale of Glamorgan, indicating that although these may be accumulations of leftover material, there was also a degree of decision making around to what was incorporated into the midden (Madgwick & Mulville 2015; Gwilt *et al.* 2016). At Scarcewater, two possible foundation deposits were made early in the construction of Roundhouse 1500 during the Middle Bronze Age: a pit below the wall of the structure contained a dark deposit, possibly an organic offering, and a lump of manganese; another pit in the south-west quadrant of the same structure contained an assemblage of 'curated' sherds of pottery, rubbing stones, a quartz crystal and burnt clay (Jones & Taylor 2010, 73). Jones and Taylor (*ibid.*, 74–8) link the deposition of older objects during the construction of the roundhouse with the tradition of including older and fragmented objects buried in earlier barrows; the objects were 'gathered together to form a meaningful and memorable foundation deposit' (cf. Jones 2008).

The importance of earlier objects in deposits is exemplified through the curation and destruction of the South Cadbury shield as a final action in a long sequence of events (see Chapter 4). At Lookout Plantation, Northumberland, a Neolithic stone axehead was several centuries old when it was deliberately damaged and deposited in the external slot of a Middle Bronze Age structure that was itself rebuilt and renewed over time (Monaghan 1994; cf. Brück 2019, 147). At Shrubsoles, Kent, an incomplete Middle Bronze Age spearhead was deposited in a Late Bronze Age enclosure ditch (Coles *et al.* 2003); wood fragments inside the spearhead socket placed the last hafting of the spearhead around 1010–820 cal BC (Taylor 2003, 42–3), suggesting the extended use of this spearhead or else the rehafting of an old object in preparation for deposition. The ditch in which it was placed was also a focus point for cremation burials and pottery, suggesting that deposition here was one of a several practices that served to legitimise a sense of place, to which the older spearhead contributed (Knight forthcoming a).

The lifecycles of houses, structures and occupied places have been linked with the lifecycles of people, which extends to the objects involved in 'event-marking deposits' (Brück 2006b, 298–9; cf. Brück 1999; Gerritsen 2003). A house may have been constructed to house a new family, for instance, or destroyed because of the death of a person. It was thus an essential part of creating, managing and expressing social identities (Gerritsen 2003). The objects deposited tended to be those used in craftworking, eating and drinking, or items of a more intimate nature, ie, those that would have been inalienably linked with individuals and communities through repeated engagements. It is striking then that weapons, which are often considered to be inalienable, personified objects, were rarely deposited in these contexts, a situation that has been noted across Atlantic Europe (Gibson 2013b, 90). The evidence from south-west Britain highlighted that the metal objects most commonly deposited included ornaments and small tools, whilst weapons and axeheads were much rarer, despite being common in contemporary hoards and as single finds. Ornaments and small tools, as well as objects such as querns, stone rubbers and pots, are artefacts that would have been engaged with regularly within settlement contexts, intrinsic to life, and these are amongst the most common depositions. The deposition of such artefacts, as well as human remains, to mark events within the settled space was a way of making tangible relatable links between people, places, and objects and required collective agency. The visual spectacles and coordinated efforts involved in constructing and deconstructing buildings, as well as the selection, fragmentation, and incorporation of inalienable material culture occasionally of some age, suggests that interactions with structures and settlements were performative and designed to be remembered. Such activities allowed people to express communal ideas about life, death, identity, space and memory within their landscapes (Gerritsen 2003; Owoc 2005; Jones 2013). Actions and specific activities were not isolated but socially-constructed, culturally-embedded and referential, building on what came before and in response to ongoing social transformations.

Metalwork destruction and deposition in the landscape

Depositional actions were also enacted in the landscape. The selection of certain locations for the deposition of metalwork throughout the Bronze Age is well-studied and a range of places were appropriate for burying artefacts (eg, Bradley 1998; 2000, 47–63; 2017; Fontijn 2002; York 2002; Cowie 2004; Yates & Bradley 2010a; 2010b; Becker 2013; Poyer 2015; Dunkin *et al.* 2020). The evidence from south-west Britain exemplifies this with hilltops, river valleys, springs, coastlines, caves, and marshes chosen at different times and with chronological and regional preferences towards certain landscapes. Landscapes have traditionally been split into 'dry' or 'wet' categories (eg, Levy 1982; Bradley 1998), but within these there are nuances that must be understood, with topographic and geological aspects coming into play for 'dry' contexts and different types of water being crucial for understanding depositions in 'wet' locations (Bradley 2000; Fontijn 2002; Yates & Bradley 2010a; 2010b; Mullin 2012, 53; Dunkin *et al.* 2020). An important consideration is the relationship between the treatment of objects and certain locations.

Weapons and wet places

Perhaps the most widely discussed association is that between Middle–Late Bronze Age weapons and watery places, particularly rivers. Walter Torbrügge was the first to draw attention to this as a widespread phenomenon in 1971 through a comparison of metalwork in major European rivers. His seminal work has since inspired a range of studies across major rivers in Europe, with complete and incomplete examples of weapons and other objects known widely (Torbrügge 1971; Harding 2000, 329–30). In Britain, many metal artefacts have been recovered from the rivers Thames (Ehrenberg 1980; York 2002) and Trent (Scurfield 1997; Davis 1999); smaller numbers are known from other British rivers (eg, Davey 1973; Cowie & Hall 2001; 2010; Mullin 2012). Jill York's (2002) analysis of later Bronze Age metalwork from the River Thames highlighted the large numbers of pieces recovered, as well as the increasing quantity of deliberately damaged material over time. However, this has encouraged the idea that metalwork was commonly destroyed and deposited in rivers, when in fact metalwork recovered directly from rivers is relatively rare. For instance, Britain's longest river, the Severn, has produced only thirteen pieces of metalwork (Mullin 2012). Moreover, when recovered, few riverine finds show signs of deliberate damage. In the South West, only 14 metal objects have been recovered from *all* watercourses and estuaries combined spanning the Early Bronze Age to Earliest Iron Age, with most metalwork deposited complete and undamaged or with minimal damage; only three of those studied showed signs of deliberate damage. Comparable situations have been observed elsewhere. None of the metalwork from the River Tay was deliberately damaged (Cowie & Hall 2010), and Scurfield (1997, 33) records that none of the 80 bronzes recovered from in or around the upper Trent valley was obviously deliberately broken. For a lower section of the River Trent valley, Davis (1999, 31) notes only one broken sword, though it is unclear if this was intentional damage. For East Anglia, Pendleton (1999, 68–72) notes only 45 or 46 pieces of metalwork derived from rivers in the region; he records only two out of six swords studied as 'ritually killed' (*ibid.*, 7).

Even if we accept that there may be some recovery bias at play here, the evidence suggests that metalwork deposition *in* British rivers, such as the Thames or the Trent, was the exception rather than the rule, and destruction was not essential to making depositions in a river acceptable. However, proximity to rivers and river valleys was indeed important, such as the concentration of Middle Bronze Age metalwork from along the River Tone. Similarly, although there was limited metalwork from *within* the Severn, Mullin (2012) identified a relatively large amount of metalwork deposited around the river. In their survey of south-east England, Yates and Bradley (2010a) identified metalwork hoards tended to be located on valley slopes and overlooking water courses; Poyer (2015) also highlights metalwork deposited close to and occasionally in major rivers and tributaries in north-east England. Adam Gwilt's (2004) assessment of Late Bronze Age hoards from south-east Wales identified concentrations of hoards on the lower slopes of river valleys and close to confluences and estuaries of rivers (cf. Gwilt *et al.* 2013). Gwilt (2004, 121) suggests a correlation between good farming land and the siting of hoards, even though hoard locations remained largely segregated from settlements sites. Alternatively, deposition may have related to rivers as boundaries or transportation routes (Scurfield 1997, 33; Fontijn 2005). Dunkin *et al.*'s (2020, 16) survey of findspots of single objects and groups of Middle–Late Bronze Age metalwork from lowland southern England found that 40% of findspots were within 200m of a river or stream. When the conditions of the finds were considered by the authors, they found that single and hoarded finds of complete Middle Bronze Age palstaves were more commonly recovered from wet locations or near water, whilst fragments were more often deposited in dry locations away from watercourses. The inverse was true of socketed axeheads, with nearly double the number of single fragmentary finds found close to waterways (*ibid.*, 13). This suggests that people had preconceived notions of where fragments should or should not be deposited and this changed through time.

One particularly striking relationship is between the accumulation and destruction of swords and spearheads and their deposition in watery locations during the Wilburton-Blackmoor metalworking assemblages *c.* 1100–900 BC (Burgess *et al.* 1972; Coombs 1975; Mörtz 2018). Just as the Bloody Pool hoard was sunk into a pool, so too were hoards of (predominantly) spearheads at Peelhill, South Lanarkshire (Coles & Scott 1963; Mörtz *et al.* forthcoming) and Willow Moor, Shropshire (Chitty 1928), deliberately bent, burnt and broken before they were buried in wet places. At Broadward, Shropshire, a large hoard of spearheads and other objects were gathered, damaged and buried at the site of a spring (Burgess *et al.* 1972; Bradley *et al.* 2015). At Duddingston Loch, Edinburgh, about 50 weapons were destroyed by exposing them to extreme heat, causing warping, melting and fragmentation, before they were deposited in the loch (Fig. 1.2; Callander 1922). In each case these must have been spectacular events, perhaps involving large pyres and communal gatherings. These deposits have often been considered the work of scrapping and metalworking activities, but Tobias Mörtz (2018; Mörtz *et al.* forthcoming) has suggested that accumulation of many weapons and the destructive actions undertaken on these objects reflected the involvement of the objects in violent interactions, with swords and spears collected following events of conflict and sacrificed in watery locations. The varied treatment of individual objects within a hoard may be a reaction to the specific biography or engagements of that object (Mörtz 2018, 180); in this sense the destruction of objects was more specific to what was known about different objects and less coordinated than, for instance, the reduction of objects for recycling in a crucible. Of course, as I highlighted in Chapter 1, weapons do not necessarily equate to violence, and destroying weapons, even those that had seen use in combat, may also have been a peaceful event. Moreover, smaller hoards and single finds of Wilburton-Blackmoor swords and spearheads have been recovered complete and incomplete, again largely from watery contexts, and this was widespread across Britain. Although there was a wider understanding of how to deposit these objects, the rationales behind destruction and deposition probably extended beyond the martial connotations of these objects to individual biographies and relations. Swords and spearheads are commonly considered inalienable, personified objects (Pearce 2013; Harding 2021, 48–9) and these were clearly symbolic offerings with water and weapons closely linked.

A hoard of deliberately destroyed weapons from Bradley Fen, Cambridgeshire, adds an interesting perspective. Here, 20 spearheads and swords, dating to *c.* 1100 BC, were deliberately damaged in various ways and deposited at the edge of a field system at a time when the area was being submerged in peat and the long-established landscape was changing (Knight & Brudenell 2020, 180–8, 213–7). These objects were thus perhaps destroyed and deposited in reaction to the changing environment; at the same time the changing environment provided a suitable arena for the deposition of this material, which accorded with broader ideas about how to treat and deposit objects. That metalwork may have been treated differently at different times within the same space is indicated by six complete or mostly complete spearheads also deposited on the boundary (*ibid.*, 181–2), which may have been part of legitimising the boundary. Depositions here imply a reflexive practice where depositional actions and the fluid nature of a specific place were interrelated. Around *c.* 1100 BC, it seems widely accepted that water was required to receive the objects and destruction was required to make the objects suitable for deposition. The process of destruction and deposition may have been a reaction to the changing landscape and an offering designed to help manage the older boundary. These examples highlight that the destruction and deposition of metalwork became a process by which a variety of situations were managed.

Whatever the interpretation, the destruction of objects during this period and their eventual placement in watery contexts were often closely linked rationales. Although destruction of objects was not necessary for placing swords and spearheads into rivers, it does seem to have been essential for placing them in bogs, lakes and marshes. This illustrates that different types of water were considered appropriate for different practices of deposition. Places like

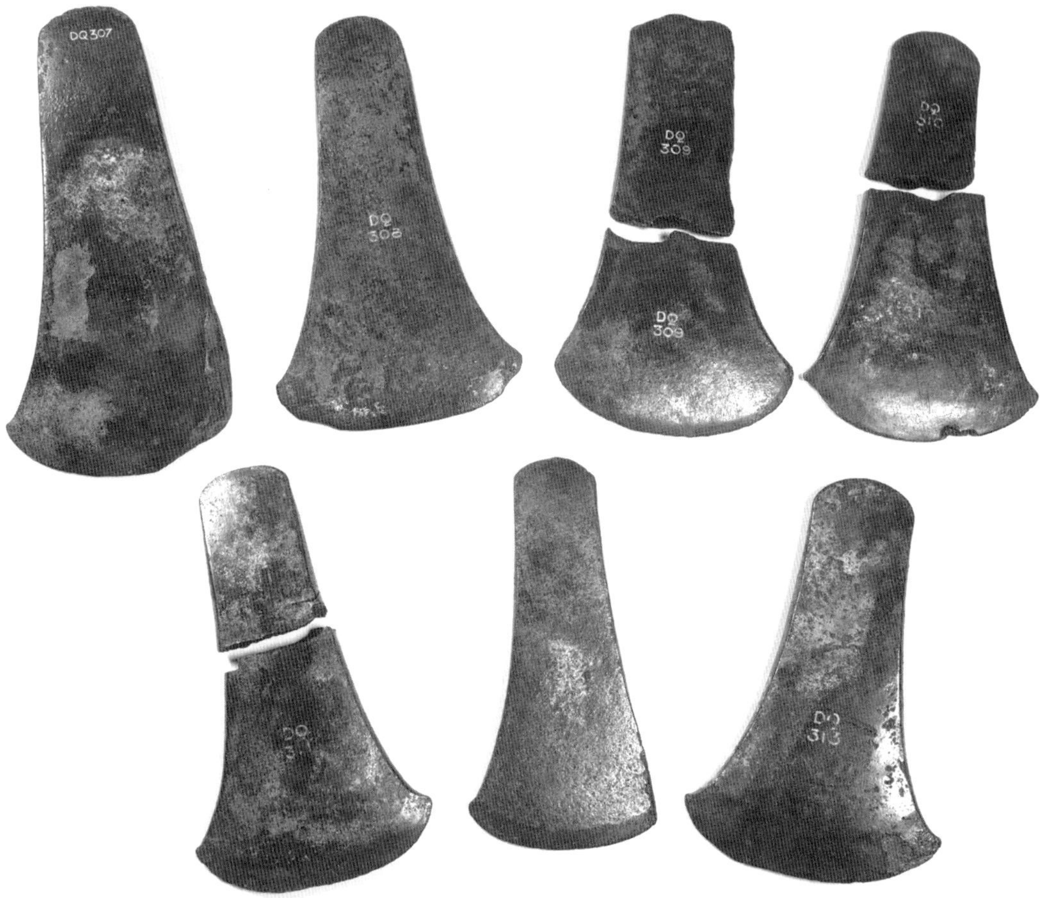

Figure 6.1: The Hill of Finglenny hoard of axeheads, Aberdeenshire © National Museums Scotland

springs, bogs and encroaching fenlands are all animate places and may have been chosen for their particular dynamic nature. Through similarities in practices across Britain, we can observe that the treatment and deposition of objects was part of a widespread ideology that changed over time and manifested itself in different ways in response to the chosen location.

Hilltops and histories

Hilltops and high places with commanding views were repeatedly selected for depositing metalwork. These were focal points for burial monuments in the earlier Bronze Age and subsequently enclosures and hillforts, but single finds and hoards were deposited in similar upland locations. Trevor Cowie (2004) has drawn attention to Scottish Early Bronze Age single finds and hoards of axeheads often positioned in striking locations, associated with rocky outcrops, passes, hills and views of a landscape or coastline. Some of these were seemingly placed in reference to earlier monuments (Cowie 2004), others may have been placed in reference to solstices and thus their placement may have held cosmological significance (Bradley *et al.* 2018). The histories of objects deposited in these places probably contributed to their eventual deposition. A hoard from Hill of Finglenny, Aberdeenshire, for instance, contained complete and deliberately broken axeheads; some were heavily worn and/or deliberately tinned (Fig. 6.1; Stevenson 1948; Cowie 2004; Moyler 2007; Crellin 2020, 218–9). This group may have been accumulated over some time (Needham 2004, 222) and was deposited under a stone on the slope of the hill, overlooking a Neolithic henge (Cowie 2004, 258). Becker (2013) has similarly highlighted the persistence of outcrops as depositional locations for Irish metalwork from the Early Bronze Age onwards, as well as their relationship with megalithic tombs. In south-west Britain, the worn and incomplete Early Bronze Age axeheads from Perranzabuloe I and Madron were recovered from hilltops with views of the coast, and a complete axehead from Broadsands was deposited close to a Neolithic tomb overlooking Tor Bay in south Devon (Knight & Chandler 2018).

The deliberate gathering of a range of objects with different histories at Finglenny recalls observations made for Middle Bronze ornament hoards, though these were predominantly recovered from lowland areas and river valleys in the South West. By contrast, single Middle Bronze Age finds from the region, mainly including palstaves and spearheads, were more common in higher places. Dunkin *et al.* (2020) similarly found that Middle–Late Bronze Age hoards and single finds, particularly fragmentary rapiers and swords, were on or close to hilltops in south-eastern England. They emphasise that these were not necessarily 'dramatic' locations but were often promontories or plateaux overlooking watercourses (*ibid.*, 15). The same is particularly true of the Late Bronze Age single finds and hoards from Devon and Cornwall, which were focused on hills and hillslopes, either associated with river valleys or views of the coasts. These were the finds that showed the clearest evidence of deliberate destruction and it seems this was part of the process for depositing these objects. That certain types of locations were persistently chosen for deposition is emphasised by the continued practice of burying Earliest Iron Age metalwork in similar locales (Chapter 5).

Bronze Age metalwork is commonly recovered from later hillfort and enclosure sites (Pearce 1976; Brück 2019, 185–6). Groups of objects from Kings Weston Down, Cadbury Castle and Ham Hill represent examples of this in the South West, but the same is seen across elsewhere, such as at Breiddin hillfort, Powys (Musson 1991), Nottingham Hill, Gloucestershire (Hall & Gingell 1974), and Danebury, Hampshire (Britton *et al.* 1984). In these places, deposits of metalwork pre-empt later sites of occupation. At Cadbury Castle, metalwork is present from the Early Bronze Age through to the Earliest Iron Age (TTNCM-F007) and the treatment of metalwork varies according to its age – the Early Bronze Age material is largely complete, whilst the later Bronze Age metalwork is more fragmentary, in common with contemporary practices. The site was repeatedly revisited for metalwork deposition ahead of the establishment of the Iron Age hillfort and several pieces of Bronze Age metalwork were reappropriated and deposited in Iron Age and later contexts. Hills are typically seen as places of defence or places where people could exert authority over an area, but Robert Johnston (2021, 210) has also argued these were places with myths and histories that people related to. Hills can of course be all these things simultaneously and in much the same way that deposits were part of the founding or decommissioning of houses, they likely played a similar role when it came to natural places. In other words, metalwork deposits served to mark these places as significant (cf. Brück 2019, 185–6) while also communicating a claim to an area and engaging with the area as an active part of the known landscape. Where later hillforts were established, it is possible that this related to long-known histories of the landscapes.

We must be careful not to stretch these various trends too far, though. As Richard Bradley (2000, 53) has emphasised, although different types of deposits were seemingly made in different places, there was in fact no overarching rationale for what was deposited when or where. This is because although many deposits may seem isolated from any nearby activity, they were not isolated, detached events but were intimately linked with the established landscape. This also relied on suitable depositional places being available: the low-lying wetlands of Somerset, for instance, provided a completely different arena for deposition than the uplands and long coastlines of Cornwall. In some cases, depositions may relate to broadly perceived ideas about the acceptable site of deposition; in others it may relate to histories of sites or objects, perceived boundary locations, or the cosmological, hydrological or topographical significance of the place itself (cf. Bradley *et al.* 2018; Dunkin *et al.* 2020). Localised depositional practices were thus enacted in landscapes that were well-known to Bronze Age communities taking diverse forms.

Selection and destruction across hoards in time and space

The evidence so far emphasises the varied selection, accumulation and occasional destruction of objects that changed across temporal and spatial dimensions. That destruction prior to deposition became more common over time and took place in different contexts is well-established, but the regional variations are less frequently noted. This regionality, however, often has a bearing on why objects were selected and treated in certain ways, giving us clues to differing relationships with metalwork. For instance, Early Bronze Age axeheads were commonly deposited complete as single finds and in hoards across Britain and Ireland (Needham 1983; Becker 2013); however, in north-east Scotland there was a clear trend towards periodically deliberately fragmenting axeheads as part of making them suitable for deposition (O'Connor 1999, 181; Jones 2010a, 112–4). This suggests a localised practice around how axeheads should be treated. Middle Bronze Age ornament-dominant hoards display similar regionalised practices towards including complete and incomplete weapons, tools and ornaments (Wilkin 2017), with clusters in certain regions and situation-appropriate choices. This theme warrants further investigation and in concluding this chapter, I want to focus on fragmentary Late Bronze Age hoards and the selective and regional aspects related to how and why objects were deliberately damaged and deposited.

Fragmentation and regional variations

The Damage Ranking System highlighted the broader ideological shift over time towards destroying objects prior to deposition in south-west Britain; similar shifts can be observed across much of the rest of Europe (Hansen 1994; Huth 1997; York 2002; Maraszek 2006; Čivilytė 2009; Rezi 2011; Dietrich 2014). However, this was more complex than a broad overview initially suggests. Although hoards deposited in the 9th–8th centuries BC tended to include highly fragmented material, this was most pronounced in certain areas within Britain, such as south-eastern England (Turner 2010a), south-east Wales (Gwilt 2004), East Anglia (Lawson 2018) and, as we have seen, western Cornwall. Further north, the practice of hoarding, level of fragmentation and range of objects within deposits were highly variable. In contrast to the large number of crushed, fragmented and blocked socketed axeheads in southern hoards, for example, contemporary deposits from north-east England and south-east Scotland often comprised large numbers of well-manufactured complete socketed axeheads, occasionally with small fragments of other objects (eg, Schmidt & Burgess 1981, pls 145, 149, 150). There were similar variations across broader areas of western Europe: fragmented hoards were common in north-western France (Briard 1965; Boulud & Fily 2009) and Portugal (Vilaça & Bottaini 2019), whilst deposition of intentionally damaged objects was rarely practised in the southern Netherlands (Fontijn 2002) or Ireland (Becker 2006, 177–8). This highlights the selective and variable nature of deliberate destruction during the Late Bronze Age that contrasts with the broader narrative generally applied to this period in Europe. Although mass deposition was a widespread ideology, destroying objects was not always the appropriate mechanism for conferring objects to the ground. This is similarly implied by the evidence from 800–600 BC where hoards were predominantly made up of complete objects, mainly axeheads, with one or two fragmentary inclusions, although some hoards also displayed more extensive signs of intentional destruction (O'Connor 2007, 64; Boughton 2015).

Selecting fragments and scales of practice

In general, hoards tended to comprise only a selection of the available metalwork repertoire, rather than the full array of objects in circulation, suggesting some adherence to an overarching principle (Needham 1988; Hansen 1991; 1994; 2012; 2013; Huth 2003; Webley *et al.* 2020, 118–20). Within fragmented Late Bronze Age hoards, certain object types were seemingly regularly excluded, whilst others were overwhelmingly predominant (Turk 1997; 2001; Hansen 2016). This varied according to region: ornaments were less common in fragmented hoards of Britain and Ireland, for instance, but more common in contemporary hoards from France and Belgium (Huth 1997; 2003; Turner 2010a; Becker 2013). In Slovenia, Peter Turk (1997; 2001; 2018) has recognised that shaft-hole axeheads were commonly selected for fragmentation and inclusion within Late Bronze Age–Early Iron Age hoarding traditions. In Late Bronze Age fragmentary hoards across Europe, there tends to be an over-representation of particular fragments of objects, such as cutting edges of axeheads or sword blades, with very few refitting pieces: these were deliberately selected for inclusion (Maraszek 2000, 215; 2006; Bradley 2005, 151–3; Becker 2013; Rezi 2011). The analysis of deliberately broken single finds from south-west Britain indicated this transcended hoards and applied to single finds as well. It was a scaled activity. One proposed explanation for this is that finds were deposited *pars pro toto*, as discussed earlier. This theory is increasingly applied to explain hoards with non-refitting fragments (eg, Hansen 1994; Fontijn 2002; 2008; Webley *et al.* 2020, 118–20). In his overview of fragmented objects in Bronze Age Europe, Svend Hansen (2016, 185–6) paralleled fragments in 'scrap' hoards with the deliberately broken token offerings at Classical Greek sanctuaries; he argued that despite no evidence of ritual structures in Central and West Europe, this practice may have been widespread. By extension, we may consider such deposits as votive offerings (*ibid.*). Although this interpretation would explain the burial of fragments of different objects, it does not account for the diversity in the character and composition in hoards, nor does it explain why some hoards contain complete and incomplete objects. In much the same way that assuming all broken hoards are scrap, there is a danger in applying a votive explanation wholesale that does not allow for the scale and intricacies of deposits. Nonetheless, the places in the landscape where deliberately broken metalwork was deposited indicates that there were guiding principles within different areas, and it seems probable that there was a symbolic element to which objects were fragmented, how they were fragmented and where they were eventually buried.

A key issue is that because many deposits of metalwork are dissociated from evidence of other practices (eg, settlement activity or burials), it becomes difficult to link these back to individuals or communities. However, if we consider that single finds and hoards may be part of a similar depositional rationale, the very size of a deposit may provide clues as to whether it represents the work of an individual, a family group or community gathering objects (cf. Hunter 1997; Knight forthcoming b); this of course raises unknowable questions surrounding ownership and whether deposited items were owned by those who buried them. However, as we saw with the hoards from Long Bredy and Stogursey, there are aspects of ownership and community input that can be gleaned, especially through the nature of fragmentation. The acts involved in forming the Long Bredy hoard seemed relatively unskilled and undertaken at personal level, whilst the fragmentation of the Stogursey hoard must have involved a metalworker and were influenced by practices across the Bristol Channel. In the opening to his book, *Bronze Age Worlds*, Robert Johnston (2021, 1–11) elaborates a similar idea in relation to the Late Bronze Age hoard from Dowris, Ireland. Johnston notes that this hoard of over 200 objects, which includes swords, spearheads, axeheads, gouges, razors, vessels, horns and crotal pendants, displays a degree of symmetry in the numbers involved. Forty-four spearheads are matched by 43 axeheads, five sword fragments are matched by four large spearheads, a cauldron is matched by a bucket, two horns are of two distinct regional types and so on (*ibid.*, 5). Some of the objects are complete, some are fragmented, some show signs of age and repair. Johnston suggests this represents the work of people gathering together and assembling objects for deposition, drawing on a series of networks and exchanges. The deposition of the hoard allowed people to establish relations between themselves, the objects involved and the place chosen at a particular time.

Blocked socketed objects also give us clues at how people selected and formed their deposits. Objects such as socketed axeheads and spearheads were occasionally 'blocked' with fragments of other objects and deposited in larger assemblages (Hansen 1996–8; Dietrich 2014; Dietrich & Mörtz 2019). In the Breage I hoard, for instance, fragments of a sword, a knife, a socketed implement and a torc were all wedged inside a broken socketed axehead (RCM-F005). Two blocked socketed axeheads were also deposited in the St Michael's Mount hoard and heavily hammered. Oliver Dietrich (2014) has suggested these may be considered 'miniature hoards' within larger hoards, indicative of individuals or smaller groups contributing to the eventual deposit. To a certain extent these blocked objects might be explained through functionalist rationales – ie, they were prepared for the crucible – but examples of axeheads blocked with gold and amber indicate a more symbolic aspect to the destruction of these axeheads and the inserted objects (Dietrich 2014). A remarkable example of this comes from Llanarmon-yn-Iâl hoard, Denbighshire, where a complete socketed axehead was deposited containing a gold 'finger-ingot', two gold link fragments and two coiled gold bracelets (Green 1983). The formation of these deposits, involving first the fragmentation of other objects and then the sometimes very forceful insertion of the fragments into sockets, suggests a coordinated process that contributed to the final deposit.

Mixed origins, mixed treatments

Moreover, combinations of different degrees of wear and destruction, mixed object origins and the selective inclusion of different pieces can highlight agency within deposits and highlights the potential for deposits to be linked with formative expressions of an event. The seemingly personal nature of the Long Bredy hoard, for instance, could be reasonably linked with the idea of an individual or a particular kind of personhood. The mixed origins and mixed practices associated with the objects within the Stogursey hoard, by contrast, were indicative of the coming together of different traditions either through exchange networks or the physical movement of people; this was supported by the undeniably south-Welsh character of the hoard. The differential treatment of objects within this hoard was seemingly linked to the known origins of the objects; objects from further away were left more complete, whilst local forms were more fragmented. The same was observed in a Late Bronze Age hoard from Le Petit-Villatte, Neuvy-sur-Barangeon, France (Milcent 1998; Bradley 2005, 155–6). In the northern Netherlands, mixed origin hoards saw the reverse treatment: here, local forms were kept intact, whilst supra-regional forms were fragmented; Arnoldussen (2015) suggests this represented a *pars pro toto* sacrifice of foreign material otherwise intended for recycling into local forms (cf. Fontijn 2008). Overall, what we observe are local, social reactions to imported material, which was considered alongside insular forms: sometimes this material was accepted, and incorporated into specific practices, sometimes this material was rejected and/or recycled or transformed into locally acceptable forms (cf. Sørensen 1987). Such relationships in the treatment of local and supra-regional object styles have yet to be given a coordinated study in Britain, but studies elsewhere indicate it warrants further investigation (eg, Sørensen 1987; Fontijn 2009; Arnoldussen 2015; Vandkilde 2017). In some cases, the style of objects clearly served to express links with different places and thus warranted an alternative, selective treatment in preparing them for deposition. This may in turn offer an explanation why some objects were left complete and others were not.

Conclusions: interpreting destroyed metalwork and deposits of meaning

There is no neat way to explain all of these temporal and spatial variations and the interpretations presented are in no way comprehensive of the inherent complexities. Each deposit was an individual manifestation and representation of widely held beliefs about what was appropriate. It resulted from localised and regional interactions and occurred in response to specific events, places and relationships. Some objects were deposited because of the death of an individual, for instance; others were the result of the exchange of metal. Moreover, deposition did not happen in isolation. It was part of a longer temporally-situated practice that served to manage past, present and future interactions with place, people and objects (Helms 2012, 111; cf. Mizoguchi 1993; Bradley 2000, 51; Needham 2001). Destruction of metalwork was the same – a practice that was socially reproduced and allowed people to manage relationships through the treatment of objects. In this chapter, I have sought to position the data analysed from south-west Britain in relation to these broader situations, predominantly drawing on case studies from Bronze Age Britain. I have deliberately not proffered one-size-fits-all explanations for why some things were destroyed and deposited, but instead tried to explore a range of possibilities drawing on the available evidence that does not assume ritual or non-ritual priorities.

However, some tools have emerged that we can utilise to engage with how we could most plausibly interpret the meaning of deposits. I draw here on the work by Fokke Gerritsen (2003) in his analysis of deposits at settlements. In seeking to recognise deposits that may have a symbolic aspect, Gerritsen (2003, 79–95) suggested symbolic deposits needed elements of three traits:

1 Recurrent patterning of the data – similar deposits of material might be made in similar places over space and time;
2 Potentially significant deposits involve objects and materials that could represent an offering, eg, whole artefacts, major parts of animal carcasses and artefacts with meaning derived from their inclusion in other contexts; and
3 The possibly public nature of a deposit (Gerritsen 2003, 83).

These three points align relatively well with some of what I have outlined for metalwork destruction and deposition so far, but we can build on them further here to apply more specifically to metalwork destruction and deposition in a range of contexts and draw together some of the conclusions of this chapter.

Firstly, the patterning of data is something I have emphasised throughout. It is one of the key traits that allows us to recognise when an object may have been deliberately destroyed, such as objects repeatedly broken in similar places (Chapter 2), and the patterns of depositions of single finds and hoards in similar locations is what allows us to recognise that some single finds are more likely to be intentionally placed than simply lost pieces (Chapter 5). The recurrence of deliberately destroyed weapons hoards within a tight chronological period across Britain *c.* 1100–900 BC is another good example of this. Such patterning of the data allows us to recognise we are dealing with intentional actions and is essential for interpreting selective deposition.

Gerritsen's second point is useful in the context of settlement deposits or isolated metalwork finds and one that is often applied, whether we are conscious of it or not. A good example is the discovery of a complete individual bronze or gold ornament lacking a context, which most people might assume represents the remains of an ephemeral deliberate personal deposit, perhaps an offering. By contrast, isolated fragments of the same ornaments are traditionally interpreted as lost metal. However, the destruction and deposition of ornaments in settlements, hoards and burials strengthens the idea that fragments elsewhere probably have some meaning behind them, as we saw for Middle Bronze Age ornaments in Chapter 4. This is not to argue that all fragments were significant, but rather they should not be quickly dismissed as stray losses, especially when they can be linked with wider patterns.

The idea of deposits in public contexts is trickier and requires us to reflect on what constitutes a public context. It may be reasonable to assume that deposits made in enclosure ditches or postholes during construction of a house are relatively public forums, and these actions were part of legitimising certain places. The treatment of an object was often part of that and where fragmented objects were included, we can consider this was an intrinsic part of constructing the deposit. However, funerals may be public or private, and depositional locations in the landscape may be known only to a select few or involve a whole community. Therefore, we must consider that recognising symbolic deposits is not limited to what was public, but also involves understanding what could have been private. The deposition itself is also distinct from the destruction event, which may also be private or public. If a metalworker was involved, as was probable for the fragmentation of much later metalwork, this may be undertaken in one location and the material gathered or transported for deposition later. The destruction itself may have been part of the routine reduction of metalwork (unless some particular technical skill is evident), and thus lacked any symbolic connotations, even if the end deposit was symbolic. Alternatively, as in the case of a cremation, the objects and body may be destroyed simultaneously and buried soon after – destruction and deposition were integrated practices with intertwined meanings. The possibly public nature of an event is part of what allows us to consider whether there may have been performative aspects involved, designed to be observed, and thus whether this was a practice through which meaning was created – a point I will come back to in the next chapter.

To Gerritsen's three categories, I wish to add a fourth, which emphasises a detailed understanding of an object's biography and treatment. This is intrinsic to all of the above. Destroyed objects showing signs of use and/or age may be interpreted in two ways: either they are worn out and no longer relevant and thus were deliberately destroyed, or they were damaged as part of ending the life of the object. This, in part, is linked to the other factors listed. For instance, many of the Late Bronze Age swords deposited in the River Thames with signs of destruction also displayed signs of use (York 2002) – the repeated choice of place and similar objects suggests these deposits were designed to end of the life of the object and/or commemorate the death of an individual with which the object was inalienable. The same is true of the South Cadbury shield (Chapter 4) or heirlooms and relics included in burials (Chapter 3). In these cases, an important point is that the original form of the object was still recognisable at the point of deposition and thus the memory of the object is preserved even through destruction; its deposition and removal from circulation may also live on in social memory. Understanding the origins of an object is also a crucial part of its biography, and by comparing the treatment of artefacts within larger assemblages, we can recognise whether the networks expressed through the forms of objects were part of establishing the meaning of a deposit. Non-local objects were often kept intact, suggesting that part of constructing and depositing the hoard was a reflection of the relations and networks represented within it. These ideas contrast significantly with small fragments of axeheads or blades that ended up in large, hoarded accumulations. In these cases, the original character of the object was not preserved, and they became dissociated from their original states and meanings through the process of destruction and accumulation. Such fragments in isolation or scattered are unlikely to represent significant deposits.

There is a danger, of course, that through these approaches one could assign meaning to any piece of fragmented metalwork, but I believe that a detailed study of these categories in relation to metalwork provides the clearest clues as to why destructive and depositional actions were undertaken. The biographies of objects, the places chosen and connections through practices were part of what helped establish destruction and deposition as important events. These aspects are what have allowed us to understand the changing approaches to metalwork in south-west Britain throughout the Bronze Age. The choices people made at a local level in this region reflected aspects of the social relations involved. These, in turn, were expressions of how these actions fit within wider patterns of metalwork destruction and deposition.

Note

1 Brück 2006b

7

Final fragments – what do the pieces tell us?

In a short piece in 2012, John Chapman posed the following two questions:

> (a) Can the identification of deliberate object fragmentation contribute to the understanding of specific deposits, sites or landscapes? (b) To what extent does the agency of humans and objects relate to structured deposition and deliberate object fragmentation? (Chapman 2012, 130)

In many respects, these reflect the core aims of this book. The deliberate destruction and deposition of Bronze Age metalwork needs to be approached from both a theoretical and a practical perspective to better understand the relationship between people and objects. Throughout I have advocated this approach, focusing as much on the material aspects of destruction and deposition as on how we might interpret these actions. The emphasis in past studies has typically been on the complete and pristine objects or those displaying exaggerated signs of destruction, but there is much to learn from the small fragments and pieces that show up isolated or in settlement ditches or contribute to large hoards. Whilst there has been an abundance of studies seeking to understand the production and use of objects, similar studies looking at the final acts committed on an object have generally been overlooked despite being the most archaeologically observable. In this final chapter, I want to return to the research aims that stimulated this study. Some of these, such as the relationships between destruction, deposition and place, have been addressed in previous chapters so I will focus specifically on three aspects: technical knowledge; performance; and object biographies associated with destruction. First, though, it is worth returning one last time to south-west Britain to assess the insights gained from studying this region.

Destruction and deposition of metalwork in south-west Britain

The general character and treatment of metalwork deposited in south-west Britain was in many ways typical of what one might expect of a region in north-western Europe. Complete and incomplete metalwork was most often deposited as single finds and associated with funerary contexts in the earlier Bronze Age, with a shift towards hoarding and deposition in specific landscape locales or associated with occupational contexts in the later periods. This included a full array of bronze weapons, tools, ornaments and casting debris, and gold artefacts, deposited in a variety of contexts and conditions. Some objects were deposited complete and freshly made, others showed signs of extensive wear and deliberate damage. The application of the Damage Ranking System and qualification of specific indicators of destruction highlighted how changes in approaches to treating metalwork transformed over time and across different areas. This proved a useful method for addressing a large amount of diverse data. Moreover, when analysed alongside specific contexts and associations it was possible to identify how destruction contributed to making selective and structured depositions possible in accordance with wider ideas. An important conclusion from this case study is that approaches to destruction and deposition were regionally varied and undertaken in response to specific situations and connections with places, as well as local traditions and interregional connections. This was apparent in different approaches to constructing and arranging Early Bronze Age burials from Cornwall to Dorset or differential Middle Bronze Age hoarding practices in the east and west of the region. Even in this small region of Bronze Age Europe, destruction and deposition could be quite varied. Some broader regionalised variations across Britain and elsewhere were illustrated in Chapter 6, further highlighting the different relationships people held with objects and traditions across space and time. This 'bottom-up' approach to the evidence usefully provides snapshots of localised interactions with metalwork and other material culture. Superficially similar actions, such as depositing weapons in wet places or fragmenting axeheads in hoards, were relational acts (cf. Fontijn 2020, 33–4). Broad ideologies were at play, but ultimately it was the individual decisions regarding the destruction of metalwork and depositional actions that allowed people to manage their lives and social worlds.

Technical knowledge, materiality and destruction

A key aspect of this was the technical knowledge involved in destroying objects and in the materiality of the objects themselves. I have placed an emphasis on this with the aim of ensuring an accurate interpretation of damage, but understanding the skills and knowledge required for destroying metalwork also helps us understand the people involved. Evidence for hot-short metalwork (ie, heating and striking bronze objects to fragment them) suggests the involvement of a metalworker, or at least an individual with a command of pyrotechnology, the necessary equipment and sound material knowledge (Knight 2017; 2019a). This represents a fairly fundamental form of destruction necessary for reducing and recycling bronze, even when undertaken for more symbolic rationales.

However, some destructive actions demonstrate greater technical abilities. Bending blades into waves or U-shapes, for instance, required an understanding of how materials would behave and what they would allow (cf. Giardino & Verly 2013). The aggrandised dirk from East Rudham, Norfolk, was bent to about 130 degrees from straight and probably required pressure to be exerted carefully and repeatedly, as well as bouts of annealing to achieve the eventual result (Needham & Wilkin in press). This was someone showing off what could be achieved and taking care not to break the object in the process; they understood the capabilities of the material and appear to have ceased bending when small cracks started to appear (Needham & Wilkin in press). By contrast, excessive and ecstatic fragmentation, bending and burning may relate to a lack of care in how things were destroyed, as seen in many later Bronze Age weapon hoards in Britain (Mörtz 2018) or accumulations in Central Europe (Nebelsick 1997; 2000).

These excessive actions nonetheless required technical knowledge on the part of the individual or group undertaking destruction: one has to know that bronze can be manipulated, snapped or melted. Technological knowledge is often considered in relation to the production and use of objects (eg, Dobres 2000; Kuijpers 2013) but rarely for destruction (though see Gabillot & Lagarde 2008; Quilliec 2008). Dobres (2000) emphasises that people were able to manage social and political relations through the production and use of objects – material and technical knowledge served practical purposes but also served to confirm one's place in and understanding of the world. The link between materiality, technology and social action is well-established (Lemonnier 1984; Pfaffenberger 1992; Dobres 2000; Brück 2006b; Robb 2010), and similar connections apply to the destruction of objects.

The regular fragmentation of objects for recycling, for instance, was essential in the *chaîne opératoire* for producing metal objects and an embodied part of being a metalsmith. Practitioners knew what temperatures were required, the best tools for the job, and how to produce the desired results most effectively. This developed and (re)asserted skills and knowledge; such acts of technical agency helped established a person's place in society – it is unlikely everybody was capable of manufacturing metal objects in the Bronze Age so possessing these skills would have been part of an individual's identity. There are similar connotations when we consider 'one-off' destruction events in preparation for deposition. In some cases, for instance the East Rudham dirk, this may have been coordinated and involved people with these select skillsets; at other times we may speculate that it was a less controlled activity where the ultimate aim was destruction and technical knowledge was perhaps less important. This is also why wear analysis and experimental archaeology are so essential for providing insights into how objects were treated.

Performing destruction and deposition

Understanding the technical processes of destruction allows us to consider the performative aspects of destruction and deposition. In the context of breaking a wine glass, Christopher Hoffman highlighted that 'the experiential component of intentional breaking is important – the noise, the mess, the unpredictability' (1999, 104). The experience is viewed as an integral part of the 'technological agency' that is constructed and expressed through the actions and knowledge inherent in breaking an object (*ibid.*). This involves understanding not only how materials will behave, but also the social implications of such an act and the world view in which it is being enacted (cf. Pollard 2001). Moreover, such events are inherently mnemonic: the ways destruction is performed and experienced will be part of what embeds events in social memory (Jones 2007; 2010b). This is particularly considered in relation to the construction and destruction of prehistoric monuments and structures, or burial rites and cremation events (eg, Downes 1999; Jones 2007; Noble 2007; Giles 2012; 2015; Brophy *et al.* 2016). For instance, Andrew Jones (2010b) highlights the burning of Neolithic monuments in northern Britain and south-west England as practices of memory formation. The destruction of structures was coupled with human sacrifice, which contributed to producing a mnemonic event that allowed places to take on new meanings (*ibid.*).

Bradley (2002, 12–4) considered bodily practices as a mode for invisible memory creation through ceremonies and destruction of material culture in prehistory. Moreover, an understanding of object biographies stresses the performance element of object deposition (Gosden & Marshall 1999, 174–5); the act of destruction that is sometimes associated with this means participants can only reexperience the object through memory, making the performance an important element (Rowlands 1993; Fontijn 2002, 35). In his study on Neolithic burnt flint axes from southern Sweden, Larsson (2000) highlighted the transformative role of fire in the destructive process and suggested that burning was part of a cosmological approach to material culture, with the destruction event intended to have a direct effect on the participants. Similarly, Henry Chapman (2018, 192–3) notes the performative elements of iconoclastic acts in the Iron Age, where the sacrifice of bodies, dismantling of structures and destruction of weapons were 'events of change' within people's lives which were enacted by individuals and groups; the performative aspect was part of what helped give meaning to the event.

However, the experiential components, and their implications, are rarely considered for Bronze Age metalwork, despite experimental work relating to the production and destruction of metalwork highlighting the fact that fire, material knowledge and specific bodily actions would all have contributed a performative element (Kuijpers 2013; Knight 2019a). An exception is the work by Andy Jones (Southampton) who emphasised 'the spectacular destruction' (2010a, 114) of Early Bronze Age metalwork in north-east Scotland, highlighting how 'the colour of objects, their biographies or exchange histories and their breakage or defacement act as vehicles for remembrance' (*ibid.*). In destroying objects, sounds, smells and sights were all part of what gave the act lasting meaning. Whilst it is impossible to understand the reactions elicited from specific acts or practices in prehistory, a better understanding of the experiential qualities of destruction has benefits. For instance, the colours of bronze at different temperatures or compositions or the sounds of fragmentation are more objective properties of the material (ie, they can be measured), even if their perception is inherently subjective. Such elements might be emphasised or reduced by the conditions in which destruction was conducted; colours would be more vivid if the metal were heated at night, whilst sounds associated with the process might be more or less dynamic in a roundhouse or an open landscape. People could have controlled these performances and heightened experiences.

A focus on the performance element of destruction emphasises this was not merely a functional action (although the outcome may have served a functional purpose), but rather the production and result of embodied practical knowledge undertaken in socially embedded contexts. The ways in which objects were damaged and the events they were involved in often served to generate memories and reinforce certain practices, whilst also highlighting the skills, social roles and significance of individuals and communities. We saw in Chapter 4 that the Taunton Union Workhouse hoard was possibly the work of a group or multiple groups of people coming together with certain objects damaged in particular ways, perhaps linked to identities. In contrast to various nearby ornament hoards that contained only complete objects, the destruction of objects in the Taunton hoard allows us to consider the pre-deposition spectacle of the hoard, with people collecting, bending, breaking and burning weapons, ornaments and tools; in turn, we can conceptualise this hoard as having a different meaning to similar contemporary deposits, and it would have stood out in social memory for its difference as well as being remembered for the physical actions involved. Similarly, although burials and funerals are coordinated affairs, serving to reinforce common beliefs about the right way to deal with death, they also possess individualistic elements that were linked to the relationship with the deceased. In some regions of Early Bronze Age Britain, it was appropriate to occasionally burn daggers on the cremation pyre; in others, daggers were dismantled beforehand and only the pommel was burned with the body (Chapter 6). Destroying the body and the object simultaneously linked the object to the person through a very performative process. All of this contributed to the construction, affirmation and negotiation of social ontologies for those involved. A similar argument has been proposed for producing and working metal objects, which required an embodied understanding of the material properties of bronze that allowed individuals to experience objects, rather than a rational understanding of precise compositions, details of hardness or exact temperatures of the fire (Kuijpers 2013; 2018). Although this cannot provide definitive answers to why objects were treated in different ways, the performance of the destruction and the stimulation of senses through actions should nonetheless be considered an inherent part of the process that allowed people to relate to objects, the processes involved and each other. Moreover, considering aspects of performance is part of what allows us to recognise that there was meaning behind the actions.

Destructive actions should of course be distinguished from the eventual depositional event, which may have had its own performative elements and served its own purposes. Sometimes objects may have been destroyed shortly before or at the point of deposition; others may have been destroyed and circulated in some way before deposition in a burial or in the landscape. Objects burned with a body entangled the destruction and transformation of people and objects. However, for the most part we rarely glimpse the post-destructive circulation of objects; wear patterns on pieces and fragments occasionally provide us with clues that we may be dealing with heirlooms or objects that enchained relations (cf. Lillios 1999; Woodward 2002). Evidence for carefully planned and coordinated depositions of a range of artefacts and materials is widespread and many of these were deliberately performative to create effective depositions that may have served to negotiate memories and relationships (Pollard 2001; 2008; Levy 2010; Helms 2012, 111). We saw this with the coordinated deconstruction of Bronze Age structures, as well as with the structured deposition of objects as single finds and within hoards. These events usually included a process of selection and accumulation that drew on the known histories of objects, people and places and were necessary for making depositions acceptable. As Mary Helms (2012, 110) puts it, Bronze Age depositions were 'carefully planned expressions of notable human activities… purposely intended to manipulate cosmic processes for the ultimate benefit of human communities.' The decision to include destroyed artefacts, or even choose to destroy them specifically for the purpose of deposition, was integral to the performance and creation of a deposition with meaning.

Biographies of destruction

This discussion highlights an important point: objects were not silent witnesses to destruction and deposition but rather they were selected, engaged with and treated in certain ways *because of* their known histories and connections. In turn, people related to objects in particular ways and this influenced how objects might be treated. Such relationships might be formed, broken and renegotiated with objects at numerous stages in their lifecycles from production through to deposition (Gell 1998, 17ff.; Dobres 1999; Pfaffenberger 1999; Robb 2010); these relationships mean objects become linked with specific people and places and it is this that makes objects inalienable (Weiner 1992).

The case of the South Cadbury shield emphasised how biographies could be intertwined with a dramatic destruction event: placing and stabbing a curated shield in a public arena was a mode for renegotiating a relationship with a socially important object, removing it from circulation to sever ties, kill the object and/or end memories. Destruction may have been a process of making an object alienable and suitable for deposition, which was also connected to the chosen place and a range of other practices undertaken nearby. Alternatively, damage and fragmentation transformed and enhanced the value of objects, making them suitable for social exchanges (Chapman 2000). Understanding how destruction was achieved adds another layer to how we can interpret an object and contributes to the overall cultural biography.

Many objects selected for destructive acts show signs of wear and may have been important because of their interactions with, and use by, the people who owned the material. This would explain the numerous trajectories of similar objects. For instance, swords might be deposited complete or damaged in rivers and watery locations or end up heavily fragmented and buried in hoards on hilltops; the eventual depositional treatment was a result of how the object was understood. At the point of deposition, it may have been an object of meaning or one that became devoid of significance. Some objects, like swords or ornaments may have been inalienable with owners, actions and/or places and perhaps even personified (Pearce 2013); destruction and deposition may have been a way of severing these links and served as acts of iconoclasm (Chapman & Geary 2013; Chapman 2018), transforming the objects into suitable forms for deposition. By contrast, objects reduced to small, undiagnostic fragments and accumulated into hoards or deposits were removed of their original meanings and connections through their destruction In discussing fragmented Late Bronze Age hoards, Brandherm and Moskal-del Hoyo suggested that '…if objects were seen as animate, a symbolic 'killing' might have been required… to transfer them from the sphere of living material culture to that of lifeless raw metal' (2014, 35; cf. Barrett & Needham 1988; Adams 2017). The places in which destruction and deposition were undertaken, as well as understanding how objects functioned in circulation and how they were treated, are intrinsic to helping us understand what underpinned the decisions taken. The best way to achieve this is through careful examination of the material, contexts and landscapes in question.

Why destroy and deposit things?

I conclude this book by returning to the question that drives so many studies into the destruction and deposition of metalwork: why? Throughout the Bronze Age, metalwork and other material culture was fragmented, bent, burnt and otherwise manipulated at different times for the purposes of recycling, offerings to the supernatural, commemorating deaths, founding structures, enchaining relationships and much more besides. As I have shown, however, this was a highly relational activity with a clear interrogation of the material culture and the circumstances of deposition required for us to present the best possible interpretations. Destruction associated with funerary contexts provides us with avenues for considering how people and objects were linked through death, for instance, whilst pieces of objects buried in postholes, pits and in the context of structures reveal how fragmenting objects was fundamental to events in the lives of settlements.

Because of these intricacies, this has not been a book trying to provide overarching answers to the question 'why' as there was clearly no single reason and to do so would flatten the complexities of the data. Instead, I have attempted to recognise and understand the meaning behind deposits through how they were brought about. I have sought to integrate the technical aspects of how things were destroyed in tandem with the ways in which they were eventually deposited. Through this, we can glean how such events varied and were performed in relation to wider processes, such as the relationships between people, objects and places, and how people used destruction and deposition to manage their understanding of the Bronze Age world. It allows us to recognise that some destructive actions were highly skilled; others may have been more commonplace, but nonetheless involved specific skills and resources. These were transformative processes for people, objects and places and enabled the creation of memories and experience through destructive actions. What we observe archaeologically represents complex and widespread practices that cannot be easily generalised across space and time but were temporally and spatially situated. Destructive and depositional actions built on embedded knowledge and were the result of long histories of how and why things were deposited. We have seen this was subject to change over time and across different regions, as destruction of metalwork became more common during certain periods of the Bronze Age and certain object types were targeted for destruction. Ultimately, the decision occasionally to destroy and deposit metalwork was a localised one in a dynamic, widely connected social world, which allowed individuals and groups to establish and enact their beliefs in relation to broader ontologies. Understanding the complexities and nuances of how metalwork was treated and deposited allows us to further our understanding of this material and these practices that formed such a central part of Bronze Age life.

Bibliography

Notes on authors' names:

References are cited with author's initials as published. However, to assist the reader in identification, in the bibliography Andy Jones (Cornwall Archaeological Unit) identified as '[Andy]', whilst Andrew Meirion Jones (Stockholm University, formerly Southampton University) identified by '[Meirion]'. {for the ease of the reader these are cited in date, not author, order}. Mark Knight (Cambridge Archaeological Unit) is always published (in cited references) as M. Knight whilst Matthew Knight (National Museums Scotland) is cited as M.G. Knight.

Adams, S. 2017. The contents and context of the Boughton Malherbe Late Bronze Age hoard. *Archaeologia Cantiana* 138, 37–64

Allen, I.M., Britton, D. & Coghlan, H.H. 1970. *Metallurgical Reports on British Irish Bronze Age Implements and Weapons in the Pitt Rivers Museum* (Occasional Papers on Technology 10). Oxford: Oxford University Press

Anderson, K. 2011. Slashing and thrusting with Late Bronze Age spears: analysis and experiment. *Antiquity* 85, 599–612. https://doi.org/10.1017/S0003598X00067983

Anderson, K. 2012. The Weapons, Warriors and Warfare of Northern Britain, c.1250 BC - 850 AD. Unpubl. PhD thesis, University of Edinburgh

Andrews, M., Polcar, T., Sofaer, J. & Pike, A.W.G. 2021. The mechanised testing and sequential wear-analysis of replica Bronze Age palstave blades. *Archaeometry*, 1–16. DOI: 10.1111/arcm.12685

Anon. 1875. The Museum, *Proceeding of the Somerset Archaeological and Natural History Society* 21, 68–70

Anon. 1881. Bronze Celts. *Transactions of the Penzance Natural History and Antiquarian Society* (1880–81), 74

Anon. 1925. *Devon and Cornwall Notes and Queries* 13 (1924–25)

Appleby, J. 2013. Temporality and the Transition to Cremation in the late third millennium to mid second millennium BC in Britain. *Cambridge Archaeological Journal* 23(1), 83–97

ApSimon, A.M. & Greenfield, E. 1972. The excavation of Bronze Age and Iron Age sites at Trevisker, St. Eval, Cornwall. *Proceedings of the Prehistoric Society* 38, 302–81

Arnoldussen, S. 2015. Something near, something far: The referencing of local and supra-regional origins in Middle- and Late Bronze Age hoards from the northern Netherlands. In P. Suchowska-Ducke, S.S. Reiter & H. Vandkilde (eds), *Forging Identities. The Mobility of Culture in Bronze Age Europe*, 2 volumes, 17–27. Oxford: British Archaeological Reports S2771

Ashbee, P. 1960. *The Bronze Age round barrow in Britain.* London: Phoenix House Ltd

Atkinson, M. 1995. A Late Bronze Age enclosure at Broomfield, Chelmsford. *Essex Archaeology and History* 26, 1–24

Barbieri, M. & Cavazzuti, C. 2014. Stone Moulds from Terramare (Northern Italy): Analytical Approach and Experimental Reproduction. *EXARC Journal* 2014/1. https://exarc.net/ark:/88735/10145

Barley, N. 1994. *Smashing Pots. Feats of Clay from Africa.* London: British Museum Press

Barrett, J.C. 1994. *Fragments from Antiquity*. Oxford: Blackwell

Barrett, J.C. 2012. Are models of Prestige Goods Economies and Conspicuous Consumption applic able to the archaeology of the Bronze to Iron Age transition in Britain? In A.M. Jones, J. Pollard, M.J. Allen & J. Gardiner (eds), *Image, Memory and Monumentality. Archaeological engagements with the material world: a celebration of the academic achievements of Professor Richard Bradley*, 6–17. Oxford: Oxbow Books

Barrett, J.C. & Needham, S.P. 1988. Production, circulation and exchange: Problems in the interpretation of Bronze Age bronzework. In J.C. Barrett & I. Kinnes (eds), *The Archaeology of Context in the Neolithic and Bronze Age: Recent trends*, 127–40. Sheffield: Department of Prehistory and Archaeology, University of Sheffield

Barrett, J.C., Bradley, R. & Green, M. 1991. *Landscape, Monuments and Society: The prehistory of Cranborne Chase.* Cambridge: Cambridge University Press

Barrett, J.C., Freeman, P.W.M. & Woodward, A. 2000. *Cadbury Castle Somerset: The later prehistoric and early historic archaeology*. London: English Heritage Archaeological Report 20

Barrowclough, D. 2014. Golden Biographies: The production, curation, fragmentation and deposition of the Armorican-Type rolled-gold bead-like ornaments found at Pendleton, Lancashire. *The Archaeological Journal* 171(1), 30–60

Basford, F. 2005. *IOW-B16625: A BRONZE AGE JEWELLERY.* Available at: https://finds.org.uk/database/artefacts/record/id/104045. [Accessed: 21 Sept 2020]

Basford, F. 2014. *IOW-0195D2: A BRONZE AGE BRACELET.* Available at: https://finds.org.uk/database/artefacts/record/id/594585 [Accessed: 22 April 2021]

Basford, F., Boughton, D. & Ellis, L. 2014. Treasure Report 2014T474. Available at: F. Basford, *IOW–2D6CBC: A IRON AGE HOARD.* Available at: https://finds.org.uk/database/artefacts/record/id/625548 [Accessed: 4 April 2021]

Becker, K. 2006. Hoards and Deposition in Bronze Age Ireland (Vols 1–3). Unpubl. PhD thesis, University College Dublin

Becker, K. 2013. Transforming Identities – new approaches to Bronze Age deposition in Ireland. *Proceedings of the Prehistoric Society* 79, 225–63. doi:10.1017/ppr.2013.8

Bell, D.R. 2019. A shifting chronology of combat damage: reassessing the evidence for use and reuse on Irish Bronze Age swords. In M.G. Knight, D. Boughton & R.E. Wilkinson (eds), *Objects of the Past in the Past. Investigating the significance of earlier artefacts in later contexts*, 152–80. Oxford: Archaeopress (Access Archaeology)

Bell, M. 1990. *Brean Down Excavations 1983–1987.* London: English Heritage Archaeological Report No. 15

Bergerbrant, S. 2007. *Bronze Age Identities: Costume, Conflict and Contact in Northern Europe 1600–1300 BC.* Lindome: Bricoleur Press

Best, J. & Woodward, A. 2012. Late Bronze Age Pottery Production: Evidence from a 12th–11th century cal BC Settlement at Tinney's Lane, Sherborne, Dorset. *Proceedings of the Prehistoric Society* 78, 207–61. doi: 10.1017/S0079497X0002716X

Bietti Sestieri, A.M., Salzani, L., Giardino, C. & Verly, G. 2013. Ritual treatment of weapons as a correlate of structural change in the Italian Late Bronze Age communities: the bronze hoard of Pila del Brancon (Nogara, Verona). *Rivista di Scienze Preistoriche* LXIII, 155–69

Bloch, M. & Parry, J. 1989. Introduction: Money and the morality of exchange. In J. Parry & M. Bloch (eds), *Money and the Morality of Exchange*, 1–32. Cambridge: Cambridge University Press

Booth, T.J. & Brück, J. 2020. Death is not the end: radiocarbon and histo-taphonomic evidence for the curation and excarnation of human remains in Bronze Age Britain. *Antiquity* 94(377), 1186–1203. doi: 10.15184/aqy.2020.152

Bordas, F. & Boulud-Gazo, S. 2018. Les dépôts métalliques de la fin de l'âge du Bronze dans le Morbihan: remarques sur quelques dépôts de l'horizon de l'épée du type en langue de carpe. *Bulletin et Mémoires du Morbihan. Société Polymathique du Morbihan* 144, 13–45

Borg, G., 2010. Warum in die Ferne schweifen? Geochemische Fakten und geologische Forschungsansätze zu Europas Goldvorkommen und zur Herkunft des Nebra-Goldes. In H. Meller & F. Bertemes (eds), *Der Griff nach den Sternen. Wie Europas Eliten zu Macht und Reichtum kamen*, Internationales Symposium Halle (Saale) 16.–21. Februar 2005, 735–50. Halle: Tagungen des Landesmuseums für Vorgeschichte

Borg, G. 2019. In search of the Golden Sky: Cornwall as the source of the gold of the Bronze Age Sky Disc of Nebra. *Journal of the Royal Institution of Cornwall* 58, 38–57

Borlase, W. 1769. *Antiquities, Historical and Monumental, of the County of Cornwall* (2nd edn). London: W. Bowyer and J. Nichols: for S. Baker and G. Leigh

Borlase, W.C. 1872. *Nænia Cornubiæ.* London: Longmans, Green, Reader and Dyer

Boughton, D. 2015. *The Early Iron Age socketed axes in Britain: A study of their typology, distribution, associations and contexts.* Unpubl. PhD thesis, University of Lancashire

Boulud, S. & Fily, M. 2009. Les dépôts métalliques de l'extrême fin du Bronze final en Bretagne: nouvelle évaluation des données à la lumière des découvertes récentes. In M.J. Roulière-Lambert, A. Daubigney, P.-Y. Milcent, M. Talon & J. Vital (eds), *De l'âge du Bronze à l'âge du Fer en France et en Europe occidentale (Xe-VIIe siècle av. J.-C.). La moyenne valleée du Rhône aux âges du Fer. Actes du XXXe colloque international de l'A.F.E.A.F., co-organisé avec l'A.P.R.A.B. (Saint-Romain-en-Gal, 26–28 mai 2006)*, 283–298. Dijon: Revue archéologique de l'Est, supplément 27

Boulud, S. & Mélin, M. 2009. Étude comparative des modalités de dépôt en milieu terrestre et en milieux humides en region armoricaine à l'âge du Bronze final. In S. Bonnardin, C. Hamon, M. Lauwers & B. Quilliec (eds), *Du matériel au spirituel. Réalités archéologiques et historiques des 'dépôts' de la Préhistoire à nos jours. XXIXe rencontres internationales d'archéologie et d'histoire d'Antibes*, 249–60. Antibes: Éditions APDCA

Bourdieu, P. 1977. Cultural reproduction and social reproduction. In J. Karabel & A.H. Halsey (eds), *Power and Ideology in Education*, 487–511. Oxford: Oxford University Press

Bradley, R. 1985. Exchange and social distance – the structure of bronze artefact distributions. *Man* 20, 692–704

Bradley, R. 1998 [1990]. *The Passage of Arms: An archaeological analysis of prehistoric hoard and votive deposits* (2nd edn). Oxford: Oxbow Books

Bradley, R. 2000. *An Archaeology of Natural Places.* London: Routledge

Bradley, R. 2002. *The Past in Prehistoric Societies.* London: Routledge

Bradley, R. 2005. *Ritual and domestic life in Prehistoric Europe.* Abingdon: Routledge

Bradley, R. 2017. *A geography of offerings. Deposits of valuables in the landscapes of Ancient Europe.* Oxford: Oxbow Books

Bradley, R. 2019. *The Prehistory of Britain and Ireland* (2nd edn). Cambridge: Cambridge University Press

Bradley, R. & Ford, D. 2004. A long distance connection in the Bronze Age: Joining fragments of a Ewart Park sword from two sites in England. In H. Roche, E. Grogan, J. Bradley, J. Coles & B. Raftery (eds), *From Megaliths to Metals: Essays in honour of George Eogan*, 174–7. Oxford: Oxbow Books

Bradley, R., Green, C. & Watson, A. 2018. The placing of Early Bronze Age metalwork deposits: New evidence from Scotland. *Oxford Journal of Archaeology* 37(2), 137–45

Bradley, R., Lewis, J., Mullin, D. & Branch, N. 2015. 'Where water wells up from the earth': Excavations at the findspot of the Late Bronze Age hoard from Broadward, Shropshire. *Antiquaries Journal* 95, 21–64

Brandherm, D. 2018. Fragmentation patterns revisited: ritual and recycling in Bronze Age depositional practice. In D. Brandherm, E. Heymans & D. Hofmann (eds), *Gifts, Goods and Money. Comparing currency and circulation systems in past societies*, 45–65. Oxford: Archaeopress Archaeology

Brandherm, D., & Moskal-del Hoyo, M. 2014. Both sides now: The carp's tongue complex revisited. *The Antiquaries Journal,* 94, 1–47. doi:10.1017/S0003581514000213

Bray, P.J. 2012. Before $_{29}$Cu became Copper: tracing the recognition and invention of metalleity in Britain and Ireland during the 3rd millennium BC. In M.J. Allen, J. Gardiner & A. Sheridan (eds), *Is there a British Chalcolithic? People place and polity in the later 3rd millennium*, 56–70. Oxford: Oxbow Books

Bray, P.J. & Pollard, A.M. 2012. A new interpretative approach to the chemistry of copper-alloy objects: source, recycling and technology. *Antiquity* 86(333), 853–67. doi: 10.1017/S0003598X00047967

Briard, J. 1965. *Les dépôts Bretons et l'Age du Bronze Atlantique.* Rennes: Travaux du Laboratoire d'anthropologie préhistorique

Briard, J. 1987. Dépôts de bronze, haches à douille, prémonnaie et fausse monnaie. In J. Bousquet, P. Naster, C. Bémont, C. Delplace, B. Fischer, K. Gruel, C. Peyre & J.-C. Richard (eds), *Mélanges offerts au docteur J.-B. Colbert de Beaulieu*, 133–43. Paris: Le Léopard d'Or

Briard, J. 1991. Le groupe de l'épée en langue de carpe en Armorique: une revision. In C. Chevillot & A. Coffyn (eds), *L'âge du Bronze atlantique, ses faciès de l'Écosse à l'Andalousie et leurs relations avec le Bronze continental et la Méditerranée, Actes du colloque de Beynac*, 125–44. Beynac-et-Cazenac: Association des Muse´es du Sarladais

Bridgford, S.D. 1997. Mightier than the pen? (An edgewise look at Irish Bronze Age swords). In J. Carman (ed.), *Material Harm. Archaeological Studies of War and Violence*, 95–115. Glasgow: Cruithne Press

Bridgford, S.D. 2000. Weapons, Warfare and Society in Britain 1250–750 BC Volume 1. Unpubl. PhD thesis, University of Sheffield

Brittain, M. & Harris, O. 2010. Enchaining arguments and fragmenting assumptions: reconsidering the fragmentation debate in archaeology. *World Archaeology* 42(4), 581–94

Britton, D., O'Connor, B. & Cunliffe, B. 1984. The Late Bronze Age hoard. In B. Cunliffe, *Danebury. An Iron Age hillfort in Hampshire. Vol 2. The excavations 1969–1978: the finds*, 335–40. London: Council for British Archaeology Research Report 52

Brophy, K., Goeckeritz, C. & MacGregor, G. 2016. Build 'N' Burn: using fire to create memorable learning experiences for the public. *Antiquity* Project Gallery 90(350): https://www.antiquity.ac.uk/projgall/brophy350 [accessed 3 May 2021]

Brown, M.A. & Blin-Stoyle, A.E. 1959. A sample analysis of British Middle and Late Bronze Age material, using optical spectrometry. *Proceedings of the Prehistoric Society* 25, 188–208

Brück, J. 1995. A place for the dead: the role of human remains in Late Bronze Age Britain. *Proceedings of the Prehistoric Society* 61, 245–77. doi: 10.1017/S0079497X00003091

Brück, J. 1999a. Ritual and rationality: some problems of interpretation in European archaeology. *European Journal of Archaeology* 2(3), 313–44

Brück, J. 1999b. Houses, lifecycles and deposition on Middle Bronze Age settlements in southern England. *Proceedings of the Prehistoric Society* 65, 145–66

Brück, J. 2004. Material metaphors. The relational construction of identity in Early Bronze Age burials in Ireland and Britain. *Journal of Social Archaeology* 4(3), 307–333

Brück, J. 2006a. Death, exchange and reproduction in the British Bronze Age. *European Journal of Archaeology* 9, 73–101

Brück, J. 2006b. Fragmentation, personhood, and the social construction of technology in the Middle and Late Bronze Age Britain. *Cambridge Archaeological Journal* 16, 297–315

Brück, J. 2007. The character of Late Bronze Age settlement in southern Britain. In C. Haselgrove & R. Pope (eds), *The Earlier Iron Age in Britain and the Near Continent*, 24–38. Oxford: Oxbow Books

Brück, J. 2009. Women, Death and Social Change in the British Bronze Age. *Norwegian Archaeological Review* 42(1), 1–23

Brück, J. 2014. Cremation, gender, and concepts of the Self in the British Early Bronze Age. In I. Kuijt, C.P. Quinn & G. Cooney (eds), *Transformation by Fire. The archaeology of cremation in cultural context*, 119–39. Tucson: University of Arizona Press

Brück, J. 2015. Gifts or commodities? Reconfiguring Bronze Age exchange in Northwest Europe. In P. Suchowska-Ducke, S.S. Reiter & H. Vandkilde (eds), *Forging Identities. The Mobility of Culture in Bronze Age Europe*, 2 volumes, 47–56. Oxford: British Archaeological Reports S2771

Brück, J. 2016. Hoards, fragmentation and exchange in the European Bronze Age. In S. Hansen, T. Vachta, & D. Neumann (eds), *Raum, Gabe, Erinnerung*, 75–92. Berlin: De Gruyter

Brück, J. 2017. Reanimating the dead: The circulation of human bone in the British Later Bronze Age. In J. Bradbury & C. Scarre (eds), *Engaging with the Dead. Exploring changing human beliefs about death, mortality and the human body,* 138–48. Oxford: Oxbow Books

Brück, J. 2019. *Personifying prehistory: Relational ontologies in Bronze Age Britain and Ireland.* Oxford: Oxford University Press

Brück, J. & Fokkens, H. 2013. Bronze Age settlements. In Fokkens & Harding 2013, 82–101

Brück, J. & Fontijn, D. 2013. The myth of the chief: Prestige goods, power, and personhood in the European Bronze Age. In Fokkens & Harding 2013, 197–215

Brunning, R. 1997. Middlezoy, Greylake, ST 3933. In C.J. Webster & R.A. Croft (eds), Somerset Archaeology 1997. *Proceedings of the Somerset Archaeological and Natural History Society* 141, 178

Brunning, R. 1998. Middlezoy, Greylake, ST393337. In C.J. Webster, (ed.), Somerset Archaeology 1998. *Proceedings of the Somerset Archaeological and Natural History Society* 142, 199

Bruns, D. & Needham, S. 2008. Mylor, Cornwall. In *Treasure Annual Report 2005/6*, 50–52, no. 69. Department of Culture, Media and Sport.

Burgess, C. 1968. The Later Bronze Age in the British Isles and North-Western France. *Archaeological Journal* 125 (1), 1–45

Burgess, C.B. 1976a. The Gwithian mould and the forerunners of South Welsh axes. In C.B. Burgess & R. Miket (eds), *Settlement and Economy in the Third and Second Millenia BC*, 69–79. Oxford: British Archaeological Reports 33

Burgess, C.B. 1976b. Burials with metalwork of the later

Bronze Age in Wales and beyond. In G.C. Boon & J.M. Lewis (eds), *Welsh Antiquity*, 81–104. Cardiff: National Museum of Wales

Burgess, C.B. 1979. A find from Boyton, Suffolk, and the end of the Bronze Age in Britain and Ireland. In C.B. Burgess & D. Coombs (eds), *Bronze Age Hoards. Some finds old and new*, 269–82. Oxford: British Archaeological Report 67

Burgess, C. & Gerloff, S. 1981. *The Dirks and Rapiers of Great Britain and Ireland.* Prähistorische Bronzefunde 4.7. Munich: C.H. Beck

Burgess, C.B., Coombs, D. & Davies, D.G. 1972. The Broadward Complex and barbed spearheads. In F.M. Lynch & C.B. Burgess (eds), *Prehistoric Man in Wales and the West; Essays in honour of Lily F. Chitty*, 211–83. Bath: Adams & Dart

Burnett, L. 2017. *SOM–81B00C: A BRONZE AGE HOARD.* Available at: https://finds.org.uk/database/artefacts/record/id/833960 [Accessed: 17 Mar 2021]

Butler, J.J. & Steegstra, H. 2003. Bronze Age metal and amber in the Netherlands (iii.2) Catalogue of the socketed axes, Part A. *Palaeohistoria* 43–44, 263–319

Butterworth, C.A. 1999. Hayne Lane. In A.P. Fitzpatrick, C.A. Butterworth & J. Grove, *Prehistoric and Roman Sites in East Devon: The A30 Honiton to Exeter improvement DBFO scheme, 1996–9* (Wessex Archaeology Report no.16), 91–129. Salisbury: Trust for Wessex Archaeology Ltd

Byard, A. 2012. *BERK-0D1A05: A BRONZE AGE JEWELLERY.* Available at: https://finds.org.uk/database/artefacts/record/id/529326. [Accessed: 21 September 2020]

Byard, A. 2015a. *BERK-F548E6: A BRONZE AGE JEWELLERY.* Available at: https://finds.org.uk/database/artefacts/record/id/701925. [Accessed: 21 September 2020]

Byard, A. 2015b. *BERK–456EE1: A BRONZE AGE HOARD.* Available at: https://finds.org.uk/database/artefacts/record/id/753607 [Accessed: 27 November 2020]

Byard, A. 2016. The Portable Antiquities Scheme in Oxfordshire, 2015. *Oxoniensia* 81, 239–46

Cabanillas de la Torre, G. & Gomez de Soto, J. 2020. Bronze hoards in the Iron Age: depositions of Armorican socketed axes in context. In H. Wendling, M. Augstein, J. Fries-Knoblach, S. Gentner, M. Kirchmayr, M. Kohle, K. Ludwig, R. Schumann, & J. Wiethold (eds), *Beiträge zur Ur- und Frühgeschichte Mitteleuropas 95. Objekt. Depot. Motiv. Kontext und Deutung von Objektniederlegungen im eisenzeitlichen Mitteleuropa*, 11–23. Weißbach: Beier and Beran

Cahill, M. 2005. Roll your own lunula. In T. Condit, C. Corlett & P. Wallace (eds), *Above and Beyond: Essays in Memory of Leo Swan*, 53–61. Dublin: Wordwell

Cahill, M. forthcoming. Reclaiming Mrs Tyrrell's field – a hoard of gold lunulae from Ballinderry, Co. Kildare. *Proceedings of the Royal Irish Academy, Section C* [accepted]

Callander, J.G. 1922. Three Bronze Age hoards recently added to the National Collection, with notes on the hoard from Duddingston Loch. *Proceedings of the Society of Antiquaries of Scotland* 56 (1921–22), 351–64

Carey, C., Jones, A.M., Allen, M.J. & Juleff, G. 2019. The social organisation of metalworking in southern England during the Beaker period and Bronze Age: absence of evidence or evidence of absence? *Internet Archaeology* 52. https://doi.org/10.11141/ia.52.4

Carlin, N. 2018. *The Beaker Phenomenon? Understanding the character and context of social practices in Ireland 2500–2000 BC.* Leiden: Sidestone Press

Caswell, E. & Roberts, B.W. 2018. Reassessing Community Cemeteries: Cremation Burials in Britain during the Middle Bronze Age (*c.* 1600–1150 cal BC). *Proceedings of the Prehistoric Society* 84, 329–57. doi: 10.1017/ppr.2018.9

Champion, T. & Jarvis, K. 1992. The Bournemouth hospital Bronze Age hoard. *Proceedings of the Dorset Natural History and Archaeological Society* 114, 253–4

Chapman, H. 2018. *Iconoclasm and later prehistory.* Abingdon: Routledge

Chapman, H. & Gearey, B. 2013. Iconoclasm in European prehistory? Breaking objects and landscapes. In S. Boldrick, L. Brubaker & R. Clay (eds), *Striking Images, Iconoclasms Past and Present*, 25–37. Farnham: Ashgate Publishing Limited

Chapman, J. 2000. *Fragmentation in Archaeology: People, places and broken objects in the prehistory of South Eastern Europe.* London: Routledge

Chapman, J. 2012. Structured deposition meets deliberate object fragmentation. *Archaeological Dialogues* 19(2), 129–33

Chapman, J. & Gaydarska, B. 2007. *Parts and Wholes. Fragmentation in prehistoric context.* Oxford: Oxbow Books

Chestnut, C. & Wilkin, N. 2014. Treasure Report 2013T482. Available at: J. Jackson, *KENT-FE9DB2: A BRONZE AGE HOARD.* Available at: https://finds.org.uk/database/artefacts/record/id/570344 [Accessed: 29 Dec 2020]

Chitty, L.F. 1928. The Willow Moor Bronze Hoard, Little Wenlock, Shropshire. *The Antiquaries Journal* 8(1), 30–47. doi: 10.1017/S0003581500057577

Čivilytė, A. 2009. *Wahl Der Waffen. Studien Zur Deutung Der Bronzezeitlichen Waffendeponierungen Im Nördlichen Mitteleuropa.* Bonn: UPA, 167

Cleary, K. 2018. Broken Bones and Broken Stones: Exploring Fragmentation in Middle and Late Bronze Age Settlement Contexts in Ireland. *European Journal of Archaeology* 21(3), 336–60. doi:10.1017/eaa.2017.61

Coffyn, A., Gomez, J. & Mohen, J.-P. 1981. *L'apogeé du Bronze atlantique: le dépôt de Vénat.* Paris: L'âge du Bronze en France 1, Picard

Coles, B. & Coles, J.M. 1986. *Sweet Track to Glastonbury. The Somerset Levels in Prehistory.* London: Thames & Hudson

Coles, J.M. 1960. Scottish Late Bronze Age metalwork: Typology, distributions and chronology. *Proceedings of the Society of Antiquaries of Scotland* 93 (1959–60), 16–134

Coles, J.M. & Scott, J.G. 1963. The Late Bronze Age hoard from Peelhill, Strathaven, Lanarkshire. *Proceedings of the Society of Antiquaries of Scotland* 96 (1962–63), 99–115

Coles, J.M., Leach, P., Minnitt, S.C., Tabor, R. & Wilson, A.S. 1999. A Later Bronze Age shield from South Cadbury, Somerset, England. *Antiquity* 73, 33–48

Coles, S., Pine, J. & Preston, S. 2003. Bronze Age and Saxon landscapes on the Isle of Sheppey: Excavations at Shrubsoles Hill, Brambledown, 1999–2001. In S. Coles, S. Hammond, J. Pine, S. Preston & A. Taylor, *Bronze Age, Roman and Saxon Sites on Shrubsoles Hill, Sheppey and at Wises Lane, Borden, Kent*, 2–55. Reading: Thames Valley Archaeological Services Ltd. Monograph 4

Colson, E. 1953. *The Makah Indians. The study of an Indian tribe in modern American society.* Manchester: Manchester University Press

Cook, M. & Dunbar, L. 2008. *Rituals, Roundhouses and Romans: Excavations at Kintore, Aberdeenshire 2000–2006*. Edinburgh: Scottish Trust for Archaeological Research

Coombs, D. 1975. Bronze Age weapon hoards in Britain. *Archaeologia Atlantica* 1.1, 49–81

Coombs, D. 1979. A Late Bronze Age hoard from Cassiobridge Farm, Watford, Hertfordshire. In C.B. Burgess & D. Coombs (eds), *Bronze Age Hoards. Some finds old and new*, 197–233. Oxford: British Archaeological Report 67

Coombs, D.G., Northover, J.P. & Maskal, J. 2004. Tower Hill Axe Hoard. In D. Miles, S. Palmer, G. Lock, C. Gosden, & A.M. Crummy (eds), *Uffington White Horse and Its Landscape: Investigations at White Horse Hill, Uffington, 1989–95 and Tower Hill, Ashbury, 1993–94*, 203–24. Oxford: Oxford Archaeology, Thames Valley Landscapes Monograph 18

Cornish, J.B. 1906. Early Man. In W. Page (ed.), *The Victoria History of the Counties of England: Cornwall Volume 1*, 353–74. London: Archibald Constable and Company Ltd

Cowie, T. 2004. Special places for special axes? Early Bronze Age metalwork from Scotland. In I.A.G. Shepherd & G. Barclay (eds), *Scotland in Ancient Europe*, 247–61. Edinburgh: Society of Antiquaries of Scotland

Cowie, T. & Hall, M. 2001. Late Bronze Age metalwork from Scottish rivers: a rediscovered sword from the River Forth near Cambus, Clackmannanshire, in its wider context. *Tayside and Fife Archaeological Journal* 7, 1–15

Cowie, T. & Hall, M. 2010. A new look at the Late Bronze Age metalwork from the Tay. In D. Strachan, *Carpow In Context. A Late Bronze Age logboat from the Tay*, 151–62. Edinburgh: Society of Antiquaries of Scotland

Craddock, P.T. 1991. The composition of Iberian Bronze Age metalwork in the British Museum. In W.A. Oddy (ed.), *Aspects of Early Metallurgy*. London: British Museum Occasional Paper No.17, 51–62

Crellin, R.J. 2020. *Change and Archaeology*. London: Routledge

Crellin, R.J., Fowler, C. & Gamble, M. 2020. Thinking outside the cist: interpreting a unique artefact assemblage from an Early Bronze Age burial on the Isle of Man. *Antiquity* 94(378), 1444–63. doi: 10.15184/aqy.2020.175

Croker, J.G. 1852. Proceedings at the meetings of the Archaeological Institute. *Archaeological Journal* 9, 185–6

Cunliffe, B. 1988. *Mount Batten, Plymouth. A prehistoric and Roman port.* Oxford: Oxford University Committee for Archaeology Monograph No.26

Cunliffe, B. 2015. Facing the Northern Ocean: The British Late Bronze and Iron Ages in their Continental Perspective. In F. Hunter (ed.), *Scotland in Later Prehistoric Europe*, 5–17. Edinburgh: Society of Antiquaries of Scotland

Cunliffe, B. & Phillipson, D.W. 1969. Excavations at Eldon's Seat, Encombe, Dorset. *Proceedings of the Prehistoric Society* 35, 191–237

Current Archaeology. 1971. Norton Fitzwarren. *Current Archaeology* 28, 116–20

Daubney, A. 2011. *LIN–76B150: A BRONZE AGE TORC*. Available at: https://finds.org.uk/database/artefacts/record/id/477589 [Accessed: 28 December 2020]

Davey, P.J. 1973. Bronze Age metalwork from Lincolnshire. *Archaeologia* 104, 51–127

Davies, A. & Webley, L. 2020. A Middle Bronze Age Enclosure and Other Prehistoric to Early Medieval Activity at Nerrols Farm, Cheddon Fitzpaine, Somerset. Archaeological Excavation Report. Oxford Archaeology: Unpubl. Report. Accessible via: https://library.oxfordarchaeology.com/5934/

Davis, R. 1999. Bronze Age metalwork from the Trent valley: Newark, Notts, to Gainsborough, Lincs. *Transactions of the Thoroton Society of Nottinghamshire* 103, 25–48

Davis, R. 2015. *The Late Bronze Age Spearheads of Britain.* Prähistorische Bronzefunde 5.7. Stuttgart: Franz Steiner Verlag

Delibes, G., Fernández Manzano, J. & Herrán, J.I. 2016. Tipología y composición de las hachas de talón ibéricas. In E. Galán, O. García-Vuelta & I. Montero-Ruiz (eds), *Hachas de talón del Museo Arqueológico Nacional. Catálogo y estudio arqueometalúrgico*, 87–133. Madrid: Ministerio de Educación, Cultura y Deporte

Denford, G. 2000. *Prehistoric and Romano-British Kimmeridge Shale* [data-set]. Available at: https://archaeologydataservice.ac.uk/archives/view/denford_na_2000/overview.cfm#intro. [Accessed: 15 May 2021] https://doi.org/10.5284/1000090

Dietrich, O. 2014. Learning from 'scrap' about Late Bronze Age hoarding practices: A biographical approach to individual acts of dedication in large metal hoards of the Carpathian Basin. *European Journal of Archaeology* 17(3), 468–86

Dietrich, O. & Mörtz, T. 2019. Sockets full of scrap? Remarks on deliberate fragmentation in Late Bronze Age metal deposits in south-eastern and north-western Europe. In D. Brandherm (ed.), *Aspects of the Bronze Age in the Atlantic Archipelago and Beyond. Proceedings from the Belfast Bronze Age Forum, 9–10 November 2013* (Archæologia Atlantica – Monographiæ III), 281–97. Hagen/Westfalen: curach bhán publications

Dobres, M.-A. 1999. Technology's links and *chaînes*: The processual unfolding of technique and technician. In M.-A. Dobres & C.R. Hoffman (eds), *The Social Dynamics of Technology: Practice, Politics, and World View*, 124–46. Washington, DC: Smithsonian Institution Press

Dobres, M.-A. 2000. *Technology* and *Social Agency*. Oxford: Blackwell Publishers

Dobson, D.P. 1931. *The Archaeology of Somerset.* London: Metheun and Co. Ltd

Dolfini, A. & Crellin, R.J. 2016. Metalwork wear analysis: the loss of innocence. *Journal of Archaeological Science* 66, 78–87

Downes, J., 1999. Cremation: a spectacle and a journey. In J. Downes & T. Pollard (eds), *The Loved Body's Corruption: Archaeological contributions to the study of human mortality*, 19–29. Glasgow: Cruithne Press

Drew, C.D. & Piggott, S. 1936. Two Bronze Age barrows excavated by Mr. Edward Cunnington. *Proceedings of the Dorset Natural History and Archaeological Society* 58, 18–25

Dunkin, D., Yates, D. & Bradley, R. 2020. The findspots of Bronze Age metalwork in lowland England: A new field study. *Oxford Journal of Archaeology* 39, 67–88. https://doi.org/10.1111/ojoa.12181

Edmonds, M. 1995. *Stone tools and society: Working Stone in the Neolithic and Bronze Age Britain.* London: Batsford

Ehrenburg, M. 1980. The occurrence of Bronze Age metalwork in the Thames: an investigation. *Transactions of the London and Middlesex Archaeological Society* 31, 1–15

Ellis, C. 2012. The excavation of a Late Bronze Age/Early Iron Age-Middle Iron Age settlement at Home Field, Down Farm, Sixpenny Handley, Dorset. *Proceedings of the Dorset Natural History and Archaeological Society* 133, 77–97

Ellis, C. & Ritchie, M. 2018. The excavation of Na Clachan Aoraidh, a four poster stone circle in northern Perthshire. *Tayside and Fife Archaeological Journal* 24, 21–38

Ellis, L., Henry, R., Holley, R., Lawson, A.J., Reavill, P., Roberts, B., Sanigar, J. & Wilkin, N. 2013. *WILT-038191: A BRONZE AGE HOARD.* Available at: https://finds.org.uk/database/artefacts/record/id/538672 [Accessed: 28 December 2020]

Eogan, G. 1983. *Hoards of the Irish Later Bronze Age.* Dublin: University College Dublin

Evans, J. 1881. *The Ancient Bronze Implements, Weapons, and Ornaments of Great Britain and Ireland.* London: Longmans, Green and Co.

Evans Pritchard, E. 1956. *Nuer Religion.* Oxford: Oxford University Press

Everden, S. date unknown. *Bronze Axe from King's Weston Hoard.* Unpubl. report stored in Bristol Museum and Art Gallery

Faulkner-Jones, R. 2016. Experiments with the replica Friarton dirk. *Tayside and Fife Archaeological Journal* 21–22, 1–6

Fitzpatrick, A. 2007. Later Bronze Age and Iron Age. In C.J. Webster (ed.), *The Archaeology of South West England: South West Archaeological Research Framework Resource Assessment and Research Agenda*, 117–44. Taunton: Somerset Heritage Service

Fleming, A. 1988. *The Dartmoor Reaves: Investigating prehistoric land divisions.* London: Batsford

Fleming, A. 2007. *The Dartmoor Reaves: Investigating prehistoric land divisions.* (2nd edn). Oxford: Windgather Press

Fokkens, H. & Harding, A.F. (eds), 2013. *The Oxford Handbook of the European Bronze Age.* Oxford: Oxford University Press

Fontijn, D.R. 2002. Sacrificial Landscapes: cultural biographies of persons, objects and 'natural' places in the Bronze Age of the Southern Netherlands, c. 2300–600 BC. *Analecta Praehistorica Leidensia, 33/34.* Leiden: Leiden University

Fontijn, D.R. 2005. Giving up weapons. In M. Parker Pearson & I.J.N. Thorpe (eds), *Warfare, Violence and Slavery* (British Archaeological Reports International Series 1374), 145–54. Oxford: Archaeopress

Fontijn, D.R. 2008. 'Traders' Hoards. Reviewing the relationship between trade and permanent deposition: the case of the Dutch Voorhout hoard. In Hamon & Quilliec 2008, 5–17

Fontijn, D.R. 2009. Land at the other end of the sea? Metalwork circulation, geographical knowledge and the significance of British/Irish imports in the Bronze Age of the Low Countries. In P. Clark (ed.), *Bronze Age Connections: Cultural contact in Prehistoric Europe*, 129–48. Oxford: Oxbow Books

Fontijn, D.R. 2020. *Economies of Destruction.* Abingdon: Routledge

Fontijn, D.R. & Roymans, J. 2019. Branded axes, thrown into a pool? The Hoogeloon hoard and the shape-based bronze economy of the north-west European Bronze Age. *Oxford Journal of Archaeology* 38(2) 164–88

Fontijn, D.R. & van der Vaart-Verschoof, S.A. 2016. Local Elites Globalized in Death: A practice approach to Early Iron Age Hallstatt C/D Chieftains' burials in northwest Europe. In T. Hodos (ed.), *The Routledge Handbook of Archaeology and Globalization*, 522–36. London: Routledge

Fontijn, D., Theunissen, L., van Os, B. & Amkreutz, L. 2012. Decorated and 'killed'? The bronze sword of Werkhoven. In C. Bakels & H. Kamermans (eds), *Analecta Praehistorica Leidensia 43/44: The End of our Fifth Decade*, 205–13. Leiden: Leiden University

Foster, J. 1986. *The Lexden Tumulus: a reappraisal of an Iron Age burial From Colchester, Essex.* Oxford: British Archaeological Reports British Series 156

Fowler, C. 2004. *An archaeology of personhood.* Abingdon: Routledge

Fowler, C. 2013. *The Emergent Past: A relational realist archaeology of Early Bronze Age mortuary practices.* Oxford: Oxbow Books

Fowler, C. 2016. Relational personhood revisited. *Cambridge Archaeological Journal* 26(3), 397–412

Fox, A. 1957. Excavations at Dean Moor 1954–6. *Transactions of the Devonshire Association* 89, 18–77

Fox, A. 1973. *South-West England 3500BC – AD600* (2nd edn). Newton Abbot: David & Charles

Frieman, C. 2012. Going to pieces at the funeral: Completeness and complexity in Early Bronze Age jet 'necklace' assemblages. *Journal of Social Archaeology* 12(3), 334–55

Gabillot, M. 2003. *Dépôts et production métallique du Bronze moyen en France nord-occidentale.* Oxford: British Archaeological Reports S1174

Gabillot, M. & Lagarde, C. 2008. Voluntary destructions of objects in Middle and Late Bronze Age hoards in France. In Hamon & Quilliec 2008, 59–65

Gates, T. 2009. Excavation of a late second/early first millennium unenclosed roundhouse at Halls Hill, near East Woodburn, Northumberland. *Archaeologia Aeliana* 38, 43–85

Gell, A. 1998. *Art and Agency: An Anthropological Theory.* Oxford: Clarendon

Gentile, V. & van Gijn, A. 2019. Anatomy of a notch: an in-depth experimental investigation and interpretation of combat traces on Bronze Age swords. *Journal of Archaeological Science* 105, 130–43. https://doi.org/10.1016/j.jas.2019.02.004

Gerloff, S. 1975. *The Early Bronze Age Daggers in Great Britain.* Prähistorische Bronzefunde 6.2. Munich: C.H. Beck

Gerritsen, F. 2003. *Local Identities. Landscape and community in the late prehistoric Meuse- Demer-Scheldt region.* Amsterdam: Amsterdam University Press. Amsterdam Archaeological Studies 9

Giardino, C. & Verly, G. 2013. Experimental tests on sword bending. In A.M. Bietti Sestieri, L. Salzani, C. Giardino & G. Verly, Ritual treatment of weapons as a correlate of structural change in the Italian Late Bronze Age communities: The bronze hoard of Pila del Brancon (Nogara, Verona), 167–9. *Rivista di Scienze Preistoriche* LXIII, 155–69

Gibson, A. 2004. Burials and Beakers: seeing beneath the veneer in late Neolithic Britain. In J. Czebreszuk (ed.), *Similar but different: Bell Beakers in Europe*, 173–92. Poznan: Adam Mickiewicz University

Gibson, C. 2013a. Out of time but not out of place. Tempo, rhythm and dynamics of inhabitation in southern England. In A. Chadwick & C. Gibson (eds), *Memory, Myth and Long-term Landscape Inhabitation*, 99–123. Oxford: Oxbow Books

Gibson, C. 2013b. Beakers into bronze: Tracing connections between western Iberia and the British Isles 2800–800 BC. In J.T. Koch & B. Cunliffe (eds), *Celtic from the West 2. Rethinking the Bronze Age and the arrival of Indo-European in Atlantic Europe*, 71–99. Oxford: Oxbow Books

Gilchrist Clark, J. 1880. Notes on a gold lunette found at Auchentaggart, Dumfriesshire, and a massive silver chain found at Whitecleugh, Lanarkshire, exhibited by his Grace the Duke of Buccleuch. *Proceedings of the Society of Antiquaries of Scotland* 14 (1879–80), 222–4

Giles, M. 2012. *A Forged Glamour. Landscape, Identity and Material Culture in the Iron Age*. Oxford: Windgather Press

Giles, M. 2015. Performing Pain, Performing Beauty: Dealing with difficult death in the Iron Age. *Cambridge Archaeological Journal* 25(3), 539–50

Gingell, C.J. 1991. The metalwork and Bronze Age burial goods. In P.J. Woodward, *The South Dorset Ridgeway. Survey and excavations 1977–84*, 102–104. Dorchester: Dorset Natural History and Archaeological Society Monograph No.8

Girke, F. & Pankhurst, A. 2011. Evoking peace and arguing harmony: An example of transcultural rhetoric in Southern Ethiopia. In C. Meyer & F. Girke (eds), *The Rhetorical Emergence of Culture*, 225–50. New York: Berghahn Books

Gomez de Soto J. 2015. Les haches à douilles de type armoricain: une production strictement de l'âge du Fer. Critique des sources documentaires afférant à leur chronologie. *Bulletin de la société préhistorique française* 112(1), 117–36

Gomez de Soto J., Marcigny C., Menez Y., Ghesquière E., Verron G. & Bourhis J.-R. 2009. Pour en finir avec le Bronze Final? Les haches à douille de type armoricain en France. In P. Barral & M.-J. Lambert (eds), *De l'âge du Bronze à l'âge du Fer en Europe occidentale (Xe – VIIe siècle av. J.-C.). La moyenne vallée du Rhône aux âges du Fer, Mai 2006, Saint-Romain-en-Gal, France*, 507–12. Dijon: RAE (Supplément à la *Revue archéologique de l'Est*, 27)

Gosden, C. & Marshall, Y. 1999. The cultural biography of objects. *World Archaeology* 31(2), 169–78

Gossip, J. 2005. Richard Lander School Development, Threemilestone, Cornwall: Archaeological Recording: Archive Report. Truro: Cornwall Council Historic Environment Service, Unpubl. report

Gossip, J. 2008. Excavations at Boden Vean, Manaccan 2008. *CBA Archaeology South-West Journal* 22, 29–31

Gossip, J. 2011. North Cornwall Sewage Treatment Works, Trevalga, North Cornwall: Excavation of a Late Bronze Age Roundhouse: Archive Report. Truro: Cornwall Council Historic Environment Service, Unpubl. report

Gossip, J. 2013. The evaluation of a multi-period prehistoric site and fogou at Boden Vean, St Anthony-in-Meneage, Cornwall, 2003. *Cornish Archaeology* 52, 1–98

Gossip, J. in press. Life outside the Round: Bronze Age and Iron Age settlement at Higher Besore and Truro College, 2004–5. In A.M. Jones & G. Kirkham (eds), *Later prehistoric settlement in Cornwall and the Isles of Scilly: Evidence from five excavations*. Oxford: Archaeopress

Gray, H.S.G. 1908. Report on the Wick Barrow Excavations, Part II. *Proceedings of the Somerset Archaeological and Natural History Society* 54, 1–78

Gray, H.S.G. 1932. Additions to the museum. *Proceedings of the Somerset Archaeological and Natural History Society* 78, lxxv–lxxxiii

Green, H.S. 1983. A Late Bronze Age gold hoard from Llanarmon-yn-Iâl, Clwyd. *The Antiquaries Journal* 63, 384–7

Green, M. 1986. Excavations in Home Field, Down Farm, Gussage St Michael. *Proceedings of the Dorset Natural History and Archaeology Society* 108, 171–3

Greeves, T. 2019. Dartmoor's sacred pools. Design in the prehistoric landscape. *Dartmoor Magazine* 137, 24–26

Grinsell, L.V. 1959. *Dorset Barrows*. Dorchester: Dorchester Natural History and Archaeological Society

Grinsell, L.V. 1961. The breaking of objects as a funerary rite. *Folklore* 72(3), 475–91

Grinsell, L.V. 1973. The breaking of objects as a funerary rite: Supplementary notes. *Folklore* 8(2), 111–14

Gutiérrez Sáez, C. & Martín Lerma, I. 2015. Traceology on metal. Use-wear marks on copper-based tools and weapons. In J.M. Marreiros, J.F. Gibaja Bao & N.F. Bicho (eds), *Use-wear and Residue Analysis in Archaeology*, 171–88. Springer International Publishing

Gutiérrez Sáez, C. & Soriano Llopis, I. 2008. La funcionalidad sobre material metálico. Bases y aplicaciones de estudio. In S. Rovira, M. García Heras, M. Gener, & I. Montero Ruiz (eds), *Actas del VII Congreso Ibérico de Arqueometría*, 432–47. Madrid: CSIC

Gwilt, A. 2003a. A Late Bronze Age Hoard from St. Nicholas, Vale of Glamorgan. Unpubl. report, Amgueddfa Cymru – National Museum Wales.

Gwilt, A. 2003b. A Late Bronze Age Hoard from Glascoed, Monmouthshire. Unpubl. report, Amgueddfa Cymru – National Museum Wales

Gwilt, A. 2004. Late Bronze Age societies (1150–600BC). Tools and weapons. In M. Aldhouse-Green & R. Howell (eds), *The Gwent County History Volume I; Gwent in Prehistory and Early History*, 111–39. Cardiff: University of Wales Press

Gwilt, A. & Lodwick, M. 2005. Treasure Case 05.15 (Wales) A Late Bronze Age hoard from Llancarfan I, Vale of Glamorgan. Unpubl. treasure report, Amgueddfa Cymru – National Museum Wales

Gwilt, A., Kucharski, K., Silvester, R. & Davis, M. 2005. A Late Bronze Age hoard from Trevalyn Farm, Rossett, Wrexham, with some observations on hoarding practice and gold bracelet weights. *Studia Celtica* 39, 27–61

Gwilt, A., Lodwick, M. & Davis, M. 2007. Burton, Wrexham: Middle Bronze Age hoard of gold adornments and bronze tools with a pot (04.2). In *Treasure Annual Report 2004*, 198–9. Department of Culture, Media and Sport

Gwilt, A., Lodwick, M. & Davis, M. 2014. Treasure Act 1996 (Case 13.01 Wales) A Late Bronze Age Hoard from Marloes & St Brides, Pembrokeshire. Unpubl. treasure report, Amgueddfa Cymru – National Museum Wales

Gwilt, A. Lodwick, M., Schlee, D., Poucher, P. & Davis, M. 2011. Treasure Act 1996 (Case 10.12 Wales) A Late Bronze Age hoard from Manorbier, Pembrokeshire. Unpubl. treasure report, Amgueddfa Cymru – National Museum Wales

Gwilt, A. Lodwick, M. & Worrell, S. 2013. Reporting finds, sharing treasures: Bronze Age metalwork discoveries from Wales. *PAST The Newsletter of the Prehistoric* Society 75 (October 2013), 10–12

Gwilt, A.T., Lodwick, M., Deacon, J., Wells., N, Madgwick, R. & Young, T. 2016. Ephemeral Abundance at Llanmaes: Exploring the residues and resonances of an Earliest Iron Age midden and its associated archaeological context in the Vale of Glamorgan. In J. Koch & B. Cunliffe (eds), *Celtic from the West 3*, 277–303. Oxford: Oxbow

Hall, M. & Gingell, C. 1974. Nottingham Hill, Gloucestershire, 1972. *Antiquity* 48 (192), 306–9

Hamon, C. & Quilliec, B. (eds), 2008. Hoards from the *Neolithic to the Metals Ages in Europe: Technical and codified practices, Annual meeting of the EAA, 2005, Cork, Ireland*, British Archaeological Reports S1758. Oxford: Archaeopress

Hansen, S. 1991. *Studien zu den Metalldeponierungen während der Urnenfelderzeit im Rhein-Main-Gebiet* (Universitätsforschungen zur prähistorischen Archäeologie 5). Bonn: Habelt

Hansen, S. 1994. *Studien zu den Metalldeponierungen während der älteren Urnenfelderzeit zwischen Rhônetal und Karpatenbecken* (Universitätsforschungen zur prähistorischen Archäeologie 21). Bonn: Habelt

Hansen, S. 1998. Migration und Kommunikation während der späten Bronzezeit. Die Depots als Quelle für ihren Nachweis. *Dacia N. S.* 40–42 (1996–98), 5–28

Hansen, S. 2012. Deposition in the Bronze Age. *Archaeological Dialogues* 19(2), 127–9

Hansen, S. 2013. Bronze Age hoards and their role in social structure: A case study from South-West Zealand. In S. Bergergrant & S. Sabatini (eds), *Counterpoint: Essays in Archaeology and Heritage Studies in Honour of Professor Kristian Kristiansen*, 179–91. Oxford: British Archaeological Reports S2508

Hansen, S. 2016. A short history of fragments in hoards of the Bronze Age. In H. Baitinger (ed.), *Materielle Kultur und Identität im spannungsfeld zwischen Mediterraner Welt und Mitteleuropa,* 185–208. Mainz: Verlag des Römisch-Germanischen Zentralmuseums

Hardaker, R. 1974. *Early Bronze Age Dagger Pommels.* Oxford: British Archaeological Reports 3

Harding, A.F. 2000. *European Societies in the Bronze Age.* Cambridge: Cambridge University Press

Harding, A.F. 2007. *Warriors and Weapons in Bronze Age Europe.* Budapest: Archaeolingua

Harding, A.F. 2013. Trade and exchange. In Fokkens & Harding 2013, 370–81

Harding, A.F. 2021. *Bronze Age Lives.* Berlin: de Gruyter

Harding, D.W., Blake, I. M. & Reynolds, P.J. 1993. *An Iron Age Settlement in Dorset: Excavation and Reconstruction.* Edinburgh: University of Edinburgh, Department of Archaeology Monograph Series

Hardman, J. 2016. An investigation into the fragmentation of archaeological tin bronze. Unpubl. undergraduate thesis, Cardiff University

Hawkes, C.F.C. 1932. The Towednack gold hoard. *Man* XXXII, 177–86

Hawkes, C.F.C. & Smith, M.A. (eds), 1955. *Inventaria Archaeologica* 2nd Set: GB.9–13. London: The Trustees of the British Museum

Helms, M.W. 2012. Nourishing a structured world with living metal in Bronze Age Europe. *World Art* 2(1), 105–18. https://doi.org/10.1080/21500894.2012.662173

Hencken, H.O. 1932. *The Archaeology of Cornwall and Scilly.* London: Methuen & Co. Ltd

Hermann, R., Crellin, R.J., Uckelmann, M., Wang, Q. & Dolfini, A. 2020a. *Bronze Age combat: an experimental approach.* Oxford: British Archaeological Reports S2967

Hermann, R., Dolfini, A., Crellin, R.J., Wang, Q. & Uckelmann, M. 2020b. Bronze Age swordsmanship: New insights from experiments and wear analysis. *Journal of Archaeological Method and Theory* 27, 1040–83. https://doi.org/10.1007/s10816-020-09451-0

Herring, P. 2000. *St Michael's Mount, Cornwall, reports on archaeological works, 1995–8.* Truro: Cornwall County Council

Hinds, K. 2011. *WILT-A74356: A BRONZE AGE HOARD.* Available at: https://finds.org.uk/database/artefacts/record/id/473204 [Accessed: 4 April 2021]

Hingley, R. 2009. Esoteric knowledge? Ancient bronze artefacts from Iron Age contexts. *Proceedings of the Prehistoric Society* 75, 143–65

Hoffman, C.R. 1999. Intentional damage as technological agency: Breaking metals in late prehistoric Spain. In M.-A. Dobres & C.R. Hoffman (eds), *The Social Dynamics of Technology: Practice, Politics, and World View*, 103–23. Washington, DC: Smithsonian Institution Press

Hood, A.A. 1873. In Proceedings. *Proceedings of the Society of Antiquaries of London* 5 (1870–3), 427–8

Hook, D. & Needham, S.P. 1989. A comparison of recent analyses of British Late Bronze Age goldwork with Irish parallels. *Jewellery Studies* 3, 15–24

Horn, C. 2011. Deliberate destruction of halberds. In Uckelmann & Mödlinger 2011, 53–65

Horn, C. 2013a. Weapons, fighters and combat: spears and swords in Early Bronze Age Scandinavia. *Danish Journal of Archaeology* 2(1), 1–25

Horn, C. 2013b. Ein alt-gefundener Stabdolch aus der Umgebung von Stolpe (Kr. Plön) am Stolper See. *Das Altertum* 58 (2), 81–98

Horn, C. 2015. Combat and change: Remarks on Early Bronze Age spears from Sweden. In P. Suchowska-Ducke, S.S. Reiter & H. Vandkilde (eds), *Forging Identities. The Mobility of Culture in Bronze Age Europe*, 2 volumes, 201–12. Oxford: British Archaeological Reports S2771

Horn, C. 2017. Combat and ritual — Wear analysis on metal halberds from the Danish Isles and the Cimbrian Peninsula. *Journal of Archaeological Science: Reports* 14, 515–29

Horn, C. & Karck, T. 2019. Weapon and tool use during the Nordic Bronze Age. *Danish Journal of Archaeology* 8, 1–20. https://doi.org/10.7146/dja.v8i0.111834

Horn, C. & von Holstein, I.C.C. 2017. Dents in our confidence: the interaction of damage and material properties in interpreting use-wear on copper-alloy weaponry. *Journal of Archaeological Science* 81, 90–100

Hughes, G. 2000, *The Lockington Gold Hoard. An Early Bronze Age barrow cemetery at Lockington, Leicestershire.* Oxford: Oxbow Books

Hunter, F. 1997. Iron Age hoarding in Scotland and northern England. In A. Gwilt & C. Haselgrove (eds), *Reconstructing Iron Age Societies: New Approaches to the British Iron Age* (Oxbow Monograph 71), 108–33. Oxford: Oxbow Books

Hurcombe, L. 2020. Experiments within experiments. Available at: https://www.youtube.com/watch?v=qW1bj-IVd-Q [Accessed 11 May 2020]

Huth, C. 1997. *Westeuropäische Horte Der Spätbronzezeit Fundbild Und Funktion*. Bonn: Universitätsverlag Regensburg GMBH

Huth, C. 2003. Poor Belgium, rich Belgium. Reflections on the nature of metalwork depositions in the Late Bronze Age and Early Iron Age. In J. Bourgeois & I. Bourgeois (eds), *Exchange and interactions. The role of the Scheldt and Meuse during the Bronze Age and the Iron Age*, 39–60. Brussels: Vlaams Kennis- en Cultuurforum

Ialongo, N. 2019. The earliest balance weights in the west: Towards an independent metrology for Bronze Age Europe. *Cambridge Archaeological Journal* 29(1), 103–24. doi: 10.1017/S0959774318000392

Ialongo, N & Lago, G. 2021. A small change revolution. Weight systems and the emergence of the first Pan-European money. *Journal of Archaeological Science* 129. https://doi.org/10.1016/j.jas.2021.105379

Johnson, N. 1980. Later Bronze Age Settlement in the South-West. In J.C. Barrett & R. Bradley (eds), *Settlement and Society in the British Later Bronze Age*, 141–80. Oxford: British Archaeological Reports 83

Johnston, R. 2021. *Bronze Age worlds: A social prehistory of Britain and Ireland*. London: Routledge

Jones, A.M. [Andy] 2005. *Cornish Bronze Age Ceremonial Landscapes c. 2500–1500BC* (British Archaeological Reports British Series 394). Oxford: BAR Publishing

Jones, A. [Meirion] 2007. *Memory and Material Culture*. Cambridge: Cambridge University Press

Jones, A.M. [Andy] 2008. Houses for the dead and cairns for the living; A reconsideration of the Early to Middle Bronze Age transition in south-west England. *Oxford Journal of Archaeology* 27, 153–74. https://doi.org/10.1111/j.1468-0092.2008.00302.x

Jones, A. Meirion, 2010a. Layers of meaning: Concealment, containment, memory and secrecy in the British Early Bronze Age. In D. Borić (ed.), *Archaeology and Memory*, 105–20. Oxford: Oxbow Books

Jones, A. Meirion, 2010b. Burning matters: Memory, violence and monumentality in the British Neolithic. In K.T. Lillios & V. Tsamis (eds), *Material Mnemonics: Everyday memory in prehistoric Europe*, 85–102. Oxford: Oxbow Books

Jones, A.M. [Andy] 2011. Without Wessex: the local character of the Early Bronze Age in the south west peninsula. In S.M. Pearce (ed.), *Recent Archaeological Work in South-Western Britain: Papers in honour of Henrietta Quinnell* (British Archaeological Reports British Series 548), 61–74. Oxford: Archaeopress

Jones, A.M. [Andy] 2012a. Going west: ceremony, barrows and cairns in the south west peninsula. In W.J. Britnell & R.J. Silvester (eds), *Reflections on the Past: Essays in honour of Frances* Lynch, 172–93. Welshpool: Cambrian Archaeological Association

Jones, A. [Meirion] 2012b. *Prehistoric Materialities: Becoming Material in Prehistoric Britain and Ireland*. Oxford: Oxford University Press

Jones, A.M. [Andy] 2013. Memory, myth, place and landscape inhabitation: a perspective from the south-west peninsula. In A. Chadwick & C. Gibson (eds), *Memory, Myth and Long-term Landscape Inhabitation*, 55–75. Oxford: Oxbow Books

Jones, A.M. [Andy] 2015. Discussion: pits, deposition, metalworking and circularity. In A.M. Jones, J. Gossip & H. Quinnell, H. (eds), *Settlement and Metalworking in the Middle Bronze Age and beyond: New evidence from Tremough, Cornwall*, 159–225. Leiden: Sidestone Press

Jones, A.M. [Andy] & Kirkham, G. 2019. Inscribing the landscape and hiding in plain view. In A.M. Jones, *Excavation of later prehistoric and Roman sites along the roue of the Newquay Strategic Road Corridor, Cornwall*, 115–45. Oxford: Archaeopress

Jones, A.M. [Andy] & Knight, M.G. forthcoming. A landscape of deposition. In A.M. Jones & M.J. Allen, *Exploration of a drowning landscape*. Oxford.

Jones A.M. [Andy] & Quinnell, H. 2008. The Farway Barrow complex in East Devon revisited', *Proceedings of the Devon Archaeological Society* 66, 27–57

Jones, A.M. [Andy] & Quinnell, H. 2011. The Neolithic and Bronze Age in Cornwall, *c.* 4000 cal BC to *c.* 1000 cal BC: an overview of recent developments. *Cornish Archaeology* 50, 197–229

Jones, A.M. [Andy] & Quinnell, H. 2013. Daggers in the West: Early Bronze Age Daggers and Knives in the South-west Peninsula. *Proceedings of the Prehistoric Society* 79, 165–91

Jones, A.M. [Andy] & Quinnell, H. 2015. The copper-alloy objects. In A.M. Jones, J. Gossip & H. Quinnell, (eds), *Settlement and Metalworking in the Middle Bronze Age and beyond: New evidence from Tremough, Cornwall*, 102–5. Leiden: Sidestone Press

Jones, A.M. [Andy] & Taylor, S.R. 2010. *Scarcewater, Pennance, Cornwall: Archaeological excavation of a Bronze Age and Roman landscape*. Oxford: British Archaeological Reports 516

Kienlin, T. & Ottaway, B.S. 1998. Flanged axes of the North-Alpine region: an assessment of the possibilities of use-wear analysis on metal artefacts. In C. Mordant, M. Pernot & V. Rychner (eds), *L'Atelier du bronzier en Europe du XXe au VIIIe siècle avant notre ère: Du mineral au metal du métal à l'objet*, 271–86. Paris: CTHS (Documents préhistoriques 10)

Kirwan, R. 1870. Notes on the prehistoric archaeology of East Devon Part III. *Report and Transactions of the Devonshire Association for the Advancement of Science, Literature and Art* 4, Part I, 295–304

Knight, M. 2021. Inventories of Routine from Must Farm. Available at: https://www.youtube.com/watch?v=c0oOaDlvMPo. [Accessed: 8 July 2021]

Knight, M.G. 2014. Masters of Mysteries or Haphazard Handymen? An assessment of the evidence for metalworkers at Bronze Age settlements in Cornwall and Devon, south-western England. *Trowel* XV, 29–41

Knight, M.G. 2017. The deliberate destruction of Late Bronze Age socketed axeheads in Cornwall. *Cornish Archaeology* 56, 203–24

Knight, M.G. 2018. The Intentional Destruction and Deposition of Bronze Age Metalwork in South West England. Unpubl. PhD thesis, University of Exeter

Knight, M.G. 2019a. Going to Pieces: Investigating the deliberate destruction of Late Bronze Age swords and spearheads. *Proceedings of the Prehistoric Society* 85, 251–72

Knight, M.G. 2019b. Doubtful associations? Assessing Bronze Age 'multi-period' hoards from northern England, Scotland and Wales. In M.G. Knight, D. Boughton, & R.E. Wilkinson (eds), 2019. *Objects of the Past in the Past. Investigating the significance of earlier artefacts in later contexts,* 19–41, Oxford: Archaeopress (Access Archaeology)

Knight, M.G. 2021. There's method in the fragments: A Damage Ranking System for Bronze Age metalwork. *European Journal of Archaeology* 24(1), 48–67. https://doi.org/10.1017/eaa.2020.21

Knight, M.G. forthcoming a. Putting 'out-of-time' metalwork in its place: commemorating and forgetting traditions through the Bronze Age metalwork of Southern Britain. In C. Gibson, D. Brown, & J. Pyzel (eds), *Making and Unmaking Memories. Mundane Mnemonics, Artificial Amnesia and Transformed Traditions.* Oxford: Archaeopress

Knight, M.G. forthcoming b. Accumulations over time. Recognising time-depth in Bronze Age and Iron Age metalwork hoards in Britain. In E. Durham, I. Bertrand, J. Hall, J. Keily & M.G. Knight (eds), *Hoarding and Deposition in Europe from Later Prehistory to the Medieval Period. Finds in Context.* Instrumentum Monographies Series

Knight, M. & Brudenell, M. 2020. *Pattern and process: Landscape prehistories from Whittlesey Brick Pits: the King's Dyke & Bradley Fen excavations 1998–2004.* Cambridge: McDonald Institute for Archaeological Research. Accessible via: https://doi.org/10.17863/CAM.55585

Knight, M.G. & Chandler, B. 2018. Two recent Bronze Age finds in Torquay Museum. *Proceedings of the Devon Archaeological Society* 76, 77–84

Knight, M.G., Boughton, D. & Wilkinson, R.E. (eds), 2019. *Objects of the Past in the Past. Investigating the significance of earlier artefacts in later contexts.* Oxford: Archaeopress (Access Archaeology)

Knight, M.G., Boughton, D. & Northover, J.P. 2021. Poolewe: The last Bronze Age hoard in Scotland? *Archaeological Journal* 178(1), 1–31. doi: 10.1080/00665983.2020.1824883

Knight, M.G., Ormrod, T. & Pearce, S. 2015. *The Bronze Age metalwork of south-western Britain.* Oxford: British Archaeological Reports 610

Kopytoff, I. 1986. The cultural biography of things: commodities as process. In A. Appadurai (ed.), *The Social Life of Things: Commodities in cultural perspective,* 64–91. Cambridge: Cambridge University Press

Kristiansen, K. 1987. Early Bronze Age burial finds. In K. Kristiansen (ed.), *Archaeological Formation Processes: the representativity of archaeological remains from Danish Prehistory,* 116–28. Copenhagen: Nationalmuseets Forlag

Kristiansen, K. 1999. Understanding Bronze Age weapon hoards: observations from the Zalkod and Vaja hoards, Northeastern Hungary. *Jósa András Múzeum Évkönyve* 41, 101–7

Kristiansen, K. 2002. The tale of the sword – swords and swordfighters in Bronze Age Europe. *Oxford Journal of Archaeology* 21(4), 319–32

Küchler, S. 1987. Malangan: Art and memory in a Melanesian society. *Man* 22(2), 238–55

Küchler, S. 2002. *Malanggan. Art, Memory and Sacrifice.* Oxford: Berg

Kuijpers, M.H.G. 2013. The sound of fire, taste of copper, feel of bronze, and colours of the cast: sensory aspects of metalworking technology. In M.L. Stig-Sørensen & K. Rebay-Salisbury (eds), *Embodied Knowledge. Perspectives on belief and technology,* 137–50. Oxford: Oxbow Books

Kuijpers, M.H.G. 2018. *An Archaeology of Skill. Metalworking skill and material specialization in Early Bronze Age Central Europe.* Abingdon: Routledge

Kuijpers, M.H.G. & Popa, C.N. 2021. The origins of money: Calculation of similarity indexes demonstrates the earliest development of commodity money in prehistoric Central Europe. *PLoS ONE* 16(1), e0240462. https://doi.org/10.1371/journal.pone.0240462

Ladle, L. 2018. *Multi-period occupation at Football Field, Worth Matravers, Dorset. Excavations 2006–2011.* Oxford: British Archaeological Reports British Series 643

Ladle, L. & Woodward, A. 2009. *Excavations at Bestwall Quarry, Wareham 1992–2005. Volume 1: The Prehistoric Landscape.* Dorchester: Dorset Natural History and Archaeological Society Monograph Series no.19

Lahiri, N. 1995. Indian metal and metal-related artefacts as cultural signifiers: an ethnographic perspective. *World Archaeology* 27(1), 116–32

Larsson, L. 2000. The passage of axes: fire transformation of flint objects in the Neolithic of southern Sweden. *Antiquity* 74, 602–10

Lawson, A.J. 2000. *Potterne, 1982–5: Animal husbandry in late Prehistoric Wiltshire.* Salisbury: Wessex Archaeology

Lawson, A.L. 2018. *Late Bronze Age Hoards: New Light on Old Norfolk Finds* (East Anglian Archaeology 166). Dereham: Historic Environment Service, Norfolk County Council

Lawson, A.J. & Farwell, D.E. 1990. Archaeological investigation following the discovery of a hoard of palstaves near New Inn Farmhouse, Marnhull, Dorset. *Proceedings of the Dorset Natural History and Archaeological Society* 112, 131–38

Le Carlier C. & Marcigny C. 2011. Nouveaux travaux sur les dépôts de l'âge du Bronze dans la Manche. *Bulletin du Groupe de Recherches Archéologiques du Cotentin* 14 (Janvier 2011), 28–31

Lemonnier, P. 1984. The Study of Material Culture Today: Toward an anthropology of technical systems. *Journal of Anthropological Archaeology* 5, 147–86

Levy, J.E. 1982. *Social and religious organization in Bronze Age Denmark. An analysis of ritual hoard finds* (British Archaeological Reports International Series 124). Oxford: British Archaeological Reports

Levy, J.E. 2010. Memory, landscape, and body in Bronze Age Denmark. In K.T. Lillios & V. Tsamis (eds), *Material Mnemonics: Everyday memory in prehistoric Europe,* 123–46. Oxford: Oxbow Books

Lillios, K.T. 1999. Objects of memory: The ethnography and archaeology of heirlooms. *Journal of Archaeological Method and Theory* 6(3), 235–62

Locock, M. 2001. A Later Bronze Age landscape on the Avon Levels: settlement, shelters and saltmarsh at Cabot Park. In J. Brück (ed.), *Bronze Age Landscapes: Tradition and Transformation,* 121–8. Oxford: Oxbow Books

Lodwick, M. 2002. A Late Bronze Age Hoard from

Llangwm, Monmouthshire. Unpubl. report, Amgueddfa Cymru – National Museum Wales

Lodwick, M. & Gwilt, A. 2002. A Late Bronze Age Hoard from 'near Cowbridge' Vale of Glamorgan. Unpubl. report, Amgueddfa Cymru – National Museum Wales

Lynch, F. 1971. Report on the re-excavation of two Bronze Age cairns in Anglesey: Bedd Branwen and Treiorwerth. *Archaeologia Cambrensis* 120, 11–83

Lynch, F. 1991. *Prehistoric Anglesey* (2nd edn). Llangefni: The Anglesey Antiquarian Society

Madgwick, R. & Mulville, J. 2015. Feasting on Forelimbs: Conspicuous consumption and identity in later prehistoric Britain. *Antiquity* 89(345), 629–44

Maraszek, R. 2000. Late Bronze Age axe hoards in western and northern Europe. In C.F.E. Pare (ed.), *Metals Make the World Go Round: The supply and circulation of metals in Bronze Age Europe*, 209–24. Oxford: Oxbow Books

Maraszek, R. 2006. *Spätbronzezeitliche Hortfundlandschaften in atlantischer und nordischer Metalltradition.* Halle: Landesamt für Denkmalpflege und Archäologie Sachsen-Anhalt, Landesmuseum fur Vorgeschichte

Marshall, A. 2011. *Experimental Archaeology: 1. Early Bronze Age Cremation Pyres; 2. Iron Age Grain Storage* (British Archaeological Reports British Series 530). Oxford: Archaeopress

Marshall, L. 1965. The !Kung Bushmen of the Kalahari Desert. In J.L. Gibbs (ed.), *Peoples of Africa*, 241–78. New York: Holt, Rinehart, and Winston

Mattingly, J., Marley, J. & Jones, A.M. 2009. Five gold rings? Early Bronze Age gold lunulae from Cornwall. Journal of the Royal Institution of Cornwall 48, 95–114

Mauss, M. 1990. *The Gift.* Translated from French by W.D. Halls. London: Routledge

May, J. 1976. *Prehistoric Lincolnshire.* Lincoln: History of Lincolnshire Committee

Maybury-Lewis, D. 1974 [1967]. *Akwẽ-Shavante Society.* Oxford: Oxford University Press

McCulloch, W.T. 1864. Notes respecting two bronze shields recently purchased for the museum of the society; and other bronze shields. *Proceedings of the Society of Antiquaries of Scotland* 5 (1862–64), 165–8

McGrail, S. 1993. Prehistoric seafaring in the Channel. In C. Scarre & F. Healy (eds), *Trade and Exchange in Prehistoric Europe*, 199–210. Oxford: Oxbow Books

McKinley, J.I. 1997. Bronze Age 'Barrows' and funerary rites and rituals of cremation. *Proceedings of the Prehistoric Society* 63, 129–45

McKinley, J.I. 2006. Cremation… the cheap option? In R. Gowland & C. Knüsel, (eds), *Social Archaeology of Funerary Remains*, 81–8. Oxford. Oxbow Books

McNeil, R. 1973. A report on the Bronze Age hoard from Wick Park, Stogursey, Somerset. *Proceedings of the Somerset Archaeological and Natural History Society* 117, 47–64

McOmish, D. 1996. East Chisenbury: Ritual and Rubbish at the British Bronze Age Iron Age Transition. *Antiquity* 70 (267), 68–76. doi:10.1017/S0003598X00082892

McOmish, D., Field, D. & Brown, G. 2010. The Late Bronze Age and Early Iron Age Midden Site at East Chisenbury, Wiltshire. *Wiltshire Archaeological & Natural History Magazine* 103, 35–101

Melheim, L. & Horn, C. 2014. Tales of hoards and swordfighters in Early Bronze Age Scandinavia: The brand new and the broken. *Norwegian Archaeological Review*, 1–24

Mercer, R. & Healy, F. 2008. *Hambledon Hill, Dorset, England. Excavation and survey of a Neolithic monument complex and its surrounding landscape. Volume 1.* Swindon: English Heritage Archaeological Reports

Miket, R. 1985. Ritual Enclosures at Whitton Hill, Northumberland. *Proceedings of the Prehistoric Society* 51(1), 137–48. doi: 10.1017/S0079497X00007064

Milcent, P.-Y. 1998. Le Petit-Villatte à Neuvy-sur-Barangeon (Cher): Lecture d'un dépôt complexe. In C. Mordant, M. Pernot & V. Rychner (eds), *L'Atelier du bronzier en Europe du XXe au VIIIe siècle avant notre ère. Tome III: Production, circulation et consummation du bronze*, 55–70. Paris: Comité des travaux historiques et scientifiques

Minnitt, S.C. & Payne, N. 2012. A hoard of Middle Bronze Age gold ornaments from Priddy, Somerset. In J.R. Trigg (ed.), *Of Things Gone but Not Forgotten. Essay in archaeology for Joan Taylor*, British Archaeological Reports S2434, 109–14. Oxford: British Archaeological Reports Publishing

Mizoguchi, K. 1993. Time in the reproduction of mortuary practices. *World Archaeology* 25(2), 223–35

Molloy, B.P.C. 2006. The role of combat weaponry in Bronze Age societies: the cases of the Aegean and Ireland in the Middle and Late Bronze Age. Unpubl. PhD Thesis, University College Dublin.

Molloy, B.P.C. 2007. What's the Bloody Point?: Bronze Age swordsmanship in Ireland and Britain. In B. Molloy (ed.), *The Cutting Edge: Studies in Ancient and Medieval Combat*, 90–111. Stroud: Tempus

Molloy, B. 2009. For Gods or men? A reappraisal of the function of Bronze Age shields. *Antiquity* 83, 1052–64

Molloy, B.P.C. 2011. Use-wear analysis and use-patterns of Bronze Age swords. In Uckelmann, & Mödlinger 2011, 67–84

Molloy, B.P.C. 2017. Hunting warriors: the transformation of weapons, combat practices and society during the Bronze Age in Ireland. *European Journal of Archaeology* 20(2), 280–316

Molloy, B.P.C. 2018. Conflict at Europe's Crossroads: analysing the social life of metal weaponry in the Bronze Age Balkans. In A. Dolfini, R.J. Crellin, C. Horn & M. Uckelmann (eds), *Prehistoric Warfare and Violence. Quantitative and qualitative approaches*, 199–224. Springer International Publishing

Monaghan, J. 1994. An unenclosed Bronze Age house site at Lookout Plantation, Northumberland. *Archaeologia Aeliana* 22, 29–41

Montero-Ruiz, I. 2016. Analisis elemental de las hachas de talon. In E. Galán, O. García-Vuelta & I. Montero-Ruiz (eds.), *Hachas de talón del Museo Arqueológico Nacional. Catálogo y estudio arqueometalúrgico*, 135–57. Madrid. Ministerio de Educación, Cultura y Deporte

Mordant, C. 2013. The Bronze Age in France. In Fokkens & Harding 2013, 571–93

Mörtz, T. 2010. Spätbronzezeitliche Waffendeponierungen Großbritanniens. *Archäologische Informationen* 33(1), 153–7

Mörtz, T. 2013. Zerteiltes Leid. Anmerkungen zur Deutung mutwilliger Beschädigungen von Metalldeponierungen der späten Bronzezeit. *Mitteilungen der Berliner*

Gesellschaft für Anthropologie, Ethnologie und Urgeschichte 34, 55–66

Mörtz, T. 2014. Erz und Erzeugnis. Bemerkungen zu den Gießformen für Schwerter der späten Bronzezeit Großbritanniens. In B. Nessel, I. Heske & D. Brandherm (eds), *Ressourcen und Rohstoffe in der Bronzezeit. Nutzung – Distribution – Kontrolle*, 61–73. Wünsdorf: Brandenburgisches Landesamt für Denkmalpflege und Archäologisches Landesmuseum

Mörtz, T. 2018. Violence and ritual in Late Bronze Age Britain: Weapon depositions and their interpretation. In C. Horn & K. Kristiansen (eds), *Warfare in Bronze Age Society*, 168–88. Cambridge: Cambridge University Press

Mörtz, T., Knight, M.G., Cowie, T. & Flint, J. forthcoming. Peelhill Farm: a possible Late Bronze Age weapon sacrifice in Lanarkshire. *Proceedings of the Society of Antiquaries of Scotland* [accepted]

Moyler, S. 2007. Life on the cutting edge: interpreting patterns of wear on Scottish Early Bronze Age axes. Unpubl. PhD thesis, University of Southampton

Mullin, D. 2012. The river has never divided us: Late Bronze Age metalwork deposits in western Britain. *Oxford Journal of Archaeology* 31, 47–57

Musson, C.R. 1991. *The Breiddin Hillfort. A later prehistoric settlement in the Welsh Marches*. London: Council for British Archaeology Research Report 76

Nebelsick, L. 1997. Auf Biegen und Brechen. Ekstatische Elemente bronzezeitlicher Materialopfer – Ein Deutungsversuch. In A. Hänsel & B. Hänsel (eds), *Gaben An Die Götter. Schätze der Bronzezeit Europas*, 35–41. Berlin: Bestandskataloge Band 4

Nebelsick, L. 2000. Rent asunder: ritual violence in Late Bronze Age hoards. In C.F.E. Pare (ed.). *Metals Make the World Go Round: The supply and circulation of metals in Bronze Age Europe*, 160–75. Oxford: Oxbow Books

Needham, S. 1980. An assemblage of Late Bronze Age metalworking debris from Dainton, Devon. *Proceedings of the Prehistoric Society* 46, 177–215

Needham, S. 1981. *The Bulford-Helsbury Manufacturing Tradition*. London: British Museum Occasional Paper No.13

Needham, S.P. 1983. *The Early Bronze Age Axeheads of central and southern England*. Unpubl. PhD thesis, Cardiff University

Needham, S.P. 1988. Selective deposition in the British Early Bronze Age. *World Archaeology* 20(2), 229–48

Needham, S. 1989a. The bronze hoard. In P. Ellis, Norton Fitzwarren hillfort: A report on the excavations by Nancy and Philip Langmaid between 1968 and 1971, 29–39. *Proceedings of the Somerset Archaeological and Natural History Society* 133, 1–74

Needham, S. 1989b. The clay mould assemblage. In P. Ellis, Norton Fitzwarren hillfort: A report on the excavations by Nancy and Philip Langmaid between 1968 and 1971, 24–9. *Proceedings of the Somerset Archaeological and Natural History Society* 133, 1–74

Needham, S. 1990a. The gold bracelets and Class B1 bracelets in Britain. In M. Bell, *Brean Down Excavations 1983–1987*, 146–50. London: English Heritage Archaeological Report 15

Needham, S.P. 1990b. *The Petters Late Bronze Age Metalwork*. London: British Museum Occasional Paper No. 70

Needham, S. 1996. Chronology and periodisation in the British Bronze Age. *Acta Archaeologica* 67, 121–40

Needham, S.P. 2000a. The gold and copper metalwork. In G. Hughes, *The Lockington Gold Hoard. An Early Bronze Age barrow cemetery at Lockington, Leicestershire*, 23–47. Oxford: Oxbow Books

Needham, S.P. 2000b. Stogursey (1), Somerset: Bronze Age gold 'basket ornament'. *Treasure Annual Report 1998–1999*, 10. Department for Culture, Media and Sport

Needham, S.P. 2000c. Power pulses across a cultural divide: Cosmologically driven acquisition between Armorica and Wessex. *Proceedings of the Prehistoric Society* 66, 151–207

Needham, S. 2001. When expediency broaches ritual intention: The flow of metal between systemic and buried domains. *The Journal of the Royal Anthropological Institute* 7(2), 275–98

Needham, S.P. 2004. Migdale-Marnoch: sunburst of Scottish metallurgy. In I.A.G. Shepherd & G.J. Barclay (eds), *Scotland in Ancient Europe: The Neolithic and Early Bronze Age of Scotland in their European Context*, 217–45. Edinburgh: Society of Antiquaries of Scotland

Needham, S. 2007a. Bronze makes a Bronze Age? Considering the systemic of Bronze Age metal use and the implications of selective deposition. In C. Burgess, P. Topping & F. Lynch (eds), *Beyond Stonehenge: Essays on the Bronze Age in Honour of Colin Burgess*, 278–87. Oxford: Oxbow Books

Needham, S. 2007b. Cirencester area, Gloucestershire: Bronze Age gold and base-metal scatter (2004 T416). In *Treasure Annual Report 2004*, 26–33. Department of Culture, Media and Sport

Needham, S. 2007c. 800BC: The Great Divide. In C. Haselgrove & R. Pope (eds), *The Earlier Iron Age in Britain and the Near Continent*, 39–63. Oxford: Oxbow Books

Needham, S. 2009. Encompassing the Sea: 'Maritories' and Bronze Age maritime interactions. In P. Clark (ed.), *Bronze Age Connections: Cultural contact in Prehistoric Europe*, 12–37. Oxford: Oxbow Books

Needham, S. 2011. Gold Basket-shaped Ornaments from Graves 7291, (Amesbury Archer) and 1236. In A.P. Fitzpatrick, *The Amesbury Archer and the Boscombe Bowmen: Bell Beaker Burials at Boscombe Down, Amesbury, Wiltshire*, 129–38. Salisbury: Wessex Archaeological Report 27

Needham, S. 2017. Assemblage, structure and meaning in bronze metalwork studies: An analysis of the British Penard assemblage. *Oxford Journal of Archaeology* 36(2), 111–56

Needham, S. & Bowman, S. 2005. Flesh-hooks, technological complexity and the Atlantic Bronze Age feasting complex. *European Journal of Archaeology* 8(2), 93–136

Needham, S. & Bridgford, S. 2013. Deposits of clay refractories for casting bronze swords. In N. Brown & M. Medlycott. *The Neolithic and Bronze Age Enclosures at Springfield Lyons, Essex: Excavations 1981–1991*, 47–74. Chelmsford: East Anglian Archaeology Report No.149

Needham, S.P. & Burgess, C. 1980. The Later Bronze Age in the Lower Thames Valley: The metalwork evidence. In J.C. Barrett & R. Bradley (eds), *Settlement and Society in the British Later Bronze Age*, 437–69. Oxford: British Archaeological Reports British Series 83

Needham, S. & Sheridan, J.A. 2014. Chalcolithic and Early Bronze Age goldwork from Britain: new finds and new perspectives. In H. Meller, E. Pernicka & R. Risch (eds), *Metals of Power: Early Gold and Silver. Proceedings of the 6th Archaeological Congress of Central Germany*, 903–941. Halle: Landesmuseum für Vorgeschichte Halle (Tagungen des Landesmuseums Band 11/2)

Needham, S. & Wilkin, N. forthcoming. British ceremonial weapons revisited: a new Plougrescant-Ommerschans dirk from East Rudham, Norfolk, and its typological, geochemical and landscape context. In L. Amkreutz & D. Fontijn (eds), *The Ommerschans hoard in context*. Leiden: Papers on Archeology of the Leiden Museum of Antiquities

Needham, S. & Woodward, A. 2008. The Clandon Barrow Finery: a Synopsis of Success in an Early Bronze Age World. *Proceedings of the Prehistoric Society* 74, 1–52. doi: 10.1017/S0079497X00000128

Needham, S. & Woodward, A. 2009. Bronze Age metalworking debris: crucible and mould fragments. In L. Ladle & A. Woodward, *Excavations at Bestwall Quarry, Wareham 1992–2005. Volume 1: The Prehistoric Landscape*, 258–8. Dorchester: Dorset Natural History and Archaeological Society Monograph Series no.19

Needham, S., Lawson, A.J. & Woodward, A. 2010. 'A noble group of barrows': Bush Barrow and the Normanton Down Early Bronze Age cemetery two centuries on. *The Antiquaries Journal* 90, 1–39. https://doi.org/10.1017/S0003581510000077

Needham, S., Parfitt, K. & Varndell, G. 2006. *The Ringlemere Cup. Precious cups and the beginning of the Channel Bronze Age*. London: The British Museum

Needham, S., Parham, D. & Frieman, C.J. 2013. *Claimed by the sea: Salcombe, Langdon Bay, and other marine finds of the Bronze Age*. York: Council for British Archaeology Research Report 173

Needham, S.P., Northover, P., Uckelmann, M. & Tabor, R. 2012. South Cadbury: The last of the bronze shields? *Archäologisches Korrespondenzblatt* 42(4), 473–91

Needham, S., Ramsey, C.B., Coombs, D., Cartwright, C. & Pettitt, P. 1997. An independent chronology for British Bronze Age metalwork: The results of the Oxford radiocarbon accelerator programme. *Archaeological Journal* 154, 55–107

Nienhuis, J., Postma, H. & Creemers, G. 2013. Four remarkable socketed axes from the Geistingen hoard. In G. Creemers (ed.), *Archaeological Contributions to Materials and Immateriality*, 8–21. Tongeren: Atuatuca 4. Publications of the Gallo Roman Museum

Noble, G. 2007. *Neolithic Scotland. Timber, Stone, Earth and Fire*. Edinburgh: Edinburgh University Press

Nord, A.G., Mattsson, E. & Tronner, K. 2005. Factors influencing the long term corrosion of bronze artefacts in soil. *Protection of Metals* 41(4), 309–16

Nordez, M. 2019. *La parure en métal de l'âge du Bronze moyen atlantique* (Mémoires de la Société préhistorique française 65). Paris: Societé préhistorique française

Northover, J.P. 1980. Appendix: The analysis of Welsh Bronze Age metalwork. In H.N. Savory, *Guide Catalogue of the Bronze Age Collections*, 229–43. Cardiff: National Museum of Wales

Northover, P. 1982a. The metallurgy of the Wilburton hoards. *Oxford Journal of Archaeology* 1, 69–109. https://doi.org/10.1111/j.1468-0092.1982.tb00299.x

Northover, P. 1982b. The exploration of the long-distance movement of bronze in Bronze and Early Iron Age Europe. *Bulletin of the Institute of Archaeology* 19, 45–72

Northover, J.P. 1988. The Late Bronze Age metalwork: general discussion. In B. Cunliffe, *Mount Batten, Plymouth. A prehistoric and Roman port*, 75–85. Oxford: Oxford University Committee for Archaeology Monograph No.26

Northover, J.P. 1989. The gold torc from St. Helier, Jersey, *Annual Bulletin of the Société Jersiaise*, 25, 112–37

Northover, J.P. & Salter, C. 1990. Analysis of a hoard of copper ingots from near Torquay. Unpubl. analytical report, University of Oxford

Nowakowski, J.A. 1998. *A30 Project, Cornwall: Archaeological Investigations along the route of the Indian Queens Bypass 1992–1994, Assessment and Updated Project Design*. Truro: Cornwall Archaeological Unit

Nowakowski, J.A. 2001. Leaving home in the Cornish Bronze Age: insights into planned abandonment processes. In J. Brück (ed.), *Bronze Age Landscapes: Tradition and Transformation*, 139–48. Oxford: Oxbow Books

Nowakowski, J.A. 2007. *Excavations of a Bronze Age landscape and a post-Roman industrial settlement 1953–1961, Gwithian, Cornwall. Volume 2*. Truro: Historic Environment Service (Projects)

O'Connor, B. 1980. *Cross-Channel Relations in the Later Bronze Age (2 vols)*. Oxford: British Archaeological Reports S91

O'Connor, B. 1999. Metal assemblage. In J.C. Barrett & R.B. Gourlay, An early metal assemblage from Dail na Caraidh, Inverness-shire, and its context. *Proceedings of the Society of Antiquaries of Scotland* 129, 172–83

O'Connor, B. 2007. Llyn Fawr Metalwork in Britain: A review. In C. Haselgrove & R. Pope (eds), *The Earlier Iron Age in Britain and the Near Continent*, 64–79. Oxford: Oxbow Books

O'Connor, B. 2009. Bronze Age Metalwork. In L. Ladle & A. Woodward, *Excavations at Bestwall Quarry, Wareham 1992–2005. Volume 1: The Prehistoric Landscape*, 272–5. Dorchester: Dorset Natural History and Archaeological Society Monograph Series no.19

O'Connor, B. 2018. Bronze Age metalwork. In L. Ladle, *Multi-period occupation at Football Field, Worth Matravers, Dorset. Excavations 2006–2011*, 192–5. Oxford: British Archaeological Reports British Series 643

O'Connor, B., Roberts, B.W. & Wilkin, N. 2017. The Ornament Horizon revisited. New and old finds of Middle Bronze Age ornaments in southern England. In T. Lachenal, C. Mordant, T. Nicolas & C. Veber (eds), *Le Bronze moyen et l'origine du Bronze final en Europe occidentale, de la Mer du Nord à la Méditerranee (XVIIe-XIIIe siècle avant notre ère)*, 169–82. Strasbourg, Mémoires d'Archéologie du Grand-Est 1

O'Flaherty, R., Gilchrist, M.D. and Cowie, T. 2011. Ceremonial or deadly serious? New insight into the function of Irish Early Bronze Age halberds. In Uckelmann & Modlinger 2011, 39–52

Olalde, I., Brace, S., Allentoft, M.E., Armit, I., Kristiansen, K., Booth, T., Rohland, N. *et al.* 2018. The Beaker Phenomenon and the Genomic Transformation of Northwest Europe. *Nature* 555(7695): 190–6. doi: 10.1038/nature25738

Oliver, V.L. 1936. Bronze Age rapiers and swords from

Dorset. *Proceedings of the Dorset Natural History and Archaeological Society* 58, 26–9

Ouvry, F. 1850. Proceedings at the meetings of the Archaeological Institute. January 4, 1850. *Archaeological Journal* 7, 64–90

Owoc, M.A. 2005. From the ground up: Agency, practice, and community in the Southwestern British Bronze Age. *Journal of Archaeological Method and Theory* 12(4), 257–81

Pankhurst, A. 2006. A peace ceremony at Arbore. In I. Strecker & J. Lydall (eds), *The Perils of Face. Essays on cultural contact, respect and self-esteem in southern Ethiopia*, 247–67. Berlin: Lit Verlag

Parcero-Oubiña, C., Armada, X.-L., Nión-Álvarez, S. & Insua, F. 2019. All together now (or not). Change, resistance and resilience in the NW Iberian Peninsula in the Bronze Age-Iron Age transition. In B.X. Currás & I. Sastre (eds), *Alternative Iron Ages. Social theory from archaeological analysis*, 151–75. London: Routledge

Pare, C.F.E. 1999. Weights and weighing in Bronze Age Central Europe. In *Eliten in der Bronzezeit. Ergebnisse zweier Kolloquien in Mainz und Athen, Teil 2* (Monographien des Romisch-Germanischen Zentralmuseums Mainz, 43(2)), 421–514. Mainz: Romisch-Germanisches Zentralmuseum

Pare, C.F.E. 2013. Weighing, commodification and money. In Fokkens & Harding 2013, 508–27

Parker Pearson, M., Sheridan, J.A., Jay, M., Chamberlain, A., Richards, M.P. & Evans, J. (eds), 2019. *The Beaker People. Isotopes, mobility and diet in prehistoric Britain* (Prehistoric Society Research Paper 7). Oxford: Oxbow Books

Paton, N. 1870. Notice of two gold ornaments found at Orton on the Spey, while cutting for the railway from Elgin to Keith in 1863. *Proceedings of the Society of Antiquaries of Scotland* 8 (1868–70), 28–33

Pearce, M. 2013. The spirit of the sword and spear. *Cambridge Archaeological Journal* 23, 55–67

Pearce, S.M. 1976. The Middle and Late Bronze Age metalwork of the South West, and its relationship to settlement. *Proceedings of the Devon Archaeological Society* 34, 17–40

Pearce, S.M. 1983. *The Bronze Age metalwork of south-western Britain*. Oxford: British Archaeological Reports 120

Pearce, S.M. 2015. The moulds and metalwork. In A.M. Jones, J. Gossip & H. Quinnell, H. (eds), *Settlement and Metalworking in the Middle Bronze Age and beyond: New evidence from Tremough, Cornwall*, 89–105. Leiden: Sidestone Press

Pendleton, C.F. 1999. *Bronze Age metalwork in Northern East Anglia. A study of its distribution and interpretation*. Oxford: British Archaeological Reports British Series 279

Penhallurick, R.D. 1986. *Tin in Antiquity*. London: The Institute of Metals

Penhallurick, R.D. 1997. The evidence for prehistoric mining in Cornwall. In P. Budd & D. Gale (eds), *Prehistoric Extractive Metallurgy in Cornwall*, 23–33. Truro: Cornwall Archaeological Unit

Perea, A. 2008. Iberian Psycho: Deliberate destruction in Bronze Age gold hoards of the Iberian peninsula. In Hamon & Quilliec, 53–8

Petersen, F. 1972. Traditions of multiple burial in Neolithic and Bronze Age England. *Archaeological Journal* 129, 22–55

Pfaffenberger, B. 1992. Social Anthropology of Technology. *Annual Review of Anthropology* 21, 491–516

Pfaffenberger, B. 1999. Worlds in the making: Technology activities and the construction of intersubjective meaning. In M.-A. Dobres & C.R. Hoffman (eds), *The Social Dynamics of Technology: Practice, Politics, and World View*, 147–64. Washington, DC: Smithsonian Institution Press

Piccardo, P., Mille, B. & Robbiola, L. 2007. Tin and copper oxides in corroded archaeological bronzes. In P. Dillmann, G. Béranger, P. Piccardo & H. Matthiesen (eds), *Corrosion of metallic heritage artefacts. Investigation, conservation and prediction for long-term behaviour*, 239–62. Cambridge: Woodhead Publishing Ltd

Pollard, J. 2001. The aesthetics of depositional practice. *World Archaeology* 33(2), 315–33. DOI: 10.1080/00438240120079316

Pollard, J. 2008. Deposition and Material Agency in the Early Neolithic of Southern Britain. In B.J. Mills & W.H. Walker (eds), *Memory Work: Archaeologies of Material Practices*, 41–59. Santa Fe: School for Advanced Research Press

Powell-Cotton, P.H.G. & Crawford, O.G.S. 1924. The Birchington hoard. *The Antiquaries Journal* 4 (3), 220–6. doi: 10.1017/S0003581500005862

Poyer, A.J. 2015. *The Topographic Setting of Bronze Age Metalwork Deposits in North East England*. Unpubl. PhD thesis, University of Sheffield

Pring, J.H. 1880. On some evidences of the occupation of the Ancient Site of Taunton by the Britons. *Archaeological Journal* 37, 94–8

Primas, M. 1997. Bronze Age Economy and Ideology: Central Europe in Focus. *Journal of European Archaeology* 5(1), 115–30, doi: 10.1179/096576697800703593

Pryor, F. 2001. *The Flag Fen Basin. Archaeology and environment of a Fenland landscape*. Swindon: English Heritage Archaeological Reports

Quilliec, B. 2008. Use, wear and damage: treatment of bronze swords before deposition. In Hamon & Quilliec 2008, 67–78

Quinn, C.P., Kujit, I. & Cooney, G. 2014. Introduction: Contextualizing cremations. In I. Kuijt, C.P. Quinn & G. Cooney (eds), *Transformation by Fire. The archaeology of cremation in cultural context*, 3–21. Tucson: University of Arizona Press

Quinnell, H. 2003. Devon Beakers: New finds, new thoughts. *Proceedings of the Devon Archaeological Society* 61, 1–20

Rahmstorf, L. 2019. Scales, weights and weight-regulated artefacts in Middle and Late Bronze Age Britain. *Antiquity* 93(371), 1197–1210. https://doi.org/ 10.15184/aqy.2018.257

Rahtz, P. 1956. Kings Weston Down Camp, Bristol, 1956. *Proceedings of the University of Bristol Spelaeological Society* 8(1), 30–8

Ramsey G. 2013. A Twisted Torc. *Archaeology Ireland* 27(3) (Autumn 2013), 26–7

Raposo, M. & Wilkin, N. 2019. Treasure Report 2015T885. Available at: F. Basford, *IOW-DDE627: A IRON AGE HOARD*. Available at: https://finds.org.uk/database/artefacts/record/id/752758 [Accessed: 4 April 2021]

Ray, V.F. 1963. *Primitive Pragmatisis: The Modoc Indians of Northern California*. Seattle: University of Washington Press

Rezi, B. 2011. Voluntary destruction and fragmentation in Late Bronze Age hoards from Central Transylvania. In S. Berecki, R.E. Németh & B. Rezi (eds), *Bronze Age Rites and Rituals in the Carpathian Basin*, 303–34. Târgu Mureş: MEGA

Richardson, I. 2017. *PAS–6DBE56: A BRONZE AGE JEWELLERY.* Available at: https://finds.org.uk/database/artefacts/record/id/833749. [Accessed 4 June 2021]

Robb, J. 2010. Beyond agency. *World Archaeology* 42(4), 493–520

Robbiola, L., Blengino, J.-M. & Fiaud, C. 1998. Morphology and mechanisms of formation of natural patinas on archaeological Cu-Sn alloys. *Corrosion Science* 40 (12), 2083–2111. https://doi.org/ 10.1016/S0010–938X(98)00096–1

Robbins, K. 2008. *NMS-A369A6: A BRONZE AGE PIN.* Available at: https://finds.org.uk/database/artefacts/record/id/241652 [Accessed: 27 September 2020]

Roberts, B.W. 2007. Adorning the living but not the dead: Understanding ornaments in Britain *c.* 1400–1100 cal BC. *Proceedings of the Prehistoric Society* 73, 135–67. doi: 10.1017/S0079497X00027328

Roberts, B.W. 2013. Britain and Ireland in the Bronze Age: Farmers in the landscape or heroes on the high seas? In Fokkens & Harding 2013, 531–49

Roberts, B.W. & Ottaway, B.S. 2003. The use and significance of socketed axes during the Late Bronze Age *European Journal of Archaeology* 6(2), 119–40

Roberts, B.W., Boughton, D., Dinwiddy, M., Doshi, N., Fitzpatrick, A.P., Hook, D., Meeks, N., Mongiatti, A., Woodward, A. & Woodward, P.J. 2015. Collapsing commodities or lavish offerings? Understanding massive metalwork deposition at Langton Matravers, Dorset, during the Bronze Age-Iron Age transition. *Oxford Journal of Archaeology* 34(4), 365–95

Roffey, S., Wilkinson, K. & Webster, C.J., 2004. Kingston St. Mary, Ivyton farm, 107–8. In T.S. Bagwell & C.J. Webster (eds), Somerset archaeology, 2004. *Proceedings of the Somerset Archaeological and Natural History Society* 148, 103–37

Rohl, B. & Needham, S. 1998. *The circulation of metal in the British Bronze Age: The application of lead isotope analysis.* London: British Museum Occasional Paper No.102

Rowlands, M.J. 1971. The archaeological interpretation of prehistoric metalworking. *World Archaeology* 3(2), 210–24

Rowlands, M.J. 1976. *The Organisation of Middle Bronze Age Metalworking.* Oxford: British Archaeological Reports 31

Rowlands, M.J. 1993. The role of memory in the transmission of culture. *World Archaeology* 25(2), 141–51

Russell, M., 2002. Excavations at Mile Oak Farm. In D. Rudling, *Downland Settlement and Land-use: the Archaeology of the Brighton Bypass*, 5–81. London: Archetype Publications

Sanford, W.A. 1865–6. Notice of a burial by cremation of the bronze period in the parish of West Buckland. *Proceedings of the Somerset Archaeological and Natural History Society* 13, 261–2

Savory, H.N. 1958. The Late Bronze Age in Wales. Some new discoveries and new interpretations. *Archaeologia Cambrensis* 107, 3–63

Savory, H.N. 1977. A new hoard of Bronze Age gold ornaments from Wales. *Archaeologia Atlantica* 2, 37–53

Schmidt, P.K. & Burgess, C.B. 1981. *The Axes of Scotland and Northern England.* Prähistoriche Bronzefunde 9.7. Munich: C.H. Beck

Scott, D.A. 2012. *Ancient Metals: Microstructures and Metallurgy Volume 1.* (2nd edn). Los Angeles: Conservation Science Press

Scurfield, C.J. 1997. Bronze Age metalwork from the River Trent in Nottinghamshire. *Transactions of the Thoroton Society of Nottinghamshire* 101, 27–57

Sheridan, J.A. 2008. Towards a fuller, more nuanced narrative of Chalcolithic and Early Bronze Age Britain 2500–1500 BC. *Bronze Age Review* 1, 57–78

Sheridan, J.A. 2010. Cremating Miss Piggy: an experimental Bronze Age style cremation. In *'A LAD O'PAIRTS'. A Day Conference in memory of Ian Shepherd to celebrate the wide contribution he made to Scottish Archaeology*, 9–12. Available at: https://citeseerx.ist.psu.edu/viewdoc/download?doi=10.1.1.465.4369&rep=rep1&type=pdf

Sheridan, J.A. 2016. The composite necklace. In A.M. Jones. *Preserved in the Peat. An extraordinary Bronze Age burial on Whitehorse Hill, Dartmoor, and its wider context*, 88–116. Oxford: Oxbow Books

Sheridan, A. & Davis, M. 2002. Investigating jet and jet-like artefacts from prehistoric Scotland. *Antiquity* 76(293), 812–25

Sheridan, A., Schulting, R., Quinnell, H. & Taylor, R. 2008. Revisiting a small passage tomb at Broadsands, Devon. *Proceedings of the Devon Archaeological Society* 6, 1–26

Shoemark, J. 2016. *SOM-AA390A: A BRONZE AGE TORC.* Available at: https://finds.org.uk/database/artefacts/record/id/774149 [Accessed: 28 Dec 2020]

Silvester, R.J. 1980. The prehistoric open settlement at Dainton, South Devon. *Proceedings of the Devon Archaeological Society* 38, 17–48

Skowranek, C. 2007. Random Places or Organized Industry? The Middle to Late Bronze Age metalworking sites in South-West England. Unpubl. MA thesis, University of Bristol

Smirke, E. 1867. Some account of the discovery of a gold cup in a barrow in Cornwall. *Archaeological Journal* 24, 189–95

Smith, M.A. 1959a. Somerset hoards and their place in the Bronze Age of Southern Britain. *Proceedings of the Prehistoric Society* 25, 144–87

Smith, M.A. (ed.), 1959b. *Inventaria Archaeologica* 7th Set: GB.42–47. London: Garraway Ltd

Smither, P (2020) *BERK–73615E: A Bronze Age unidentified object.* Available at: https://finds.org.uk/database/artefacts/record/id/1010526 [Accessed 21 May 2021]

Sommerfeld, C. 1994. *Gerätegeld Sichel. Studien zur monetären Struktur bronzezeitlicher Horte im nördlichen Mitteleuropa* (Vorgeschichtliche Forschungen 19). Berlin: de Gruyter

Sørensen, M.-L.S. 1987. Material order and cultural classification: the role of bronze objects in the transition from Bronze Age to Iron Age in Scandinavia. In I. Hodder (ed.), *The Archaeology of Contextual Meanings*, 90–101. Cambridge: Cambridge University Press

Soriano Llopis, I. & Gutiérrez Sáez, C. 2009. Use-wear analysis on metal: the influence of raw material and metallurgical production processes. In *Archaeometallurgy in Europe, Proceedings of the 2nd Conference (Aquileia 2007)*, 115–24. Milan: Associazione Italiana di Metallurgia

Standish, C.D., Dhuime, B., Hawkesworth, C.J. & Pike, A.W.G. 2015. A non-local source of Irish Chalcolithic and Early Bronze Age gold. *Proceedings of the Prehistoric Society* 81, 149–77. doi: 10.1017/ppr.2015.4

Stanton, Y.C. 1984. The hoard of South Wales or 'Stogursey' axes from St Mellons, South Glamorgan: A preliminary statement. *Bulletin of the Board of Celtic Studies* 31(III), 191–5

Stayt, H.A. 1931. *The BaVenda*. Oxford: Oxford University Press

Staniaszek, B.E.P. & Northover, J.P. 1983. The properties of leaded bronze alloys. In A. Aspinall & S.E. Warren (eds), *The Proceedings of the 22nd Symposium on Archaeometry held at the University of Bradford, Bradford, U.K. 30th March–3rd April 1982*, 262–72. Bradford: Schools of Physics and Archaeological Sciences, University of Bradford

Stevenson, R.B.K. 1948. Notes on some prehistoric objects. *Proceedings of the Society of Antiquaries of Scotland* 82 (1947–8), 292–5

Stradling, W. 1854. A young turf-bearer's find in the Turbaries. *Proceedings of the Somerset Archaeological and Natural History Society* 5(ii), 91–4

Sturgess, J. & Lawson-Jones, A. 2006. *Bronze Age Gwithian Revisited. Archaeological Excavations Between 1956 and 1961 in Cornwall. Volume 1*. Truro: Historic Environment Service (Projects)

Tabor, R. 2008. *Cadbury Castle: The hillfort and landscapes*. Stroud: The History Press

Tarbay, J.G. 2017. The Late Bronze Age hoard from Oltárc Márki Hill: analysis of prehistoric manipulations, selective fragmentation and non-ritual violence. *Zalai Múzeum* 23, 73–138

Taylor, J.J. 1994. The first golden age of Europe was in Ireland and Britain. *Ulster Journal of Archaeology* 57, 37–60

Taylor, J.J. 1999. The Colaton Raleigh gold bracelet hoard and its significance to the interpretation of the later Bronze Age. *Proceedings of the Devon Archaeological Society* 57, 205–18

Taylor, R. 2003. The spearhead. In In S. Coles, S. Hammond, J. Pine, S. Preston & A. Taylor, *Bronze Age, Roman and Saxon Sites on Shrubsoles Hill, Sheppey and at Wises Lane, Borden, Kent*, 42–3. Reading: Thames Valley Archaeological Services Ltd. Monograph 4

Taylor, R.J. 1980. An Armorican socketed axe from the sea off Chesil Beach, Dorset. *Archaeologia Atlantica* 3, 133–7

Taylor, R.J. 1982. The hoard from West Buckland, Somerset, *The Antiquaries Journal* 62(1), 13–7. doi: 10.1017/S0003581500003954

Thomas, R. 1989. The Bronze-Iron Transition in Southern England. In M.L. Stig-Sørensen & R. Thomas (eds), *The Bronze-Iron Age Transition in Europe: Aspects of Continuity and Change in European Societies, c. 1200–500BC (British Archaeological Reports International Series S483)*, 263–86. Oxford: British Archaeological Reports

Thompson, T. 2015. Fire and the body: Fire and the people. In T. Thompson (ed.), *The Archaeology of Cremation. Burned human remains in funerary studies*, 1–17. Oxford: Oxbow Books

Tilley, C. 1999. *Metaphor and material culture*. Oxford: Blackwell Publishers

Timberlake, S. 2009. Copper mining and metal production at the beginning of the British Bronze Age. In P. Clark (ed.), *Bronze Age Connections: Cultural contact in Prehistoric Europe*, 94–121. Oxford: Oxbow Books

Torbrügge, W. 1971. Vor- und frühgeschichtliche Flußfunde. Zur Ordnung und Bestimmung einer Denkmälergruppe. *Bericht der Römisch-Germanischen Kommission*. Bände 51–52 (1970–71), 1–146

Tratman, E.K. 1923. First report on Kings Weston Down, Bristol. *Proceedings of the University of Bristol Spelaeological Society* 2(1) (1922–23), 76–82

Tratman, E.K. 1926. Second report on Kings Weston Down, Bristol. *Proceedings of the University of Bristol Spelaeological Society* 2(3), 238–43

Trevarthen, C.H. 2016. *DOR-31AD21: A BRONZE AGE HOARD*. Available at: https://finds.org.uk/database/artefacts/record/id/798297 [Accessed: 29 Dec 2020]

Tronner, K., Nord, A.G. & Borg, G.Ch. 1995. Corrosion of archaeological bronze artefacts in acidic soil. *Water, Air and Soil Pollution* 85, 2725–30

Tucker, C. 1855. Antiquities and works of art exhibited. *Archaeological Journal* 12, 84–5

Tucker, C. 1867. Notices of antiquities of bronze found in Devonshire. *Archaeological Journal* 24(1), 110–22

Turk, P. 1997. Das Depot eines Bronzegeißers aus Slowenien - Opfer oder Materiallager? In A. Hänsel & B. Hänsel (eds), *Gaben An Die Götter. Schätze der Bronzezeit Europas*, 49–52. Berlin: Bestandskataloge Band 4

Turk, P. 2001. Some aspects of new Late Bronze Age and Early Iron Age hoard-finds from Central Slovenia. In A. Lippert (ed.), *Die Drau- Mur- und Raab-Region im 1. vorchristlichen Jahrtausend. Akten des internationalen und interdisziplinären Symposiums vom 26. bis 29. April 2000 in Bad Radkersburg*, 155–64. Bonn: Habelt

Turk, P. 2018. Early Iron Age hoards from central and western Slovenia. In E. Borgna, P. Càssola Guida & S. Corazza (eds), *Preistoria e Protostoria del Caput Adriae*, 397–406. Firenze: Istituto Italiano di Preistoria e Protostori

Turner, L. 2010a. *A Re-interpretation of the Late Bronze Age Metalwork Hoards of Essex and Kent: Volume 1* (British Archaeological Reports British Series 507). Oxford: John & Erica Hedges

Turner, L. 2010b. *A Re-interpretation of the Late Bronze Age Metalwork Hoards of Essex and Kent: Volume 2* (British Archaeological Reports British Series 507). Oxford: John & Erica Hedges

Tyacke, A. 2007. *CORN-E2DD57: A Bronze Age flat axehead*. Available at: https://finds.org.uk/database/artefacts/record/id/158111 [Accessed 12 December 2020]

Tyacke, A. 2008. *CORN-B6B241: A BRONZE AGE TORC*. Available at: https://finds.org.uk/database/artefacts/record/id/218583 [Accessed: 4 May 2020]

Tylecote, R. 1986. *The Prehistory of Metallurgy in the British Isles*. London: The Institute of Metals

Tyrrell, R. 2009. *BUC-C07E88: A BRONZE AGE TORC*. Available at: https://finds.org.uk/database/artefacts/record/id/266606 [Accessed: 2 September 2020]

Uckelmann, M. 2011. The function of Bronze Age shields. In Uckelmann & Mödlinger 2011, 187–99

Uckelmann, M. 2012. *Die Schilde der Bronzezeit in Nord-, West- und Zentraleuropa*. Prähistorische Bronzefunde 3.4. Stuttgart: Franz Steiner Verlag

Uckelmann, M. 2020. A Newly Discovered Later Bronze-Age Shield from Woodstock. *Oxoniensia* 85, 267–75

Uckelmann, M. & Mödlinger, M. (eds), 2011. *Bronze Age Warfare: Manufacture and Use of Weaponry*. British Archaeological Reports S2255. Oxford: Archaeopress

Van der Noort, R., Blue, L., Harding, A.F., Hurcombe, L., Hansen, T.M., Wetherelt, A., Wittamore, J. & Wyke, A. 2014. *Morgawr*: an experimental Bronze Age-type sewn-plank craft based on the Ferriby boats. *The International Journal of Nautical Archaeology* 43(2), 292–313

Van der Vaart-Verschoof, S. 2017. *Fragmenting the Chieftain. A practice-based study of Early Iron Age Hallstatt C elite burials of the Low Countries.*Leiden: Sidestone Press

Van der Vaart-Verschoof, S. & Schumann, R. 2020. Connected by more than exceptional imports: Performance and identity in Hallstatt C/D Elite burials of the Low Countries. *European Journal of Archaeology* 23(1), 22–42. doi: 10.1017/eaa.2019.44

Vandkilde, H. 2017. *The Metal Hoard from Pile in Scania, Sweden. Place, Things, Time, Metals and Worlds around 2000 BCE*. Aarhus: Aarhus University Press & The Swedish History Museum

Verney, A. 1991. La production en série d'objets métalliques à l'âge du Bronze: les dépôts de la Chapelle-du-Bois-des-Faulx (Eure). *Matières et figure, Etudes et travaux, Ecole du Louvre, Ecole du Patrimoine*, 117–35. Paris: La Documentation Française

Vilaça, R. & Bottaini, C. 2019. Breaking metals and handling ideas about Bronze Age hoards from Western Iberia. Material patterns, invisible behaviors and possible interpretations. In A.C. Valera (ed.), *Fragmentation and depositions in pre and proto-historical Portugal (Lisbon, 14 October 2017)*, 125–39. Lisbon: Núcleo de Investigação Arqueológica (Nia). Era Arqueologia S.A.

Waddington, K.E. 2009. *Re-assembling the Bronze Age: Exploring the Southern British Midden Sites*. Unpubl. PhD thesis, Cardiff University

Waddington, K. Bayliss, A., Higham, T., Madgwick, R. & Sharples, N. 2019. Histories of deposition: creating chronologies for the Late Bronze Age-Early Iron Age transition in Southern Britain. *Archaeological Journal* 176(1), 84–133. doi: 10.1080/00665983.2018.1504859

Wainwright, G.J. & Smith, K. 1980. The Shaugh Moor Project: Second Report The Enclosure. *Proceedings of the Prehistoric Society* 46, 65–122. doi: 10.1017/S0079497X00009348

Walker, K. 2018. *Axe-heads and Identity*. Oxford: Archaeopress

Wall, J. 1987. The role of daggers in Early Bronze Age Britain: The evidence of wear analysis. *Oxford Journal of Archaeology* 6(1), 115–8

Wang, Q. & Ottaway, B.S. 2004. *Casting Experiments and Microstructure of Archaeologically Relevant Bronzes*. Oxford: British Archaeological Reports S1131

Wang, Q., Strekopytov, S., Roberts, B.W. & Wilkin, N. 2016. Tin ingots from a probable Bronze Age shipwreck off the coast of Salcombe, Devon: composition and microstructure. *Journal of Archaeological Science* 67, 80–92

Wang, Q., Strekopytov, S. & Roberts, B.W. 2018. Copper ingots from a probable Bronze Age shipwreck off the coast of Salcombe, Devon: Composition and microstructure. *Journal of Archaeological Science* 97, 102–17. Doi: 10.1016/j.jas.2018.07.002

Warden, K., Caswell, E. & Roberts, B.W. 2016. Funerary fragments between the rivers: analysing the evidence for the dead in the Tyne-Forth region during the Late Bronze Age (*c.* 1150–800 BC). In R. Crellin, C. Fowler & R. Tipping (eds), *Prehistory without Borders. The prehistoric archaeology of the Tyne-Forth region*, 156–67. Oxford: Oxbow Books

Warner, R. & Cahill M. 2012. The Downpatrick hoard: an analytical reconsideration. In J.R. Trigg (ed.), *Of Things Gone But Not Forgotten. Essay in archaeology for Joan Taylor*, British Archaeological Reports S2434, 95–108. Oxford: British Archaeological Reports Publishing

Watts, S.R. 2014. *The Life and Death of Querns*. Southampton: The Highfield Press

Way, A. 1869. Antiquities of bronze found in Devonshire. *Archaeological Journal* 26(1), 339–51

Webley, L. 2007. Using and abandoning roundhouses: a reinterpretation of the evidence from Late Bronze Age-Early Iron Age southern England. *Oxford Journal of Archaeology* 26(2), 127–44

Webley, L. & Adams, S. 2016. Material Genealogies: Bronze moulds and their castings in Later Bronze Age Britain. *Proceedings of the Prehistoric Society* 82, 323–40

Webley, L., Adams, S. & Brück, J. 2020. *The social context of technology: Non-ferrous metalworking in later prehistoric Britain and Ireland* (Prehistoric Society Research Paper Series 11). Oxford: Oxbow Books

Weiner, A.B. 1992. *Inalienable possessions. The paradox of keeping-while-giving*. Oxford: University of California Press

Wessex Archaeology. 2014. *Kingsmead Quarry, Horton*. Available at: https://www.wessexarch.co.uk/our-work/kingsmead-quarry-horton. [Accessed 4 June 2021]

Whitley, M. 1943. Excavations at Chalbury Camp, Dorset, 1939. *The Antiquaries Journal* 23, 98–121. doi: 10.1017/S000358150001636X

Wickstead, H. 2008. *Theorising Tenure: Land division and identity in later prehistoric Dartmoor, south-west Britain*. British Archaeological Reports 465. Oxford: Archaeopress

Wilkin, N. 2017. Combination, composition and context: readdressing British Middle Bronze Age ornament hoards (*c.* 1400–1100 cal. BC). In T.F. Martin & R. Weetch (eds), *Dress and Society: Contributions from Archaeology*, 14–47. Oxford: Oxbow Books

Wilkin, N. 2019. Treasure report 2017 T1170. Available at: C. Hayward Trevarthen, *DOR-813231: A BRONZE AGE HOARD*. Available at: https://finds.org.uk/database/artefacts/record/id/878796 [Accessed: 24 Nov 2020]

Williams, R.A. & Le Carlier de Veslud, C. 2019. Boom and bust in Bronze Age Britain: major copper production from the Great Orme mine and European trade, *c.* 1600–1400 BC. *Antiquity* 93(371), 1178–96. https://doi.org/10.15184/aqy.2019.130

Wiseman, R. 2018. Random accumulation and breaking: The formation of Bronze Age scrap hoards in England and Wales. *Journal of Archaeological Science* 90, 39–49

Woodward, A. 2000. The prehistoric pottery. In G. Hughes, *The Lockington Gold Hoard. An Early Bronze Age barrow cemetery at Lockington, Leicestershire*, 48–61. Oxford: Oxbow Books

Woodward, A. 2002. Beads and beakers: Heirlooms and relics in the British Early Bronze Age. *Antiquity* 76, 1040–7

Woodward, A. 2009. The pottery. In L. Ladle & A. Woodward, *Excavations at Bestwall Quarry, Wareham 1992–2005. Volume 1: The Prehistoric Landscape*, 200–71. Dorchester: Dorset Natural History and Archaeological Society Monograph Series no.19

Woodward, A. & Hunter, J. 2015. *Ritual In Early Bronze Age Grave Goods*. Oxford: Oxbow Books

Woodward, A., Hunter, J., Ixer, R., Maltby, M., Potts, P.J., Webb, P.C., Watson. J.S. & Jones, M.C. 2005. Ritual in some Early Bronze Age grave goods. *Archaeological Journal* 162(1), 31–64

Woodward, P.J. 2000. The Late Bronze Age gold neckrings from Chickerell: An interim note. *Proceedings of the Dorset Natural History and Archaeological Society* 122, 145–8

Wright, E. 2021. Beyond cremation: Theorising fire in funerary contexts. *Journal of Archaeological Science: Reports* 38. https://doi.org/10.1016/j.jasrep.2021.102953

Yates, D. & Bradley, R. 2010a. The siting of metalwork hoards in the Bronze Age of South-East England. *The Antiquaries Journal* 90, 41–72

Yates, D. & Bradley, R. 2010b. Still water, hidden depths: the deposition of Bronze Age metalwork in the English Fenland. *Antiquity* 84, 405–15

York, J. 2002. The life cycle of Bronze Age metalwork from the Thames. *Oxford Journal of Archaeology* 21(1), 77–92

Young, T. 2013. Assessment of bronze casting debris from Banwell, North Somerset. GeoArch 2013/17. Unpubl. report. Accessible via: https://www.geoarch.co.uk/reports/2013–17%20Casting%20debris%20from%20Banwell.pdf

Index

Page references in italics denote pages with images, numbers prefixed t indicate pages with tables. For full details of all objects and deposits please see Archaeology Data Service: https://doi.org/10.5284/1090300.